WOMEN'S ORIENTS:
ENGLISH WOMEN AND THE MIDDLE EAST, 1718–1918

Women's Orients: English Women and the Middle East, 1718–1918

Sexuality, Religion and Work

Billie Melman

Ann Arbor
The University of Michigan Press

Copyright © 1992 by Billie Melman

All rights reserved

Published in the United States of America by
The University of Michigan Press

1995 1994 1993 1992   4 3 2 1

Printed in Hong Kong

Library of Congress Cataloging-in-Publication Data
Melman, Billie.
    Women's Orients, English women and the Middle East, 1718–1918 :
sexuality, religion, and work / Billie Melman.
        p.   cm.
    Includes index.
    ISBN 0–472–10332–6 (alk.)
    1. Orientalists—Great Britain—Biography.   2. Women authors,
English—18th century—Attitudes.   3. Women authors, English—19th
century—Attitudes.   4. Middle East—Study and teaching—History.
5. Ethnology—Middle East—History.   I. Title.
DS61.7.A1M45   1992
956'.0072—dc20   91–32433
                                                                          CIP

to my parents Glila and Samuel Rosenzweig

Contents

List of Plates

1. Women and the Banks of the Nile. Israel Museum, Jerusalem.
2. Lepers in Jerusalem c. 1885. Israel Museum, Jerusalem.
3. Nubian woman with *marghile*, probably 1880. Israel Museum, Jerusalem.
4. Arab woman in an outing dress c. 1885. Studio Bonfils, Beirut. Probably taken by Marie Lydie (Studio Bonfils 1837–1918), one of the very few women photographers active in the 1870s and 1880s.
5. Beduin encampment near Jericho c. 1885. Israel Museum, Jerusalem.
6. Courtyard of a Jewish House in Damascus, c. 1875. Studio Bonfils. The courtyard is described by Isabel Burton and Mary Mackintosh. Israel Museum, Jerusalem.
7. Beduin Vegetable Vendors c. 1885. Studio Bonfils. Israel Museum, Jerusalem.
8. Arab woman on a donkey, 1880s. Israel Museum, Jerusalem.
9. A corner of the vegetable market, Jerusalem, 1908. The Israel Museum, Jerusalem.
10. The mill, 'primitive' (sic) method of grinding, 1908. Israel Museum, Jerusalem.
11. Emmeline Lott c. 1865, from Emmeline Lott's *Harem Life in Egypt and Constantinople* Vol. I, 1865. The Bodleian Library.
12. Moslem (sic) women attired in *mandrils* and *izzars*. The Bodleian Library.
13. 'Mosque of Sultan Valide' features unveiled women, which is quite rare, from Pardo, *The Beauties of the Bosphorous*. The Bodleian Library.
14. (above left) Turkish lady in yashmak or feradjen from M. Lucy Garnett's *The Turkish People*, 1909.
15. (top right) Stamboul Jewess and Jewess in *izzar* from Matilda M. Cubley *The Hills and Plains of Palestine*, The Bodleian Library.

List of Abbreviations

AA	*American Antiquary*
AE	Amelia Edwards' Papers, University College, London, Science Division
AT	*Athenaeum*
BM	*Blackwood Magazine*
BSR	Benevolent Society for the Relief of Poor Jewish Women in Childbirth
CI	*Christian Intelligenzer*
CM	*Cornhill Magazine*
CMS	Church Missionary Society
DS	Dorcas Society (Jerusalem)
EEF	Egypt Exploration Fund
EEFAR	*Egypt Exploration, Reports of Annual General Meetings and Balance Sheets*
ER	*Eclectic Review*
EJ	*Englishwoman's Journal*
FEM	Female Education Mission
FR	*Fortnightly Review*
GJ	*Geographical Journal* (see RGSP)
ISA	Israel State Archives
JI	*Jewish Intelligence*
JLS	Jerusalem Literary Society
LJS	London Society for the Promotion of Knowledge Amongst the Jews
PEF	Palestine Exploration Fund
PEQ	*Palestine Exploration Quarterly, Embodying the Quarterly Statement of the PEF and the British School of Archaeology in Jerusalem*
PMLA	Publications of Modern Language Association
RA	*Revue Archeologique*
RAS	Royal Asiatic Society
RGS	Royal Geographical Society
RGSP	*Proceedings of the Royal Geographical Society and Monthly Record of Geography* and from 1888 *The Geographical Journal, Including the Proceedings of the Royal Geographical Society*

SS   Sarah Society (Jerusalem)
WA   Jacob Wharman Archive and Library
WR   *Westminster Review*

List of Figures and Tables

Figures

Tables

Note on Transcription

For Ottoman I have followed standard modern Turkish. For the usage and spelling of the terms harem and *haremlik* see note 3 to Chapter 2, p. 348.

Preface

Women's Orients is a case of academic serendipity. Like Sir Horace Walpole's happy three princes of Serendip I made unexpected discoveries quite by accident. I had intended to write a book on women travellers to the Middle East. But the volume of neglected writings by women on that region and their unknown work in it, diverted me from the intended route and caused me to widen the topic and include ethnographers, missionaries, pilgrims and scientists. At the same time my perspective became more focused. The result is an attempt to look at the ways in which gender and class influenced the European perception and representation of the 'other' and more broadly at how non-hegemonic groups in a culture, or a society, perceive subordinate peoples, or races, or classes.

Along my own circuitous journey I received guidance and direction from generous colleagues: fellow historians of Europe and the Middle East (they would, I am sure, resent the epithets 'orientalists' and 'area specialists'), feminist historians, literary critics and geographers.

My longest-standing debt is to Shulamit Volkov and John A. Sutherland who, both, read the final draft of the manuscript and made many helpful suggestions. Joel Kraemer, Ehud R. Toledano and David Trotter read scrupulously the part on the women's literature on harems and saved me from a number of muddles and errors. Conversation with George L. Mosse and Gertrude Himmelfarb helped me develop some of the ideas on the relationship between Victorian sexuality and popular discussion on the Orient, as well as between popular religion and Orientalism. I am indebted to Zvi Razi and Dan Eshet for their commonsensical advice and assistance with the quantification of biographical data on writers.

Fellows and colleagues at the Center for European Studies at Harvard, where I was Visiting Fellow in 1989–90, unstintingly lent of their time and counsel. I am particularly grateful to Margaret Higonnet, most careful of readers, for comments on Part Four of the book; to Sonya Michel for her support; to members of the Study Group on Women in Western Europe; to Simon Schama and finally to Abby Collins for her hospitality. Bill Kovach, curator of the Nieman Foundation and the devoted staff at Walter Lippmann

House, have shown many kindnesses and made the completion of the manuscript possible. Special thanks are due to David Prochaska, Helena Michie, Leila Kinney, Zeynep Celik, Martin Kramer, Steve Daniels, Ruth Kark, Joshua Ben-Arieh, Martin Kramer and Sarah Kochav.

A brief version of chapters 2–4 appeared in the *Mediterranean Historical Review*, Vol. 4, December 1984, in a double-feature entitled 'Desexualising the Orient'. Diluted versions of chapters 3–6 were the basis for papers given at Harvard, at the Study Group on Women in Western Europe and at a conference on Women and Colonisation in April 1990.

Archivists and librarians helped cut through red tape and discover neglected manuscripts. Mrs Kelly, archivist at the Royal Geographical Society, London was particularly helpful. Rupert Chapman III, Secretary and Acting Director of the Palestine Exploration Fund permitted me to read and quote from, the Minutes of the Jerusalem Literary Society and his unpublished paper on 'Archaeology and the Holy Land'. I am also grateful to the staffs at the Egypt Exploration Fund; the Department of Rare Manuscripts at the Sciences Library at University College, London; to T. J. H. James, Director of the EEF and the Department of Egyptian Antiquities at the British Museum, for permission to quote from Amelia Edwards' unpublished lecture on 'The Social and Political Position of Women in Ancient Egypt'; the Librarian at the Manuscript room at the British Library; Ms Elsie Logan of the Anglican Israel Foundation and Nisan Peres, Curator of Photography at the Israel Museum. I should like to express my gratitude to Nathan and Eva Schur and Jacob Wharman, collectors of travel-literature on Palestine and the Near East, who opened their libraries for me and shared with me their encyclopedic knowledge on the eighteenth- and nineteenth-century travelogues. Ken Herzog and Suzan Moffatt, two IBM wizards, turned an unreadable manuscript to a neat typescript. The devoted Suzan in particular remained calm in the face of a deadline and worked through weekends to help finish this book.

At Macmillan I am inbebted to Frances Arnold and Margaret Cannon for their faith in the book. My deep appreciation goes to Anthony Grahame, my editor, for his patience. The preparation of the last stages of this book coincided with the missile attacks on Tel-Aviv – not an ideal time for finishing off any project. His commitment helped in carrying the work through to its conclusion.

Last but first comes Yossi Melman, my fellow-traveller, whose love and support sustained me through the years of research, writing and teaching full-time. If there is any one reader to whom this book is particularly addressed, it is to him.

BILLIE MELMAN

Introduction

I rediscovered in Islam the world I myself
had come from; Islam is the West of the East.
                    Claude Lévi-Strauss, *Tristes Tropiques*.[1]

LADY STANHOPE'S SECOND BURIAL

Sometime during the first week of February 1989, a strange burial
took place in the small British cemetery at Abey near Beirut.
There was no body, since the time of death was June 1838. And
what the years had left had been ravaged by treasure-hunters and
grave-robbers. So that the remains of what had been Lady Hester
Lucy Stanhope, niece of William Pitt, traveller and eccentric, 'Queen
of the Orient', and at last a pauper and recluse, now barely filled
a despatch-box. Her skull and assorted bones, exhumed early in
1988, then offered for sale to a few uninterested British officials,
then recovered by the Red-Cross, were finally laid to rest.[2]

Hester Stanhope's burial, unburial and re-burial are intriguingly
symbolic and may serve to illustrate informed and popular attitudes to the place and role of women in the British experience
of the eastern Mediterranean, indeed in the colonial experience as
such. Historians and students of culture alike relegate women to
the periphery of imperialist culture and the tradition of 'empire',
the assumption being that the female experience of the Western
expansion and domination outside Europe had been subsumed in
a hegemonic and homogeneously patriarchal tradition.[3]

This book is about the West's gaze at its 'other' and the influence
through time of gender and class on Europe's perspective of the
culturally and ethnically different. More specifically I am interested
in the ways in which Western women experienced the Middle
East, in their contacts with Middle Eastern women, in the limits
of their vision of the 'elsewhere' and representations of it. Could
women, conventionally identified in the Christian West as the 'other
within',[4] develop their own notion of the 'other without', of peoples,
or races or – for that matter – classes outside a dominant culture?

1

And how indeed do politically and economically marginal groups (minorities is an inadequate term) perceive what the dominant culture defines as 'different'? Are these groups the passive receptacles of the common idiom and common ideas, or do they actually articulate their own notion about the 'other' 'elsewhere'? Put somewhat differently, did gender and socio-economic differences matter more than the national, religious and racial ones? Was women's experience of modern colonialism subsumed in the newly 'invented tradition' of an expanding empire (Hobsawm's term), or did they develop a separate, feminine experience? To hope to answer all or some of these questions may seem crazily ambitious. Nevertheless they need to be asked, if only to broaden our understanding of that uneasy situation described by James Clifford as being 'in culture', while looking at another.

BOUNDARIES AND DEFINITIONS

Historically my study is confined to the eighteenth and nineteenth centuries, more precisely to the period between 1718 and 1918. The slicing of an historical continuum into periods and centuries is, of course, arbitrary and tidy-minded. My section is probably both and may seem rather eccentric, for it appears to 'leave the politics out'.[5] I begin a century before the awakening of Western political interest in the eastern Mediterranean, decades before the revival of scholarly interest in the Mediterranean Orient and the discovery of the languages and culture of what Raymond Schwab calls the 'integral Orient' that is Persia and India. Actually my starting point is the piratical publication, in London, of a collection of anonymous letters on 'Turkey' by a 'Lady' identified by a few as Lady Mary Wortley Montagu, the very first example of a secular work by a woman about the Muslim Orient.[6] Montagu set the terms of an alternative, gender-specific discourse on the Middle East, one which evolved alongside the dominant discussion, which nowadays is described as Orientalism. Her *Letters* acquired the status of an authority on things oriental, a text of reference and a model and had enormous impact on women and men travellers throughout the nineteenth century. Indeed the history of the reception of the *Letters* (which is studied in Chapters 3 and 4) may tell us a great deal about how a text becomes an authority, how canonicity is decided, and how a community of writers and readers participate in a discourse.

I do not proceed beyond the First World War even though Mediterranean travel continued after it and the involvement of the Western Powers in the Middle East assumed more direct forms after the war than before it. The war effectively solved the 'Eastern-Question', dissolved the Ottoman Empire, and reshaped the Middle East. It also dealt travel, as an individualised form of exchange between cultures and part of middle-class *Bildung*, its *coup-de-grâce*. As Paul Fussell wryly puts it, tourism, not literary travel, is the characteristic form of the inter-war seasonal migration to the South.[7] Finally the Great War brought to a close the 'Age of Empire' and the supremacy, in Europe, of the *bourgeoisie*, intimately connected with the imperialist experience. And it is with the lives and work of middle-class women, and a few men, that this study is concerned.

Geographically, too, my study has its limits. In the first place I include only the experience and writing of British women and a few American ones who had special impact in Britain. Not because I think the French or German writing unimportant. Nor because I fail to recognise that comparison is a powerful methodological tool, but because parochialism may be healthy, especially in areas of study like 'Orientalism' or 'Europe and its others' that are given to generalisation. For the very rationale of my own study is that Europe's concept and representation of the Orient were not unified. That there was, indeed, a plurality of notions and images of the 'other'; that the discourse about things oriental was polyphonic and that the experience of the eastern Mediterranean was heterogeneous and not, or not only, political.

Another self imposed boundary has to do with my usage of the terms 'Middle East' and 'Orient'. They are employed in this book interchangeably, sometimes simply as *geographical names*,[8] to designate the territories, under Ottoman rule, in Europe, Asia Minor, Mesopotamia or modern Iraq, the province of Syria (including Syria and the modern Lebanon), Palestine and the Arabian Peninsula and Egypt. The terms 'Near' and 'Middle East' are, of course, relatively new and had not been used before 1902. And I am well aware that the 'Orient' is not a fact, nor merely a geographical region, but a politically and culturally charged *topos*. But the two terms have become common currency and to argue against them would serve no purpose.[9]

But something *has* to be said about the 'imaginary geography'[10] of the Orient as opposed to the natural one. The former is a perspective, or a notion that derives from an epistemology that divides the world into two asymmetrical parts: the West and the East, Europe and the Orient. This is what came to be known as Orientalism.

Now Orientalism is, of course, an umbrella that covers diverse and numerous meanings. It is an academic system, or 'network'; it is a style and an aesthetic; it is a 'discourse': the manipulative amassing of information about the Middle East by a politically and economically superior West, the classification of that knowledge and categorisation of the different and its reconstructuring.[11] The Orient – in a paraphrase on Marx – cannot represent itself: so it needs to be represented.[12] It cannot speak for itself, therefore it is 'spoken for'. It is interpreted, by the purveyors of knowledge and agents of power. In a still broader sense Orientalism is used synecdochially as a metaphor for a representation of the other that is based on a hierarchical relationship between an hegemonic and a subordinate group (another race or sex, or religious minority). Throughout the book Orientalism is used in a catholic and inclusive manner, rather than exclusively to denote some or all of the four meanings.

A NOTE ON THE HISTORIOGRAPHY

There is, it is generally assumed, an intimate relationship between Orientalism and patriarchalism, between colonisation and the domination over women in the 'metropolitan' West. This relationship is structural and central to each of the four meanings of Orientalism. Discourse on the empire informed that on sexuality and gender. And the inarticulateness of the Orient stands for the silence of marginalised groups in the *bourgeois* West: women, the poor, racial minorities. The analogy between European women and non-Europeans is quite common in popular Victorian and Edwardian idiom and also in the new scientific discourse on race (notably biological anthropology and phrenology).[13] So Orientalism is characterised as a variant on 'male gender dominance, or patriarchy, in metropolitan societies'.[14] For the West feminised the East and eroticised it. Like the female body in the West, the Orient served as the site of mixed feelings, attraction and repulsion; intimacy and a sense of distance. And for a long stretch of time, a particularly *longue durée*, the odalisk, the domestic despot and the harem had been the most repeated, most enduring *topoi* of the Muslim eastern Mediterranean. Both the historiography now bracketed 'ethnocentric' and the 'alternative', 'post-colonial' historiography of the political and cultural exchanges between Europe and the Middle East, assume a changelessness in the myth of the Orient. Admittedly a few historians, notably Norman Daniel and, following in his footsteps, Dorothee Meltitzki and R. W. Southern, allow a linear development, or progress, in Europe's notion of the other: from the 'simple' image of the alien in early anti-Saracen polemical writing, to the more complex notion which developed after the Crusades, to the secular images dating from the Reformation and the Enlightenment, to the imperialist *topos*.[15] But the changes allowed are of emphasis, not substance.[16] Thus the Flaubertian paradigm of the positional relations (literally and metaphorically as it were) between the Turkish *'alimah Küçück Hanîm*, and her master/lover, Flaubert himself, is elevated to a metaphor for the hierarchical relations between the Occident and Orient.

Ironically the critics of Orientalism and ethnocentric scholarship carry on the very tradition which they condemn. For these critics write out gender and class. The Orient is depicted as a man's place, and the empire as a male space, the *locus* of male character-building and 'career' (this last a paraphrase on Disraeli's idiom in his mystical novel *Tancred*). The imperialist experience and tradition are presented as androcentric. In Edward Said's script of the exchange between the West and the East, the occidental interpretation of the Orient is a symbolic act of appropriation from which Western women are excluded. Flaubert knows Egypt as he knows *Küçück Hanîm*. There were, it is conceded, distinguished women explorers, missionaries and pilgrims, even a few women orientalists. But they were 'emergency men' operating within a male tradition, imitating men's ideas and behavior, 'subsumed' in the hegemonic cultural apparatus.[17] Look at Gertrude Lowthian Bell, arch-imperialist and anti-Suffragist, or at Flora Shaw, Lady Luggard, Colonial correspondent of the *Times* and supporter of Britain's intervention in Egypt. And note Amelia Blanford Edwards, promoter of the new science of Egyptology and founder of the Egypt Exploration Fund, who always referred to herself in the de-gendered, impersonal 'the author' (but to her female travel companions in the diminutive 'Lady' or 'the Bride').

Class, too, is written out by students of Orientalism. Discourse on the Orient is conventionally presented as unified, authoritative and, to use Bakhtin's term, monoglot. 'Monoglot' designates the omniscient authorial voice of Flaubert and, by analogy, a dominant, unified idiom or language. The term seems particularly apt because the French novelist's representation of the East has been recently elevated to a metaphor for ethnocentric cross-cultural representation. The Western voice, then, is identified as one of authority – cultural and political authority. The discussion on things oriental was carried on and orchestrated by an intellectual élite (academic specialists, writers and artists), political and economic interests.[18]

It is significant that feminist criticism too reduces the European experience of the geographically and culturally different to the Flaubertian paradigm of unequal power and that feminist writers on imperialism assign to women a passive role. Indeed the very analogy between patriarchalism and imperialism leaves little room for the possibility of the evolution of a gender-specific experience of the 'other'. Thus anthropologists – like Callaway, Etienne and Leacock and the Ardeners – and literary critics – Stevenson, de Groot, Pucci – all subscribe to the 'post-colonial' *post-mortem* analysis discussed above (the surgical metaphor seems apt). Historians, with the exception of a very few, have neglected to look at the relations between imperialism and gender.[19] Yet the study of the Western women's Orient has a meaning beyond the discovery of new evidence, the unearthing of the debris of unknown lives and of an experience 'hidden from history'. Historians dealing with the subject are not merely archaelogists or (to carry the analogy with Lady Stanhope's burial further) treasure-hunters. New evidence may be used to develop a new perspective on the relations between Europe and its 'others' and redefine these relations in terms which are not mostly political. The traditional and new historiography discussed earlier interpret the cross-cultural exchange in political terms and locate it in the context of a conflict for supremacy. It is precisely because of that that women are omitted from the histories of Orientalism and imperialism. Once these phenomena are perceived as the discourses of hegemony, they are located in the centres of power in the public sphere and hence defined as 'masculine' or 'patriarchal' (Said's term). Women, associated with social rather than political history, are admitted to the experience of the empire only as spectators, or as victims. Through the study of their role as actors in this experience a better understanding of cross-cultural relations in the colonial era may be reached. And, of course, such an understanding is neither a justification, nor a vindication, of Europe's attitudes towards its subordinate peoples, only a historicisation.

THE SCOPE OF WOMEN'S WRITING

My own argument is simple but, I hope, not simpleminded. Europe's attitude towards the Orient was neither unified nor monolithic. Nor did it progress (or regress) linearly. Nor did it necessarily derive from a binary vision sharply dividing the world into asymmetrical oppositions: male–female; West–East, white–non-white and Christian–Muslim, nor from that universal propensity to 'think in pairs'. I argue that in the eighteenth century there emerged an alternative view of the Orient which developed, during the nineteenth century, alongside the dominant one. The new view, which is expressed in diverse images that are in many ways more complex than the orientalist *topos*, is found in the mammoth body of writings by women travellers to and residents in, the Middle East and which so far have received very little attention. Richard Bevis in his *Bibliotheca Cisorientalia*, the most complete checklist of travel books in English about the Middle East, lists some 245 printed works by 187 women between 1821 and 1914 (compared to only four before 1821). And his remarkable inventory is by no means exhaustive. It excludes works not defined as 'travelogues' (works of missionaries, scientific or 'specialist' works) and articles – of which there are many hundreds. And it does not record unprinted materials – diaries, letters, etc.[20] I was fortunate to come across over a hundred uncatalogued book-length publications, and many more papers read to the scientific organisations with an interest in the Middle East and private records. And what can be found in the archives of the Royal Geographical Society, the Palestine and Egypt Exploration Funds and the missionary archives – notably the archives of the biggest Evangelical missions, the Church Missionary Society (CMS) and the London Society for the Promotion of Knowledge Amongst the Jews (LJS) – is probably only a part of what was actually written. Like the unclaimed remains of Lady Stanhope, these women's writing had to be exhumed, sorted and brought to light.

Let me make myself quite clear. It is not as a historian of Middle Eastern society that I approach and look at the writings – for I am not qualified to do that. It is rather as a student of the shifts and mutations in Western sensibilities, particularly the sensibilities of the Western European middle-classes, that I propose to look at the materials. And these materials present a plurality of discourse which is *sui-generis* and which differs from the dominant idiom. Travel and the encounter with systems of behaviour, manners and morals, most notably with the systems of polygamy, concubinage and the sequestration of females, resulted in analogy between the polygamous Orient and the travelling women's own monogamous society. And analogy led to self-criticism rather than cultural smugness and sometimes resulted in an identification with the other that cut across the barriers of religion, culture and ethnicity. Western women's writing on 'other' women then substitutes a sense of solidarity of gender for sexual and racial superiority. And even outside the harem, the women's experience of the Middle East was quite novel and challenged middle-class gender-ideology. Travel was a culturally meaningful gesture. It was, Fussell notes, a emancipating experience. And travel-writing constituted a break away from the precepts and aesthetics of the very notion of separate, masculine and feminine spaces.

A GENERAL MAP: WOMEN'S TRAVEL IN THE MEDITERRANEAN

In contrast to the hegemonic orientalist discussion, women's discourse on the Orient evolved outside the main locations of 'metropolitan' knowledge and power (Foucault's well-known term). For until the very end of the period I examine, women had been excluded from the communities of specialists and the guilds devoted to the learning of 'things oriental' and associated with the more aggressive forms of Britain's expansion overseas. Thus the Royal Geographical Society (RGS), the biggest and most reputable promoter of Victorian and Edwardian exploration and geographical studies, admitted women as fellows only in 1913, after two decades of a vigorous campaign inside the Society and in the national press.[21] So that female explorers of Mesopotamia, of *Arabia Deserta* and *Arabia Felix*, like Lady Anne Noel Blunt, Gertrude Bell and Mabel Virginia Bent, were allowed to read papers to the General Quarterly Meetings of the RGS but not to vote or hold office. And significantly, even after admission only 77 women joined in, a minority of less than five per cent of the members. Some women travellers preferred to join the Royal Asiatic Society (RAS), which had admitted females earlier, and the Scottish RGS.[22]

It is significant that women acquired representation and power in the voluntary, non-specialist societies with interest in the Middle East and in the Evangelical proselytising organisations. Both kinds of organisations were less directly connected with imperialist policies. Both were based on subscription and informal work. Both had allegiance to emotional, 'vital' religion. And both represented the 'new' oriental 'sciences' of Biblical and field Archaeology and Egyptology which had burgeoned outside the universities (see Chapter 1).

The extraordinary career of the twin Scottish scholars Agnes Lewis Smith and Margaret Gibson Dunlop may give us a clue to the nature of the relations between the academic community of orientalists and those women who made the Orient a career. The eccentric twins – nicknamed the Giblewes – embarked on their career when in their early fifties, in 1891–2. Almost immediately they discovered, transcribed and deciphered the Sinai Palimpsest (now known as the Lewis Codex) the earliest Syriac, or Aramaic translation of the Gospels. Their discovery revolutionised Biblical criticism and the comparative study of Semitic languages. The sisters were duly recognised as prominent linguists and lexicographers. Between 1893 and 1914 (they were then well into their eighties) they published 43 works. They were showered with honorary degrees in almost every Western country except Britain.[23] In fact they were constantly criticised by professional orientalists, the pundits of Cambridge. Amelia Edwards' uneasy relations with the Department of Egyptian Antiquities at the British Museum – that repository of oriental treasures looted by excavators, soldiers and tourists – manifest the same characteristics as the relations of the twins with orientalist authority.[24]

In short 'feminine' interest in the Orient did not assume institutional forms. It evolved outside formal networks of power and organisations and clubs. That interest was channeled into one cultural form in particular – travel.

It has recently become the fashion to look at travel as a form of domination. The occidental traveller's gaze, the explorer's eye, has been made an emblem of the unequal relations between Europe and the Orient. So much so that another aspect of exploration is forgotten: the comparison between self and 'other', between societies and between cultures, that travel makes possible. For it was the broadening of Europe's horizons, as Claude Lévi-Strauss usefully reminds us, that enabled Europeans to realise the diversity of human experience and the relativeness of systems of values and morals and of human organisations.[25]

The explorer's gaze, however, had been generically and literally, man's gaze. For until the eighteenth century, travel outside Europe was a male experience. And most relevant to this book the *voyage-en-orient* was man's voyage in man's lands. There is no secular tradition of female travel before Montagu's 'Embassy Letters'. And there is no model of a female narrative of a journey outside the chronicle of the pilgrimage.

What little evidence that we do have about women's travel to the eastern Mediterranean before 1717 suggests that it was exclusively religious. The modern 'secular' discourse erupted after more than fifteen centuries of silence. Richard Bevis lists only one travelogue by a woman between 1500 and 1763 and three between 1763 and 1801, compared with some 240 books between 1801 and 1911. And a *millennium* separates the pilgrimages of the great religious travellers of the Late Roman Empire and Montagu's *Letters*. This silence was interrupted only twice, first in the eighth century, in the first English travelogue, Huceburg of Eichstätt's *Odoporicon Sancti Wilibardi* (which is not a personal record but a transcription of the story of a male traveller and an authority in the Church, St. Willibard) then, for the second time, around 1420, in the transcription, by a man, of the pilgrimage of Margery Kempe of Lynn, an illiterate mystic, unrecognised by central religious authority.[26]

So not only the volume of the work produced by women from the eighteenth century, but the very phenomenon of female Mediterranean travel, was quite new. Yet clearly to separate the gender-specific from the culturally generic, 'feminine' interest in the Orient from the general interest in things oriental would be misguided and misleading. What is so intriguing about the feminine discourse is not its 'separateness' but the dynamic interchange between it and the hegemonic orientalist culture. We may look at the new phenomenon as part of the curiosity about the Mediterranean Orient, which arose about the time of Napoleon's conquest of Egypt in 1798. The general interest and that attitude towards the Mediterranean described by John Pemble as 'the Mediterranean passion' became features of Victorian and Edwardian culture.[27] Books about the region became one of the mainstays of the Victorian publishing industry. The presses plied an insatiable reading-public with *Sketches*, and *Gleanings; Glimpses* and *Illustrations; Impressions* and *Accounts* about the Classical and Muslim Mediterranean, the ancient and modern Orient and the sacred and the profane East, from *Diaries, Tours, Wanderings, Rambles* and *Residences* in the quarters of the East. And accounts of travel enjoyed an enormous popularity decades after the emergence of such alternative forms of representation of the Orient as the guide-book, dating from Murray's *Handbook* on Turkey (dated 1847) and the mass-produced photograph (dating c. 1890). Moreover literary travel presents only a fraction of the historic experience of travel in the Orient. The period after Napoleon's defeat and the Napoleonic wars is characterised by a move away from grand- to mass-tourism, a move that can be adequately described as the *embourgeoisement* of Eastern travel. The journey to the Middle East became a part of the education and *Bildung* of the *bourgeoisie*. And, I argue, Mediterranean travel was integrated into the female *Bildung*. As I show in Chapter 1, the overwhelming majority of travel writers came from a middle-class background. Even the rise of organised tourism in the mid-1860s did not make the eastern Mediterranean affordable to the lower middle-class. A Thomas Cook's organised package to the Holy Land averaged 31 shillings a day and included accommodation, a *dragoman* or translator, a military escort and provisions (imported from Britain, and agreeable to occidental stomachs). Such a sum put the Orient beyond the reach of the *petite bourgeoisie*.[28] (Dickens's fulsome Meagles, it will be remembered, did not proceed beyond Rome. Nonetheless they did display bits of brand new mummies on their mantlepiece, together with pieces of the ceiling of the Sistine Chapel.)

Improvements in maritime and land-transport made travel easier than ever before and affordable to the *bourgeoisie*. Sea-crossing under steam had become an established feature of Mediterranean travel after 1830. By the early 1840s there were regular Peninsular and Oriental passenger services from Southampton, connecting Britain with western and north-eastern Mediterranean ports (Malaga, Marseilles, Genova, Brindisi, Naples). By the 1850s, there were weekly departures from Southampton to Malaga and fortnightly departures to Alexandria. The P&O competed with continental lines, notably the Austrian Lloyd (*Lloyd Triestino*) and the (much less popular) French *Messagerie Orientale* which did not admit women passengers until 1868. Finally, the construction of stretches of railways between eastern Mediterranean ports and the hinterland, between Alexandria and Cairo, and between Jaffa and Jerusalem (in 1892) made the *voyage-en-orient* almost as easy as travel on the continent.

Of course improvements in the modes of travel and material changes in general do not, in themselves, account for the explosion of travel-literature about the Middle East nor for the development of gender-specific features of travel and the travelogue. Did the Orient have special allure for women? Did the pattern of their travel to, or life in, the Middle East significantly differ from those of men? In short, to borrow Disraeli's term again, did there emerge an 'Eastern' female 'career'?

Let there be no misunderstanding. By 'writing in' gender and class, I do not propose to 'write out' politics, nor history-as-a-narrative. The women's experience of the Orient was private rather than 'civic' or public, individual rather than institutionalised and finally it was a-political. Yet to de-politicise that experience and relegate it to the private sphere, outside the context of modern imperialism, would be as myopic as the attempt to reduce Orientalism to a tool of power politics. Clearly the development of Mediterranean travel and the Mediterranean travelogue, as well as the rise of scientific interest in that area, were influenced by if not causally related to, Britain's intervention in the Middle East.

The politics of the 'Eastern Question' and its strategies, both direct and indirect, military, economic and cultural, have received ample attention. Suffice it to isolate here those changes in the relations between the West and the Middle East and in the policies of the Ottoman Empire that, more directly than others, impinged on the nature of travel.[29] First is the opening up of parts of the Middle East to Western influence on a pragmatic as well as an ideological level. Military defeat and the decline of Turkey as a European and later a Mediterranean power, made élites inside that Empire aware that military superiority was related to modernisation and industrialisation and to advances in technology. The aftermath of the defeat of Mehmet Ali (in which the European powers of course played a major role), and the era of reforms following that defeat and known as the *Tanzimat* (1839–76), are characterised by westernisation and modernisation. Obviously 'openness' was relative and pragmatic and was dictated by a politically dominant West. Second, and related to the first change, is the policy – albeit not always the practice – *inside* the empire, of tolerance towards religious minorities and non-Ottoman Christians. The new policy of tolerance climaxes in the legislation to end discrimination against Christians in the 1850s. The *Hatt-i Hümayün* of 1856 granted minorities religious and civil liberties denied them before. More important, the *firman* dated *Muharram* 1267 (1850) changed the status of protestants, by officially recognising them as a community, thus legalising the conversion of Christian Ottomans to protestantism.

Tolerance of central authority increased the proselytising and philanthropic activity of Anglicans in the Middle East, attracting a new species of a traveller, the millenarian Evangelical with a vocation in the East.[30] Travellers' reports attest that prejudice against Christians was fairly common. But by and large the safety of *Franks* (that is local Christians) and westerners was the norm. Sightseeing, even of places forbidden to infidels, was made possible. The early travellers, before the *Tanzimat* era, often took considerable risks by penetrating the precincts of sacred mosques. In 1818 Sarah Belzoni, who travelled alone from Egypt to Palestine, succeeded in getting into the Haram el-Sharif or Mount Temple and even reached the Aqsa Mosque, disguised as a young Arab male.[31] Lady Hester Lucy Stanhope visited Damascene mosques dressed up as a young mameluke and about two decades later,[32] the less eccentric and much less adventurous Julia Sophia Pardoe attended night prayers at Aga Sophia in male attire.[33] A few years later there was no difficulty for tourists to obtain a royal *firman* to visit sacred places and they were provided with escorts. Thus Georgina Dawson-Damer remarks in 1843 that, notwithstanding a few local demonstrations of hostility towards westerners, the overall attitude of Turks and Arabs was one of tolerance.[34] Certain sacred places, of course, remained unseen (Mecca and the tombs of Patriarchs in Hebron, which even tourists armed with the imperial permission were not allowed to enter). On the whole, however, the Orient was not only accessible to Europeans but a safer place to Christians.

The third political factor that made travel easier than ever before was the entrenchment of the related systems of capitulations and consular representation. Both these systems date back to the period of Ottoman political supremacy. Economic capitulations were first granted by Sultan Suleiman the Magnificent, at the height of the empire's power. During the nineteenth century legal and economic concessions to foreigners became a barely disguised form of imperialism. The local influence of consuls was growing in direct proportion to the weakening of the central administration. And European residents and travellers registered in their consulates, represented by these offices and often protected by them, acknowledged no other authority in the Middle East.[35]

My argument, however, is that the politicisation of West-Eastern relations, which may explain away the growing of interest in the Orient, does not account for the rapid growth of female travel in the Mediterranean. In what remains of this Introduction I characterise women's travel and models of travel-writing before Montagu's *Letters*, then, in general terms, discuss the 'invention' of a tradition, or rather traditions of female travel in the nineteenth century, and the elements in these traditions of continuity with, and break from, the older forms of Orientalist authority.

FROM THE *PEREGRINATIO POR CHRISTO* TO *CURIOSITAS*: THREE MODES OF MODERN TRAVEL

The single most important shift in the eighteenth and nineteenth century is the move away from one exclusive model of feminine travel to a plurality of models, a move that I relate to the secularisation of the alternative oriental experience. I use 'secularisation' in the everyday sense of the term, denoting the breaking of the grip of religious institutions over the lives of individual men and women and the weakening of the institutions of the Church. But I qualify this usage by saying that secularisation by no means implies the death of religion, rather its privatisation, a take-over as it were of institutions and hierarchies by groups outside the Church – women for example. Indeed, the 'feminisation of religion' in the nineteenth century is conventionally associated with secularisation.

Before the eighteenth century the only tradition of female travel was religious. To be sure, there are examples of women tourists who were not pilgrims (Aphra Behn's own irreverent 'pilgrimage' to Surinam, at the end of the seventeenth century immediately springs to mind). And there are secular accounts of travel – both real and imaginary – before Montagu's. But they are episodes which do not form a tradition. It was the pilgrimage, both as actual experience and 'emplotted' narrative that offered women a model of feminine travel as well as a female model of the *persona* (both historic and fictive) of the traveller/narrator. Certainly, the pilgrimage was the oldest and popularly the best-known form of *rapport* with the Middle East. Moreover, as both Christian Zacher and Jonathan Sumption argue, the religious voyage to holy places was secularised before the Reformation and the scientific revolution of the seventeenth century.[36] For medieval men and women the journey to shrines and sepulchres fulfilled social needs as well as spiritual ones.

Yet the *peregrinatio por christo* as an actuality and as metaphor for the Christian life had certain generically feminine aspects. The *peregrinus* was a generic rather than a literal term. So that the pilgrimage was a culturally legitimate mode of travel for women. The religious or vocational trip to the Orient licensed degrees of freedom: a freedom of movement that was not usual in Western societies, an escape from social constraints, even from family. Margery Kempe of Lynn forsook her husband, her marital duties, even her duties as mother, to travel to Rome and Jerusalem and gain the Christian man's destination. Above all the pilgrimage was an alternative to domesticity and the sequestration of celibate women (either in religious communities or, according to the eastern Pachomian ideal, *outside* the community).[37] Last, but not least, the unChristian *curiositas* or interest in the rare, the exotic and foreign, a thing particularly condemned in females (for it had been Eve's *curiositas* that had brought on the Fall and the *damnosa hereditas*), was tolerated in the context of a pilgrimage. Thus the pious and simple-minded Egaria, the late fourth-century Galician nun, whose *Itinerarium* is the only record of female pilgrimage before Kempe's which came down to us, describes – together with the sepulchres she visited and cults and liturgies she observed – local customs and manners. Significantly she is addressing a female audience, the good sisters in her nunnery in Spain.

Naturally the practice of pilgrimage died down in the West even before the Reformation. And I do not propose here that the women travellers in the eighteenth and nineteenth century consciously continued the medieval tradition of religious travel. Indeed none of the Victorian evangelicals that I discuss even heard of Egaria (whose *Itinerario*, in fact, was discovered only in 1884), let alone of Jerome's female acolytes Paula and Eustochium, or of the two Melanias, *Senior* and *Minor*, pilgrims and founders of convents on the Mount of Olives, outside Jerusalem, or of Poemenia, the Nile traveller, or of Sylvia of Aquitaine, or of Huceburg of Eichstätt. And only a few Greek and Syriac scholars like Gibson and Lewis were aware of the part played by the Empresses Helena and Eudocia in the late Roman and early medieval pilgrimage movement.

What is significant is that the pilgrimage as image and a metaphor lived on in the literary imagination and in popular idiom *after* the Reformation. Bunyan's *Pilgrim's Progress* informed virtually all travellers to the Middle East, regardless of their denomination.[38] In 1880, Anne Noel Blunt, recently converted to the Catholic faith, models her classic *Pilgrimage to Nejd* on Bunyan's pilgrimage. And two decades earlier Frances Power Cobbe, feminist and philanthropist, an Evangelical turned agnostic, eulogises the puritan allegory of the journey. The pilgrimage, she insists, is an image which every child carries with him or her. A journey to the holy places in the East is vicariously experienced by every English reading youth. And Harriet Martineau, Britain's most successful female political writer and an experienced traveller who, like Cobbe, abandoned the Church after a Middle Eastern tour, nevertheless acknowledges the tradition of the pilgrimage.[39]

More important, the concept and practice of a vocational journey were acquiring novel and modern meanings. As I show in Chapters 6–7, evangelicalism and evangelical gender ideology, which stressed the moral superiority of women, sanctioned a career in 'the world'. So that those parts of the empire identified with the Scriptures were particularly appealing to religiously motivated women. At any time between 1886 (when the CMS first employed female missionaries) and the outbreak of the First World War, there were more women than men missionaries in any of the evangelical Middle Eastern missions, except in Turkish Arabia. There was a majority of women in non-evangelical organisations too (see Chapter 1). And the statistics of the missions do not include the enormous religious and educational work of women for women and children that was carried on informally and voluntarily outside the evangelising bodies. One of the corollaries of this work is the development of the evangelical ethnographic writing and the evangelical travelogue on the Middle East, genres which have allegiances with, yet depart from, the traditional *peregrinatio*.

The other two models of writing are to be discussed in terms of change, rather than continuity. The eighteenth and nineteenth centuries saw the rise and evolution of two distinctly female artefacts which I call 'harem literature' and the feminine 'travelogue proper'. By harem literature I mean writing concerned, mainly or wholly, with the material conditions of life and everyday domestic experience of Muslim women. Harem literature was written by travellers but is, by no means, travel literature. For the narrative of the journey is characteristically subordinated to the interest in customs, manners and morals. More significantly harem literature as its very name implies focuses on the private life rather than on the public, civic, or political one. And its *locus* is the separate female space of the *haremlik*, the women and children's quarters in the segregated household. Harem literature, I argue, presents the most serious challenge to Orientalist and patriarchal authority. For what characterises the women's representation of the different is a sense of familiarity and sympathy with the other. Let me be clear. I do not argue that female observers of and writers on, the *vie intime* were innocent of prejudice or that cultural smugness which characterised the Victorian or Edwardian abroad. Indeed they were believers in Western 'values', in progress, in the cultural supremacy of Europe, sometimes in the empire. As I stressed earlier, the alternative discourse on the Orient did not evolve as a *separate* tradition, precisely because – contrary to the belief of a few exponents of 'gynocentrics' – there was no historical separatist women's culture. Rather gender-specific representations of the other developed alongside the traditional, patriarchal *topoi* and images. What is culturally significant about harem literature is its resistance to the essentialist *topos* of the sensual Orient and the mythically libidinous *orientale*.

By 'travelogue proper' I mean the narrative of a progress from one spot to another, in an open landscape. By definition, then, the very *locus* of the travel account is non-domestic and had been popularly identified, until the nineteenth century, as 'masculine'. To be sure, travel is a universal theme. And the apposition of 'home' and the 'world', domestic happiness and the journey of quest (that apposition noted by Northrop Frye), is archetypal and appears in different cultures at different times. Indeed appositional 'pairs' of the house and the open road, the garden and the 'natural' non-domestic landscape, the hearth and the river, Penelope and Odysseus, a feminised static place and a dynamic space – all these dominated the epic tradition as well as the tradition of the novel and informed the Western imagination *before* the evolution in the eighteenth century of the *bourgeois* ideology of domesticity.[40]

What is relevant to an historian is that harem literature and the feminine travelogue on the Orient were shaped during the very period when gender ideology and the definition of private and public, 'feminine' and 'masculine' spaces, reached their most elaborate forms. And both the new genres challenge not only Orientalist authority but the ideology and the aesthetics of the concept of separate spheres. Harem literature, drawing on experience rather than 'external' textual authority as well as on comparison between cultures, is a critique on Western patriarchy and the position of women in the West. And travel literature by women, indeed the very experience of travel *ipso facto*, subvert gender ideology and the ethoses of domesticity. Writing a travelogue involved a redefinition of the feminine space and sphere of action. And the new genre anatomises the tension between the emancipating effects of travel in what had been literally and metaphorically man's land and culturally dominant notions of femininity (see Chapters 10–12).

Clearly there is a good deal of overlap between the two new models of writing, to be related to the two different kinds of experience of the Middle East: the generically 'feminine' experience of the sympathetic ethnographer and that of the traveller. Thus books with 'customs and manners' for their main subject quite often contained extracts of logs or narratives of travel. And travelogues proper contained conventionally comprise ethnographic accounts. To take a few examples: Montagu's *Letters*; Julia Sophia Pardoe's *City of the Sultan* and the *Domestic Manners of the Turks* (1837); Mary Eliza Rogers' *Domestic Life in Palestine* (1863); Isabel Burton's *Intimate Life in Syria* (1875); Sophia Lane Poole's *The Englishwoman in Egypt* (1844); Annie Jane Harvey's *Turkish Harems and Circassian Homes* (1859) and Caroline Paine's *Tent and Harem* (1859). All these are domestic ethnographies that include sequences of travel. Similarly voyage accounts like Amelia Edwards' *A Thousand Miles Up the Nile* (1873); Amy Fullerton's *Lady's Ride Through Palestine and Syria* (1872); Blunt's *Pilgrimage to Nejd* (1880) and Adella Goodrich-Freer's *In a Syrian Saddle* (1904), as do many other travelogues, include descriptions of harems and the life of women.

ON METHOD AND STRUCTURE

Awareness of the diversity of experience and plurality of discourses, the polyphonic quality of the discussion on the Orient, dictated the organisation of the material. For notwithstanding a number of structural unities, the women's discourse is multivocal. And it presents this diversity of idiom that is a condition of what Bakhtin called 'heteroglossia', the usage, in one culture, of a number of equally significant 'languages' or currencies. There is no 'narrative', strictly speaking. But the presence of 'actors' – individual travellers and writers who are active agents rather than passive characters entrapped in the machinery of structures – is emphasised. Shifts and mutations through time in Western sensibilities are as important as models and patterns. I trace changes from the Augustan to the Victorian then to the Edwardian eras. Consequently the book is arranged chronologically and by theme. Individuals and groups are important and audible (a departure, it will be noted, from the Foucauldian mechanism of discourse and the impersonal study of mentalités).

Part I is a prosopography of travel which analyses the impact of gender on writing about and work in the eastern Mediterranean. This part is about the locations of the alternative female discourse on the Orient, mainly about the relation between the central 'metropolitan' sites of knowledge and authority and the periphery inhabited by the amateur scholar of oriental subjects. Evidence drawing on the quantitative analysis of the literary careers of some 84 authors is collated with examples – the study of unusual lives and oriental careers. Part II, the largest in the book, is devoted to harem literature, the most radical and most innovative of the women's genres. I first examine the writers' filiations and affiliations with tradition and mainstream orientalist authority. Then I proceed to innovation, those elements of discontinuity with hegemonic attitudes to, and representations of, the Middle East. The eighteenth- and later nineteenth-century representations of the *haremlik* and Turkish and Arab women are examined in detail in Chapters 3–6. I begin with the Augustan model of the harem in the works of Lady Mary Wortley Montagu and Elisabeth Craven, margravine of Anspach. Then I proceed to the Victorian and Edwardian writing on oriental women. Certain unities transcend the differences between individual writers and between particular groups of writers. First and most important is the unity of time. There is a significant divide between the eighteenth and nineteenth centuries, predictably in the treatment of sexuality, the sexuality of Eastern women and, indirectly, the writers' own. The Augustan writers, despite their break away from Enlightenment perceptions of womanhood are fascinated with sexuality. The Victorians are more equivocal and their ambivalence evinces itself in elaborate stratagems and stylistic devices that helped the writers come to terms with 'forbidden' subjects. Apart from the 'great divide', between Augustans and Victorians, there are smaller but nonetheless detectable fences which distinguish the early and middle-Victorians from those writing after the 1870s and from the Edwardian writers. Suffice to say here that the farther we get into the nineteenth century the greater the writers' interest in the common people and in life outside the Turkish-Circassian élites, an interest which is traceable to contemporary ethnographic studies of the lower classes in Britain itself and of the 'condition of England question'. And the farther we get into the Victorian era, the more conspicuous the idealisation of the harem and the comparison between it and the *bourgeois* home.

Connected with the desexualisation of the harem in the nineteenth

century is the de-politicisation of the domestic sphere, a trend that
goes back to the Augustan writers. The analogy between domestic and political economy, between patriarchalism and political
tyranny, between the rights of the woman and the citizen, an
analogy that is so pertinent in the Enlightenment discussion on
the origins of government, virtually disappears in the nineteenth
century. Of course, the women travellers had political views, and
most relevant here, they had views about the 'Eastern Question'
and Britain's foreign policy. But the salient characteristic of harem
literature is that it is a-political. Salient because, the nature and
trajectory of the more 'traditional' discourse about the Middle East
were distinctly political. Modern imperialism politicised, more than
ever, the relations between Britain and the Middle East.

To turn away from the 'historical' unities to the structural ones,
those characteristics common to a group, or groups of travellers,
to different communities of writers within the larger group of
gender and class. The most coherent and subsequently most easily
identifiable category of travellers/writers is that of evangelical
proselytisers. The secularisation and feminisation of religion, especially evangelicalism, influenced representations of the domestic
and civic, or political world; of the harem and non-domestic historical landscapes of the Orient. Part III focuses on the expansion
of the religious discourse on the Middle East and the modernisation and secularisation, themselves the results of evangelical
revivalism, of the old model of the pilgrimage. Both the actual
work and the writings of evangelicals are examined. The life and
activities of a community of missionaries and philanthropists in
mid nineteenth-century Palestine are reconstructed. Then representations of domestic life and Biblical landscapes are analysed.

Part IV moves from the domestic to the public, from ethnography
to travel-literature proper, from the *haremlik* to the road and the
caravan. I examine the break away from the religious model in the
writings of Harriet Martineau, Amelia Edwards and a group of specialists with interests and careers related to the new orientalist sciences of Egyptology, Biblical and field archaeology and linguistics.
Last, I look at 'writing couples', the orientalist pairs who travelled
and worked together in the Middle East. A number of the women
authors were married to men who were distinguished authorities
on the Middle East. These pairs not only worked together but
produced co-written accounts of their experiences. The co-produced
travelogue more than any other artefact anatomises the question

of authority, of the tension between tradition and innovation, and between the orientalist and the alternative discourse. At the centre of this chapter is the work of Anne Noel Blunt and Wilfrid Scawen Blunt, husband and wife, anti-imperialists, Arabists, co-travellers. The work of other couples experiencing the Middle East together are also referred to (Isabel and Richard Burton; Theodore and Mabel Bent and Georgina and Friedrich Max Müller *et al.*). Gertrude Bell and Lady Stanhope are omitted not because their lives and Middle Eastern careers are insignificant but because the two writers received so much scholarly and popular attention. And I chose to let the less audible voices of travellers speak.

The ideal reader to whom this book is addressed will follow the argument from beginning to end. However the design of the narrative makes it relatively easy for readers who find the journey too long, or too tedious, to pick up any of the four parts as something self-contained. Thus readers interested in the sociology of travel and travel-literature would concentrate on Part I and those interested in the history of sexuality and in cross-cultural representation on Part II. Part III particularly addresses historians of evangelicalism and the relations between popular religion and imperialism.

One last note on discipline and method. The student of the shifts and mutations in popular sensibilities, what Raymond Williams sensitively described as 'the structure of feeling',[41] is caught between the *Scylla* of analysis of structures and patterns and the *Charybdis* of the select example. He or she may find themselves entrapped between narrative and analysis, between the notable and the common, the 'old' history and the 'new'. My own work, and, I believe, women's history in general, grew from these two kinds of history. Indeed I may even be accused of drawing on them indiscriminately. For in Chapters 3, 10, 11 and 12 I am attentive to the voices of individuals and the group is muted. In Chapters 4–9, the group or groups of writers are more audible than the individual, and I focus on themes, key-words and formulaic representations. Moreover I mix different kinds of evidence – private records and published mass-circulation books, fiction, specialised 'scientific' writing and statistics from the records of organisations. This magpie's promiscuity, Arnaldo Momigliano, has warned us, is the bane of the antiquarian and the bad historian.[42]

If my mixture of materials and of narrative and analysis is 'promiscuous', this is by choice and not by default. Biography and the study of structures are not mutually exclusive, nor are the study of human actors and plots and that of 'discourses'. And the estrangement between 'cultural' resources, like texts and 'social' documents, is in the minds of historian, not in historical reality. A work about the plurality and diversity of experiences and idioms would benefit from a combination of traditional and novel approaches.

Part I

Orientalism, Travel and Gender

1

A Prosopography of Travel, 1763–1914

She considered – or at any rate so expressed herself – that peas could not grow very well without sticks, and could only grow unsupported, but could also make their way about the world without any encumbrance of sticks whatsoever. She did not intend, she said, to rival Ida Pfeiffer, seeing that she was attached to society in a manner almost more than moderate; but she had no idea of being prevented from seeing anything she wished to see because she had neither father, nor husband, nor brother available for the purpose of escort.

Anthony Trollope, 'An Unprotected Female at the Pyramids'.[1]

STRATEGIES AND METHODS

Trollope's delightful, if unkind, portrayal of the 'unprotected' Victorian female abroad is, surprisingly enough, still prevalent. The complex relationship between travel and gender is, conventionally, reduced to Trollopian stereotypes. Women travellers remain classified into 'independent', 'professional' or 'semi-professional' explorers, or writers (exemplified by Ida Pfeiffer) and peripatetic spinsters, redundant both at home and in the expatriate colony abroad. The first class of travellers – comprising women like Gertrude Bell, Amelia Blanford Edwards, Marianne North and Freya Stark – is characterised as 'atypical', an exception from an otherwise patriarchal culture of exploration and, therefore, of little significance to the historian.[2] The second class of travelers is, to be sure, more typical and is thought to reflect the changing status of women in British society. But the enormous literary output produced by amateurs is reckoned worthless and consequently largely ignored.

Tourists like Trollope's Sabina Dawkins remain objects of ridicule, or are benignly neglected. And it is assumed that their experience of the Orient is subsumed in that of their husbands or brothers; that the women's Eastern careers are relative and their role 'supportive'.[3]

Not even decades of women's studies, nor the recent upsurge of popular interest in travel, have dispelled the familiar Trollopian notion about the Western female in the Middle East. Indeed Western travel as such is seen as a literary phenomenon, rather than as a social and cultural one. Professional historians – with few notable exceptions like John Pemble – are not particularly interested in travellers.[4] The field is left to biographers (whether the writers of monographs, or the compilers of collections of biographies of travellers) and literary critics,[5] and is balkanised by television and the press.[6]

I propose to examine the scope of travel to, and writing about, the Middle East between 1763 – which saw the publication of Mary Wortley Montagu's 'Embassy Letters', the first *secular* text by a woman on the Orient – and the outbreak of the First World War in 1914. Further, I attempt to locate travel-writing in the context of the relations between gender and genre. My source material is a quantitative study of structural features of travel, which draws on the collation of biographical information, from diverse sources. My argument is that women's travel, travel as such, is a social phenomenon as well as a cultural one and that, throughout the eighteenth and nineteenth century, this phenomenon was integrated in the *bourgeois Bildung* and *bourgeois* life-style, methods of livelihood and gender-ideology. It is time to rid ourselves of terms like 'middle-class travel', 'aristocratic travel', '*bourgeois* tourism' and so on. They are relative and imprecise and tell us very little about the impact on travel, of the construction of class and gender. A prosopography of travel, drawing on a group-portrait of travellers, will locate them in the broader cultural and literary context.

A few words of qualification. First, it is not my intention to substitute a quantitative analysis for the close-reading of texts. Nor do I propose to supplant historical and literary examples by structures. This part of the book constitutes a supplement – and a necessary one, I would argue, – to what follows it. The explorers and tourists, missionaries and ethnographers whose patterns of career is my source material, are more than the component parts of structures. They are actors, with individual experiences and attitudes. It is vital to bear this in mind and not allow impersonal forces and structural processes to write out the protagonists from the drama. For this reason the discussion of the book-market is generously supplemented by detailed history cases, select examples which spotlight the larger picture.

A second qualification. My study of the travellers' biographies is by no means complete. Rather it is a preliminary sketch hopefully to be followed by extended studies of the social aspects of Orientalism.

In contrast to classical studies of nineteenth-century literary élites, like Williams and Altick's, or very recent works on the gender-sociology of literature like Tuchman and Fortin's,[7] merely collecting the biographical information about travel-writers posed a problem. I was able to draw on the Dictionary of National Biography and other authoritative collections of biography for only about one-third of the writers; most of the names in my sample were never canonised, not even as 'middle-brow', or 'minor' authors. Information, then, had to be extracted from elsewhere, from a variety of biographical and non-biographical sources which may roughly be classified into three types: autobiographical sources; listings and catalogues of works; and the records of societies with special interest in the Middle East.

Travel-books, it is commonly agreed, are in more than one sense autobiographical. They are reconstructions by a narrative 'I' – that may of course be very personal, or impersonal, of a slice of life, or lives. Some students of women's autobiographical writing have pointed out that women's sense of the past is collective rather than individual, emphasising relations to others. In other words, the 'feminine' autobiography does not comfortably fit Olney's classical definition of the genre as a statement of individualism by a 'separate I'.[8] As will be shown in Part IV, women tend to relate their own experience of travel to that of others and develop a number of stratagems and ploys to avoid individualist narrative. A number of travelogues do not simply relate the story of a slice of life but are, also, *Bildung* stories.[9] Much may be gleaned from the texts about the *Bildungsheld* or *protagonist* of the history of travel, about her development and personal and professional choices. Harriet Martineau's *Eastern Life Present and Past* (1846), Amelia Blanford Edwards' *A Thousand Miles Up the Nile* (1873), Emily Anne Beaufort's *Egyptian Sepulchres and Syrian Shrines* (1863) – not to mention Elisabeth Ann Finn's *Home in the Holy Land* and her *Third Year in Jerusalem* (1863 and 1866); Adella Goodrich-Freer's *In a*

Syrian Saddle (1900), Baroness Herbert's *Cradle Lands* (probably 1864) and numerous other narratives of travel – are also *Bildungsromans*. Of course, travelogues draw on purely autobiographical materials, usually not intended for publication, such as notes, journals, logs, letters and so on. In published versions, prefaces or introduction are particularly rich in biographical detail. But more often than not the preparatory notes are designed to conceal rather than reveal the real purpose of travel, the nature of the journey and its circumstances.

Notwithstanding, information about social background, family status and methods of livelihood or work can usually be gleaned from the texts themselves. Travellers sometimes wrote auto-biographies. Elisabeth Craven, margravine of Anspach; Harriet Martineau; Julia Pardoe; Elisabeth Ann Finn; Isabel Burton; Fanny Janet Blunt; Marianne North; Margaret Fountaine, are but a few examples.[10] Other travellers were written about in monographs, articles and popular contemporary collections of biographies. Missionaries, in particular, were featured in the publications of the evangelising societies. As is shown in Chapters 6 and 7, the evangelical hagiographies of peripatetic missionaries make it possible to recover the life of a forgotten group of travellers, barely known to us. Suffice to mention here evangelisers in Syria like Elisabeth Bowen Thompson and Augusta Mentor Mott, missionaries to Persia like Mary S. R. Bird and Fidelia Fisk; proselytisers active in Palestine, like Jane Walker-Arnott, Caroline Cooper and Mary Louisa Whately, the enormously influential missionary to Egypt.[11]

The vast biographical information has been collated with data from the records of the orientalist societies. The Victorian ethno-graphic and geographical societies – amateur *and* scientific, religious *and* anti-clerical – were the bodies principally responsible for the purveyance and dissemination of data on non-European cultures. These bodies commissioned explorers and missionaries to collect information, then classified it, processed the data and disseminated knowledge to diverse audiences. Naturally the control of infor-mation involved status, authority and power.[12] Thus the activity of individual writers, in or alongside the metropolitan centres of knowledge and power, reveals a great deal about the élites of professional orientalists, but also about the relationships between specialists and amateurs and between writing and reading publics. The records of the societies – reports of proceedings, subscription lists and official statements – are mines of information about par-ticipating individuals as well.

Four societies, each representing a different organisational pattern, a different approach to 'science', a different attitude towards religion, and, finally, a different gender-policy, were selected here: the Royal Geographical Society (RGS); the Palestine Exploration Fund (PEF); the Egypt Exploration Fund (EEF) and the Jerusalem Literary Society (JLS). Of the four, the RGS, founded by a charter in 1832, is the only homogeneous body: socially, professionally and sexually.[13] Though non-partisan, the RGS identified itself with Britain's imperialist politics, maintaining connections with army circles, notably the admiralty. Victorian exploration was never a purely scientific enterprise and constituted a part of Britain's expansionist drive. Like all male clubs the RGS persistently refused membership to women. They were admitted as fellows as late as 1913, after nearly three decades of agitation, manipulations and discussion inside the Society's governing bodies and the national press.[14] Informally, however, women working in connection with the RGS were permitted to appear before its general meetings and publish in its periodicals.

The PEF (founded in 1865) and EEF (started in 1882) represent two similar variants of the amateur voluntary association with a fundamental religious ideology and purpose.[15] Both were based on subscriptions and donations, both were inclusive and non-denominational (but nevertheless overwhelmingly Anglican societies), and neither officially discriminated against women. The EEF was founded and, until 1892, practically run by a woman, Amelia Blanford Edwards. The three societies are self-designated 'scientific'. But the Victorian usage of the word 'science' is rather loose and certainly different from our own post-Kuhnian notion of it. For 'science' could denote every field of inquiry and writing outside the Humanities, or more specifically the natural sciences, or the new and non-academic *Wissenschaft*, apparently based on empirical and value-free investigation. This last category applies to Biblical geography and Biblical archaeology, indeed to the semi-scientific inquiry of the Holy Land. The PEF is ostensibly committed to the 'principles of scientific investigation', but its numerous addresses to the public do not even pretend to conform to the Baconian concept of neutral and moral-free experimentation. Indeed the very purpose of scientific interest in Palestine was to corroborate religion, not to undermine it. The EEF was more connected with the rise of archaeology and historical geography as academic disciplines, based upon empirical (field) research, methods of classification and methodical

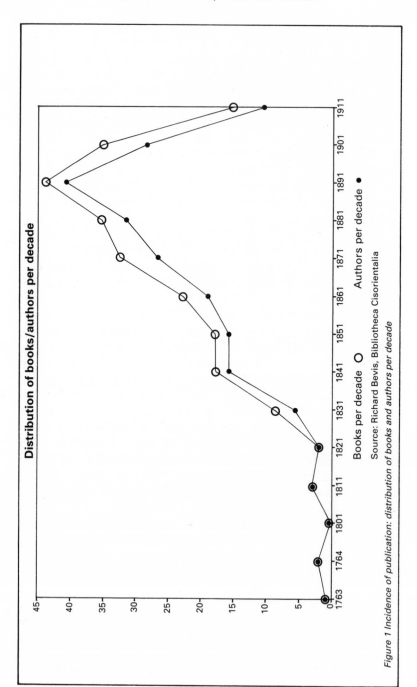

Figure 1 Incidence of publication: distribution of books and authors per decade

organisation of data.[16] The Jerusalem Literary Society may be taken as exemplar of the provincial or colonial amateur society, an anti-quarian body, devoted to the collection of raw ethnographic and archaeological data.[17] The JLS admitted women and, of the four societies, had the closest relations with the 'ordinary' travellers and residents in the Middle East.

Finally, the catalogues of the Societies and the British Library Catalogue (BLC) were used to substantiate information obtained elsewhere, on literary activity, specialisation and careers. Following Williams' example (in his *Long Revolution*) an inventory, listing printed books about the Middle East was taken as the basis of the analysis of structures of travel and the travellers' collective biography. Richard Bevis' *Bibliotheca Cisorientalia*, a richly annotated inventory of orientalist scholarship and travel-literature between 1500 and 1914, particularly suited my purposes.[18] Its flaws not-withstanding, Bevis' is the most inclusive catalogue available of works in English about the Middle East. Starting from it, I set on the tortuous and often unrewarding search for information.

MAPPING THE FIELD: PRINTED BOOKS, 1763–1914

It sometimes occurs that quantitative analyses and researches of structures corroborate, rather than reverse, those general impres-sions, or vague, commonly-held assumptions which are so despised by social historians. Bevis' list happily verifies what literary critics and culturalists had always suspected namely, that travel, before the nineteenth century, was an exclusively androcentric experience and the travelogue a male genre. The invasion of the field by women during the nineteenth century was ignored. Of Bevis' figure of 245 published books, by 187 women, 4 appeared between 1500 and 1821 and the rest, 241, were issued over a period of 90 years (1821–1911).[19] The nine decades present an interesting hyperbola. As Figure I clearly shows, three decades of slow but steady rise in the incidence of publications (1821–1851) are followed by a dramatic curve, manifest in a cascade of works, climaxing in 1891 and then tapering down. The figure for 1911–1920 is lower than that for 1821–30. The decline in the incidence of publications undoubtedly reflects global political curves. The First World War interrupted regular communications between Europe and the eastern Medi-terranean, effectively stopping travel. Moreover, during the war the publishing industry suffered one of its worse ever slumps. However, the changes in the graph are also attributable to shifts in the nature of travel which are not political and which should be connected to the changing relations between tourism and gender. The curve illustrating 'distribution of authors' follows, though a little less dramatically, that of the incidence of 'publication per decade'.

It would be myopic to present the pace and scope of the writings as gender-specific. Indeed the change from 1821 to 1920 is not a classic example of the feminisation of a literary genre, a term which is applied to the 'take over' of an artefact, previously dominated by men, its occupation, then appropriation by the invaders. The so-called 'invasion' of the 'high-brow' novel by women in the middle decades of the nineteenth century and its subsequent re-appropriation by men-of-letters (recently described by Tuchman and Fortin), are spuriously comparable with the entrance of women into the field of travel-writing.[20] Numerically, Mediterranean literary travel was not feminised. The majority of writers were men. Reliable nineteenth-century listings of travel books, notably Reinhold Röhricht's *Bibliotheca Geographia Palestinae* (1888), confirm this.[21] The flourishing of travel-writing by women is evidently a manifestation of the bonanza of the commercial travelogue on the eastern Mediterranean.[22] Comparison with male travel is not enough. To assess change over time, to grasp the novelty of the phenomenon, we need to look backward. Set against the long period of inactivity that had preceded it the outburst in the nineteenth century constitutes what can only be called an eruption. Material, mainly political changes, discussed in detail in the Introduction, contributed to (rather than determined) the rise of Mediterranean travel. It is more than a coincidence that the breakthrough in the decade 1841–50, shown in Figure 1, almost exactly overlaps with the aftermath of the demise of Mehmet Ali and the beginning of the intervention, on an unprecedented scale, of the Western powers in the Ottoman Empire. The central curve, from the fourth to the eighth decade, roughly coincides with the era of reforms in the Ottoman Empire (*Tanzimat*) and the revolution of transport which made the eastern Mediterranean easily accessible to Europeans. Yet, as already argued, political changes and changes in the material conditions of travel do not account for those traits of the *voyage-en-orient* which are new and gender specific. Did the Orient have special allure for women? Was there a feminine pattern of travel, distinguishable from the culturally predominant one? Did there evolve a female 'Eastern career'?

PATTERNS OF TRAVEL AND WORK

My prosopography of travel is somewhat less than the sum of the biographies of the 187 odd female authors on Bevis' incomplete list. I was able, with some difficulties, to compile the biographies of 84 authors, or 53 per cent of the list, a large enough sample which covers the entire period of study. The questions asked about the biographies fall into five major categories: family status, social origin, method of livelihood or occupation, the nature and trajectory of travel and last but, perhaps most important, the class or kind of publication, according to subject matter and prospective audience. A few of these categories need to be refined before proceeding.

'Occupation' or 'method of livelihood' are particularly problematic covering, as they do, both paid and non-paid work. As has been argued in the past, orthodox, especially Marxist definitions of work as waged labour, write out gender and do not adequately describe women's work. Even after industrialisation and the separation of the home from the work place, female labour remained largely individual, unregulated and based in the home. Work does not necessarily denote paid work, certainly not in middle-class contexts.[23] On the contrary. The *bourgeois* woman's work was a 'vocation', a duty or a mission. As F. K. Prochaska has shown, for middle-class Victorian women philanthropy was not merely a pastime, nor an outlet to frustrated energies, but a full-time occupation which apprenticed women in careers which were socially and sometimes politically meaningful.[24] A number of travellers in the sample were engaged, full-time, in voluntary work. Even missionaries formally affiliated to the larger evangelical organisations and employed by them, often travelled to the Middle East at their own expense, living on their own incomes. As the smug official historian of the Church Missionary Society puts it: 'God raised up Christian ladies with private means'[25] to work in his vineyard. Beside vocational work, that is paid missionary work and private philanthropy, 'occupation' comprises two other sub-categories: specialised writing requiring a training of sorts, usually in the burgeoning new non-academic orientalist sciences, and non-specialised writing, for majority audiences. The tripartite classification into 'vocational',

Table 1   Women travellers, 1719–1918: distribution by marital and social status, occupation, types and journey and publication.

A: Family status	no.	%
unmarried	23	27.4
married	53	63.1
unknown	8	9.5

B: Social Status		
titled	14	16.7
upper middle	25	29.8
middle middle	42	50.0
lower middle	1	1.2
uncertain	2	2.4

C: Occupation		
specialist	25	29.8
vocational	13	15.5
non-specialised	46	54.8

D: Journey		
specialised	27	32.1
vocational	9	10.7
travel	36	42.9
tourism	11	13.1
uncertain	1	

E: Authors, by subject		
specialist	20	23.8
religious	4	4.8
general	59	70.2
uncertain	1	1.2

'general' or 'non-specialised' and 'specialised' was found particularly useful and was applied to 'occupation' as well as to the two other major categories 'nature of travel' and 'class', or type of writing. Except that in the case of the second category, 'tourism'[26] and 'travel' are substituted for 'general' or 'non-specialised' travel (see Table 1).

In contradistinction to the stereotype of the peripatetic spinster abroad, the object of numerous Victorian literary spoofs and some recent journalistic and scholarly efforts, the typical traveller/writer in my sample is married. Table 1A clearly shows that a significant 53, or 63 per cent of the authors were married, only 23, or 27.45 per cent were single and the marital status of 8 or a mere 9.5 per cent cannot be ascertained. In point of fact the 63 per cent married authors may be defined as 'auxiliary travellers', or, in supporting roles, as spouses or siblings. They had not chosen an

'Eastern career', but went to the Orient as the help-mates of career-diplomats, soldiers, missionaries, colonisers and scholars. It appears that travel, far from emancipating middle-class women, reproduced dominant structures of hierarchy, notably the familial structure with its distinct gender-roles. However, 'supporting' or 'auxiliary' are empty titles. Some of the most distinguished travellers and greatest literary innovators superficially fit in the classification of 'help-mates'. Lady Mary Wortley Montagu accompanied the unfortunate and forgotten Edward Wortley on his embassy to the Sublime Porte; Isabel Burton was the wife and help-mate (she would rather prefer 'mate') of Richard Francis Burton, the most versatile and prolific Victorian travel writer and, between 1871 and 1875, Britain's Consul to Damascus; Elisabeth Ann Finn was married to James Finn, Britain's most controversial Consul to Jerusalem; Fanny Janet Blunt married the Consul to Smyrna. And there is much more. Mabel Bent, Sophia Lane Poole, Georgina Max-Müller, Elisabeth Bensley, Agnes Lewis Smith and Margaret Gibson Dunlop were married or otherwise related to prominent orientalists and Biblical scholars. Lane Poole was the sister of Edward William Lane, the greatest authority on contemporary Egypt and Max-Müller was the wife of Europe's foremost comparative philologist. Anne Noel Blunt, wife of the Arabist and poet Wilfrid Scawen Blunt and, probably, the single most impressive example of a woman explorer in the Middle East before Gertrude Bell, did not initiate any of her first six journeys to that area. She merely followed the peripatetic Blunt, whom she reverently calls, in her journals, 'master'.[27] My argument is that an initial supporting role by no means precludes the development of an independent career, let alone a generic experience of travel. This is the case with each and every one of the cases cited above and quite a few others besides. Who now remembers the Honourable Edward Wortley? Probably a very few diplomatic historians.

Travel was a middle-class phenomenon. Women's travel exclusively so. No longer aristocratic, or 'gentrified', a part of the nobleman's classic *grand tour*, the *voyage-en-orient* was becoming a distinctly *bourgeois* practice. The process of *embourgeoisement*, however, even in the era of Thomas Cook's organised packages to Palestine and Egypt (the first of which took place in 1869, a short time before the opening of the Suez Canal), did not extend to the lower middle-classes. But within certain social *milieux*, notably the middle, middle-class, travel was becoming established as a part of the female, as well as the male education and *Bildung*.

To exactly define 'social status' reasonably continuous kinds of family were listed and then divided into 'titled' houses: upper middle-class, middle-middle and lower-middle class. The sub categories are nobility (in the narrow legal sense of the term), county families (gentry is too open a term in the nineteenth century), higher clergy, 'intellectual aristocracy' and top professions, army families and big business. All except 'nobility' are entered under upper middle-class. There follow medium business, lower clergy and the professions, and then finally trade. As Table 1B indicates, an impressive 80.1 per cent came from the bottom three categories. A little over 29 per cent of the writers came from county and upper middle-class families. Notable examples are Gertrude Lowthian Bell, with a manufacturing, gentrified background and a network of family connections in the metropolitan 'intellectual aristocracy' (Noel Annan's term);[28] Emily Beaufort (at the time of her travels she had not yet married Viscount Strangford) and Frances Power Cobbe, of Anglo-Irish landed background. Examples of the upper middle-class are: Lucie Duff-Gordon, wife of a civil-servant and daughter of a jurist and barrister and the famous blue-stocking Sarah Austin and Mary Louisa Whately, daughter of the Archbishop of Dublin (C.O.E).

An overwhelming 50 per cent of the writers came from middle middle-class background: clerical (typically dissenting) families, provincial business, or manufacturing and the professions, below the leading London élite.[29] Harriet Martineau is a very good exemplar of a professional writer with a provincial dissenting background. Isabella Bird-Bishop, Margaret Fountaine (the well-known entomologist) and the Gibson-Lewis twins represent the comfortably off, Broad-Church section. Elisabeth Ann Finn, on the other hand, comes from an Evangelical missionary background. Amelia Edwards comes from a banking family and Julia Sophia Pardoe from an army background. In the whole of my sample there is a single, untypical example of a *petit-bourgeoise*. This is the delightful Eliza Fay, an adventurer and embezzler, whose *Letters from India* (comprising sections on Egypt) was sold, posthumously, to the *Calcutta Gazette*, to pay off her debts. Fay's example may serve to illustrate the way in which travel became a status symbol and a symbol of social mobility, and was integrated in the feminine *Bildung*. In the stylised *apologia*, preceding the *Letters*, Fay explains she did not venture to publish earlier. In the past: 'a woman who was not conscious of possessing decided genius or superior knowledge could not be induced to leave the harmless tenor of her way and render herself amenable to the pains and penalties generally inflicted on female author-ships'.[30] Obviously her approach to travel is frankly entrepre-neurial.

> Many unpretending females, who fearless of the critical press that once attended the voyage, venture to launch their little books on the vast ocean through which amusement or instruction is conveyed to a reading-public: the wit of Fielding is no longer held *in terrorem* and the delineations of Smollett would apply them in vain . . . A female author is no longer regarded as an object of derision, nor is she wounded by unkind reproof from the Lords of creation.[31]

Fay's *apologia* is both a pastiche on contemporary discussion on travel-literature and a feminist statement. The butt of her criticism are Fielding and Smollett, two prominent novelists who shaped the travelogue. Her use of the metaphor of the sea-voyage, to describe both her own travel experience and the narrative of travel, is immensely revealing. Fay rose from humble origins to respectability, becoming a textile merchant and the owner of a ship. The illegitimate daughter of a maidservant and an unknown father, she married above her station, a barrister who was advocate of the Supreme Court at Calcutta. Thus travel and life in the colonies made and unmade Fay's career, reputation and fortune. And at the end of an extraordinary life she shrewdly notes that a fortune is to be made from travel-writing. A female too can launch a 'book' on the 'vast ocean' of literature.

The top of the greasy social pole is, throughout the nineteenth century, considerably less crowded than the crammed middle. Only 14, or 16.5 per cent, of the authors come from families which can be classified as 'noble' (in the narrow, legal sense of this term) or 'aristocratic' (denoting the hereditary group of the bigger landed families, below the peerage). Seven per cent only belong to the former category and significantly two of them are the (only) eighteenth-century examples in the sample: Lady Mary Wortley Montagu (1689–1763), daughter of the fifth earl and first duke of Kingestone and Elisabeth Craven, margravine of Anspach, daugh-ter of the fourth earl of Berkeley, wife of William, later earl of Craven and then married to Frederick Christian Charles, margrave of Brandenburg, Bareith and Anspach. Among the nineteenth-century examples are: Hester Lucy Stanhope, (1776–1839) daughter of the third earl of Stanhope and niece of Pitt the Younger; Harriet Catherine Egerton, Lady Ellesmere (1800–1860), daughter of Charles Granville and wife of the first earl of Ellesmere and Frances Vane, marchioness of Londonderry, heiress to Sir Henry Vane-Tempest and wife of Charles William Stuart, third marquis of Londonderry. But like the Cockney traveller, the aristocratic tourist, maliciously attacked by Thackeray in his *Book of Snobs*, is untypical. Feminine literary travel was, almost exclusively, *bourgeois*.

'Social status' and 'work' are almost inextricable and, together, bear on the nature of travel and type of publication. What immediately strikes us about the women's oriental career is its amateur character. Work is related to education, albeit one which is typically informal. A self-taught woman could and often did specialise in one of the new amateur orientalist sciences that burgeoned outside the universities. The work cannot narrowly be defined as a profession, because it did not involve formal training, nor a collective sense of status and identity of its pursuers. The characteristic Middle Eastern career, then, illustrates the traits of women's work outside the industrial working-class: it is not rigidly defined; it is informal and only rarely centrally controlled or institutionalised; it is individual; it can be done at home or, from home and, subsequently, it does not seriously challenge Victorian gender ideology and the middle-class ethos of domesticity. It is, in short, quasi, or proto-professional. The figures in Table 1C speak for themselves: 69 authors, or slightly over 70 per cent, pursued non-specialised careers. Significantly, this figure divides, unequally, between non-specialised writing, 49, or 54.8 per cent, the single largest category of occupation in the sample and vocational work 13, or 15.5 per cent of the sample. The significant figure of 25 specialists (29.8 per cent) corroborates the earlier argument about the character of women's work.

A relatively large number of travellers were affiliated to the burgeoning scientific societies and wrote for specialist audiences, which were smaller and more homogeneous than the larger fiction and miscellany reading-public, the target of non-professional, miscellaneous writers. It is no coincidence that there were women ethnographers (notably evangelical ethnographers) but no anthropologists, at the very time that physical anthropology and field studies of exotic cultures were emerging as separate disciplines. Women were botanists, entomologists and botanical painters, but there were no women geologists and hardly any zoologists. They were Biblical archaeologists and Egyptologists, but no philologists or Bible´ critics; amateur geographers, but no topographers (an occupation dominated by the military corps of the Royal Engineers, first surveyors of Palestine).[32] Take, for example archaeology and Egyptology, both emerging in the 1880s and 1890s as disciplines, still lacking a methodology and research techniques and struggling for recognition as 'sciences'.[33] The proportion of women among the scholars of Egypt's antiquities and archaeologists and antiquarians active in Egypt and Palestine is astonishing. Amelia Blanford Edwards (1831–92); Lady Helen Mary Tirard (the first woman to serve on the Committee of the EEF); Annie Quibele Abernethie (1862–1927); Grace Mary Crowfoot (1878–1951); Marie (Fanny) Corbaux (1812–1882); Mary Brodrick (died 1933); Kate and Nora Christina Griffith; Janet Gourlay, not to mention Agnes Lewis and Margaret Dunlop, are but a few examples. It is significant that the cohort of writers born after 1850 received a university education, or a higher education of sorts.

Before assembling the data on occupation, the types of career and the two remaining categories, which cover the nature of travel and classification of writing, another word of caution. Neither 'nature of travel', nor 'type of writing' are precise categories. Both resist definition and quantification. What sometimes is stated by the travel-writer as the purpose of the journey may be either a rationalisation of motives, or excuses for ambitions which are less readily articulated. Even experienced and confident writers are cryptic about their purposes or aims and resort to convention and bathos.

Beyond the stiffly clichéd preface is, usually, an elusive residuum of explanation for the lure of the Orient. Harriet Martineau and Amelia Edwards, both established as professional novelists and essayists *before* their Eastern journeys, each, respectively, states that these journeys were merely diversions; that they are neither serious nor scholarly pursuits; that the travelogues based upon them are not carefully planned and executed constructs but unpremeditated, rather innocuous artefacts. Yet both writers prepared themselves before, during and after the actual journey, for its literary reconstruction. Both took on punishing reading courses in the classics, in Biblical archaeology and Egyptology (Edwards taught herself to read hieroglyphs). For both, the journey was a watershed in a literary career, indeed in their lives. Martineau's travels precipitated her transformation from Necessarian Unitarian to a Positivist. As for Edwards, she abandoned fiction and embarked on – to her – a totally new occupation: the study of Egypt's history, ancient language and antiquities, the organisation of a new scientific society and the propagation of the new science of Egyptology. The preface to her *A Thousand Miles Up the Nile* (1873) which Edwards left in the revised second edition, states that she 'drifted hither [to Egypt] by accident, with no excuse of health, or business, or any serious object whatever; and had just taken refuge in Egypt as one might turn aside into the Burlington Arcade or the *Passage des Panoramas* – to get out of the rain.'[34] One finds it difficult to imagine the formidable Edwards drifting anywhere. And, like Martineau, or the equally diffident Emily Beaufort and Anne Blunt, she (Edwards) encumbers her scholarly, carefully constructed narration of an 'unserious' journey with notes and references to impress upon the reader her own seriousness. Blunt, in fact, conceals the real purpose of her various journeys and that purpose must be sought in her journals and pocket-diaries. So 'nature of travel' is a compromise, between the confusingly ambiguous professed motives, and the pattern of occupation during the journey.

The correlation between occupation and nature of travel is revealing: 42.9 per cent may be classified as 'travellers' (including long-time residents) touring the Middle East in a party, or on their own, but not on an organised package. Another 13 per cent are tourists, typically Cook's tourists, or 'Cookites' as they are collectively known, less individualistic, and, obviously, pertaining to the category of mass, commercialised tourism, rather than travel. Together, the two categories add up to nearly 56 per cent, a figure which matches that of non-specialist writers, catering for large, heterogeneous audiences. Yet there is a significant change over time, clearly evident in Figures 2 and 3, which illustrates the shift from traditional female work and writing to a more modern pattern of quasi- or semi-professional careers. The older, traditional pattern in which writing and philanthropy predominate, is supplanted by a newer one, in which specialisation becomes all-important. One notes that the change is quite dramatic and climaxes in the decade 1891–90, when the number of specialist journeys rises and, for the first time, actually exceeds 'travel', 'tourism' and 'religious journeys'.

Two structures or patterns of Eastern career emerge. The first is non-specialist travel, combined with a writing career. The second pattern is a semi-professional, quasi-scientific career, connected with the new branches of Bible and oriental studies, themselves devoted to the authentication of the Scriptures as historically accurate texts and the rise of quasi-scientific, voluntary evangelising societies. Ample evidence outside Bevis' list and my sample supports this conjecture. The proportion of women in the new societies, propagating the newer sciences of Biblical Archaeology, geography and naturalism is impressive, particularly when it is compared with the proportion in the older, male-dominated scientific clubs, such as the RGS. In the Palestine Exploration Fund there is a rise from an initial one per cent of female subscribers in 1865, to seven per cent in 1868 to 17.2 per cent at the beginning of 1869. In 1875 the figure stabilises to remain a little over 20 per cent (there are 22.5 per cent in 1877; 20.5 per cent in 1888; 22 per cent in 1895 and 18.92 per cent in 1901).[35] The reason why the proportion never rises above about a fifth of the subscriptions may well be that the PEF had its affiliated female organisation, the Ladies' Association in Aide of (the) Palestine Exploration Fund or LAPEF, for short (my abbreviation). The Ladies' Association was started in 1875, at the time of one of the PEF's worse-ever financial crises (it had had quite a few) and was master-minded by the formidable Elisabeth Ann Finn. Finn, a well known Evangelical with a millenarian bent, philanthropist amongst the Jews and philosemite and an authority on mid-century Palestine, responded to the request of Sir Walter Besant, the Fund's secretary, to mobilise 'ladies', known for their love of the Bible and things Biblical, to help out the parent-body. Initially a fund-raising organisation, the LAPEF soon took off. At peak times, during the late 1870s, it had over 12 local branches and 300 members. It disappears from the Society's Quarterly Statements in 1881, exactly at the time when the proportion of females in the parent organisation rises. Several Scottish Ladies' Associations, however, persist till 1890. Significantly the LAPEF concentrated on work among women, distributing pamphlets, organising Palestine bazaars, convening ladies' meetings aimed to bring the 'work we are doing in Palestine before those who can best be reached by drawing room meetings'.[36]

The figures for the EEF are even more impressive. There are merely five women, or 7.6 per cent on the very first list of subscribers, launching the Fund. In 1884, a year later, there is a sudden rise to 25.7 per cent in England alone. The figure for 1886 is 37 per cent, for 1887 37.4 per cent and for 1905 38 per cent. In 1911, when total subscription slumps from 1530 to 983, the proportion of the women slightly rises to reach its peak, a little over 39 per cent. In the antiquarian Jerusalem Literary Society, the origin, in Palestine, of the PEF, the proportion of women members hardly ever falls below fifty per cent.[37]

The patterns of travel and career correspond with the kinds of women's work and method of livelihood which were wholly reconcilable with Victorian gender ideology. Writing and philanthropy were women's vocations, 'proper' tasks for ladies. Generically 'feminine', both occupations were outward manifestations of inner female qualities and aptitudes and corroborated, rather than challenged, the *bourgeois* ethos of the separateness of the sexes. The famous typology of gender, at the centre of this ethos, stresses women's impressionability; their unlimited capacity for 'empathy' and identification with the 'other' (a child, man, the pauper, the non-regenerate) their sensitivity to detail, rather than the whole; their genius as collectors of evidence, rather than analysts.[38]

It is precisely these qualities that have been appreciated in the ethnographer (as against the modern anthropologist), the antiquarian (as against an historian), and the travel-writer and the novelist. So, the women's entrance into a discourse previously perceived as 'masculine' could be conceptualised and ideologically legitimised. Certainly, travel, both in the literal and metaphorical meaning of this word, signified a break-away from the 'home', apotheosising those values inscribed in the woman. Yet travel-writing was done from home. The log, or journal or epistolary travelogue usually – like the domestic novel – were prepared for publication at home. And, as Frances Power Cobbe shrewdly notes in 1863, to the 'unprotected', solitary female abroad, the tent too was 'home', invested with middle-class values.[39] Travel brought together, both for the travel/narrator and the reader (travelling vicariously), hitherto two separated spaces: the domestic, or private and the public or civic, 'home' and the 'world'. Leonore Davidoff aptly describes the tensions between, and overlapping of, these two spaces as 'negotiable relations'.[40] For the very notion of separateness, of gender-specific qualities and aptitudes, which are naturally 'feminine', legitimised the evolution of new kinds of public work, yet one that was related intimately to the real and symbolic home.

The third pattern of Middle Eastern travel presents another example of the negotiability of socialised and symbolic spaces. Missionary work and philanthropy were gradually becoming attractive and respectable occupations. Evidently both fit in the category of 'woman's work'; particularly the evangelical concept of work. According to evangelical gender ideology, which will be discussed in detail in Part IV, women are particularly equipped for a spiritual, evangelist occupation such as proselytising among women. Naturally religious, specially close to Christ, 'first at the cross and last at the sepulchre', women possess his two humane traits: self-sacrifice and the service of others. Christ-like, women are mediators between the thiswordly and the spiritual and otherwordly. They are the saviours of the *homo economicus et sensualis* from a corrupting materialistic and crassly sensual life in an increasingly competitive society. Evangelical ideology and propaganda as well as the secularised stereotype of the 'Angel in the House', deriving from this ideology, encouraged women to go out of the home and into the world as apostles of Christian humanity and carriers of moral and social reforms.[41] The guardian of the family hearth was natural candidate for an evangeliser or a reformer. And as F. K. Prochaska has shown, religious gender ideology is one of the main causes for the invasion – for 'invasion' is an apt metaphor here – of Victorian charity organisations by middle-class women.

As already mentioned, a whole section of this book (Part IV) is devoted to vocational travel and religious work in, and writing about, Palestine and Syria. It suffices here to outline the borders of the work in the Middle East. Although missionaries and pilgrims add up to merely a fifth of Bevis' list, their work typifies certain general patterns of behaviour of the Englishwoman abroad. Virtually every one of the writers I came across enacted at one point or another in her Eastern career the conventionalised feminine role of the Christian 'lady bountiful', ministering to the poor or attending the sick and elderly; initiating indigenous women in the domestic sciences; distributing Bibles and, more practicably food, or clothes and, sometimes, openly sermonising. Emily Ann Beaufort and her sister aided Druse and Christian women during the first hostilities in Lebanon in 1861; Isabel Burton distributed medicines and foodstuffs to Syrian villagers. Jane Digby El-Mezrab (Lady Ellenborough) regularly supplied the Bedouin clan of the Anayza with staples and was renowned, throughout the Syrian desert, for her healing powers. Earlier Hester Stanhope played similar roles for the Druse of Mount Lebanon. Mary Eliza Rogers, Elisabeth Ann Finn, Mathilda Cubley, Elisabeth Bowen Thompson, Augusta Mentor-Mott and Mary Louisa Whately were each involved in philanthropic activities aiding indigenous women and children.

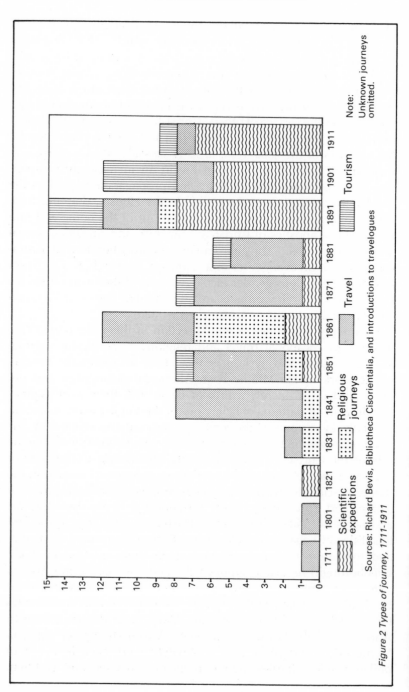

Figure 2 Types of journey, 1711-1911

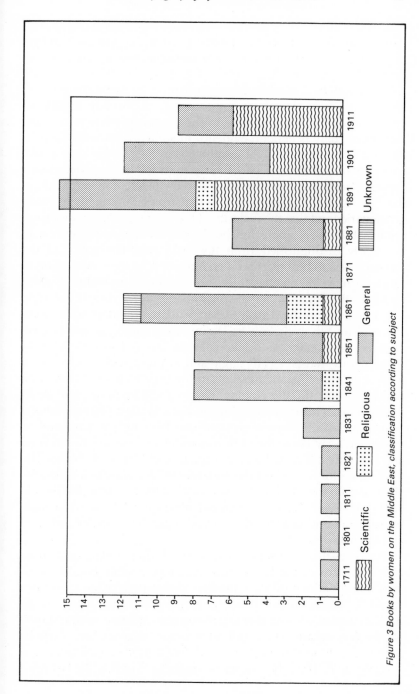

Figure 3 Books by women on the Middle East, classification according to subject

And Anne Blunt, Mary Mackintosh, Lucie Duff-Gordon and even the apostate Adella Goodrich-Freer offered advice and medical care to *fallahin* and Bedouins and were distinguished as 'hakims', or doctors.[42]

It may well be argued that the female traveller merely transferred abroad her domestic role at home, simply duplicating traditional gender roles. Yet there is more to the enormous missionary drive than that. There is enough evidence to show that women preponderated in the bigger Anglican missions in the Middle East. In fact contemporary estimates, particularly from the last two decades of the nineteenth century and the decade before the outbreak of the First World War, demonstrate that women outnumbered men missionaries and that the majority of the females in the missionising organisations were single. Indeed the female missionary career may be clearly distinguished from the male one. The policy of the missions was to hire married men but single women. According to Julius Richter, the nineteenth-century authority on Middle Eastern missions, the figures of female missionaries, for Syria and Palestine are: 19 (of 20), in the British Syrian Schools, an independent body founded by Elisabeth Bowen Thompson; 5 (of 10) in the English Friends' Missionary Association; 29 (of 56) in the CMS, plus 13 missionaries' wives; 29 (15 single and 14 missionaries' wives) of a total of 44 in the Asiatic missions of the London Jews Society (LJS) which did not officially employ women and 4 (of 6) respectively in the Edinburgh Missionary Society and Jane Walker-Arnott's Tabitha School, at Jaffa.[43] Altogether, there are 175 single women and 58 missionaries' wives in the 24 British and American societies in Syria and Palestine, compared with 99 ordained and lay missionaries. The total figure for Egypt and the Sudan is 161 females compared with 108 males. In the whole of the Middle East the figure for the decade 1891–1900 is 450 single female missionaries and 229 married female missionaries and missionaries' wives, compared with 380 ordained and lay male ones.[44]

One notes that the process mapped by Richter and by contemporary historians of the Evangelical missions, notably Eugene Stock (CMS) and Gidney (LJS), is inverse to that perceptible in Figures 2 and 3. It appears that religious work, rather than being on the decline, expanded. And that expansion is particularly manifest during the very decades characterised before as 'secular'. Yet, as will be seen later, vocational work too underwent professionalisation and specialisation. The cohort of missionaries born during the last third of the nineteenth century were trained and formally educated. The traditional pattern of pilgrimage was retained, but religious travel was secularised and acquired a thisworldly social significance. In other words the *peregrinato* developed into a career.

It is significant that the outburst of missionary activities abroad coincides with and manifests, a wider 'feminine' interest in the Middle East. Even the misogynist metropolitan missions shrewdly capitalised on this interest. Standard histories of the CMS and LJS emphasise that women are possessed of a 'natural', generic interest in the land of the Bible. Women, devoid of theological education, are reckoned specially susceptible to evangelical millenarian beliefs and to literal Biblism, with its emphasis on the historical veracity of the Scriptures. Critics of Bibliotary, from Coleridge and George Eliot to Martineau, condemn female enthusiasm about Middle Eastern Geography (I have in mind Eliot's attack on devout 'ladies'). And Frances Power Cobbe, an evangelical turned agnostic, exhorts women to follow in the footsteps of Bunyan's Christian (not his meek Christina) and those of the crusaders, to recover faith and a meaning to their lives.[45]

The Evangelical propaganda was effective. The Eastern, or Levantine missions boast of the highest proportion of female subscribers. The proportion in the CMS rises from a 17 per cent in 1824 to 44 per cent in 1900, and in the JLS the proportion is 59 per cent.[46]

Late in the day, the metropolitan missionary establishment acknowledged that women field-workers were an enormous asset to the missions, particularly in polygamous and segregated societies. Only women, it was realised, could penetrate the harem, or *purdah*, or even the monogamous, non-segregated, nonetheless closed, non-Muslim household. Only women had access to information concerning the life of oriental women and children. Only the truly Christian women could reach out to the non-regenerate ones and only the former could precipitate domestic and moral reform in the polygamous Middle East. Thus the rise of new career-opportunities, deriving yet breaking away from traditional patterns of vocational work, was accompanied by a redefinition of the purposes and roles of the religious, evangelical travelogue (see Chapters 6–7).

Any taxonomy will have obvious flaws. My sampling and classification of travel and structuring of patterns and trends, may contain more flaws than comparable attempts in neighbouring disciplines. There is, of course, a good deal of overlapping, of diverse categories:

between 'nature of travel' and 'occupation' and, between sub-categories like 'travel' and 'tourism', 'specialised' and 'professional' writing and so on. Most scientific travellers, to cite but one illustration, had a religious axe to grind. The new orientalist societies were religiously motivated, broad-churches in the inclusive sense of the term (the PEF prided themselves on being non-denominational), but nonetheless 'churches', sometimes narrowly evangelical. The under-representation of certain patterns – mainly religious travel and a religious Eastern career – was discussed earlier. More serious than all this is the dehumanisation, in the taxonomic presentation of evidence, of the historical phenomenon and the failure to convey to modern readers the experience of individuals. For the structural changes mapped earlier were made by human actors: explorers, missionaries and scientists, adventurers and package tourists. And their experiences of the Orient were as diverse as their writing.

To restore the human aspect to our overview of travel, we need to turn to the particular and, perhaps, atypical that is, to the select historical example.

SOME EASTERN CAREERS: LITERARY TRAVELLERS

Of the only two eighteenth-century authors in the sample, Elisabeth Craven, margravine of Anspach, is the less known (though unlike some of her sister-travellers she received her slice of immortality in an entry in the *DNB*). She may be adequately described as a playwright and woman-of letters. Like her model, Lady Montagu, Craven did not write for money, which she chronically needed. Like Montagu, she came from the nobility, marrying into it, twice, first the sixth earl of Craven then, her benefactor and protector Frederick Charles Alexander, margrave of Brandenburg, Anspach and Bareith (sic), Duke of Prussia and Count of Sayen. What set Craven on a course of travel and life as an expatriate was her legal separation from her husband and six children and the financial difficulties resulting on the separation. Craven was deprived of her jointure, perhaps because technically she had been the 'injuring party'. 'She has been', as Walpole delicately puts it, '*infinitamente* indescreet'.[47] Her literary and dramatic career actually preceded her career as traveller. Her first comedy, *Somnanbule*, printed in one of Walpole's periodicals, went on the stage at Newmarket, for a charitable purpose, in 1778. The hilarious *Modern Anecdotes of the Family of Kinrerrankotspakengatchdern, a Tale of Christmas,* a knockabout burlesque on German pomposity, followed a year later. *The Silver Tankard* and *Princess of Georgia* ran at the Haymarket Theatre and Covent Garden respectively (1781). A decade of travel and remarriage finally rehabilitated the disgraced Craven and made possible her return to respectable society.

Elisabeth Craven indeed was a protected female. And in a sense more literal than Trollope's. Throughout her adult life she was supported by influential male friends who appreciated her spark and talent. Interestingly, however, her voyage to the Crimea and Istanbul, the basis for *Journey through the Crimea to Constantinople,* published in an expensive quarto edition in 1789, was solitary, self-financed and truly adventurous. The book is not (as is erroneously believed) addressed to her German benefactor, but to a fictitious male-friend and, in the context of Craven's scandalous life, this is a bold statement. The journey itself was perilous. Craven used public transport and lodged in disreputable inns. She had no escort except one incompetent servant. She did not enjoy the pomp and ceremony, characterising aristocratic travellers on their *grand tour,* and she chose the overland route from Hungary to Istanbul, via Russia and the Crimea, avoided by most eighteenth century travellers. The more cautious Montagu had proceeded from Hungary through the Ottoman occupied Balkans to Asia-Minor. For Craven travel meant emancipation from economic and social restrictions. She typifies the non-professional aristocratic adventurer, of the days before travel became a specialised and increasingly commercialised phenomenon. Her book too, is aimed at a select readership, the *cognoscenti,* purchasers of lucrative productions which were beyond the reach of the English common reader.

It is precisely here, at the juncture of types of travel and travel-writing with the travelogue reading-public, that Craven differs from her nineteenth-century successors. For they, especially those among the writers who were not specialists, wrote for profit, with an eye to an expanding market-place and a readership with an insatiable appetite for vicarious travel. It is significant that for quite a few of these writers their Eastern voyage was the booster to a literary career, if not a turning-point in their professional and personal lives. An early and now regrettably forgotten example is Julia Sophia Pardoe (1806–1862), a very popular travel-writer and historical novelist.[48] Pardoe, born to an army family of Portuguese (possibly Jewish) origin had written before her fateful journey, with her retired father, to Istanbul in 1835. But her breakthrough came after the appearance in 1837 of the *Domestic Manners of the Turks in 1836*, probably the most detailed, most sympathetic description of the Turkish élite before the *Tanzimat*, or reform era. Two factional works on Turkey, *Romance of the Harem* (1839) and *Beauties of the Bosphorus* (1839) appeared in rapid succession and were followed, rather late in Pardoe's career, by an expurgated 'family edition' of Petis de la Croix's *Persian Nights* (1857). In the interval Pardoe, tied to Bentley, the 'women's publisher', produced some of her best-selling historical novels: *Louis XIV and the Court of France in the Seventeenth Century* (1847); *The Court and Reign of Francis I* (1849) and *The Life and Memoirs of Marie de Medici*, each of which brought her a handsome advance of 300 pounds.[49] Two years before her death Pardoe, who had never married, received a civil list pension.

Harriet Martineau, born four years before Pardoe, is a better known example. She is in fact the most celebrated, most successful and, over the decade between the Reform Bill of 1832 and the early 1840s, the most politically influential female writer in Britain. Of a Unitarian manufacturing family at Norwich, Martineau began to write for a living in her early twenties. Her industry is astonishing: a number of novels, numerous magazine and newspaper-articles, religious essays and, best known – the popular series, or 'illustrations' of economic and social topics: *Illustrations to Political Economy* (1832–1835) of which up to 10,000 copies sold monthly; *Illustrations to Taxation* and *Illustrations to the Poor Laws* (1845), commissioned by the Society for the Diffusion of Useful Knowledge and, notwithstanding her own Radical views, by a Whig administration. Evidently Martineau reached wide audiences and, in contrast to the typical Victorian author in the sample, aimed, particularly in her early work, at the working-class market. *Eastern Life Present and Past* is her fourth travel-book, following a popular guide to the Lake District and the much overrated *Society in America* and *Prospect of Western Travel*, published in 1836–8 and usually compared with De Tocqueville's classic *Democracy in America*. In *Eastern Life*, the journey to and through, the Middle East is used as a skeleton for an ambitious (too ambitious, one might say) study in comparative religion, an attempt to track down the evolution of faith from tribal animism and fetishism, through polytheism, through 'immature' monotheistic beliefs (Martineau's epithets) like Judaism to the 'mature' Christian and Muslim faiths and, finally, to a progressive deism.[50] Eastern travel and the production of *Eastern Life* were the turning point in Martineau's biography. It was immediately after the journey that she abandoned her rational, Necessarian brand of Unitarianism for Positivism, soon to become Comte's first populariser in Britain and his first translator.

It is difficult to imagine two lives and two experiences of the Middle East entirely different as those of Martineau and Lucie Duff-Gordon, née Austin. For Martineau, despite her Radical reformism, despite her advocation of diverse causes and despite her conversion to Positivism, was to remain, all her life, a small-town dissenter with that type's intolerance towards the social or cultural 'other'. Duff-Gordon was not a political figure, nor a reformer. And her secular education and upbringing are markedly different from Martineau's Unitarian background. Nonetheless Duff-Gordon was a true liberal and humanitarian. And her books on nineteenth-century Egypt are exemplars of tolerance and a sense of cultural relativeness.

Socially too, the two writers are different. Born in London in 1821, to well-connected intellectual and Radical parents, Lucie Austin moved in literary circles and the milieu of the Philosophical Radicals. After her marriage in 1846 to Alexander Duff-Gordon, a Treasury official and court officer, she set a *salon* which attracted *literati* like Kinglake; Thackeray and Tennyson (who used her as model for the *Princess*) and the adoring Meredith (who portrayed her as Lady Jocelyn in *Evan Harrington*).

What drove her abroad was – conventionally enough – poor health. She first went to the Cape of Good Hope, then in 1860 arrived at Egypt where she was to remain until her death in 1869. Unlike most Europeans, Duff-Gordon could not afford to live in the westernised Frank neighbourhood in Cairo, or Alexandria. Money difficulties – which had dogged the Gordons throughout their married life – climate and a marked antipathy to the cosmopolitan community in the Delta cities, drove her to the upper Nile, to Luxor, where she lived *à l'arabe*, in a crumbling hut which formed a part of a temple in Luxor's pharaonic *Necropolis*. She was immensely revered by the local *fallahin*. And she lived to become a tourist attraction, visited by travellers on their way to the First Cataract. Her years in Egypt produced two volumes of letters, published in 1865 and posthumously in 1869. And if there is travel writing that is not ethnocentric and is anti- or counter-orientalist, it is to be found in these volumes.

The career and work of Amelia Ann Blanford Edwards spuriously resemble those of Martineau's. For Edwards was more versatile and her history combines two different patterns of travel and writing: non-specialist literary and journalistic career and semi-professional work in one of the emerging amateur sciences. The change from the first, traditionally feminine occupation to the second occurred in the 1870s, at the start of the period of transition in women's travel, discussed earlier.[51]

Amelia Edwards was born in London in 1831, to a banking family with an East-Anglican gentry background. She displayed extraordinary precocity in writing, having her first poem published when she was seven and her first story when she was twelve. Like Martineau before her, Edwards was forced into a writing career by her family's financial difficulties. She slowly built a reputation as a producer of ghost tales for magazines. In the late 1850s she was employed on the staff of the *Saturday Review* and the *Morning Post* and went on writing novels, at the pace of one every two years. Altogether she published eight and, at least one of them, *Barbara's History* (1864), became a popular success. Reviewers particularly liked her independent and adventurous women characters. Her promising career as a novelist was interrupted by the single most important event of her life, a trip to Egypt in 1873. Thereafter, Edwards became a passionate enthusiast for everything to do with ancient Egypt. In 1882 she co-founded the EEF and was its Honorary Secretary and later Vice-President.

Between the publication of her scholarly *A Thousand Miles Up the Nile* in 1877 and her death in 1891 the prolific Edwards produced an astonishing number of popular articles to publicise the excavation work done by Flinders Petrie and Naville in the Delta region. She contributed some 100 pieces to the *Academy* alone and many more to the *Bulletin of the American Geographical Society; Harper's Monthly* and the *E.E.F. Archaeological Reports*, not to mention the national dailies. Nor is that all. As unpaid Honorary Secretary to the Fund, Edwards took care of the EEF's correspondence, raised funds, enlisted hundreds of subscribers and, amidst all this activity, found time for lecture tours. By legacy she helped found the first English chair of Egyptology at University College, London. Untypical as it may appear, then, Edwards' history spotlights the patterns of life and career of an entire group of travellers, the new orientalists of the last quarter of the century.

WORKING IN GOD'S VINEYARD: EVANGELICAL CAREERS

By way of introduction to the missionary experience and *Weltans-chauung*, we may first study the separate but parallel lives of four rather obscure evangelisers: Mary Louisa Whately; Jane Walker-Arnott; Elisabeth Bowen Thompson and Augusta Mentor-Mott. Their careers overlap, covering as they do, the period 1861–1880 (with the exception of Walker-Arnott who remained active until 1911). Their lives cross and give us clues to the drive, aspirations and thinking of a much wider group of missionaries, working inside, or in connection with, the large missions and, through that group, to the views on the Orient of middle-class evangelical women.

Mary Louisa Whately, philanthropist, educator, proselytiser and amateur ethnographer was renowned in church circles during her life-time. She is the subject of a hagiography, a number of obituaries, and is referred to, in passing, by a few travellers.[52] These materials, together with her own writings – she produced nine books about Egypt – make it possible to build up an almost complete history. Whately was particularly equipped for an evangelical career abroad. Her background is solidly episcopal. Her anti-Erastian and anti-Evangelical father was Archbishop of Dublin (C.O.E.). But very early in life, Mary Whately came close to the low-church and almost immediately became involved in philanthropic work. She received her apprenticeship in work with the unregenerate, in the Evangelical Rugged Schools. She moved from Dublin to London, to the CMS's base in Rome and then, in 1860, arrived in Egypt. She was to stay in that country for 22 years, symbolically until the occupation. In Cairo, Whately started on, singlehandedly, first at her own expense then relying on contributors in Britain, a network of schools for girls. Only after material success came were the CMS prepared to back up the project. Whately's schools were to become the basis of primary education for non-Protestant Christians in Egypt, catering mainly for Greek-Orthodox and Copts. Whately, like most evangelical ethnographers, is extremely knowledgeable about the Coptic and Greek-Orthodox communities. About Muslims, particularly Muslim women, she knows little and cares less. Her fortunately infrequent lapses on polygamy, concubinage and the harem-system in general, are diatribes on Muslim lasciviousness, spiced with second-hand stories on a few Cairene households. First-hand information she has very little.

The history of Jane Walker-Arnott touches on Whately's at more than one point.[53] Walker-Arnott, or Miss W-A, as she is commonly referred to by her contemporaries, was between 1860 and 1862 a superintendent in Whately's schools. And it was from Whately that she learnt how to apply the system and methods of education of the English urban poor to the Middle Eastern context, an experiment characterised by the confluence of notions of race and class. W-A's life is not documented. So her story had to be patiently unravelled from materials at the Tabitha School, her school in Jaffa, still active today, and the Jewish Mission Committee, Church of Scotland.

W-A had not Whately's religious pedigree. In fact she came from a secular and scientific family. Her father was a Regius Professor of Botany at the University of Edinburgh who gave his daughters an education quite advanced for Victorian, upper middle-class girls (the curriculum included the natural sciences). Legend has it that the invalid W-A went to Egypt for her health – she was in fact dispatched there to die. But she never got to Cairo and, instead, sailed to Jaffa. She was to remain in that city, intermittently, for 48 years, until her death in 1911. Jaffa in 1860, when W-A arrived there (according to the unlikely official COS version, she was then 15!), was not a missionary's paradise. It was not a holy place, had a few relics, was relatively open to Western influences and had a multinational, religiously heterogeneous population. A short time before W-A's arrival an attempt of a missionary of the CMS, the Reverend Cruse, to set-up a girls' school, failed dismally. After a year in Jaffa, and her two years as teacher in Cairo, W-A opened in 1863 the Tabitha School for girls, with the purpose of taking in day-scholars and boarders, apprenticing them in a useful profession (the cloth-industry, naturally) and indoctrinating them in a true Christian faith. In March 1863 the school had 14 scholars, at the end of the year 50 and a year later, despite the cholera epidemic, over 200. Money came from two sources, voluntary ladies' associations in the neighbourhood of Glasgow, and, more substantially, from Thomas Cook and Son, Kings of the Eastern tourist packages. Cook purchased the ground for a new school, had it built and, for eighteen years, maintained a number of Arab scholars, at his own expense.

The pattern which appears in Whately's history repeats itself in the story of W-A and, as I shall show in Chapter 7, is structural. Characteristic female missionary work is carried on not inside the missionary societies, but alongside them. Cooperation follows success in the field and institutional support is informal. There is no defined policy concerning women's work. But, eventually, the

individual or individually initiated projects are co-opted by the
bigger missions. Whately passed on the schools to the CMS, W-A
to the COS mission and there are numerous other similar cases.

The parallel lives and careers of Elisabeth Bowen Thompson
and Augusta Mentor-Mott, two sisters-in-law, and fellow-workers,
elude the models of travel described earlier. Both started as 'help-
mates', the supporting wives of missionary husbands. Thompson
followed her own husband, a physician, to Antioch and her sister
and brother-in-law made Southern Syria their basis. When the
Crimean War broke out, Dr. Bowen Thompson joined the army
as a surgeon and was killed in service. It was after his death that
Elisabeth Bowen Thompson started on an entirely new career of a
scope far greater than any of the couple's earlier projects. After
the massacres of 1860, she established girls' schools for Maronite
refugees, first in Beirut, then in Damascus, then in Zahleh, Baalbek
and Sidon and Tripoli. At first, the schools were maintained at her
own expense, but after her death, in 1870, a society in aid of the
Syrian schools started a fund, with the enormous yearly sum of 9000
pounds, presumably the largest amount of money at the disposal
of any single mission in the entire province of Syria, save the
Presbyterian Board. The network of schools spread fast. In 1902
there were 56 institutions, with a total of 4,262 pupils, 20 women
missionaries, 128 Syrian female teachers, not to mention the numerous Bible classes, employing 25 native teachers, a teacher-training
centre for natives and the training of Bible-women (there were 170
of them in Beirut alone).[54] Bowen-Thompson, quite neglected by the
bigger missions, had support from other quarters. She was granted
a *firman* by the Sultan, permitting the Society to establish schools all
over Syria and, shortly before her death, was personally presented
by him with a village, near Baalbek, which was to help maintain the
schools.

The four devout lives studied here illustrate the possibilities, for
married and single women, in a religious career in the Middle
East. These lives also illustrate the process of secularisation of
the traditional model of the *peregrinatio*. The pilgrimage, before
the eighteenth century, the only model of female travel, changed
radically. Evangelical gender-ideology shaped the travel and work
of women in the sample and outside it. The nineteenth-century
religious experience of the Middle East was more complex and
varied than the medieval one, the latter gaining from the relationship between belief and the new scientific investigation of the

places with Biblical and religious associations. About a fourth of the travellers produced specialist work. A larger proportion were active in many ways in the scientific, semi-religious societies with interest in the Middle East. Moreover, the very nature of religious experience itself changed. Travel was not merely a pilgrimage. Certainly the *voyage-en-orient* was, for the believers, an intensely emotional experience. But benevolent or missionary work was a *public* rather than an inward, private activity and had distinct social and cultural functions.

Neither the collective biography of travel, nor individual travel biographies, stand on their own. Nor does the collated evidence, assembling taxonomy and biography. Caught between the tyranny of 'structures' and the arbitrary nature of the select example, the student of sensibilities must turn to the texts.

Part II

The Women's Harem: Autonomy, Sexuality and Solidarity

2

Harem Literature, 1763–1914: Tradition and Innovation

... that crucial moment in modern thought when, thanks to the great voyages of discovery, a human community which had believed itself to be complete and in its final form suddenly learned ... that it was not alone, that it was part of a greater whole, and that, in order to achieve self-knowledge, it must first of all contemplate its recognisable image in this mirror.

Claude Lévi-Strauss, *Tristes Tropiques*.[1]

The reader will perceive with pleasure that we are approaching an interesting theme, the first question of mankind to the wanderer 'what are the women like'?

Richard Francis Burton, *Personal narrative of a Pilgrimage to Al-Madinah and Meccah*.[2]

WESTERN IMAGES OF THE HAREM

The harem[3] had always pricked the imagination of Western people. The desire to penetrate – if only vicariously – the women's quarters in the Muslim house, to know more about oriental females, had surpassed the prurience of the *voyeur*.[4] This desire had exceeded the curiosity of mankind about the unfamiliar and exotic; it had eclipsed the interest of Europeans, from the age of the great geographical discoveries, in the sexual manners and morals of non-Europeans.[5] Students of exoticism and Orientalism have noted the *longevity* of the *topos* of the harem and its endurance in the face of political and cultural changes. From the earliest encounters between Christians and Muslims till the present, the harem as the *locus* of an exotic and abnormal sexuality fascinated Westerners. It came to be regarded as a microcosmic Middle East, apotheosising the two characteristics perceived as essentially oriental: sensuality and violence. As Norman Daniel has argued, this particular combination of sexuality and the oppression of women appealed to the West because of its obvious political aspect.[6] From the Enlightenment onwards, the harem came to be not merely a psychosexual symbol, but a metaphor for injustice in civil society and the state and arbitrary government.

Of course, the origins of the harem system – that is the combination of the seclusion of females with polygamy and concubinage – are in the pre-Islamic era.[7] Polygamy, concubinage and various forms of segregation had been practised in Mediterranean societies *before* the Arab conquest of the Middle East.[8] The Greeks had sequestered females in separate *gynecea*. The Hebrews had been polygamists. Evangelical missionaries who, throughout the nineteenth century, preached the abolition of the harem well knew that the Scriptures abounded with examples of plural marriages. Indeed nowhere in the Old or New Testament is polygamy explicitly prohibited – except once, in St. Paul's admonition to bishops and deacons not to espouse more than one wife at a time.[9]

The pre- or non-Islamic origins of plural marriage and seclusion were, by the beginning of the nineteenth century, fairly widely known in the West. Veiling and sequestration as travellers and ethnographers often noted, had not been enjoined in the Koran and even the *Hadith* (or tradition) had not been very clear on these related practices. Certainly seclusion was a later development, limited to the urban commercial class and probably copied by the Arab conquerors from the vanquished populations. The early Ottoman Sultans modelled the *harem-i hümâyûn*, or Imperial Harem, on the Byzantine *gynecea*. The usage of eunuchs also had been Byzantine.[10]

Notwithstanding, polygamy and seclusion came to be identified with the Muslim eastern Mediterranean. Significantly, the harem more than the Indian *Zenana* or the Chinese customs of concubinage, conjured in the West a cluster of powerful images. In contradistinction to other forms of non-monogamous sexuality, encountered by Europeans, the harem system had been rarely idealised. Polygamy and 'promiscuity' in the Far-East, in equatorial societies or in the antipodes had been elevated to models of natural sensuality or pre-Lapsarian innocence.[11] The *haremlik* (or women and children's quarters in the Ottoman house) was not a utopian place, nor the *locus* of innocent sexuality, not even to 'polygamists' like Montesquieu and Diderot. Indeed the *haremlik* had occupied a special place in the sexual geography of travellers, ethnographers and thinkers. There are a few reasons for this. First is the proximity of the Middle East to Europe. Second, and related to the first, is the political threat which, over a long stretch of time, the Ottoman Empire had presented to the West. To be sure, after the Battle of Lepanto (1572) coexistence with the 'Turks' became generally peaceful. Nevertheless even after its decline, first as a European then as a Mediterranean power, the Ottoman Empire remained a factor in European politics. The third reason for the endurance of the *topos* of the sensual Orient has to do with the special status of Islam as one of the three great revealed religions of the world. As Daniel and Hourani have emphasised, Muslim society and culture had never been seen as the relics of underdeveloped civilisations, as curiosities alone. Rather, Islam had presented an alternative to Christianity.[12] We may extend this observation to the European obsession with sexuality in Islam. The harem was appealing and, at the same time, threatening *because* it seemed an alternative to the Western, Pauline-Augustinian model of sexuality. As Chapters 3–5 demonstrate, eyewitness representations of Muslim women and the *haremlik* illustrate this mixed attitude of attraction and repulsion.

I already argued that studies of Orientalism – whether the so-called 'post colonial' historiography, or feminist criticism – understate changes in the myth of the harem while overstating the androcentric character of that myth. It was recently argued that representations of the harem had been exercises in 'male voyeuristic pleasure.[13] Or, as Joana de Groot put it, the writers and painters who popularised the notion of the promiscuous Orient 'were defined by their masculinity, their class and their European culture. They dealt with Middle Eastern societies as males from professional, gentry or middle-class background.'[14] However to reduce exoticism to a male fantasy is to write out gender and class. It is precisely the influence of both that determined the approach of women to the 'other.' I would argue that these women's Orient is a *locus* that is markedly different from that of orientalists. Women travellers and ethnographers domesticated the exotic or, put slightly differently, these women normalised and humanised the harem. Harem literature, I further argue, presents us with two related processes: the comparison between Western and Middle Eastern culture and criticism on the West. The encounter with a non- monogamous system of sexuality that denies women public freedoms, often resulted in analogy between the position of Muslim women and women in Britain. In what follows harem literature is considered as a challenge both to traditional notions on the Orient and to middle-class gender ideology in the West.

The culturally most significant feature of the women's writings is that these are eyewitness descriptions. The vast literature on harem life constitutes a substantial body of ethnographic evidence, the first of its kind, on regions which before the appearance of Montagu's *Letters* had been *terra incognita* to Westerners. Men's writings on harems did not draw on an observable reality, 'seen' on the spot. Typically these writings relied on texts – literary texts, polemical literature, travellers' accounts. With very few exceptions, the *haremlik* was sealed to European men. First-hand information on Middle Eastern women characteristically derived from male informants. It is significant that representations based on experience largely drew on sexual encounters between Western men and oriental women. Much has been made of Flaubert's liaison with Kücük Hanîm, of Loti's affair with Aeizadé, of Lane's relationship with Nefise, of Burton's adventures with prostitutes. The Flaubertian paradigm of sexual exploitation and colonisation has been blown out of proportion. There is no evidence that commercial sex was the characteristic form of communication between colonisers and colonised.

Cross-cultural representation in harem literature is free of the insurmountable barrier of sex and sexual taboos. Moreover, the eyewitness accounts are also characterised by what students of the evolution of ethnographic authority call 'intersubjective relation', that is a communication, or an exchange of sorts, between the observer and his or her 'informant'. The very presence of eyewitnesses on the scene they describe transforms them from onlookers – gazing from a distance upon a remote, exotic object – to observers.[15] As observers, women became engaged in the phenomena, or people, they described; they took part in the ordinary activities of Muslim women and in the rituals observed in harems. This kind of participant observation, as part of an intersubjective process, distinguishes harem literature from the more general discussion in Europe, on the exotic.

Certainly 'observing,' or 'seeing', are pre-programmed activities. Of course women were as prejudiced as men travellers. As Chapters 6–9 illustrate, participant observation often displays religious and racial prejudice. Some of the women studied in this book were myopically ethnocentric. Curiously it is feminists like Harriet Martineau and Amelia Edwards, who present the most glaring examples of racism and cultural narcissism. Conservatives like Mary Lucy Garnett, Anne Bowman and Anne Noel Blunt could view the harem from an historic rather than moral angle.

To juxtapose a female experience of the harem with male fantasy, the commitment of women ethnographers to observable fact with the orientalist's veneration of texts would be not only myopic but unintelligent. Travellers, regardless of sex, or class or education did not operate in an informational vacuum. Men and women had experienced the Orient literarily before visiting the geographical Middle East; they brought with them to that region images, propagated by a long literary tradition. In order to comprehend how radically different harem literature is from this tradition we shall first have to examine affiliations with the main authorities on the Orient.

THREE LITERARY AUTHORITIES: ELEMENTS OF CONTIGUITY

Most eighteenth- and nineteenth-century writers could have recourse to three disparate but confluent kinds of texts. First and most influential is the *Thousand and One Nights*, or *Alf Layla wa-Layla*, commonly known to Western readers as the *Arabian Nights Entertainment*. That compilation of texts, originally transmitted orally and amassed and transcribed over, at least, eight centuries, had become a definitive text in French and English before it was ever printed in Arabic. The first printed Arabic collection, known as 'Calcutta I,' appeared only in 1814–18, a little over a century after the publication of the first French and English transcriptions. Other printed versions in the Arabic, notably the 'Bulak' version and the manuscripts known as 'Calcutta II' and 'Breslau' (collectively as Zer) appeared between 1825 and 1872. Western audiences became familiar with the imaginary, exotic harem through Antoine Galland's immensely popular *Mille et une nuits* which appeared in twelve volumes between 1707–14.[16] Thus when in 1717 Lady Mary Wortley Montagu embarked on her journey to Istanbul, she was thoroughly read in Galland's transcription. Like virtually all eighteenth- and early nineteenth-century travellers Lady Montagu used Galland as a reference text, a source of ethnographic data to be cited as authority, a repository of ready anecdotes, types, and plots. However, her reverence of the canonical text is rhetorical and strategic, as we shall see later.

Galland's version retained its status long after his death, actually until the publication, between 1838 and 1841, of Edward William Lane's transcription of the *Nights*. Both versions are technically clean. Galland's franchicised text leaves out the bawdy in the original Arabic, systematically omitting what he thought improper and unsuitable to the 'polite reader'. And even Lane's admirers would consent that his own expurgated, massively annotated and savagely cut edition (it comprises less than one-third of the original source) is, indeed, different from the original. It seems that the Victorian reading-public found even Galland's euphemism too hard to stomach. The *Mille et une nuits* could not be read in a family circle. Galland's translation was bracketed 'foreign' and 'unEnglish' and, therefore, dangerous to British readers. Stanley Lane Poole, Lane's nephew and the editor of the 1859 edition of the *Arabian Nights*, puts the book into its proper perspective: 'The translation of Galland with all its lameness, puerility and indecency; gained them [the tales] a hold which has never been relaxed; and it only required the appearance of a scholar-like and readable translation, freed from these defects, to make them genuinely accepted in English families.[17] Lane's undisputed status as scholar and the technical cleanliness of his version made this version appealing to heterogenous and diverse audiences, outside the literary or professional elites. The new *Arabian Nights* did not offend Victorian notions of propriety and was reckoned suitable even to audiences traditionally regarded as uncritical and easily impressionable; women, adolescent girls and children. The *Nights*, as Thackeray observed, had reached even young ladies' academies together, incidentally, with Gutherie's harmless Geography.[18] Of course, *Vanity Fair* is about the corrupt Regency, but Thackeray was addressing a Victorian audience. And he shrewdly noted the indelible affects of the tales on half-educated, easily impressionable juvenile females.

Unabridged versions, loyal to the frankly bawdy original, appeared only towards the end of the period under discussion. John Payne's translation and Burton's mammoth *Complete and Literal Translation*, including 17 volumes, were published in 1882–84 and

1884–86 respectively, and reached limited audiences: oriental scholars and pornographers and collectors of *erotica*, attracted by Burton's *Notes* and his notorious *Terminal Essay* on oriental sexuality. Given the language and content of these translations, it is highly unlikely that women read them. And we may assume that female readerships had access only to the earlier 'clean' versions. But expurgated or literal, the *Arabian Nights* conjured up female stereotypes and stereotypes of feminine sexuality which had a tremendous affect on Victorian readers and writers.

Descriptions of women in the tales are conveniently arranged in two classic categories of victims and aggressors, that is, negative *topoi* embodying the vices traditionally associated with female nature.[19] The women pertaining to the last category are faithless and fickle, lewd and promiscuous, dangerously perfidious and, sometimes, violent. Sheherezad herself, the narrator who became a model to modern female writers, alludes classification. She is pure. Significantly, her own marriage to the Sultan is not consummated. She is impressively erudite. But her vast knowledge on sexual matters derives, not from experience, but from books. Sheherezad recounts salacious stories, in a sexually neutral or male voice that is curiously detached.[20] The frame story itself, as Pucci notes, sets the tone for the rest of the collection. King Shahzaman's queen befouls his bed with a black slave. His brother Shahriyar too is betrayed by an unfaithful wife. On their journey to Samarkand the two kings are accosted by a lewd hag who bids them copulate with her in turn. In the notorious 'Tale of the Enscrolled Prince', the ruler's wife leaves his bed every night, to copulate with a leprous black who abuses her and forces her to eat rat-stew. The entire episode is reconstructed in high-falutin archaic language by an obviously delighted Burton. 'I will not keep company with thee nor will I glue my body with thy body and strum and belly-bump. Dost thou play fast and loose with us, thou cracked pot, that we may satisfy thy dirty lusts? Stinkard! bitch! vilest of the vile.'[21]

Galland's audience and Lane's Victorian readers remained blissfully ignorant of episodes like that. But the Victorians had their fair share of generalisations and clichés concerning oriental females and the harem. Readers were invited to share with the translators/censors in the scopic pleasure of the narrator of the original Arabic text. Note how Lane handles the episode of the queen and the black slave which in the Victorian context was not only sexually, but racially explosive.

having returned to the palace to fetch [something which he had forgotten] he [Shahzaman] beheld his wife sleeping in his bed, and attended by a male negro slave, who had fallen asleep by her side. On beholding this scene the world became black before his eyes; and he said within himself, if this is the case when I have not departed from the city, what will be the conduct of this vile woman while I am adjuring with my brother.[22]

This is a feat of euphemism. Nevertheless Lane's euphemisms ('attended by a male negro slave'), the suggestiveness of the entire scene, particularly appealed to contemporary audiences. His version was more widely effective than Burton's explicit literalism. The former version made it possible for readers to have it both ways: to experience the exotic vicariously and, at the same time, remain 'clean,' exactly like the voyeuristic narrator in the text. Ultimately, translations like Galland and Lane's domesticated the harem and 'normalised' it.

Throughout the eighteenth and early nineteenth century the *Arabian Nights* had enjoyed the status not only of a literary classic, a canonical artifice, but also of an ethnographic source. Orientalists habitually infer from the medieval texts, to contemporary societies; from domestic manners in the time of Harun-al-Rashid, to the Egyptian household around the middle of the nineteenth century. The title-page of the first edition of François petis de la Croix' *Persian and Turkish Tales*, which appeared immediately after Galland's work, reads:

Here is no Heap of extravagant Ideas collected together, but the Manners of several Nations, composed on purpose for Delight . . . taken from things that are real, and Customs that are always in use.[23]

The assumption being that oriental customs are changeless. Lane, writing 120 years after Galland and de la Croix, echoes their words. The interest in the collection is, according to Lane, not so much in the stories themselves, but in the 'fullness and fidelity with which they describe the characters, manners and customs of the Arabs',[24] including their sexual manners and customs. The very realism of the scholarly and naturalist text fixes notions of the harem as a static, changeless construct.

Travellers borrowed massively from the *Arabian Nights*. Yet, from

Montagu onwards, their reading of the text becomes increasingly critical. And they are conscious of the difference between observable reality and fantasy, fact and fiction. More important, the writers of harem literature are very critical about the value of the *Nights* as ethnographic and historical sources. Take for example Montagu herself. In a pseudo-letter to her sister, Lady Mar, she comments: 'Now do I fancy that you imagine I have entertained you all this while with a relation that has (at last) received many Embellishments from my hand. this is but too like (says you) The Arabian Tales; these embroide'd napkins, and a jewel as large as a Turkey's egg.'[25] The self irony in the passage and Montagu's implied criticism, on herself – a writer who is, in fact, a copyist of a well-known text; on her sister who, Montagu assumes, is familiar with the text and, finally, on Galland – is very revealing. And unlike Montagu, the real and fictional Lady Mar is not a particularly educated woman. Nonetheless, Montagu assumes that Lady Mar is discriminate enough to sift out the real from the congeries of facts, half-truths and fantasies. Over a century later, Julia Sophia Pardoe takes on the argument exactly where Montagu left it off. Pardoe knew enough about the oriental-tale industry to doubt the ethnographic value of Galland. She herself was to publish an abridged family edition of the *Turkish Tales* in 1858. In her earlier first-hand account of Istanbul on the eve of the *Tanzimat* (*City of the Sultan* (1837), Pardoe insists on the importance of eye-witness reports on the domestic life of the Ottomans.

> There is no intimate knowledge of domestic life, and hence the cause of the tissue of fables which, like those of Sheherezad have created *genii* and enchanters *ab ovo usque ad male* in every account of the East. The European mind has become so imbued with the ideal of Oriental mysteriousness, mysticism, and magnificence, and it has been so long accustomed to pillow its faith on the marvels and metaphors . . . that it is to be doubted whether it will willingly cast off its associations, and suffer itself to be undeceived.[26]

Pardoe assumes a role which is diametrically opposite to that of the female narrator in the *Arabian Nights*. Sheherezad deceives a credulous and beguiled male audience. The task of the modern traveller is, according to Pardoe, to 'undeceive' the readership and instruct Europeans about intimate life and manners.

To turn to the second literary inheritance. Adjacent to the *Nights* and comparable translations from Arabic, Turkish and Persian manuscripts, is that corpus of writings collectively known as 'oriental tales'. This mobile and rather open term, first used critically by Marie de Mesteer and Martha Pike Conant,[27] covers the vast body of prose or verse literature on oriental themes set in the East and uses the frame structure of the *Alf-lyla*. Beyond these common features it is convenient to distinguish four forms. They are: the oriental romance; the fantastic tale of magic and supernatural phenomena; the didactic, moralistic tale with a pedagogic moral; and, last, the philosophical tale which uses travel as a metaphor for cross-cultural representation and the notion of the relativeness of cultural norms. Voltaire's *Zadig* and *Candide* and Montesquieu's *Lettres persanes* are notable examples of tales of philosophical travel. It is mainly the first and the last categories which directly concern us.[28]

Galland's international success marks the beginning of a flourishing literary industry, capitalising on a new literary phenomenon. Translations from genuine manuscripts and pseudo oriental tales, manufactured by Western orientalists, catered for every taste. High upon the heels of Galland's success appeared de la Croix' *Turkish and Persian Tales*. The Abbé de Bignon's *History of Abdallah, the Son of the Hanif* appeared in 1713. Thomas Simon Gueullette's series of stories, set in the Orient, came out between 1716 and 1736. A typical title reads: *A Thousand and One Quarter Hours, Being Tartarian Tales . . . The Dreams of Men Awake*. Most French versions were immediately translated into English. And British writers quickly saw the market value of 'oriental' literature. Examples abound. William Collins' *Oriental Eclogues*, 'written originally for the Entertainment of the Ladies of Tauris' appeared in 1757. Hawkesworth followed with *Almoran and Hamet* (1760) and was succeeded by Ridley and Frances Sheridan, whose popular *History of Nourjehad* appeared in 1767. Romantic tales featuring European women captives in harems were extremely popular. The anonymous *Female Captive, A Narrative of Facts which Happened in Barbary* saw publication in 1769.[29] Later examples include *The Fair Syrian* which appeared in 1787 and 'Monk' Lewis' *The Anaconda*, published in 1808 with the subtitle 'Romantic Tales'.

It was in 1786, after the appearance of William Beckford's *History of the Caliph Vathek*, that the oriental tale became canonised. *Vathek*, written in French and translated into English by Beckford and Henley, is a combination of implausible erotic fantasy with orientalist erudition and ethnographic detail. The grandson of the legendary Harun al-Rashid, Wathik (anglicised as Vathek), is the prototypical oriental despot. He is licentious and gluttonous, 'much addicted to women and the pleasures of the table'.[30] His domestic tyranny is more than matched by his despotic rule. Beckford's usage of the harem as metaphor for corrupt government, evidently modelled on the political metaphor of the *philosophes*, is transparent.

The harem in *Vathek* is a *voyeur's* paradise. Occupying the fifth wing of the caliph's sumptuous palace, it is appropriately called 'the Retreat of Mirth, or the Dangerous' and it is: 'frequented by troops of young females as beautiful as the Houri's and not less seducing, who never failed to receive the caresses of all whom he allowed to approach them'.[31]

Beckford's use of authorities is as important as his representation of the exotic. He draws on authentic sources – *Orientalia* in the original Arabic and Persian, or in translation and travellers' accounts. The prodigious notes to *Vathek* exceed the tale and form a sub-text whose rationale is to establish Beckford's own status as omniscient scholar and narrator. His citationary rhetoric was to be emulated by numerous imitators. Accuracy in detail is the primary requirement of the oriental tale. The wilder and more fatuous the fantasy, the more realistically it is presented. Early examples abound with reference to ethnographic authority. Coleridge draws on Bruce's *Travels* for ethnographic detail in *Kubla Khan, The Religious Musings* and, possibly, in *The Ancient Mariner*. Erasmus Darwin freely borrows from the same source in the *Botanic Garden*, notably in the parts on 'The Economy of Vegetation'. Southey resorts to travel-books in the composition of his oriental epic *Thalaba the Destroyer* (1803). The poem has, at least, thirteen references to Thomas Shaw's *Travels in Egypt*. Byron's famous verse-tales of oriental love *The Giaour* and *The Bride of Abydos* are encumbered with references. Thomas Moore's immensely popular *Lalah Rook* is massively annotated. And Keats, Shelley and Tennyson in *Hyperion, Alastar* and *Recollections of the Arabian Nights* draw on Galland, Beckford and on travel-accounts.[32]

The oriental philosophical tale has certain contiguities with the romantic tale set in the East. Not least among these contiguities is the rhetorical use of citation and of ethnographic literature. The philosophical tale belongs to an historic genre that evolved during the Enlightenment: the secular quest of a truth (or truths) which is reached after many tribulations and through error and trial. The theme of the philosophical tale is cultural differentiation and the relativeness of systems of moral and of social structures. In the prototypical tale, exemplified in Giovanni Marana's *Espion turque* and the *Lettres persanes*, an enlightened oriental tourist visits a European capital, observes people, customs and manners, European society and polity. Significantly the traditional roles of the observer and the observed, of the traveller as 'seer' and those 'seen' by him, are reversed. Thus, instead of the omniscient, omnipresent European representing savages we have a noble savage, or a benighted heathen, commenting on the state of civilization. Hogarth's figures of black servants, in his pictorial satires on Augustan society, are silent commentators on its corrupt morals. And Montesquieu's Usbeq in the *Lettres persanes* is a critic of society and the state. The demonised Muslim of the Middle Ages and the Renaissance is transformed into a positive, often idealised type. He is the interpreter of human society in its diversity.[33]

It is important to note that discussion of sexuality is central to the philosophical tale, because tolerance of the sexually different is the ultimate test of the openness of the *philosophes* or the enlightened traveller. Indeed sexuality becomes a metaphor for geographical and cultural diversity. It is not surprising that the harem attracted the *philosophes*. They did not regard it merely as a trope but as one of several alternative familial and social structures. Middle Eastern polygamy was, to Europeans, more real and more easily conceivable than the non-monogamous practices of the Haitians or the native Australasians. Usbeq's harem in the *Lettres persanes* (1721) can be an alternative to promiscuous monogamy in contemporary France. Similarly in Marana's *Espion turque*, Montesquieu's blue-print, the sexual codes and attitudes towards sexuality of the French, are ridiculed and criticised. Voltaire's Candide and his mentor Pengalose are rather tolerant towards the habits of the Turks and Dr. Johnson's Rasselas and Imlac, to take a comparable English example of philosophical travellers, are very broad-minded.

Thus the influence of travel accounts extends not only to imaginative literature, but to the comparative study of society, religion and sexuality. The expansion of exploration and travel resulted in a forceful critique on the Europocentric vision of the world. For example, it was realised that systems of sexuality varied, according to place and time. Monogamy was not universal. Nor was the Pauline-Augustinian idea of chastity. Indeed, the reports of travellers suggested that the monogamous family was untypical. As David Hume and Lord Kames note, the majority of humankind was not monogamous.[34]

The novelty of eighteenth-century utterances concerning polygamy and the seclusion of women is not in the defence of the non monogamous family, for it had been defended from the Reformation, but in a historical and moral-free approach to the sexually different. Earlier polygamists, notably the Anabaptists, based their polemic on the Scriptures. The Patriarchs were polygamists. Hence monogamy is a Catholic aberration, or corruption.[35] Travellers and philosophical, armchair ethnographers approached the harem historically, as a social and economic construct, shaped by geographical and climatological conditions (climatological interpretations of sexual diversity are peculiar to French thinkers).

The new tolerance notwithstanding, the Enlightenment did not desexualise the harem. Rather the contrary. It was precisely the new licence to publicly discuss sex that revitalised the traditional *topoi* of the lascivious *odalik* (known to Europeans as *odalisk*) and the harem. Note that in the famous fifth book of Montesquieu's *De l'esprit des lois* (1748) it is the nature of the Eastern female, her very physicality, her innate lasciviousness that makes her so dangerous.[35] So much so, that her seclusion is to her own good as well as to the good of society at large. Paradoxically, Montesquieu's *odalik* resembles her predecessor, the seductive *houri* of the anti-Saracen polemic. Like all oriental females the *philosoph's odalik* is essentialised and objectified. She is, as Pucci brilliantly shows, an object of vicarious pleasure. The scopic experience of the *voyeur* substitutes for real sex.[36] The *odalik* embodies the essence of the feminised Orient, sensuality and violence. At the same time she embodies the 'other' of the ideal man-of-letters of the Enlightenment. She is enslaved by her sex and imprisoned by her femininity. And she is expressionless. In Diderot's lewd tale *Bijoux indiscrets* the sensual pleasure of oriental females is interpreted by an oriental despot. Sultan Mangogul possesses a magic ring which allows him to appropriate the intimate lives of his concubines. When the ring is turned upon a woman, her own 'jewel,' or *genitalia*, reveals through images and words their mistress' most secret desires. Alexander Pope's letters to Lady Mary Wortley Montagu, sent to her during her absence from England between 1717 and 1718, manifest similar attitudes to the *orientale*. In a paragraph which moves from the covertly erotic to the openly bawdy, Pope describes the passage

of Lady Montagu from Christian territory to a Muslim terrestrial
paradise.

> [you will soon be] in the land of Jealosy, where the unhappy
> women converse but with Eunuchs, and where the very cucum-
> bers are brought cutt [sic]. I expect to hear an exact account how,
> and at what place, you leave one Article of Faith, after another
> as you approach near to Turkey.[37]

Proceeding from the 'area of sin and Fornication [sic]', Lady
Montagu should soon arrive at the 'free region of Adultery':

> I shall hear how the very first night you lay in Pera you had a
> Vision of Mahomet's Paradise, and happily awaked without a
> soul. For which blessed instant the beautiful Body was left at full
> liberty to perform all the agreeable functions it was made for.[38]

Of the three kinds of authority discussed here, travel-literature
was, probably, the most vulnerable to criticism. For only very few of
the men tourists actually penetrated Muslim houses. Those who did
cross over from the *selamlik*, or the men's quarters, the public part of
the house, to the *haremlik*, were even fewer. But travellers, especially
before the eighteenth century, when the boundaries between truth
and untruth had not been set, lied or exaggerated. There are many
examples of that kind of 'travellers' lies' (Percy G. Adams's term)[39]
and it is, perhaps, worth citing those writers who claimed to have
proceeded beyond the 'gate of felicity' separating the Ottoman
Sultans' harem at *Topkapi* from the Second Court of the palace.
The Third Court with its women's quarters and the quarters of
black eunuchs were the most impenetrable territory in the Ottoman
Empire and, before the nineteenth century, were hermetically sealed
to adult males other than the Sultan himself, his sons and the black
eunuchs.[40] The Italian physician Domenico Hierosolimitano, who
stayed in Istanbul between 1580 and 1589, saw parts of the Third
Court, but not its inhabitants.[41] Thomas Dallaway, an organ-builder
sent by Queen Elizabeth I in 1580 to present the Sultan with musical
instruments, gazed upon a group of *odaliks* playing with a ball in
the palace's gardens and was overcome with emotion.[42] And Sir
George Courthope peopled the same gardens (they were empty
when he saw them) with naked concubines, and even imagined
the Sultan shooting them with pellets that stuck on their flesh.[43]

THE CRITICISM ON TRAVELLERS

But deception, or the stretching or varnishing of the truth, are not the only flaws of the descriptions of non-witnesses. The narrative of men travellers has other flaws: citation, or reference to textual authority substitutes for first-hand information. Moreover, the narrative is rhetorical rather than descriptive or representational and the reader is hectored with general information, obtainable from external authorities (reports of earlier travellers, the *Nights* and oriental fiction). Last, the accounts tend to be vague and anecdotal rather than circumstantial, and lack the realistic detail characteristic of descriptions of public spaces. Even reliable authors like the Baron de Tott in the eighteenth century, and Adolphus Slade or Lane in the nineteenth, are rather thin on life inside the harem and on its intimate aspects.

A few of the travellers admit to their ignorance and even acknowledge their indebtedness to female informants. Thus Dallaway, in a moment of truth, disclosed the fact that he had obtained information about the high-harems at Istanbul from the wives of Frank merchants at Pera: 'From such opportunities all accurate information concerning the *interior* of the palaces must be collected, and to such I am at present indebted'.[44] He somehow managed to glance at unveiled females, he claims, but his comments on 'the symmetry of their faces', their 'stooping' and the 'elegance of their countenance,' suspiciously resemble comparable remarks in Lady Montagu's *Letters*.[45] A few years after Dallaway, William Hunter Crane admits that: 'with regard to the women, you must depend on the accounts of others, as no men, but to whom they belong, is ever permitted to see them.'[46] The great Lane himself becomes somewhat awkward in passages on harems and Egyptian women. He devotes a whole chapter in his *Manners and Customs of the Modern Egyptians* to these topics, but is reticent on the intimate life of women. In a rather convoluted passage Lane explains that:

For a person who has become familiar with male Muslim society in Cairo, without marrying, it is not difficult as might be imagined by a stranger to obtain, directly and indirectly, correct and ample information respecting the conditions and habits of women. Many husbands of the middle-classes and some of the higher orders, freely talk of the affairs of the hareem with one who professes to agree with them in their general moral sentiments, if they have not to converse through the medium of interpreter.[47]

His statement amounts to an admission that his information is derived exclusively from male sources. In fact, Lane himself was well aware of the inadequacy of his own accounts on women, and urged his sister, Sophia Lane Poole (who had lived in Lane's Cairene harem), to write a companion-volume to the *Modern Egyptians* that would focus on life inside the harems of Egypt's Circassian-Turkish élite. The book, appropriately entitled *The Englishwoman in Egypt, Letters from Cairo Written During a Residence there in 1842/3/4* (1844), is particularly informative on women of the upper classes.

Like Lane, James Silk Buckingham writes on women in rather general terms which disclose an uneasiness. In a chapter on daily life in Mosul in *Travels in Mesopotamia* (1827) Buckingham generalises on the license of women of the Ottoman Empire. *'It is said'* he states, 'that women of the highest conditions *sometimes* grant assignations at . . . houses [brothels] and this, *indeed cannot be denied, the facility* of clandestine meetings is much greater in Turkish cities . . . than in any Metropolis' (my emphasis).[48] Despite his allusions to the Ottoman women's propensity to vice, Buckingham is, uncharacteristically, cautious. Note the reservations in the passages quoted above: 'it is said' . . . 'cannot be denied' etc. Even the great Burton, known for his encyclopedic knowledge on exotic sexuality, is less confident when he writes on women. Despite his mastery of oriental languages and dialects, despite his familiarity with Arab, Indian and Ottoman sources, despite the fact that he travelled through Egypt and the Hijaz disguised as a Muslim physician (which made contact with local women relatively easy), Burton could not penetrate the private world of Middle Eastern women. And his writings on harems manifest exactly the same flaws as those of the lesser authors. Burton does not inform us even about the unsecluded and independent Bedouin women. He admits, albeit reluctantly, that in his capacity as a physician he 'heard much but saw little' of harems.[49] And he infers from medieval or pre-Islamic sources to the contemporary Hijaz, or Egypt; and by doing so de-historicises the harem. Burton, Lane and Buckingham may be taken as representative examples. Their writings on Muslim women, like the writing of most Western travellers, did not derive from participant observation. This is, perhaps, the reason why so many of the travellers/ethnographers lack what Lévi-Strauss regards as the essential characteristic of ethnographic literature, an empathy towards the object of research that develops as a result of intersubjective relations between the observer and those he observes and that sense of common humanity shared between the 'I' with its cultural 'other'.[50]

Women writers from Lady Montagu onwards openly criticise male representations of the domestic sphere. Take for instance her comment in a letter, dated April 1717, to Lady Mar: 'Now I am a little acquainted with their ways, I cannot forbear admiring either the exemplary discretion or the extreme stupidity of all the writers that have given accounts of 'em [the Turkish women]'.[51] Over a century later, Pardoe elaborates on the same theme in a long, self-conscious passage on the difficulties of travellers to the Middle East. She distinguishes between difficulties that *can* be surmounted – prejudices, ignorance, the barrier of language and those difficulties which are insurmountable. The Ottomans, observes Pardoe, are 'private people'. And they will not welcome strange men into their own houses, let alone to the 'private' portions of the house. It remains for female writers like herself 'mere woman that I am,' to describe the private and intimate aspects of life.[52] Less self-assured, nevertheless equally revealing, is Sophia Lane Poole's first letter in her *Englishwoman in Egypt*. Lane Poole defines her role as writer, *vis-à-vis* that of her celebrated brother, thus distinguishing between a male and a female sphere of interest. 'The fact that I could see things accessible only to a Lady,' she confides in her audience, 'suggested to him [Lane] the idea that I might both gratify my curiosity and collect much information of a novel and interesting nature'.[53] And as late as 1871, Annie Harvey, one of the better chroniclers of life within the foreign colony at Istanbul, notes in her *Turkish Harems and Circassian Homes*, that the harems of the élite are impenetrable. Almost. Well-connected travellers like Harvey herself could gain access into the 'best establishments' and inform armchair travellers about the 'forbidden' portion of the Eastern house.[54] Decades after Harvey, Anna Bowman Dodd defines the weaknesses of masculine narrative. Interrupting her description of a dinner in one of the palaces of the Sultan, Bowman recalls an incident which involves her brother who, after having seen the Sultan at the Paris Exhibition of 1867, wrote back to her that the Sublime Porte looked like anyone else. The appalled Bowman remembers even 'at this distance of years what impatient, scornful disgust these laconic lines brought with them . . . as proving masculine dullness of vision and limitations in elaboration of detail'.[55]

By the second part of the nineteenth century the notion that the 'private' or *vie intime* is women's sphere is well established, hence the fact that harem literature is, *sui-generis*, 'women's literature', had become widespread. The best illustration to this is that the association between gender and travel had filtered down, from the travelogue to mass-circulation guidebooks. The guides urged 'lady travellers' to visit Middle Eastern private houses. Indeed a visit to a harem became *de rigueur* to Englishwomen. Murray, the leading publisher of travel literature and guides on the Mediterranean, is partly responsible for the commercialisation of the harem. The firm's first guide on the Middle East, combining the Ionian Islands, Asia Minor and Istanbul, has no reference to women, or to harems. The 1847 edition, comprising 'Turkey in Europe', Asia Minor, Armenia, and 'Mesopotamia,' includes a section on harems with a special address to 'lady travellers,' followed by an account of a visit to a house in Istanbul 'from the pen of a lady'.[56] In the 1871 edition lady travellers are warned not to depend on the British ambassador to the Sublime Porte, or the Consul General to Istanbul, to procure for them introductions to 'Turkish ladies'. Instead, tourists are advised to try and 'acquire Turkish female friends'.[57] Even the misogynist Royal Geographical Society included in its standard *Hints for Travellers* a section on the diversity of forms of marriage and sexuality with passages on Muslim polygamy and concubinage. Significantly, the entire section addresses not specialist audiences (professional geographers and anthropologists) but amateur travellers – women and men.[58]

Certainly, the diffusion of the 'feminine' eyewitness account from the literary travelogue down to popular guide-books may be interpreted as the ultimate proof of the commercialisation of the exotic. The harem, it may well be argued, became a mass-market commodity. And the female participant observers ultimately repeat the process of the objectification of the Orient, began by Galland. However, as Chapters 3–6 clearly demonstrate, this is not the case. The Western women's harem is not an image in an occidental 'archive' of the exotic. That harem is an image of the familiar, it is rarely a monolith and is never merely an objectified commodity.

3

The Eighteenth-Century Harem (1717–89): Lady Montagu, Lady Craven and the Genealogy of Comparative 'Morals'

It is a great problem for men to decide whether it is more advantageous to allow women their freedom, or to deprive them of it. It seems to me that there is a great deal to be said both for and against. If the Europeans say that it is ungener-ous to make those we love unhappy, the Asians retort that it is ignoble for men to renounce the authority that Nature gave them over women.

> Rica to Ibben, at Smyrna, Montesquieu,
> *Persian Letters*, Letter 38.[1]

What is commonly call'd Barbarous is but a different mode of Civility.

> L. Addison.[2]

As to their Morality or good Conduct, I can say like Arlequin 'tis just as 'tis with you, and the Turkish Ladys don't commit one Sin the less for not being Christians.

> Lady Mary Wortley Montagu, to Lady Mar,
> Adrianople, 1 April 1717.[3]

'NOVELTIE' AND TRADITION

It is very convenient to associate a new genre, especially one that

77

has not yet been recognised, with one particular date and a single work. This legitimises the work and lends it certain respectability. Certainly, the question of paternity can be settled. What easier, then, than to date the female literature on the harem from 1763, the year of the posthumous publication of Lady Mary Wortley Montagu's famous Turkish Embassy *Letters*,[4] describing her travels in Europe and the Ottoman Empire? For these letters are, arguably, the first example of a secular account, by a woman, on the Muslim Orient. And they concentrate on the position of Ottoman women and domestic manners. And, happily for the lexicographer of literary 'genres' and *mentalité*, Lady Montagu's work represents a wider consciousness of the comparativeness of 'morality' (her own term, designating sexual morals) and the relativeness of Western European values. Last, but not least, the *Letters* exude an aura of broad-mindedness and tolerance towards the Ottomans, indeed towards Europe's religious and cultural 'other' as such. Lady Montagu's letters, in short, may be appropriately designated a key text, the corner-stone in the new, alternative discourse that developed in the West on the Middle East.

There is, undoubtedly, much that is true in what is said above. Yet the production of the *Letters* and their impact on different readerships, at different points in time, present a few provocative questions. These questions concern periodisation (what are the chronological limits of harem literature); the location of the *Letters vis-à-vis* the literary traditions and the *mentalités* described in Chapter 2 and, most relevant here, the impact of the text on travel-writers and the wider audience. To evaluate *historically* the influence and status of the first modern description, by an eyewitness, of *actual* harems, we shall have to tell the story of its reading, or rather *readings* by actual audiences, as well as the fictive audiences implied in the text. Then we shall have to isolate certain images of the Orient and compare those images with older ones, or with eighteenth-century *topoi* of the Orient. In what follows I reconstruct the history of the *Letters* and their reception in the eighteenth century and try to separate what in Lady Montagu's attitudes towards sexuality is novel from what is more 'traditional'. As the title of this chapter suggests, in a final analysis, the harem in her letters embodies certain new and radical ideas about the position of women in the Ottoman Empire and, more important, in Britain.

The production and reception of the letters conveniently present three phases.[5] The first and shortest phase parallels the *actual* journey from London to Istanbul, the stay there and the return journey (1 August 1716–1 November 1718). Lady Montagu accompanied her husband, the Whig politician Edward Wortley Montagu, who had been appointed ambassador extraordinary of George I to Sultan Ahmet III and representative of the Levant Company to the Sublime Porte. Wortley Montagu, as is well known, had been entrusted with the task of mediator between the Porte and Emperor Charles VII. The embassy utterly failed, Montagu was recalled back a year after his arrival at Istanbul, and his career practically terminated.[6] While the embassy lasted, however, Lady Montagu had access to the households of the Turkish-Circassian military and official élites at Edirne (Adrianople, Ahmet III's second capital) and Istanbul. And the original letters, sent to female and male correspondents, drew on the log she kept daily and which, unfortunately, was entirely burnt by Lady Montagu's daughter and literary executioner, Lady Bute. The second, much longer phase, lasting until 1763, saw a two-sided change in the text: from actual letters to a limited readership, to pseudo-letters to fictive addressees, being aimed at a wider, more varied audience. The letters, it will be recalled, still remained unprinted, but circulated in manuscript among the London wits and *literati*, and selected extracts of the text appeared both in Britain and abroad.

With these changes came a meaningful transformation not only in the characters of the 'recipients' – 'characters' based on 'real' people but dramatised and fictionalised – but also in the *persona* of the writer. The actual Lady Montagu, an aristocrat, a progressive Whig and a rising wit, was present in the text. And – as a number of pamphlets and blurbs circulating in London testify – she could be easily identified by her readers. But she evidently developed into a fictional narrator, assuming diverse voices and different masks to convey to her audience different points of view, in accordance with the person (or character) she addressed. And the recipients of the letters were no longer merely 'real' readers, but 'implied' ones as well (I am using Wayne Booth's term), characterised and fictional-ised. The actual letters, then, were transformed into a chronological, linearly evolving narrative of travel, in epistolary form, a common enough form in the eighteenth century. Altogether, there are 15 recipients of 52 pseudo-letters, and 12 of these recipients are female. This exceptionally varied gallery of readers (less numerous than the 20 addressees in Richardson's later *Clarissa*, but then *Clarissa* has 600 letters as against Montagu's merely 52) of different sexes, classes and social and political status, authenticates a kaleidoscopic and unprejudiced view of Istanbul.

The most significant correlation is between the topics and style of the letters and the gender of recipients. Those letters addressed to named (historical) women and to unnamed ones, focus on the life of Ottoman women. Uneducated recipients, like the unnamed 'Lady-' are treated to pictorial and excessively descriptive representations of Cttoman households.[7] Better educated female recipients like Frances Pierrepont, Lady Mar, Montagu's sister and second wife of the Jacobite rebel, 7th earl of Mar, retain their descriptiveness but develop the idea of tolerance, emphasising the analogy between tolerance towards sexual manners and morals and the toleration of political opposition.[8] This analogy is not coincidental. The Pierrepont sisters were identified with opposing political camps. Lady Montagu was a staunch Whig and Hanoverian and very close to court circles, especially to the coterie of the Prince of Wales (actually Caroline, the Regent's wife is one of her correspondents). Moreover, at one time she contributed to the Whig press, writing anonymously to Walpole's organ, *the Nonsense of Commonsense*. Lady Mar, on the other hand, was the wife of the military leader of the opposition to the new succession and the Settlement of 1711. All this accounts for the comparison between the 'home' and the polity and the politicisation of sexual issues in the letters to Lady Mar (I shall discuss this topic in detail later). Letters to the male recipients also deal with the harem, but in a significantly different manner and style. The harem appears in letters to Alexander Pope and Abbé Conti,[9] a progressive churchman and cosmopolitan minor thinker, then living in Paris. The letters to Conti, the best in the batch, are modelled on the philosophical tale and develop the notions of the relativeness of beliefs and values implied in the letters to Lady Mar.

Early commentators on the manuscript focused their attention on the gender of the writer and the generically novel approach to foreign lands and cultures, of a female traveller. This is Mary Astell, highchurch, Tory essayist and the first exponent in modern Britain of female education, in an address to the reader which prefaced the Montagu manuscript.[10] The fact that an 'address' was prefixed to an unprinted text is in itself significant and possibly points at the relations between the readership and the author.

I confess I am malicious enough to desire that the world should see to how much better purpose the Ladys travel than their Lords, and that whilst it is surfeited with Male Travels, all in the same Tone and Stuft with the same Trifles, a Lady has the skill to strike out a New path and Embellish a worn-out Subject with Vivacity and Spirit.[11]

Publishers and printers – who made a little fortune of piratised editions of extracts of the letters – were fast to drum up the new image of the female traveller to Turkey. A reproduction of a letter to Abbé Conti presented an engraving of Lady Montagu in her Turkish dress, the caption being a four-line doggerel which reads:

> Let men who glory in their better sense
> Read, hear and learn Humility from hence;
> No more let them Superior Wisdom boast,
> They can but equal M-nt-g-e at most.[12]

Astell and the anonymous printer make the same point as Abbé Conti and his friend, the *savant* Nicolas-François Remond in the actual correspondence: the *experience* of Turkey largely depends on the sex (and class) of the traveller. Being a woman enabled Lady Montagu to cover certain areas which had before been *terra incognita* to male travellers, and to approach these areas from a *novel* angle. It is a point that is carried farther in the letters themselves.

To return now to the third and longest phase in the history of the 'Embassy Letters', a phase which begins with actual publication and ends with the outbreak of the First World War and the decline of travel to the Orient. Walter Benjamin would describe the change which now took place as one from 'original' artefact to reproduction.[13] The circle of readers in the 1760s was certainly wider than in, say, the 1730s or 1740s. But the letters were not, and were not meant to be, *popular* literature. The first printed edition unashamedly catered for an aristocratic and cosmopolitan readership. The exasperatingly long title is immensely revealing: *Letters of the Right Honourable Lady m-y w-y m-e: written during her Travels in Europe, Asia and Africa, to Persons of Distinction, Men of Letters & c. in Different Parts of Europe, Which Contain, Among Other Curious Relations, Accounts of the Policy and Manners of the Turks; Drawn from Sources that Have Been Inaccessible to Other Travellers.* Note the undisguised snob-appeal and the emphasis on the value of new, and hitherto 'inaccessible' sources, implying mainly female sources. The impact of the letters on Victorian writers is beyond the chronological scope of this chapter and shall be treated in Chapter 4. Suffice it to note here that after publication the relationship between readers and text took yet another important turn. Those readers who documented their reactions were, themselves, travel-writers, who in their own turn, described the harem. And in the alternative system of information about and interpretation of the Middle East, the 'Embassy Letters' acquired a status and authority comparable with those of Galland's *Nights*, in the more traditional discourse. The single most important fact about the history of the reception of the *Letters* in the nineteenth century is that their readers were, themselves, writers and their own work, a commentary on Montagu's model. I shall stop the narrative here but resume it in Chapter 4, and now fix on the scene of the eighteenth century.

The tension between 'noveltie', or 'invention' and 'tradition', between change and continuity in the images of the harem, dominates the text. Lady Montagu, despite the eulogies of the early commentators, does not present herself as the narrator of what is absolutely novel in an informational vacuum. Rather, her text predisposes the reader to specific kinds of reception, by explicit utterances, covert messages and various allusions.[14] Very subtly, the letters on the Ottoman women are designed to evoke commonly shared notions, prejudices even, on the Orient. Then the 'older' authorities on the Middle East, notably Galland's text and travellers' reports, are critically reviewed, and mercilessly dissected. Then on the basis of this criticism and Montagu's own personal experience, a new edifice of notions about morals is erected. Female readers are assumed to be differently prejudiced (and educated) than the male ones. As mentioned before, even the least knowledgeable and most credulous among the women addressees, and those who receive the most sensational reports on harems, are assumed to be familiar with Galland's transcription of the *Nights* and even with a few travel-books.

Montagu herself had mastered both the *Arabian Nights* and François Petis de la Croix's *Milles et un jours* (1710–12), commonly known as the *Persian Tales* and, before and during her journey, had embarked on a Jesuitical syllabus that included the Koran, in the French version, and practically every available report in English and French on the Ottoman Empire (notably the works of travellers like Paul Rycaut, Richard Knolles, François Thevenot, George Sandys, Aaron Hill, Dumont and G. F. Gemelli-Carreri),[15] not to mention the classics (Montagu's command of Latin was noted in her own days) and Turkish prose and poetry which, by the middle of 1717, she could study in the original.[16]

Montagu, then, was better equipped than most travellers to Turkey. And as is shown by Halsband, she had utilised the various literary traditions on the Orient. She drew on Galland and La Croix and her letters to Pope and Conti on the Edirne area and the coast of Asia Minor are still considered a feat of classical scholarship. On those travellers whose works she had admired (Sandys and Gemelli-Carreri) Montagu drew heavily. Nevertheless she criticises all non-classical authorities, both individually and collectively, openly and indirectly, for the ignorance these authorities disclose, for their prejudice and inaccuracy. And not only the substance of the writings on modern Turkey is criticised, but their *style* as well. Thus the reputed learning of Rycaut and Knolles is lampooned. They hector the reader with unnecessary information and bore. As for Montagu herself, she affects to sacrifice learning for wit (which, as the *Letters* themselves show, she did not): 'I'll show you', she writes, 't'is not want of learning that I forbear writing [sic] all these bright things [e.g. the history of Istanbul and the Sultans]. I could also, with little trouble, turn over Knolles and Sir Paul Rycaut to give you a list of Turkish Emperors'.[17] Ignorance and lying, however, are far worse than the inelegant parading of learning. And, of course, it was the travellers' ignorance about, and prejudice against, the morality of the Ottomans that particularly made them an easy target. Characteristically, it is the less educated audience, fictionalised in the unknown 'Lady—', the most susceptible to the influence of stories and inventions, who is warned against travellers:

> I see you have taken your Idea of Turkey from that worthy author Dumont, who has writ with equal ignorance and confidence. 'Tis a particular pleasure to me to have to read the voyages to the Levant, which are generally so far remov'd from Truth and so full of Absurdytiys I am very well diverted with 'em. They never fail giving you an account of the Women, which 'tis certain they never saw, and talking very wisely of the Genius of the men, into whose company they were never admitted.[18]

Time and again, Western notions about sexual morals are exposed as a system of misinformation – resulting from ignorance and prejudice. 'Now I am a little acquainted with their ways', writes Montagu to Lady Mar, in a letter dated 1 April 1717, 'I cannot forbare admiring the exemplary discretion or extreme stupidity of all writers that have given accounts of 'em.'[19] 'Acquaintance', then, is the key. Personal experience, not external authorities, make a report accurate. And for Montagu, accuracy and an unbiased approach to a foreign, 'other' culture are vital. Moreover, the Ottoman home, the *locus* of the intimate and private, is elevated from the merely picturesque and erotically exciting, to a pivotal place in the discussion of Ottoman culture and society. The reliable representation of the private, becomes the *litmus-test* to the travellers' credibility and his or her tolerance towards the more public areas of life: the government, the administration, economy and public (as against private) religion.

The relation between 'acquaintance' (that is Montagu's own experience of the harem) and external, traditional authority varies. In the letters addressed to Abbé Conti and Alexander Pope, Montagu utilises and, at the same time, challenges traditional images and precepts, not so much in imaginative literature and travel-books as in non-fictional writing concerning Islam. It is assumed that the male readers are conversant with classical texts. They are expected to be, at least, superficially familiar with the Koran and also with the political writings of Whig thinkers.[20]

I have already mentioned that the reading-matter of the female-correspondents which is implied in the text is lighter. The letters addressed to these correspondents have a few other generic characteristics. First is the centrality of personal experience. Second, and related to the first, is the representational nature of the narrative. This, for instance, is exemplified in the descriptions of domestic spaces, particularly the households of the élite, both in Istanbul and Edirne (the finest exemplars are the descriptions of the *haremlik* at the palace of Arnaut Halil Pasha (1655–1733), Grand Vizier of Ahmet III; the Edirne and Istanbul households of Ahmet's Kâhya, or 'second in command', and the palace of Sultan Hafise (misspelled by as Montagu as Hafife), favorite *kadine* of the deceased Sultan Mustafa III).[21] Apart from physical representation the 'female' parts of the travelogue are marked by a significant change from the real traveller, to the fictional *persona* of narrator. There is no mistaking the female identity of that *persona*, particularly because Montagu, who takes pains to dim national and religious attributes, consciously emphasises gender. Montagu is, in fact, the first in a long succession of women travellers, to have affected oriental dress and manners. Now the disguise, or mask, is somewhat puzzling. Because it may appear as mere attitudinising. This seems to be the case in a letter to Lady Mar, in which Montagu indulges in two and a half pages of description of her Turkish costume, which can be seen in the several engravings and oil-paintings that present her in this costume.[22] Yet the disguise implies a deeper change, albeit only a temporary one, in the traveller's identity. Montagu often emerged from the comparative security of Christian and cosmopolitan Pera to Istanbul proper, disguised as an Ottoman woman. She particularly delighted in veiling herself. And, paradoxically, the *yashmak* enabled her a freedom of movement denied to uncovered Christian females, or to male travellers.

LIBERTY BEHIND THE VEIL

The usage of the veil, in both the literal and metaphorical sense, is significant. The metaphor for the oriental woman's subjection is now reversed to stand for 'Liberty': 'Y'll wonder madam', Montagu writes to Lady Bristol, in a letter dated 10 April 1718, 'to hear me add that I have been there' [at Istanbul 'proper'] very often. The *asmak* or Turkish veil [sic], is become not only very easy but agreeable to me, and if it was not, I would be content to endure some inconveniency to content a passion so powerful with me as Curiosity',[23] and, in another letter, to the unnamed 'Countess——': 'I ramble everyday, wrap'd up in my *ferige* and *asmak*, about Constantinople and amuse my self with seeing all that is curious in it.'[24] Apart from its well-known anthropological aspects, masquerading as one's cultural 'other' is a literary device. And in the context of an epistolary travelogue on the Orient, the device is especially evocative. For all of Montagu's earlier readers were familiar with Harun al-Rashid, the insomniac Caliph, forever on the lookout for the bizarre and curious and a 'diverting story' (a combination which Lady Montagu often used). Like the Caliph, the fictive and, probably, the real Montagu roams the streets of an oriental city. Moreover, she, a female and a Christian, embodies the two 'types' of narrator in the original *Nights*: Sheherezad, the inventor of tales and the 'framer' of the collection, who gives the myriad of 'framed' anecdotes a shape, and the Caliph, the omniscient, omnipresent *voyeur*, who, unseen, sees and experiences what others cannot.[25] However, Montagu's narrator/traveller, unlike Galland's Caliph, or the lewd Sultan in Diderot's *Bijoux indiscrets*, or Usbeq, in the *Lettres persanes*, is not a *voyeur* who is actually absent from the scene of action, but observes it from the outside. The fictional Montagu is a witness. It was what she had seen of women's life in Istanbul that formed the basis of what is, perhaps, her most famous generalisation about their freedom. The following is from a letter to Lady Mar and is to be found at the end of a passage in which Montagu abuses her male predecessors and contemporaries. And it is the second (and by no means the last) time that she elaborates on the subject:

> 'Tis very easy to see they have more Liberty than we have, no Woman of what rank so ever being permitted to go in the streets without 2 muslins, one that covers her face all but her Eyes and another that hides the whole dress of her head . . . You may guess how effectually this disguises them, that there is no distinguishing the great Lady from her Slave, and 'tis impossible for the most jealous Husband to know his Wife when he meets her, and no Man dare either touch or follow a Woman in the Street. This perpetual Masquerade gives them entire Liberty of following their Inclinations without danger of Discovery.[26]

As Robert Halsband has noted, the paradox of liberty in bondage is driven *ad-captandum*.[27] What is important, however, is not Montagu's 'sincerity', whether she *actually* thought the veiled Ottoman women freer than their Western European sisters (which she seemed to), but her usage of 'Liberty' (invariably capitalised in the text). For Montagu, as well as for her only eighteenth-century disciple, Lady Elisabeth Craven, margravine of Anspach, a professional playwright who in 1785 travelled *alone* to Istanbul, 'Liberty' spelt out *sexual freedom*. And it meant one's ability to follow one's 'inclination' and 'indulge' oneself (Montagu's words) in that inclination, regardless of one's sex. Certainly Montagu was not entirely original. A few (male) travellers before her had commented upon the advantages of the veil. Du Loir and Robert Withers in particular had noted that the *yashmak* offered Ottoman women kinds of freedom denied to the Christian woman.[28] Like these predecessors Montagu was aware that infidelity could have incurred death to the adulteress. What is novel in her usage of the metaphor of the veil is the notion that 'Liberty' – that is a moral-free and natural sexual conduct – is applicable to both sexes.

Montagu put the metaphor of the *yashmak* in circulation. Craven, after her, elaborated that metaphor, as many a Victorian writer would do:

> As to women, as many, if not more than men, are to be seen in the streets – but they look like walking mummies – A large loose robe of dark green cloth covers them from the neck to the ground, over that a large piece of muslin, which wraps the shoulders and the arms, another which goes over the head and eyes; judge, Sir, if all these coverings do not confound all shape or air so much, that men or women, princesses or slaves, may be concealed from them. I think I never saw a country where women may enjoy so much liberty, and free from all reproach as in Turkey.[29]

Unlike Montagu, Craven was no Turkophile. Nor was she particularly interested in the *haremlik*. She discloses a preference for 'Nature', or picturesque landscapes and rather dislikes man-made spaces. The change in aesthetic sensibilities, from the Augustan to the Romantic is perceptible. Equally perceptible is the change in the sensibilities of the aristocratic traveller. Craven writes in the last decade of the eighteenth century, when the Evangelical assault on public morality was well on its way. She notes the visibility of women of all classes in a public space: 'women . . . are to be seen in the streets'. In the Augustan vocabulary, certainly in the Victorian idiom, 'walking the streets' is virtually synonymous with prostitution. Yet, according to Craven, veiling not only liberates Ottoman women sexually, but makes them more mobile than their English sisters. Paradoxically the *yashmak* guarantees degrees of public freedom. Coming from the Turkophobe Craven, the passages on the freedom of women are particularly convincing. Moreover, Craven introduces into the discussion on the condition of women another detail, the custom of putting a pair of slippers outside the door separating the *haremlik* from the *selamlik* (the men's quarters and public part of the Turkish house), to signify the women's wish for privacy.[30] And, as with the *yashmak*, the *çedik-pabuç* (the yellow slipper for indoor wear) is used as metaphor and symbol for freedom. For the late eighteenth-century writer, the negative sense of 'Liberty', or the woman's right to privacy, designated by the slippers, is more important than the earlier sense of the word, 'freedom for', the 'positive' pursuit of one's inclination, symbolised by the veil. The Victorian writers preferred Craven's metaphor to that of Montagu's. Because for the Victorians the married woman's right to freedom from sexual exploitation *within* marriage was particularly important.

Significantly the two eighteenth-century writers associate sexual freedom with economic independence. They both maintain that the upper-class Ottoman woman is economically as well as sexually free. Thus Montagu: 'Neither have they [the Ottoman women] to apprehend from the resentment of their Husbands, those Ladys that are rich having all their money in their own hands, which they take with'em upon a divorce with an addition which he is oblig'd to give 'em).'[31] And Craven: 'The Turks in their conduct towards our sex are an example to all other nations – A Turk has his head cut off – his papers are examined – every thing in his house seized – but his wife is provided for.'[32] The obsession with the freedom of the Ottoman women and the comparative bondage of the Western ones, has a poignantly personal angle. For both Montagu and Craven were, throughout their lives, economically vulnerable. And there is abundant evidence that Montagu's first circle of readers (the audience with access to the manuscript), and Craven's public, were both aware of the writers' pecuniary problems.[33] The position of both writers was characteristic and manifested the disabilities of married women, disabilities against which even aristocrats were not immune. Lady Montagu's marriage had not been settled, that is, no prenuptial agreement had been signed to secure her 'portion' in case of dissolution by divorce, or separation. When a few years after their return from Istanbul she separated from Wortley, she became propertyless and depended entirely on Wortley's good will. Craven's case was even more severe. Legally separated from William Craven, later sixth earl of Craven, she had been grudged her jointure and forcibly separated from her seven children. And her travelogue is a vindication of her *status* as legal wife and mother – the introduction being an attack on her husband, and tyrannical husbands in general.[34]

As with the passage on veiling and masquerade, the description of the *hammam*, or public bath, was elevated by the Victorians to a *text of reference*. The texts, of course, are different in that the passage on veils is openly polemical and self-consciously rhetorical. And, despite Montagu's emphasis on 'acquaintance', information on items of dress could be obtained from external authorities, not the least from travelogues. Montagu's description of bathers in Sophia's public *hammam* is, on the other hand, richly representational. And, there is little doubt that she had actually witnessed and participated in the scenes that she later described. Different as they are, the two texts have in common the sophisticated usage of dress and undress as both metaphors for and symbols of, varying degrees of freedom and the relation of individuals to Nature (Montagu's own term, denoting, not so much the natural world as against man-made environment, but human inclination, basically the inclination of the body and senses).

Now in Western imagination the *hammam* came to apotheosise the sensual, effeminate Orient. Never actually penetrated by male travellers, the women's public-baths were identified as the *loci sensuales* in the erotically charged landscape of the Orient. For the female bathers combined two of the oriental woman's traditional characteristics: over-sexuality and the easterner's propensity towards indolence. It is significant that the early eighteenth-century term for 'public-bath', the italianate *bagnio*, used to designate a brothel (the *bagnios* and *serails* which mushroomed in London in the early part of the eighteenth century, in fact catered to specialised tastes such as flagellation).[35] Montagu herself uses the italianate form in her description of the bath in Sophia. The description itself was to become a blue-print, interpreted and challenged by nineteenth-century travellers, and an inspiration to painters of the Orientalist school, notably Ingres, whose *Bain Turc*, 1862, shows the influence of Montagu's piece. Ingres copied the piece into his notebook, using the French translation of the 1805 edition of the *Letters*.

Lady Montagu refers to her representation of the bathers as 'Novelty', thereby legitimising any 'innovation', that is fictionalisation, on the part of the narrator. From then on she proceeds in a matter-of-fact way, with attention to the minutest detail; the layout of the building; the different stages of bathing, cooling, massaging and toilette; and only then does she embark on what was to become, with justice, one of the most controversial pieces in the modern literature on the Orient and which is worth quoting at length.

> *I was in my travelling Habit, which is a riding dress,* and certainly appear'd very extraordinary to them, yet there was not one of'em that shew'd the least surprise or impertinent Curiosity, but receiv'd me with all the obliging civility possible. I know not one European Court where the Ladys would have behav'd them selves in so polite a manner to a stranger. I believe on the whole there were 200 Women and yet none of those disdainful smiles or

satyric whispers that never fail in our assemblys when any body appears that is not dress'd exactly in fashion. They repeated over and over to me, *Uzelle, pek uzelle,* which is nothing but, charming, very charming. The first sofas were covered with Cushions and rich Carpets, on which sat the Ladys, and on the 2nd their slaves behind'em, but without any distinction of rank by their dress, all being *in the state of nature,* that is, in plain English, stark naked, without any Beauty or deffect [sic] conceal'd, yet there was not the least wanton smile or immodest Gesture amongst'em. They walk'd and mov'd with the same majestic Grace which Milton describes of our General Mother. There are many amongst them exactly proportion'd as ever any Goddess was drawn by pencil of Guido or Titian, and most of their skins shineingly [sic] white, only adorn'd by their beautiful Hair . . . I was convinc'd of the Truth of a Reflexion that I had often made, that if 'twas the fashion to go naked, the face would be hardly observed . . . To tell you the Truth, I had wickedness enough to wish secretly that Mr. Gervase [Charles Jervase (1675–1739) – portrait-painter and friend of the London wits. In 1710 he painted Montagu dressed as a shepherdess] could have been there invisible. I fancy it would have very much improv'd his art to see so many fine Women naked in different postures, some in conversation, some working, others drinking Cofee or sherbet, and many negligently lying on their Cushions while their slaves (generally pritty girls of 17 or 18) were employed in braiding their hair . . . (my emphasis)[36]

After expanding on the social functions of the bath (a meeting place, the women's 'coffee-house') Montagu, in a few suggestive phrases, describes how she herself, was addressed by the Turks: 'The Lady that seem'd the most considerable amongst them entreated me to sit by her and would fain have undress'd me for the bath. I excus'd my selfe with some difficulty, they being all so earnest in perswading [sic] me. *I was at last forced to open my skirt and shew them my stays, which satisfy'd them very well, for I saw they believ'd I was so lock'd up in that machine that it was not in my power to open it, which Contrivance they attributed to my Husband'* (my emphasis).[37]

Before getting to the passage on the naked Miltonic Graces that had pleasantly titillated the Augustans and incensed the Victorians, a word on Montagu's opening. As already mentioned her reference to 'novelty' is a defense mechanism, aimed at the reader's faith and the build-up of her image as truthful traveller. For the early eighteenth-century reader the Ottoman female bathers were possibly as exotic and 'foreign' as the inhabitants of the South-Sea Islands, or the celebrated Patagonian Giants of even earlier travel-stories. Yet the appearance of the bathers, it seems, does not draw from the lips of the narrator a single utterance regarding their strangeness. Significantly the roles of traveller and 'foreigner' are reversed. And the very first sentences are about Montagu's own strangeness and 'otherness'. It is she, the covered European, that seems extraordinary and exotic – not to the Turkish bathers, but to herself. And her elaborate dress and underwear are more suggestive than the nakedness of the bathers. The Ottomans, for their part, *tolerate* her apparel and refrain from impolite comment. In fact, they are far more broad-minded and enlightened than the seemingly more advanced Western women. The reversal of the roles of observer and his or her object of observation, plus the fact that both happen to be female, together make for a small artistic (and cultural) feat. Certainly the eyewitness derives scopic pleasure from what she sees. But so do those seen by her. The bathers are both actors and spectators, politely directing their gaze at the traveller. Montagu manages to be ironic through a piece that smacks of self-conscious and smug broad-mindedness, which the reader implied in the text (also a woman) is invited to share.

Equally important is the balance between 'truth' and 'lie'. Montagu did not describe the bath as she had actually seen it. Most later descriptions testify that the Ottoman women never bathed in the nude, but covered themselves with linen-wrappers (I have come across only one reference to nudity in the bath, in Sophia Lane Poole's description of one high-class establishment in Cairo in 1842). And the statuesque Miltonic Eves are not exactly living women. They are rather, figures in a Neo-Classical *tableau vivant* (note the reference to Charles Jervase). But then, eighteenth-century readers would not have expected a representation described as 'novelty' to be absolutely realistic. In the eyes of that readership, both the analogue with classical standards and aesthetic values, and with *Paradise Lost* are in order. Also in order is the combination of decorousness and sensuality. The important words in the Augustan body-language are 'propriety', 'civility', 'politeness', all key-terms in the Enlightenment discourse on sexuality. Characteristically sensuality (and in the last passage on 'stays' sexual attraction) is expressed in an aesthetic and sometimes elevated language, brimful of undercurrent sensations. In contrast

to the erotic Oriental tale, Montagu offers her readers a refined
sensuality. There is nothing offensive or rude in her writing.
Rather she tames the exotic and normalises it. Her message of
individual sexual freedom and tolerance is especially pronounced
in the juxtaposition of 'nature' and 'machinery', or mechanism. The
Ottoman women are 'natural', because they indulge their senses and
bodies. It is the Western travellers, not the orientals, who need to be
released from imprisonment in a torturous 'machinery'.

The letters on women to Alexander Pope and Abbé Conti (together
with a few notes to Conti's friend, the French *savant* Nicolas-
François Remond) differ in form, style and manner from those
letters addressed to female correspondents. Montagu the narrator
changes from the female traveller, the collector of information and
story-teller, to the *philosophical traveller*, comparing social and political organisations and systems of morality. She is a classical scholar
and linguist. And her purpose is not merely to inform and divert her
readers but also to offer a critique on British attitudes to women and,
in a broader context, on Christian notions of womanhood and sexual
morals and manners.

The topic of the relative freedom of Ottoman women is first
brought on in a letter to Alexander Pope, dated 1 February 1717.
In the letter Montagu describes a dispute between herself and
her host in Belgrade, a (probably) factional scribe and philologist,
whom she calls Achmet-Beg [sic]. Montagu and her host discuss
matters 'concerning the differences of our Customs, particularly
the confinements of Women. He assures me there is nothing at
all in it; only, says he, we have the advantage that when our
Wives cheat us, no body knows it'.[38] The form of discourse is
appropriate. The comparativeness of diverse systems of marriage
as well as private and public behaviours, and the consciousness of
a pluralism of sexual codes are debated between an enlightened
Christian and an equally enlightened Muslim. The fact that the
first is a female and the second a male, makes the scene even
more *piquant* (particularly when the reader is Pope . . .), for in
traditional writing on the Orient, the typical relationship between
a Christian and a Muslim of opposite sexes is of a more intimate
nature. The description of a *rational* exchange on the position of
women, implies the possibility of a dialogue that cuts across sex,
religion and culture. Being the aristocrat she is, Montagu assures
both her addressee (and prospective readers) that Achmet-Beg is 'a
man of quality',[39] more polite than most Christians of a comparable

background and class. In the relevant letters to Abbé Conti, the Muslim divine is dropped to be replaced by a Catholic priest. Abbé Conti may have been – like his female *disputant* – a broadminded cosmopolitan. Still he is identified, through the *Letters*, with the official position of the Roman Catholic Church regarding women, sex and matrimony. Most important, Conti is sometimes identified with the Pauline-Augustinian negative attitudes to marriage and St. Paul's preference of virginity to matrimony. The most brilliant and merciless attack on the Church and churchmen is to be found in a letter that is not in the manuscript of the 'Embassy Letters' and which dates from February 1718. The letter in question, creating a stir both in literary Paris and London, was published separately in 1718 and 1719 (under the title *The Genuine Copy of a Letter Written from Constantinople by an English Lady . . .* , a second edition appearing in 1719 and reprinted in 1766 in the *Gentleman's Magazine* and the *Annual Register*). The letter had been triggered off by Conti's query about the spiritual status of Muslim women and their share in the after-life and the Islamic paradise. Montagu erroneously opined that the marital status of women influenced their spiritual status and that virgins and widows were excluded from paradise. It is, however, what follows these observations that directly concerns us here:

> Women, says he, [the Prophet] not being capable to manage Affairs of State, nor to support the Fatigues of War, God has not order'd them to govern or reform the World; but he has entrusted them with an Office which is not less honourable, even that of multiplying the human Race; And such as, out of Malice or Laziness, do not make it their Business to bear or to breed Children, fulfil not the Duty of their Vocation, and rebel against the Commands of God. Here are Maxims for you, prodigiously contrary to those of your *Convents*. What will become of your Saint *Catharines*, your Saint *Theresas*, your Saint *Claras*, and the whole Bead-roll of your *holy Virgins and Widows*? who, if they are to be judged by this System of Virtue, will be found to have been infamous Creatures, that past their whole Lives in a most abominable Libertinism. (emphases in text)[40]

Montagu's message comes through clear enough. Virtue, in particular female virtue, is a relative, not absolute value. Chastity

for women is not a universal notion. Nor should it be particularly commended. Celibacy and purity which are, in one religion,
sanctified, may be regarded in another as sinful and contrary to
nature and woman's vocation. The reference to the three saints
(Montagu significantly picks up three virgins: Saint Clara, Saint
Catherine, presumably of Sienna – Catherine of Genova being, at
one time, married – and Saint Theresa of Avilla) as 'libertines' and
'infamous' dissipators is audacious and provocative, even in the
rationalist anti-Clerical philosophical travelogue, or its equivalent,
the philosophical oriental tale. The text, it shall be recalled, is
very early, earlier than Montesquieu's comparable harem-cycle in
the *Lettres persanes* (1721), certainly much earlier than Voltaire's
celebrated anti-Clerical diatribes (and Voltaire admired the letters).
Nor is the letter atypical. For the gist of what is said in it is
repeated *ad captandum* in the collection itself. One example from
29 May 1717 is characteristic: 'This [the supposed exclusion of
widows from paradise] is a piece of theology very different from
that which teaches nothing to be more acceptable to God than a
perpetual Virginity. Which Divinity is most rational I leave you to
determine'.[41] There seems to be very little doubt as to Montagu's
view.

Montagu's latitudinarianism is typically limited. Her praise of
Islam is rather conventional and rhetorical. For the *Letters*, as much
as they are a vindication of the Ottoman women's morality and
Muslim morals in general, are pronouncedly anti-Catholic. Praise
of the tolerance of the Turks was a stick which Protestants – well
before the Enlightenment – used to beat with Catholic intolerance.
Those extracts in the *Letters* which describe the Catholic states and
principalities in Central Europe abound with derisory remarks
on Catholic theology, liturgy and ritual. It is, however, for the
religious orders, particularly the female ones, that Montagu's most
biting criticism is reserved. Convents are compared with prisons.
Life-long virginity is condemned as *sinful* because it is 'unnatural'.
The analogue between the *haremlik* and the convent, so common in
Victorian travelogues would be unacceptable to the two Augustan
writers. Anti-Catholicism, of course, had political aspects, of which
the readers of the manuscript had been aware. Montagu, as already
mentioned, was committed to the central idea and the politics of
the Act of Toleration (1699), which had excluded Catholics from
politics, and to the Settlement of 1711. Like most Whigs before 1745
she dreaded 'papists' and regarded them as the enemy within. She

could afford to be more tolerant towards an 'other without' that had ceased to threaten the society and polity she lived in. The condemnation of Catholic morality and the Pauline doctrine by a Whig that professes tolerance is, therefore, the result of a political more than a religious bias.

As with religion, so with sexual morals, Montagu's latitudinarianism may appear conventional. As Roy Porter has pointed out, the preoccupation, throughout the Enlightenment, with the freedom of the individual, licenced certain changes towards sexuality and its organisation and regulation. First, sex became more discussable. Yet, at the same time, discourse on sexuality was refined and highly stylised. Montagu's description of the bathers is, as already mentioned, one exemplar.[42] Second, and more important, sex was dissociated from Sin and was increasingly perceived as part of the economy of Nature. Third and related to the second change, the natural man was encouraged to freely pursue his sexual freedom. Yet not the natural woman. Because as both Porter and Susan Moller Okin, and a few other have shown, the tolerance of Enlightenment thinkers extended only as far as man. Woman was treated in a somewhat ambiguous way. The generic term 'man' was used literally.[43] The notion of liberty (in *Whig* writing, rather *liberties*) applied to Western Man alone with an emphasis on the 'M'. 'Liberty' for the woman clashed with an approach that saw her mainly in terms of her sex and productivity. Sexual freedom for women would certainly endanger the family. Thus, whereas natural man was free to pursue his will, the natural woman was perceived (within certain limits) largely as mother and wife. And purity in females was valued as in the Pauline doctrine and still considered as vital in the monogamous family.

In the *Letters* Montagu certainly does not advocate equality between women and men. Not even indirectly. And she emphasises not the similarities, but the differences between Ottoman men and women and between women and men in general. The Ottoman women are constantly characterised as *mothers*. And throughout the letters their attitudes to children, in fact the attitudes of Ottoman society in general to children, are marked out. 'In this country', opines Montagu, in a letter to her friend Anne Thistlethwayte, 't'is more despicable to be marry'd and not fruitful, than 'tis with us to be fruitful before marriage'.[44] Islam is a rational and thisworldly religion, with a practical morality that recognises the nature and vocation of man (in the generic sense of the word). Certainly the chastity of Ottoman females is guarded. Certainly adultery is severely punished. But chastity as such is not an ideal, nor is celibacy a way of life. And the Ottomans *are* free from the notion of Sin.

Let there be no misunderstanding. The idea of 'liberty' for women that is presented in the letters is limited. Nowhere in the travelogue is 'equality' even contemplated. And it would take two more decades for Montagu to actually preach equality in education opportunities and even in 'government' (in the recently discovered pamphlet entitled – *Women not Inferior to Men*, probably written in 1735). The 'Embassy Letters' base any claim for liberty on dissimilarities between the sexes, that is on the traditional doctrine of the separateness of the 'spheres', a tradition which, as has already been shown, was upheld by the Enlightenment thinkers.

Notwithstanding the emphasis upon 'vocation' and 'nature', Montagu breaks away from standard notions about women and morality. The 'Liberty' offered by the veil and polygamy is real, constituting a freedom of movement, sexual freedom and a certain degree of economic independence. Montagu insists that women, as well as men, have sexual appetites and that both should be able to pursue these appetites. Most important, however, she seems to be able to break away from the aesthetics and central idea underlying the discourse, in the West, on the harem and oriental (Muslim) 'morality'. For she effectively dissociates the question of the position of women, from political and social dominance. In short, for Montagu and, following her, Craven, polygamy and seclusion by no means purport subjection and a low status for women. And, by the same token monogamy – especially when buttressed by women's legal and economic disabilities and the Christian 'double standard' – does not guarantee freedom. In fact, plural marriage and segregation have never precluded various degrees of personal freedom and the freedom of a group.

As already mentioned, Montagu was not the first Westerner to favourably describe polygamy. Nor would she be the last. In point of fact polygamy had been advocated *at least* from the Reformation. Admittedly the 'polygamists' had been a tiny and insignificant minority that had tended to congregate in the fringes of radical and mainstream Protestantism had been like the Catholic Church, vehemently anti-polygamist (that is it objected to male and female plural marriages). But the dissenting voices had some resonance, particularly when, from the seventeenth century onwards, travellers came to encounter non-monogamous cultures and societies.[45] As is well known travellers had tended to glorify the terrestrial sensual paradise of noble savages. And the farther the sin- and moral-free a society was, the better. Enlightenment thinkers borrowed from travellers and ethnographers and by the time the *Letters* saw publication, there was growing tolerance towards the sexually different. Yet polygyny, concubinage and promiscuousness, especially in diachronic, historical societies, fairly well known to Westerners, such as the Ottoman, were invariably associated with tyranny and the subjection of females. And even the staunchest 'polygamists' saw both the basis and justification for plural marriage in female nature and, at the same time, agreed that polygamy perpetuated the inferiority of women and their low status. The best exemplar to this is, of course, Montesquieu's harem-cycle in his *Letters* and book V of the *De l'esprit de lois*. Usbeq is, after all, a petty tyrant. And his concubines are slaves. Exoticism and voyeurism apart, the *Letters* are a vindication of Western values and Western individual and political freedoms. Montagu, on the other hand, severs the vindication of the harem from the accepted notions of freedom. Significantly the paradox of the *yashmak* ends thus: 'Upon the whole, I look upon the Turkish Women as the only free people in the Empire. The very *Divan* pays a respect to 'em, and the Grand Signor himself, when a Bassa is executed, never violates the privileges of the Harem which remains unsearch'd entire to the Widow'. And on those *atypical* cases that polygamy is practiced, the polygamous husband 'is spoken of as a Libertine, or what we should call a Rake'.[46]

What is most significant about the severance of polygamy and 'tyranny' is the de-politicisation of the harem. The domestic economy is not analogous to that of an Empire. The *haremlik* is not a microcosmic state but rather the reverse of the state. And the Turkish husband, or slave-owner – unlike Montesquieu's Usbeq – is not a diminutive Sultan. Moreover, despite the trappings of the eighteenth-century oriental tale, despite the neo-classical conventions, despite the use of the polemics of the Enlightenment, Montagu's harem is neither a merely exotic place, nor a philosopher's Utopia. It is in fact not dissimilar to the aristocratic household in Britain, at that time. In other words: the harem is neither different nor foreign. And it is that quality which transcends Montagu's sometimes conventional representation and makes her so tolerant. 'The manners of mankind,' she summarises a letter to Lady Mar, 'do not differ so widely as our voyage writers would make us believe, perhaps it would be more entertaining to add a few surprising customs of my own Invention, but nothing seems to me so agreeable as truth. and I believe nothing so acceptable to you.'[48] Yet Montagu's Victorian readers found her 'invention' pernicious and her 'truth' disagreeable.

4

Exorcising Sheherezad: The Victorians and the Harem

We are Turks with the affections of our women; and have them made subscribe to our doctrine too. We let their bodies go abroad liberally enough, with smiles and ringlets and pink bonnets to disguise them instead of veils and yakmaks [sic]. But their souls must be seen by only one man, and they obey not unwillingly, and consent to remain at home as our slaves . . .

> William Makepeace Thackeray, *Vanity Fair*.[1]

The European mind has become so imbued with ideas of Oriental mysteriousness, mysticism and magnificence, and it has been so long accustomed to pillow its faith on the marvels and metaphors of tourists, that it is to be doubted whether it will willingly cast off its old associations, and suffer itself to be undeceived.

> Julia Sophia Pardoe, *The City of the Sultan and the domestic manners of the Turks in 1836 (1837)*.[2]

CHANGES IN SENSIBILITIES

The most important, most dramatic change that took place in the literature on harems in the nineteenth century is the desexualisation of the Augustan notion of liberty and the domestication of the Orient. This change roughly coincides with, rather than causally relates to, the perceptible shift away from aristocratic travel towards what may conveniently be described as the *embourgeoisement* of the voyage to the eastern Mediterranean countries. Certainly, Lady Montagu was

99

to remain, throughout the Victorian era, an authority on private life and the position of women. And the 'Embassy Letters' retained their status as a reference text, a status almost equal to that of Galland's *Nuits*. The *Letters* fired the imagination of many a writer and painter[3] and influenced some of the best, most reliable travellers to Istanbul – Julia Sophia Pardoe; Amelia Bythinia Hornby; Frances Vane, marchioness of Londonderry and Georgina Dawson-Damer. To men writers, denied access to harems, Montagu's descriptions were a mine of information.[4] Yet, increasingly, the Augustan writer was becoming a source of embarrassment. The Victorians were not always amused by Montagu's sensual representation of Ottoman women and her shameless advocation of 'licence'.

Montagu was criticised on two grounds: latitudinarian attitude towards sexual excesses, and excessive interest in the lives of the rich and powerful, to the exclusion of the ordinary people. The association between class and morality is characteristic and immensely revealing. For criticism on aristocratic behaviours, manners and codes, especially sexual codes, is an important component of *bourgeois* culture and the evolving middle-class ethos. Julia Pardoe, a Turkophile, a traveller, a writer of popular histories and, probably, Montagu's most loyal disciple, is uncomfortable with the earlier writer's famous passages on the *hammam*. 'I should be unjust', confides Pardoe, 'did I not declare that I witnessed none of the *unnecessary* and *unwanton* exposure described by Lady M. W. Montagu. Either the fair Ambassadress was present at a particular ceremony, or the Turkish ladies have become more *delicate*, and *fastidious* in their ideas of *propriety*' (my emphasis).[5] This is doubtful. It was probably Pardoe and her readers that had become obsessed with 'propriety' and 'delicacy', two key-words in polite Victorian discourse about women and female sexuality. Emmeline Lott, one time governess of Ibrahim, son of Ismail Pasha from Ismail's second *kadin*, is incensed not only by Montagu's 'indelicacy', but also by her lack of interest in the daily life of women, outside the salons of Audience. 'Her handsome train', writes Lott, 'Lady Ambassadress as she was, swept but across the splendid carpeted floors of those Noble Salons of Audience, all of which had been, as is invariably the custom, well "swept and garnished" for her reception. The interiors of the Harems were to the aristocratic Augustan, *terra incognita*.'[6]

The middle-class writers of the nineteenth century revaluated the 'position of women's' question and that of sexual morality, projecting onto the harem *bourgeois* gender ideology. The *embourgeoisement* of the image of the *orientale* also involved a shift of the focus of interest away from élites, to the middle classes and even the populace, and from the exotic and unusual to the ordinary. The Imperial and Viceregal palaces and the abodes of the rich still attracted writers and readers. Pardoe and Lott focus on the life of the élite. Writers, however, were becoming increasingly sensitive to the diversity of familial structures within the system generally known as 'harem'. The Victorians banished the exotic, to recreate the harem in the image of the middle-class 'home': domestic, feminine and autonomous. This is not to say that Victorian travel writers were impervious to the sexual aspect of the harem. Indeed nineteenth-century attitudes to female sexuality are far more ambivalent and more complex than the Augustan attitude. In order to come to terms with their own experience of women's life in the Middle East, the Victorians developed an elaborate rhetoric and generic stratagems of observation and representation, that Chapters 5 and 6 examine in detail.

RHETORIC AND REPRESENTATION, A PRELIMINARY NOTE

Conveniently enough the 'position of women's' question and that of 'morality' are approached *directly* and *generally* as well as *indirectly*, in what may be described as 'representation'.[7] By direct approach I mean general information, or statements, directly addressed to the reader, by an authoritative narrative 'I', or an impersonal voice. The travelogue, of course, abounds with non-descriptive parts that aim to inform on the legal status of women; their economic position; the regulation of sexuality – especially segregation, plural marriages and concubinage; the life-cycle of females; attitudes to children; culinary habits, hygiene and so on. General information on these topics does not necessarily draw on evidence gathered 'on the spot', but is derived from external authorities – for example, ethnographic studies by earlier travellers (female and male). Nor are the direct and overtly rhetorical general parts of the narrative peculiar to harem literature. And, of course, 'general' information is not value-free, but reflects the informer's sympathies and prejudices.

Much more complex than the straightforwardly rhetorical, informative parts of the narrative are the descriptive ones, those parts which profess to rely exclusively on the personal participant observation as part of an intersubjective experience. The tag of these eyewitness descriptions is obsession with detail. They are excessively representational, an excess that is unusual even in a genre like the travelogue, whose primary requirement is accuracy in geographical and ethnographic detail. Let there be no misunderstanding. Excess is not indiscriminate. Indeed, the travellers and amateur ethnographers were selective in the choice of material. Certain areas in the *vie privée* appeared to need careful authentication. Other areas were treated in temperance, yet others were abstained from altogether. This overall approach to another culture and the writers' strategies of cross-cultural representation may be described as 'synecdochical'. The participant observer cannot reconstruct a culture in its totality. He or she cannot record all that was seen 'on the spot'. Instead they select a detail: a custom, an institution, a ritual, a group of people. The detail is then used to evoke the cultural whole.[8] The subject matter of the representational parts is manners, particularly the social behaviour of Muslim women, though it is difficult to separate manners from the system of conventional rules which regulate personal behaviour in society, what the Augustans had designated 'civility' (Mary Montagu's term) and the Victorians referred to as 'respectability'. Ottoman society in general, and the harem in particular, were based on a rigid and elaborate etiquette that resisted change.[9] And rules and etiquette defined and regulated the conduct and manners of individuals, groups and sexes in private and in public.

From the mass of detail on women's private and public life four themes emerge. The first theme is the features of the *orientale* and her physique. The second is costume: dress and undress are used rhetorically and metaphorically as tropes and symbols of women's status and their position in society at large. Third is eating and table-manners, a particularly large category that comprises cookery, dietary habits, table etiquette, the nurture of infants and children, and so on. Fourth and last is hygiene, especially personal hygiene. All the themes may be characterised by their ambiguous status in the discussion on women; they were all increasingly associated with feminine sexuality and the female body. Detailed physical descriptions of women were introduced into mainstream literature only between the 1840s and 1860s.[10] As for naturalist activities like eating and washing, both became privatised and were conspicuously absent in the novel, and equivocally treated in sub-genres like literature of conduct and manuals for women.[11] The writers on harems resort to physical representation to tame the exotic and normalise it. At the same time these writers use description as a code. Their euphemistic body-language speaks what they cannot state explicitly. The elaborate physical detail substitutes for delicate subjects, particularly the sexual aspects of the harem system, and the travellers' own sexuality. This substitution could work because the writers and their readers shared a language, aesthetic conventions and an ideology that formed a system of meaning.[12] The readers were able to 'translate' the idiom of the travellers and read into the descriptive excess of the literature on harems. For both the groups abundant, yet discriminate detail was a means to come to terms with an unfamiliar system of sexuality and reconcile this system with *bourgeois* gender ideology. In the remainder of this chapter I first deal with the general informational parts on women, then proceed to examine the narrational ones, focusing on the four problematic themes. In Chapter 5, I proceed in exactly the same manner to discuss the harem system and relations between the private and the public. Are the two narratives compatible? Do the eye-witness descriptions *complement* the rhetoric of domesticity, or do the strategies of representation subvert the apparent denial of sexuality? Either way, the juxtaposition of the two discourses will be revealing.

DEGREES OF FREEDOM: FROM 'LIBERTY' TO 'AUTONOMY'

In the autumn of 1849 Miss Florence Nightingale and party descended upon the city of Alexandria. They visited the main tourist attractions, including the Great Mosque, where Miss Nightingale disguised herself as an Egyptian woman. The experience was horrific.

> I felt like the hypocrite in Dante's hell, with the leaden cap on – it was like hell to me. I began to be uncertain whether I was a Christian woman, and have never been so thankful as being so as since that moment. That quarter of an hour seemed to reveal to one what it is to be a woman in these countries . . . God save them, for it is hopeless life.[13]

From personal experience Nightingale passes on to the more general theme of the condition of women in Egypt, lumping together fragments of information on etiquette, custom and religion: 'In the large harems, there are 200 to 300 wives and 4 to 5 children; but she [the Egyptian woman] is not a wife, nor a mother; she cannot sit down in the presence of her son; her husband is her master, and her only occupation is beautifying herself . . . She becomes his real wife only at his caprice, by a paper given to her, then she is satisfied to believe that she will stay at the gate of paradise.'[14] Nightingale then opines in a voice that is anything but neutral: 'the woman . . . has more to suffer here than the man, both in heart, and in spirit, and in body.'[15]

There is not one single fact in Nightingale's catalogue of 'laws' and 'customs' that is free of error. But her general comments are worth quoting because they are untypical. The majority of her contemporaries did not regard Muslim women as 'sufferers', or victims, the passive objects of sexual exploitation and social and political dominance in a patriarchal society. Far from this. Characteristically, observers of the harem and women's lives were impressed that the Muslim women, regardless of class, or place, enjoyed various degrees of freedom – legally, economically and in every-day life. Moreover, by and large, throughout the Victorian and the Edwardian eras, the prevailing opinion was that in certain areas, the Muslim women were freer than their Western European sisters. The Victorians inherited from their Augustan predecessors the notion of liberty 'behind the veil', but modulated 'liberty' to suit their own *bourgeois* sensibilities.

Comments on the Muslim women's freedom are legion and examples can be multiplied. In the late 1820s, Catherine Elwood, in her *Journey Overland from England to India*, opines that: 'The Turkish ladies are under no greater restraint than princesses and ladys of rank in our country, and the homage that is paid to them [is] infinitely greater.'[16] She is 'well pleased' with the position of Arab women as well, and thinks 'The women in Arabia . . . [are] apparently allowed more freedom than in Egypt . . . they [the women in Hodeida] [were] permitted to walk out and . . . whenever they pleased,' a privilege sometimes denied to Elwood's own country-women.[17] A decade later, the Turkophile Pardoe declares that: 'If, as we are all prone to believe, freedom be happiness, then are Turkish women happiest, for they are the freest individuals in the Empire. It is the fashion in Europe to pity the women of the East; but it is ignorance of their real position alone that engenders so misplaced an exhibition of sentiment.'[18] The emphasis on 'happiness' as the sole criterion to judge organisations and institutions, smacks of popular Utilitarian idiom. From a Utilitarian point of view, *harems* are justifiable: they make Ottoman women 'happy' – that is, they are useful and do not cause 'suffering'. Six years after Pardoe, Sophia Lane Poole deplores the effects of seclusion on females, nevertheless approves of the segregation of the married, the implication being that excessive freedom is, to women, pernicious.[19]

The status-minded Victorians were very sensitive to the fact that 'liberty', or more accurately in the British context 'liberties', could not be dissociated from class. From the 1850s (when Mediterranean travel became cheaper and widely popular) interest in women of the middle echelons of society and the *fallahin* class increased. Travellers still visited and described the households of the élite, but there is a perceptible shift away from the rich and powerful, to the 'people'. The shift is, I think, parallel to the growth of interest of the Victorians in the 'condition of England problem' and the economic and moral welfare of the working classes. In fact the travellers who compare between the *hanim*, or *odalik*, of the merchant class and the Victorian lady, very often make analogies between the position of women of the poorer classes and that of working-class women in Britain.

Travellers, both male and female, were unanimous that the position of Muslim women was in inverse relation to social and economic status: the 'lower' the *economic* class, the 'higher' the status of the woman, the greater her role in the family economy and the fewer the restrictions on her. Outside the élite women seemed to enjoy public freedoms. Seclusion was not strictly enforced. And outside the cities the veil was an exception, rather than the rule. Tourists who penetrated the hinterland of Turkish Asia, or the Upper Nile Valley, were impressed by the freedom of peasant women. Lucie Duff-Gordon, writing in 1869 from Luxor, insists that husbands of the *fallahin* class allow their womanfolk great freedom and even tolerate infidelity.[20] Indeed, the *fallah* of the Upper Nile is more 'liberal' than the British gentleman (of *any* class) and the *fallahah* freer than the British working-woman: 'I believe', expounds Duff-Gordon, 'that very forgiving husbands are commoner here than everywhere. The whole idea is founded on the verse of the Koran, incessantly quoted: "The woman is made of the man, but the man is made for the woman", *ergo*, the obligations of chastity are equal, *ergo*, as the men find it difficult, they argue that the women do the same.'[21] Gordon, in fact, showed that she could live up to her liberal notions. For she had witnessed a love affair between Lucy, her English maid and Gordon's Egyptian factotum, that resulted in an illegitimate pregnancy. Gordon's report on the affair, including her own role as midwife and nurse 'in a boat and frightened sick by it all', is remarkably cool: 'she was delivered without a twinge and did admirably'.[22] There is not a shred of evidence that Gordon preached to her maid, or manservant. And, what's more important, there is not a single reference to Muslim promiscuity.

Even the Radical Gordon, however, never publicly advocated 'free-love'. Nor did any of her sister-travellers. For, in contrast to Montagu, the Victorians did not interpret 'liberty' as 'sexual freedom', or licence. Indeed they desexualised liberty. And they depoliticised this term. Their notion of it was broader than the Augustan one and combined economic and legal *rights* with custom and etiquette that, together, guaranteed to women, of different classes, freedom from sexual exploitation. Significantly, the Victorians fixed their attention on the married woman, or, on the mother, whether the legally married, or the unmarried one. The interest in the marital status of the Muslim woman, it seems, reflects the contemporary discussion in Britain on the rights of the married woman. In 1857, following a well orchestrated Feminist campaign, divorce was legalised and made civil, and in 1882 married women were granted property rights.[23] Interestingly the travellers' intense interest in legal and economic rights of the *hanîm* persists down to the First World War, long after the debate in Britain had shifted from those issues to that of political rights.

Even more significant are the comparisons between married Muslim and married Englishwomen. One notable, yet characteristic, example of the interest in domestic freedom is to be found in the writings of Mary Lucy Garnett on Turkey. Garnett is important because she was the first ethnographer to have devoted a whole study to women in a Middle Eastern country. Her *Women of Turkey, and their Folklore*, which summarises a few years' research in that country, appeared in 1893 and was the first in the series of works on folklore and folk-life, the last of which, *Home Life in Turkey*,[24] came out in 1909. The complete edition of *Women in Turkey* (cheap editions were published in 1893 and 1907) is the closest to 'modern' ethnography that can be found in the corpus of texts on customs and manners. The book is a comparative study of women in Turkey, in Europe and Asia, based on intensive field-work. Garnett discusses the life and position of Christian women (Greek, Armenian, Bulgarian and Frank, that is European women), Jews and, of course, Muslim women, the latter group occupying the largest part of the book. This part is subdivided into sections on Kurds, Circassians, Yuruks, Albanians, Tartars and, of course, Ottoman women. The conclusion of Garnett's richly documented study is stated in unequivocal terms in a later publication, *Home Life in Turkey*: 'with regard to their legal status, Turkish women, as above pointed out, already possess all *legal, personal* and *propriety rights* necessary to give them a social position equal if not superior to that of European women generally.'[25]

Nor is that all. *Women in Turkey* itself concludes with an eulogy on the Muslim women's freedom, followed by an astonishing diatribe against the Liberal state and the movement for women's suffrage. Montagu and Craven criticised the Christian double sexual standard, relating anti-feminist attitudes to the historical misogynism of the Church. Garnett, on the other hand, connects the low status of women in the West, particularly in Britain, not to religion but to the secular doctrine of Liberalism, especially to the Liberal tradition of interpreting 'freedom' mainly in legal and political terms. Her main butt is John Stuart Mill and his *Subjection of Women*, the basic Liberal text on the women's question, canonised by nineteenth-century feminists. She (wrongly) criticises Mill for assuming that women are universally subjected. Garnett particularly objects to the Utilitarian remedy for social evils: legislation and regulation by state intervention. Liberalism, tidy-mindedly, equates 'freedom' with the removal of some legal disabilities. But the 'women's problem' is social and economic and not legal and political.

> I trust also that the reader who reflects on the facts contained in the preceding pages will realise how false is the assumption of Mill and his disciples that Woman {sic} has everywhere and at all times, been in a position of slavish subjection to Man {sic}. The respective spheres of men and women of the various nationalities I have attempted to describe are regulated mainly by the special social and economic conditions necessitating a rigid exclusion of women, and others allowing them an extraordinary degree of independence. The subjection of women in the East is consequently, as far as it exists, the result of such conditions, rather than the legal and religious enactments.[26]

Garnett seems to be aware of the differences in legal and social *status*, on the one hand, and variations in social and economic *conditions* on the other. [27] She would not infer the actual position of women in actual harems from Islamic law and exhortations.[28] And, like most women travellers, she would depend on the *particular example* and *individual experience* acquired in direct contacts with local women and not on general rules and laws, nor merely on traditional textual authorities. Take, for instance, her interpretation of the married women's freedom. 'Freedom' means rights within the law, but also privileges guaranteed by etiquette and a system of manners and human relations ('propriety'), *and* the freedom acquired in certain (economic and social) conditions. These four components are stressed in the discussion of divorce; property rights and the custody of, and guardianship over, children.

To begin with divorce. The easiness with which Muslim marriage could be dissolved did not shock all writers. Naturally enough, the *talaq*, or divorce, initiated by the man outside the courts of law drew forth a great deal of comment.[29] But so did the fact that the divorced woman retained what property she had brought into the marriage, plus the balance of her *mahr* and was supported during the *'iddah*, or 'safety period' of three months before remarriage. [30] The Victorians were impressed because even unilateral divorce did not necessarily bring about destitution, or an eviction from the family home (the late eighteenth-century example of such an eviction, Lady Craven's, immediately springs to mind).[31] Much attention is paid to the two other *bilateral* forms of divorce that needed to be ratified in court: the *faskh* (or judicial separation) and the *'khul* (or divorce by mutual consent in which the woman gives up her property rights. The literal translation of *'khul* is 'renouncing'). To argue now that women did not usually make use of either the first, or the second, and that the man's right to divorce his wife was abused, is beside the point and seemed so to a few nineteenth-century travellers.[32] The gist of their rhetoric is that Muslim marriages *are in theory dissoluble* and *can* be dissolved on the woman's initiative, or by mutual consent. In Britain, as the travellers were well aware, the wife had to have two grounds to sue for a divorce. Divorce by mutual consent did not exist before 1936.[33] More important, the social implications of divorce in Muslim countries were far less severe than in Victorian Britain. The divorced Ottoman or Arab woman was not a declassé. Divorce, like slavery, was not a permanent condition, but a temporary and transitory one. The divorced wife – like the slave – lived within, not outside the family.[34] Certainly divorce was not looked down on as a moral disgrace.

Economically, the married Muslim woman seemed to be superior to her middle-class British sister. For the *hanim*, or wife, was a legal person and could, in theory, hold property, appear before the courts and enter contracts.[35] By Common Law the married woman was *femme couverte*. Having entered into a contract with the other party in marriage, she had ceased to legally exist, forfeiting her right to sue, or be sued, be liable for debts and, most significantly, hold, or discharge of property in her own right. To be sure, both within the Common Law *and* Equity there had developed a mechanism that enabled wives to retain their property. But, as most students of the legal status of women have agreed, those mechanisms had been accessible to a tiny minority, until the Married Women's Property Law of 1882.[36] No wonder that many a writer regarded the right to hold property, that is economic independence, as a palliative to easy divorce and polygamy. As Fanny Janet Blunt, whose *People of Turkey*, covers a period of 25 years' residence in that country puts it: 'should a lady possess any property the husband cannot assume any right over it, nor over any of the rest of her belongings. The wisdom and generosity of this . . . cannot be too highly commended.'[37] An Ottoman woman, it is pointed, can inherit without trustees, sue or be sued independently of her husband and *plead* because: 'No doctrine of *couverture* exists for her.'[38] What is astonishing is that this last comment postdates the reform of 1882, when *couverture* was all but buried. Blunt and Garnett's sensitivity to women's disabilities in Britain suffused their picture of the married Muslim woman. (For the right to own property was often a fiction. Muslim women had little chance against brothers, husbands and even sons.)

To the Victorians, the relation between money and sex was pertinent. Property guaranteed freedom from sexual exploitation; lack of property made a woman sexually vulnerable. Virtually no traveller who writes on slavery fails to stress the important distinction between slaves that are the property of a wife, and those slaves owned by the husband.[39] Many women of the upper classes purchased Circassians and Georgians – infants were in special demand – raised them up and educated them. To be sure, the motives of amateur slave-dealers were not exactly altruistic. Great profits were to be made from trafficking, especially after the slave-trade had been officially abolished (1885). Female slaves were also a well provided-for labour-force, as well as status symbols.[40] I shall discuss attitudes to slavery in detail in Chapter 5. What is of relevance here is that the wife's slaves were inviolable, as was, by analogy, her property. They seemed to the writers not only better provided for than the domestic female servant in the Western *bourgeois* household, but better protected than the servant from sexual exploitation. Pardoe tells with relish how Nazip Hanim, favourite slave of Esma Sultan, independent and unruly sister of Sultan Ahmet III, thrice refused his lucrative offer to enter the Imperial *haremlik* as *kadin*, preferring the 'liberty of the harem of her protectress and the comparative independence of her present position to the gilded captivity' in the palace of Topkapi. Even 'the most powerful man in the whole of the Turkish Empire', concludes Pardoe, cannot compromise the virtue – and by analogy *property* – that is lawfully woman's.[41]

'Propriety' was a word specially dear to the heart of the British middle classes. And the liberties of married Muslim women – both the liberties granted in the law and those privileges guaranteed by custom – were buttressed by what Garnett designated 'laws of propriety'. Propriety, it was noted with satisfaction, forbade the husband, who saw the *çedik pabuç* (yellow slippers for indoor wear) on the threshold of the *haremlik*, to enter that part of his house. The custom – first noted, it will be recalled, by Craven in 1785 fascinated the Victorians. For example Pardoe:

> It is also a fact that though the Turk has an undoubted right to enter the apartments of his wives at all hours, it is a privilege of which he very rarely, I may almost say, never, avails himself. One room in the harem is appropriated to the master of the house, and therein he awaits the appearance of the individual with whom he wishes to converse, and who is summoned to his presence by a slave. Should he, on passing to his apartment, see slippers at the foot of the stairs, *he cannot, under any pretense, intrude himself on the harem*; it is a liberty that every woman in the Empire would resent. (my emphasis)[42]

Note the very deliberate selection of phrases like 'very rarely', 'almost never' and so on, that are added to Craven's bare notation of facts. Also significant is the distinction between law (or right), and 'privilege' (or liberty). By right the Turk is polygamous and his wives are his chattels. But a system of 'civility' protects them from intrusion – sexual, or otherwise – into their privacy. To converse – read 'cohabit' – with a *hanim*, or an *odalik*, is, according to Pardoe, man's 'privilege', not his 'right'. Most important, however, is the break away from the eighteenth-century interpretation of 'liberty'.

'Liberty' for the Augustans is licence, the liberty to indulge the natural sexual drives. To the Victorians it is freedom *from* sex, within marriage. Woman's *privacy* within her own sphere and her control on her own body. Privacy and immunity from 'physical tyranny' (Mrs W. M. Ramsay's words) were idealised because they were not self-evident rights.[43] The privacy of the married Englishwoman was not protected, as many an observer commented (marital rights, incidentally, were enforceable by Common Law). Indeed the Ottoman wife enjoyed greater autonomy over her own person than the English. And the former – regardless of status and class – was universally respected. Thus Mrs W. M. Ramsay argues that women of the poorer classes, in the remotest spots in Anatolia (she was particularly referring to the neighbourhood of Afyonkarahisar), enjoyed 'liberty'. And, she adds, 'the ordinary Turkish husband does not appear to avail himself often of his *legal* right to tyrannise over his better self than the British husband does – less oftener in fact. Cases of brutality on the part of man towards his wife are a hundred times commoner among the lower classes of this country than they are in Turkey.'[44] The shift from 'liberty' to 'autonomy', from the eighteenth-century positive definition of freedom, to the essentially Liberal negative interpretation ('freedom from'), is significant. Undoubtedly this shift evinces the awareness of middle-class writers of their inability to control their own bodies and to regulate productivity.

The *hanîm's* liberties were by no means limited to the enclosed domestic sphere. Ottoman and Arab women, even of the élite, it was noted, enjoyed a freedom of movement guaranteed by the veil. Most significant, they were *free of* intrusion. As I later show, the veil in the eighteenth century, the symbol of *licence*, was transformed by the Victorians into a trope for female virtue and respectability. Travellers repeatedly comment on the safety of the streets of Turkey and Egypt's big cities.[45] A woman, observes Pardoe, is much safer in Istanbul than in the slums of London. She herself visited St. Sophia and the Mosque of Sultan Ahmet at midnight. In London, a similar adventure would have been unthinkable.

The Victorians' notion of liberty is, then, far more complex than that of their eighteenth-century model. 'Liberty' in its later usage is a versatile word that covers many meanings and extends beyond the domestic sphere. The term denotes a degree of economic independence, certain legal rights and those 'freedoms' derived from custom and etiquette, mainly the *freedom from sex*. Autonomy or *'liberty from'* is the keynote to our understanding of that term in the Victorian Liberal context. It is ironic that anti-Liberals and anti-Feminists, like Mary Lucy Garnett and Anna Bowman Dodd, chose to approach the topic of the 'Muslim women's freedom' in the very terms used by Mill. It now remains to see whether *actual* Muslim women seemed to the travellers autonomous individuals, liberated from sex, and from an enslaving sexuality.

PHYSIOGNOMY, CHARACTER, DRESS AND UNDRESS

In the early summer of 1785, the playwright, essayist and traveller, Elisabeth, Lady Craven, briefly saw the inside of a public bath at Athens. Her description of Ottoman and Greek bathers superficially resembles that of her famous model, Lady Montagu. Both authors are commonsensical; both are very sensitive to physical detail and neither is embarrassed by 'nature', their euphemism for 'nude', and the attitude of oriental females to it. The similarity, however, stops here. For Craven, who, as already shown (see Chapter 3) is tolerant towards the 'morality' of the Ottomans, seems to depart from the latitudinarian Augustan concept of cultural diversity. She adopts a serious tone that already anticipates that of the early Victorian writers and nineteenth-century middle-class morality. For one thing, in the passage on the bath, Craven cuts herself away from the moral-free aestheticism of Montagu's famous *tableau vivant*, which presents the bathers in Sophia in 1717. For another, Craven, uncharacteristically, abandons the classical analogues and the neo-classical terminology with that terminology's emphasis on terms like 'harmony', 'order' and 'proportion', inherited from Montagu and utilised by Craven elsewhere. For, in contrast to Montagu's statuesque Miltonic Eves, Craven's bathers are merely obese women. Their nakedness disgusts her. And her reaction is frank enough: 'I never saw so many fat women at once together, nor fat ones at that.'[46] Also in the later description the women are sallow. And their sallowness (Montagu's idols are very fair) and obesity allude to some inner characteristics – a sensuality that borders on lewdness, a vulgarity and a propensity towards idleness.[47]

This early example, from the pen of an aristocrat, already antici-pates the shift from a moral-free representation of the body towards physical representation charged with morality and middle-class ideology. Nowhere is the change in the sensibilities of the writers

– both the writers as a group and as individuals – as perceptible and easily discernible as in the somatic descriptions of Muslim women.

I have already mentioned that physical description is one of the most important conventions of a genre that stresses the experience of the eye-witness and participant observation, at the expense of the authority of the written precedence. The real and believable (especially at the beginning of the nineteenth century, when only a few writers had actually penetrated into the *haremlik*), was that which had been seen. And physical description was probably the most common and acceptable, as well as the most economic way to represent character which was not supposed to develop in time. The travel-writers were not merely describing. They were *physiognomists*, that is, they used human features and expressions and the human physique to judge oriental 'nature', whether the character of individual oriental woman, or the moral state of Middle Eastern society. For the human expression, to cite Johann Kaspar Lavater, the inventor of the popular 'science' of physiognomy, is 'an index not merely to emotional response or to intellectual capacity but, most important, to the possibilities of moral life'.[48] Inner characteristics and values were then inferred from outward appearance. Physical detail provides clues to morals and, at the same time, conveys to the reader social and moral beliefs concerning feminine sexuality.

As is well known, physiognomy as means to characterisation, particularly the characterisation of females, is one of the conventions of the Victorian novel. As Helena Michie, Jeanne Fahnestock and Julie F. Codell[49] have shown, physiognomy was used in the novel, in sub-genres like etiquette-books and in painting. By the 1860s there developed conventional standards of female beauty and womanly behaviour which, themselves, reflected middle-class notions of femininity. Elisabeth Eastlake, in an article published in 1851 in the *Quarterly Review*, distinguished between the female and male physiognomy and varieties of expressions as well as between permanent characteristics and the changes which time brings on the human face. 'Every sex and every age of life,' she argues, 'has a physiognomy proper to itself, and only to be rightly defined by its dissimilarity of another. Each has a beauty after its kind, which it belongs to the artist to observe.'[50] Parallel to the 'norms' and ideal images there gradually evolved a set of equally conventionalised 'deviations' ('irregularities' as Fahnestock would call it), associated with the 'unusual', 'unwomanly' heroine, a woman who is assertive and whose assertiveness is, usually, connected with an endangering sensuality.[51]

The travel writers had used the device of physiognomy before and to a greater extent than, novelists. Physical detail and physiognomy are introduced by the earlier travellers in the 1820s and 1830s. At the time that characterisation by physiognomy reached its vogue in realistic fiction and in painting (notably in the works of the Pre-Raphaelites) around the middle of the century, it had already become a cliché in harem literature.

Obsession with elaborate physical detail is, of course, generic. It characterises travel-literature and ethnographic writing in general. Yet in harem literature these characteristics have another, more important purpose. They were stratagems, developed to help the writers and the Victorian readership to come to terms with that area in Middle Eastern life which had been most problematic: sexuality.

The earlier examples, from the 1820s and 1830s, still manifest allegiance to the eighteenth-century tradition. There are, already, very detailed descriptions, but these descriptions are, consciously, not very realistic. A typical exemplar is Julia Pardoe, whose *City of the Sultan in 1836*, the best documented book by a woman on Istanbul in the early days of the *Tanzimat*, abounds with long, itemised descriptions that may seem excessive to the modern reader. Pardoe's fascination with detail, her wordiness and 'romantic' relish in the picturesque and sensational, received attention from contemporary critics.[52] In her own introduction to the *City* she distinguishes between the nineteenth-century obsession with value-free 'bare' facts, and the reader's need for entertainment and escapism. Very shrewdly Pardoe designates the first phenomenon 'Utilitarianism' and the second 'romance'. Her own ambition is to combine the two: to demythisise the Orient, in order to *inform* the reader, but, at the same time, to appeal to the imagination.[53] The result may be artificial, a garrulous account that, realistic detail notwithstanding, falls back on the style of Montagu and Galland. This is the case with a chapter devoted to the Istanbul household of Scodra Pasha (Mustafa Pasha, of the Albanian house of Scutari), the famous rebel who, before surrendering to the grand Visier Reshid Pasha (1831), had virtually ruled the entire province between the Adriatic and the Aegean. The harem is presented as a typical example of the traditional Ottoman home. Pardoe briefly notices several female figures then fixes on the central 'character', *Heymine Hanim*, eldest daughter of the exiled rebel.

How shall I describe the beautiful Heymine Hanoum [sic]? How paint the soft, sweet, sleepy loveliness of the Pasha's daughter? she was just sixteen, at the Age when Oriental beauty is at its height, and Oriental gracefulness unsurpassed by any gracefulness on earth. Her slight, willow-like, figure – her dark deep eyes, long and lustrous, with lashes edging like silken fringes, their snowy and vein-traced lids – her luxuriant hair, black as the wing of the raven – her white and dazzling teeth – and the sweet but firm expression of her beautifully formed mouth.[54]

Pardoe's itemised catalogue of clichés (dark oriental 'eyes', soft skin, dazzling teeth, streaming hair) is followed by a biography of the *hanîm* and the (obligatory) description of her costume (one page is devoted to the head-dress alone). Significantly the descriptions of women in households of the merchant-classes, especially outside Istanbul, are realistic and less wordy than the representations of the women of the élites. The 'ordinary' *hanîm* and *odalik* is de-exoticised. Note, for example this picture of the young wife of the *cadi* of Çekirge (spelt Tzèkerghé) in Bursa, a few hours after the birth of her first-born. Pardoe is ushered into a noisy room, packed with women singers and players. Facing her is the new mother, lying in state on the *yataklik* (a couch of wood ornamented with mother-of-pearl) under an improvised canopy formed of cashmere shawls, bathing scarfs and gold and silver tissue, the whole being fastened together with head-dresses of coloured gauze.

As I entered, she was flinging over her child a small coverlet of crimson velvet, most gorgeously wrought with gold; and as the sleeves of her striped silk antrey and gauze chemisette fell back to her elbow, her *white and dimpled arms* circled by bracelets of brilliants, and her small hands glittering with jewelled rings, were revealed in all their beauty. Her dark hair was braided in twenty or thirty small plaits, that fell far below her waist, as she lent against a cushion similar to that on which she had pillowed her infant. *Her throat was encircled by several rows of immense pearls*, whence depended a diamond star, nesting upon her bosom; her chemisette was delicately edged by a gold beading; and met at the bottom of her bust, where her vest was confined by a costly shawl. Her head-dress, of blue gauze worked with silver, was studded with diamond sprays, and ornamented with a fringe of large gold coins, which fell upon her shoulders, and almost concealed her brilliant ear-rings. Her satin antrey was of the most lively colours, and her salva were of pale pink silk, sprinkled with silver spots . . . Previously to her confinement, she had plucked out the whole of her eyebrows, and had replaced them by two strips of black dye, raised about an inch higher upon the forehead. This is a common habit with the Turkish women on great occasions . . . [55]

Pardoe, effectively, uses physiognomy synecdochially. A part of the body (the hair, the arm, the eyes) is dismembered from the whole then made to symbolise another thing. Significantly she fixes on 'a dimpled arm', the 'throat', 'the bosom', parts of the body which, in the 1830s, were almost unmentionable in mainstream discourse, in which they were associated with sensuality (the much later example of Maggie Tullivar's dimpled arm in George Eliot's *Mill on the Floss* immediately springs to mind). There is a plethora of examples in Pardoe's own work, as well as in the work of other travellers, to the deliberate extensive use of synecdoche, to the stereotyping of oriental features and, subsequently, oriental character. Eyes-'dark', 'almond-shaped' and 'soft' are referred to by virtually every observer.[56] A number of writers comment on eyebrows, and the Ottoman women's custom of plucking the hair above the eye and blackening it.[57] Hair and head-dress receive special attention as does the skin.[58]

The appliance of cosmetics is universally noted and not always tolerated – yet it is never implied that the attempt to perfect nature is immoral, or gross (in Victorian writing, it will be recalled, the 'public woman' only, the prostitute or, her equivalent, the actress, are allowed 'paint'). To pick a few examples at random. In 1848 Lady Amelia Bythinia Hornby refers to the 'highest perfection of physical beauty' achieved by Ottoman women who 'make their skins as snow white and their eyebrows as jet black as possible' and that 'when young their skin is literally as white as their veils, with the faintest tinge of pink on the cheek'.[59] Less than a decade earlier, Marianne Young Postans is more critical. In her *Facts and Fictions Illustrative of Oriental Character*, a three-volume reproduction of articles originally appearing in the *Asiatic Journal*, she devotes a chapter to high harems in Cairo. The chapter draws mainly on her own visit to the harem of Sami Pasha, late governor of the Citadel of Cairo, at the time of Mehmet Ali. Rather conventionally, Postans includes a long, itemised description of the Pasha's wife, marking out certain

physical features, for stereotypical characterisation, then moves on
to the appliance of cosmetics by women of the Turkish-Circassian
élite. 'Faces naturally pretty, were reduced laughable by misapplied
care to render them more beautiful; the fine dark eyebrow was
painted in a broad arch of light sienna [*Henna*] extending from the
temple to the centre of the nose, a large circle, like a black wafer,
was stained on the forehead and the cheeks were highly rouged,
while they emulated the inner leaves of a full blown rose; not red
but a delicate tint used to its fullest strength. This combination of
pink, black and white gave a most Grimaldi-like [Joseph Grimaldi
(1779–1837) – celebrated clown-pantomimist who first appeared as
an infant dancer at Sadler's Wells, and acted there and at Drury
Lane for many years. He had a son of the same name, who died
in 1863. Grimaldi's memoirs were edited by Dickens in 1838, with
illustrations by Cruikshank.] appearance to the face of my friend
and its singularity was increased rather than diminished by their
head-dresses.'[60]

By the 1860s and 1870s, the stylised, conventional physical representation had diffused to semi-documentary *logs*, or to works on
local 'customs and manners', with emphasis on the lives of the
common people. Mary Eliza Rogers' *Domestic Life in Palestine* (1863),
probably the best authority on every-day life in that country in the
1850s and 1860s, may be taken as an example. Rogers' Palestine
has nothing of Pardoe's factional Istanbul and her descriptions
are, usually, matter-of-fact. Yet Rogers often breaks the narrative
and adopts conventional characterisation by itemised description,
physiognomy and synecdoche. The following is from a chapter
devoted to a visit of the womenfolk of Saleh Beg of Haifa with
whom she developed warm and sustained relationships. Rogers
fixes on Helweh, youngest wife of Saleh-Beg, who sits before
her. The seemingly ingenuous episode is artistically constructed.
Rogers' choice of theme is brilliant: a European woman paints a
Muslim female model. Muslim women did not sit for painters.
For 'sitting', or having one's image taken, was immodest, not least
because it involved exposing one's face. Virtually every Orientalist
painter had great difficulties obtaining live female models (Hunt
and Gérôme's sitters were European). Evidently, Helweh could sit
for Rogers only because the latter was a woman. Thus a sexually
dangerous exchange, between the observer/artist and the mod-
el/object is diffused and reduced to a domestic episode. A gifted
engraver and water-colourist, Rogers portrays the Arab woman in

picture-and word-images. Helweh, it may seem, is 'framed' by the painter/narrator, who 'freezes' the living person on canvas and in the written description. Yet Rogers' sympathy towards the Beg's women, her warmth and the feel of trust and comradeship, break through conventional detail.

> Helweh came shyly to see the drawing, and she asked me if I drew her because she was the prettiest. I told her that I should like to draw any one who would sit near to the door, where the sunlight was streaming in. Then the others took the same seat in turn, and I made two more sketches, but Helweh was by far the prettiest . . . She wore yellow silk trousers, ornamented at the sides with black silk braid. Her yellow pointed slippers were turned up at the toes. She wore no stockings. Her black velvet jacket was embroidered beautifully with gold thread, and a purple, red and green shawl twisted round her waist rather low, served for a girdle. A wide collar of gold coins encircled her throat, and a little, shallow, red cloth cap was arranged coquettishly on one side of her well-shaped head. A long tassel, springing from perforated gold balls, hang from it. Her hair, intertwined with silk braid, was divided into nine plaits and fell straight over her shoulders. Little jewels and pearls were fastened to it. Round her head, over her red cloth cap, or tarbush, she wore strings of pearls and coins of diamond and emerald sprays, and little bunches of red, yellow and violet everlasting flowers, which grow wild on the hills in Palestine.[61]

Rogers then proceeds to a few select details: 'She had large, dark eyes. The eyebrows were painted thickly, and the eyelids edged with kohl. She had spots of blue dye on her chest, and on her chin, and a blue star tattooed on her forehead'.[62]

Ugliness, deformity and obesity (as distinct from mere plumpness which is favourably, or neutrally, noted) are typically associated with old-age. The moralistic tenor of this association is transparent. A life that is devoted to 'Nature', that is natural, physical appetites and to the flesh has not, cannot, have only its rewards. The high class *odalik* ages prematurely. Her physique deteriorates. Often she degenerates mentally as well as physically. Revealingly, comment on the physical deterioration of the Muslim women – and it *is* abundant – is typically characteristic of descriptions of the public bath. I shall, therefore, discuss treatment of this subject in the section on attitudes to personal and public hygiene.

Dress and undress are enormously important and used as metaphors for autonomy (or the lack of it) and sexuality. Articles of dress, like certain features are, quite often, singled out, treated separately and, sometimes, fetishised. In Victorian class-culture dress was a mark of class, gender and sexuality. Dress distinguished the rich from the poor, the respectable from the unrespectable, the pure from the impure and, most important here, women from men. The elaborate dress of the *bourgeois* matron and the equally elaborate apparel of the prostitute symbolised their place in society. In Victorian body-language dress and undress, like the female physiognomy, expressed class and character.

Exotic foreign costume, endowed with an even greater symbolism, fascinated travel-writers and apparently also the travelogue reading-public. In the first place oriental costume, since the publication of Galland's *Mille et une nuits*, presented the exotic and picturesque at its most elaborate. The dress as well as the physique of Middle Eastern women seemed entirely different from those of middle-class Victorians. Observers made most of the difference between the Ottoman and (very elaborate) Druse head-dress and the bonnet, that symbol of middle-class propriety and feminine decorum; between the loose garments of the *odaliks* and the English-woman's corsets; between slippers and high-laced boots; between bare and gloved hands; between unveiled and veiled faces. A significant number of the travellers affected oriental dress during their stay in the Middle East and, in a few cases, after their return to Europe. Julia Pardoe, Sophia Lane Poole, Isabel Burton, Anne Blunt and Isabella Bird Bishop are the best known examples.

Martineau's admonition, in her *Eastern Life, Present and Past*, against Western women's adoption of an Arab dress is an exception that helps illustrate the rule. Masquerading as *orientales* and exchanging articles of dress between English and Ottoman or Arab women are common practices. Emmeline Lott and Ellen Chennels, governesses in the Viceregal harems of Ismail Pasha, each describe how the Pasha's *odaliks* ransacked the British governess's wardrobes, parading European articles of dress and, most embarrassingly, underwear.[63] Mary Eliza Rogers humorously tells how the women in the *haremlik* of 'Yassin-Bey', at Haifa were astonished at the sight of her own skin 'coming off' her hands. These women, who had never before seen a European, let alone one wearing kid gloves, made Rogers pull off and put on her gloves again and again.[64] Of course, such descriptions are condescending enough: the uncorseted, gloveless, bonnetless, bootless Muslim *is* patronised. Yet the reversal of roles of the tourist/observer and her object of observation is very suggestive. Western costume is as exotic and 'different' as oriental dress. Dress, like manners and morals, varies. In the second half of the nineteenth century, European fashions, in dress, furniture and decoration, conquered over the harems of the Turkish-Circassian élite in Istanbul and Cairo. The travellers lamented the change. They invariably condemn imitation of Western (usually French) costume.[65] And the europeanised *hanîm* and *odalik* in garish chintz is an undignified spectacle, a symbol of an indiscriminate aping of the West, and is a subject of pity and ridicule.

Preoccupation with costume has a second, important reason. Dress and undress retain their earlier Augustan symbolic significance. Dress reflects the social and economic position of Muslim women and their place inside and outside the home. More significantly, costume could be used to encode the Victorian notions of autonomy and sexuality. Two articles of dress in particular, the *yashmak* and the *ferace* (a long, loose coat reaching from the shoulders to the ground, made in various colours and in woolen fabrics, satin or taffeta) are singled out and elevated to metaphors for the changing notion of personal liberty. In the earlier usages, both the veil and the long hood retain their original Augustan meaning. They are metaphors for licence and artful seductiveness. The yashmak *facilitates* rather than hinders eye and verbal contact between women and men. Julia Pardoe, in many passages on outdoor excursions of the inmates of high-class harems, opines that the *yashmak* is used to seduce males.[66] Two decades later Amelia Bythinia Hornby describes a group of women with their slaves, picnicking in the 'Valley of the Sweet Waters', near Therapia. She arranges her objects picturesquely, under plane-trees, noting that 'nothing' . . . could be more strikingly beautiful than these clusters of women by trees and fountain . . . their jet-black eyes shining through their white veils . . . The white yashmaks contrast prettily with all the colours.'[67] As late as 1871, Annie Harvey, in her *Turkish Harems and Circassian Homes*, argues that 'so coquettishly is the transparent muslin folded over the nose and mouth, so tenderly does it veil the forehead, that the delicate cloud seems but to heighten and increase each charm. Far, very far is it from hiding the features from the profaning gaze of men.'[68] Tourists to Egypt commented that the unbecoming Egyptian outdoor cover, which effectively concealed the face, was not universally donned.[69]

Around the middle of the nineteenth century there is a perceptible change. The veil is divested of its sexual, erotic meanings and is associated with privacy, autonomy and the inviolability of the female body. In the big cities veiling protects females from harassment. Outside the urban centres women rarely affect the *yashmak*.[70] The veil no longer symbolises *subjection* and sexuality but autonomy or, freedom *from* sexual exploitation. Thus a year after the outbreak of the First World War, Elisabeth Goodnow warns in her *Women of Egypt*, that: 'the modern Egyptian woman . . . does not care to unveil herself.'[71] Goodnow, like a few other writers, objects to the suppression of the veil, in the same way that she objects to imported ideas and behaviours.

Fairly early in the nineteenth century another article of dress, for *indoor wear*, is specially marked out and fetishised. The *çedik pabuç*, or yellow slippers for indoor wear, acquire a symbolic meaning. When put on the threshold of the *haremlik*, the slippers signified the inmates' wish for privacy. Husbands and owners, virtually all travellers note, invariably respect the custom. The Ottoman woman's right to refuse conjugal sex appealed to the Victorians. As Pardoe and Fanny Janet Blunt remark, married middle- and lower-class Englishwomen had no such privacy, and had little control on reproduction.[72] The *haremlik*, seemed more protected from intrusion than the middle-class parlour.

An opprobrious reference to the veil is not very common. Even missionaries who did see physical segregation as a symbol of the degraded position of Muslim women are ambivalent about veiling. For this custom could be and was explained as an illustration of Biblical practices at the age of the Patriarchs.[73] Thus Florence Nightingale's analogue, made in 1854, between the Egyptian veil and the leaden caps of the hypocrites in Dante's *Inferno, is* not typical, yet helps illustrate the more characteristic attitudes of mid nineteenth-century travellers to seclusion.[74]

Obsession with the physical appearance of Muslim women persisted down to the First World War. Clearly that obsession cannot be explained away merely as a generic convention, characteristic of a literary form that particularly depends on ethnographic detail. The travel-writers seem to have responded to a certain larger demand. It is very significant that not even the emergence of comparable, *non-verbal* forms of representation – such as photography – killed off the verbal description of oriental characters. As a number of students of Western photography in the Orient have shown, by the 1880s and 1890s photographs (specially studio-made ones) and post-cards of 'orientals' had become mass-produced commodities.[75] The market, both in France and England, could offer cheap reproductions of photographs, and photographed sketches of oriental people and landscapes. The persistence of a literature on the harem with emphasis on physical description probably had other reasons. First, elaborate stratagems – the 'straightforward descriptions', characterisation by physiognomy and inference from the select detail, synecdoche – all could help the writers distance themselves and their readers from sensitive sexual issues. The extraordinarily long and detailed descriptions of Muslim women were buttressed by equally detailed representation of houses, furniture and domestic manners. The overall effect on the reader of this mass of realistic detail probably was to domesticate the alien. Moreover, reference to sensuality by euphemistic detail was a Victorian convention. Physiognomy and synecdoche enabled the writers to imply what they could not in propriety explicitly say. Reference to the sensuality of Eastern women is indirect. I came across very few examples that fix on 'sensual', or corporeal 'countenance' or 'expression'. Even the very critical Nightingale who described Egyptian harems in a Dantesque language, mercilessly attacking oriental morals, emphasises that the faces of some *odaliks* had nothing sensual in them.

'THE ETERNAL OR UNSATIATING BANQUET': EATING, FOOD AND TABLE-MANNERS

'In the first of these [the wings of Vathek's palace] were tables continually covered with the most exquisite dainties; which were supplied both by night and by day, according to their constant consumption, whilst the most delicious wines and the choicest cordials flowed forth from a hundred fountains that were never exhausted. This palace was called the Eternal or unsatiating Banquet.'[76] The voice is William Beckford's. But the words are not characteristically his. For food and eating are portent symbols in traditional imaginative and polemical literature on the Middle East. And, significantly, these symbols have been associated with, indeed have become inseparable from, the image of the Orient as

locus sensualis and that of orientals as generically lascivious. Gluttony accompanies lasciviousness. And both manifest the Muslim's
propensity to excess. And, it was repeatedly argued, Islam itself was
a thisworldly, materialist religion that actually encouraged physical
excesses in the believers. Of course, the association between food
and sexuality is universal, but is characteristically Christian. For to
Christians the combination of gluttony and promiscuity has always
seemed pernicious. *Lust* and *Gluttony* – both vices of the flesh (and
both associated with the Original Sin) – are two of the *Seven Deadly
Sins* – discussed in polemical church literature and, from, at least,
the thirteenth century, in popular texts.[77] The archetype of the
amorous and omnivorous oriental male, whose palate is rich and
exotic, was inflated in the *Mille et une nuits* and from thence passed
on to, and was circulated by, numerous writers and travellers.[78]
There are many examples to that *topos* but Beckford's Vathek, the
capricious tyrant, 'much addicted to women and the pleasures of the
table', [79] immediately springs to mind. Vathek's female counterpart
is the sensual *orientale*, with insatiable appetite for men and food.[80]

It may first appear that the women travellers copied the secularised notion of eating as sin. References to excessive, irregular and
undisciplined eating are scattered in harem literature, particularly
in descriptions of the harems of the élite. There is, also, negative
comment on the nutrition of children. Isabel Burton, in 1875, argues
that peasant-children in the neighbourhood of Damascus, chronically suffered dietary deficiencies caused by an imbalanced diet.[81]
Fanny Janet Blunt claims in a chapter devoted to 'Food' in her
Turkey and its People that the diet of infants, of all classes, is too
rich and their appetite pampered. According to Blunt, intemperate
eating is one of the causes for the high rate of infant mortality in
that country.[82] Amelia Bythinia Hornby even planned to translate
manuals for women into Turkish, to teach the Turks the principles
of cookery, wholesome nutrition and the 'domestic sciences'.[83] So
widespread became the allusions to the ignorance of upper and
middle-class Ottomans regarding cookery and housekeeping, that
Mary Lucy Garnett protested against the notion of the indolent,
'sweet-eating' wife, whose sole function in life is to sexually gratify
her master.[84]

The descriptive parts of the narrative, however, are far more
complex and present an attitude to food and the female body that,
in the Victorian cultural context, is quite revolutionary. Characteristically, the same writers who, in the 'general' rhetorical parts

condemn gluttony, represent eating neutrally or sympathetically (Julia Pardoe is one example). The obsession with food and table manners should be located in a wider cultural context. For modern Europeans, as Claude Lévi-Strauss has pointed out, eating habits do not constitute the free code that they do, or rather did, for exotic societies. During the nineteenth century the *bourgeoisie* was opting for some habits, transmitting certain cultural messages and prohibiting others.[85] The Victorians increasingly associated food and eating with gender, class and sexuality. Literary and medical discourse gendered eating and presented it as a masculine activity. To eat was 'unfeminine'. As Helena Michie succinctly puts it, the Victorian Lady was, literally and metaphorically, expelled from the table and was required to be anorectic.[86]

It is precisely this background that makes the treatment of eating and food in harem literature culturally significant. *Bourgeois* culture transformed eating to a private, asocial activity. In descriptions of harems, eating is the main way in which women, of different religions and cultures, interact. Food is socialised. The table, or *sofra* (a tray on a collapsible basis, around which the party of diners squat), is the centre of feminine activity and the *locus* of intersubjective contacts that cut across the hierarchy of the *haremlik*, that of class and across culture. The following is a description of Julia Pardoe's first meal in Turkey, in the winter of 1835. The household she represents is that of a respectable merchant and – according to her – characteristic of the abodes of the urban middle-class. What Pardoe painstakingly reconstructs is the *iftar*, or the meal concluding the daily fast in *Ramadan*.

at the centre of the floor was spread a carpet, on which stood a frame, about two feet in height, supporting an immense round plated tray, with the edge slightly raised. In the centre of the tray was placed a capacious white basin, filled with a kind of cold bread soup; and around it were ranged a circle of small porcelain saucers, filled with sliced cheese, anchovies, caviar and sweetmeats of every description: among them were scattered spoons of box-wood, and goblets of pink and white sherbet, whose rose-scented contents perfumed the apartment. The outer range of the tray was covered with fragments of unleavened bread, torn asunder; and portions of the Ramazan cake, a dry, close, sickly kind of paste, glazed with whites of eggs, and strewed over with aniseeds . . . As soon as the serious

business of the repast really commenced . . . and [we] squatted
down with our feet under the round dinner tray, having on our
laps linen napkins of about two yards in length richly fringed;
the room was literally filled with slaves . . . Fish, embedded in
rice, followed the side or rather circle saucers . . . With the fish,
the spoons came into play, and all were immersed in the same
dish; but I must not omit to add that this custom is rendered
less revolting than it would otherwise be, by the fact that each
individual is careful, should the *plat* be partaken of a second time
(a rare occurrence, however, from the rapidity with which they
are changed), always to confine herself to one spot. The meat and
poultry were eaten with the fingers, each individual fishing up, or
breaking away, what pleased her eye; and several of them tearing
a portion asunder, and handing one of the pieces to me as a courtesy, with which, be it remarked, *par parenthesie*, I should joyfully
have dispensed. Nineteen dishes, of fish, flesh, fowl, pastry and
creams, succeeding each other in the most heterogenous manner
– the salt following the sweet, and the stew preceding the custard
– were terminated by a pyramid of pillauf. I had the perseverance
to sit out this elaborate culinary exhibition; an exertion which is,
however, by no means required of anyone, by the observance
of Turkish courtesy. Gastronomy is no science in the East, and
gourmands are unknown; the Osmanlis only eat to live, they
do not live to eat; and the variety of their dishes originates in
a tacit care to provide against individual disgusts, while the
rapidity with which they are changed sufficiently demonstrates
their want of inclination to indulge individual excesses . . . the
instant that an individual has satisfied his appetite, he rises
without comment or apology, washes his hands, and resumes
his pipe or his occupation.[87]

I do not quote the description in its entirety (altogether there are
seven pages on the *iftar* alone). But the passage above is quite typical
and represents widely shared attitudes towards oriental food and
table-manners. The photographic attention to detail, the precision,
Pardoe's overall attitude and respect to the habits of the 'other' and
last, but not least, the tolerant *rationalisation* of eating (the immense
variety of dishes is 'economical' and 'useful'), all of them make for
a sympathetic representation. But there is much more. For Pardoe
breaks, violates even, every single rule in the middle-class code,
regulating female behaviour. Indeed she reverses the language of

food and sexuality. The very description of women consuming food is unusual. The Victorians stereotyped appetite and eating as masculine. Lack of appetite and the refusal of food were reckoned 'feminine'. The novel, conduct books and cookery-books and (as recently shown by Joan Brumberg) medical texts, depict women as food providers and preparers and men, as food consumers.[88] The gentlewoman, of course, was not supposed to prepare the food herself but was exhorted to supervise those who did. Women, traditionally the controllers of food, could exercise their power through the appetite, or the lack of it.[89] And, as a few historians of food and a number of anthropologists have argued, the distinction between feeders and those who are fed and the association between gender and food, is universal and cross-cultural and characterised different societies ('primitive' as well as 'modern') at different places and in different times.[90] In harem literature women, *of all classes*, are eaters. In fact, in works on the Ottoman and Egyptian urban élites and the middle classes, women are hardly ever depicted as feeders. This particularly applies to the Imperial and Viceregal Harems where, of course, food had been prepared by men, outside the women's quarters, and brought into the forbidden apartments by the eunuchs.[91]

But even in accounts of the household of the merchant classes it is unusual to find descriptions of women cooking. This is particularly significant because women's work is discussed in detail (see Chapter 5). It is the preparing of food that is under-represented. Furthermore women in the harems eat in public, whereas in Victorian fiction, particularly the realistic social novel, they do it usually furtively and in private. Hunger in Pardoe's and other accounts is acted publicly – *both* by local women *and* by the travellers themselves. A healthy appetite is not considered 'improper', or 'unladylike'. Moreover, the Ottomans or Arabs consume food that is rich and heavy and was usually referred to as 'men's food'. Muslim women are carnivorous, and digest *meat* – universally believed to arouse sexual feelings, aggravate lust and cause somatic disorders. Women gorge themselves with 'intemperate' and 'exotic' dishes, thought by the Victorians to endanger the female constitution: very sweet, or very spicy food. It will be recalled that even the unconventional, sensual and unladylike Becky Sharp cannot stomach oriental food. She is made sick by Jos Sedley's chili. Her more virtuous sisters, Amelia Sedley, Dickens's anorectic Amy Dorrit and Mrs Gaskell's Mary Burton, would wisely avoid it.[92]

Specially offensive to *bourgeois* sensibilities were undisciplined eating, analogous to undisciplined, unregulated sexuality,[93] and the mixing together of different kinds of food, differently cooked and differently processed, in what Pardoe calls 'the most heterogenous manner'.[94] Indeed the classification of food, especially the distinction between 'natural' and 'cooked', or artificial products, completely disappear. Specially sensitive travellers could not stomach the combination of the sweet with salty, the cooked and roasted, the raw (the habit of eating fresh vegetables was specially noted) and boiled. Emmeline Lott, for example, watches, amazed, the succession of dishes that rapidly appear on and disappear from the table in Ismail Pasha's *haremlik*. For the benefit of her readers every variety of food is itemised and the whole quoted in the form of a menu.

– Soup, made from sheep's shanks or fowls, having rice and forcemeat balls (made of the crumbs of bread left on the trays).
– Legs of mutton (which are as small as the lamb of Italy), roasted, and stuffed with the kernels of ground-nuts, onions, raisins, spice and sugar.
– Tomatoes, scooped out and filled with meat, rice, and spice.
– Cucumbers, dressed in a similar manner.
– Boiled cucumbers, small vegetable-marrows, onions, and pieces of fowl, all mixed up together.
– Broad Beans, boiled in their shells, from which the bean is removed at table, and then eaten.
– . . . Cutlets fried in syrup with spice.
– Boiled fowls.[95]

Twelve more dishes are listed, most of them meats, or *viands*, in the author's gentile expression. The indigestive Lott took to her room and a diet of tea and biscuits, and remained constipated to the end of her unsuccessful stay in Egypt. She was no favourite among the members of the harem. Most travellers, however, seem to have tolerated and enjoyed the oriental *cuisine*. Georgina Dawson-Damer, regally received in the harem of Shami Bey, secretary to Mehmet Ali, openly enjoys the royal feast. Anne Noel Blunt, includes in her *Pilgrimage to Nejd* two recipes for locusts, a staple ingredient in the diet of the nomad tribes in the Arabian Peninsula. And she describes, with special relish, a meal in which her Bedouin escort consume a hyena, whose belly is full of (the still undigested) insects.[96]

Implicitly, and in explicit language, the travellers dissociate eating from sin, thus desexualising oriental women. Even Lott herself, who describes the Royal children and the manual workers in Ismail's palaces as carnivorous animals, reluctantly admits that the Khediv's concubines, that is, those individuals whose role is sexual, are 'refined', 'delicate', and can boast of the best table-manners.[97] Eating thus is feminised. It is legitimised and is not represented as a vice, or an 'indulgence' of the senses. It is, rather, a natural and rational activity (recall Pardoe's intricate rationalisation of culinary habits in the *City of the Sultan*). And it does not denote undiscipline. On the contrary, visitors to the high-harems – Pardoe, Lott herself, Hornby, Vane, Harvey, Young-Postans and a few others – note that in those establishments eating and non-eating had been rigidly regulated.[98]

In the high-class Turkish household the number of meals was restricted to two, the *kahvalti*, or breakfast, usually served at 11 a.m. and the *yemek*, taken at sunset. The custom was imitated in Egyptian harems too. During Ramadan, eating and fasting were particularly ritualised. Throughout the elaborate meals the rule of silence was observed. The table was quitted by the person who had finished her repast and mere 'indulgence' was not encouraged.[99] And, most impressive, rules of hygiene were observed by means of the traditional ablutions before and after meals. Outside the households of the élites, eating was a *necessity*. And travellers passing through rural Palestine, or Anatolia, or in the desert routes of today's Iraq, were grateful to and openly admired the hospitality of local women. How many Englishwomen, wonders Anne Blunt, would welcome into their houses and to their tables, unknown guests, as the Bedouins of the isolated Oasis of Jof, in the North of the Arabian Peninsula.[100]

It is 'at the table', that the Bedouin or Arab woman is at her best. And sometimes she is more self-controlled, more tolerant and more courteous than the female tourist. Mary Eliza Rogers, for instance, reverses the roles of the observer and the observed. In *Domestic Life in Palestine* she gives a few accounts of meals in Muslim, Jewish, Druse and Christian houses. The following is from a much longer description of the harem and womenfolk of the Muslim house of Hadi, a clan which in the 1850s practically ruled the Jabal Nablus area in the eastern part of the country, not far from Jerusalem. Instead of showing herself looking at or down on the native women, Rogers has them watching her in the role of exotic foreigner. It is the

English gentlewoman, not the Arab peasants, who is 'different' and bizarre. There is a more than spurious similarity between this scene and Montagu's brilliant exercise in role reversal in her description of the public baths of Sophia. Rogers' message is clear. Differences in habits should be interpreted as differences in environment. They are tantamount to differences in language. It is evident to Rogers, as it was to Montagu before her, that the Eastern women are far more tolerant towards the Western tourist than the latter is towards them. The entire harem watches in silent amazement how the un-gentile Rogers devours an enormous meal:

> I was glad to see something to eat, for I was very hungry. The tray was soon quite covered with the following dishes: – a small metal dish of fried eggs – a wooden bowl of lebben, or sour milk – a bowl of sweet cream made of goat's milk – a dish of very stiff starch, like *blanc mange*, sweetened with roseleaf candy, with almonds and pistachio nuts chopped up in it – a long dish of rice boiled in butter, with little pieces of fried mutton all over the top – a plate of walnuts, dried fruits, sugared almonds and lemon-peel. A black slave . . . stood by me, holding a silver saucer in her hand, filled with water, ready for me to drink whenever I wished for it. There was not a knife or even a spoon to be seen, . . . [but] they soon perceived that I was not much accustomed to that mode of eating, so they brought me a large wooden cooking spoon, at which the little ones laughed heartily. I wished the ladies to eat with me but they would not . . . [101]

There follow ablutions, then the women and children and finally the slaves partake of the food and the *chibouque* is passed between the women. Note Rogers' smoking in public. Smoking, like meat-eating, was considered masculine and was characteristically associated with male or public places: the club, the pub or the study. In Victorian fiction only really dissolute women smoke. Yet in harem literature smoking is domesticated and feminised. Indeed quite a few travellers took to smoking. Rogers herself, Elisabeth Finn, Lucy Stanhope and Isabel Burton smoked. And Mrs Bird-Bishop and Harriet Martineau, these two paragons of propriety, became quite addicted to the *chibouque*.

Comparing with representations of female physiognomy and costume and the usage of body-language, the treatment of table-manners is neutral and moral-free. It is also markedly tolerant.

Food and eating are dissociated from sexuality. And traditional *topoi*, notably that of the gluttonous *odalik*, are discarded. More significant even, the travellers challenge the *bourgeois* code and redefine the borders of feminine *social* behaviour. The case with physical hygiene, as shall be seen, is quite different.

HYGIENE AND MORALITY

Without doubt, the most problematic, most delicate, of the four subjects of physical representation, is hygiene. The travellers' attitudes to cleanliness and uncleanliness are equivocal and reflect social and sexual anxiety.

In mainstream Victorian discourse 'cleanliness' and 'uncleanliness', 'filth' and 'purity', are terms supercharged with notions of class and gender, the two often being interrelated. Physical cleanliness, especially in women, signified sexual purity. Uncleanliness implied impurity and a pernicious and de-stabilising sexuality that threatened the social and even the political order. The association between purity and gender (exactly like that between gender and food) is neither typically Victorian nor particularly *bourgeois*, but universal and cross-cultural. In traditional, synchronic societies, as both Lévi-Strauss and Mary Douglas have shown, women are perceived as pollutants. They are impure, the agents of disease and of social and cosmic disorder. Hence the system of taboos concerning menstruation and the personal hygiene of women in general.[102] In modern society, according to Douglas, women are transformed to symbols of purity, stability and order. Douglas' distinction between the modern and the traditional is not always applicable to the Victorian context of class relations, or of relations between races and cultures. The Victorians associated purity with middle-class women. Working-class ones, particularly prostitutes, were identified as pollutants. They were, to repeat the historian Lackey's paraphrase on St Augustine, the very 'cesspools in the palace', veritable sewers, the transmitters of filth, disease and disorder.[103] Moreover, in the minds of the Victorians the pure was intimately connected with the impure, the filthy and promiscuous, with the sexually innocent. The working-class prostitute protected the virtuous *bourgeois* wife and mother from male lust. Yet, at the same time the former threatened the health and integrity of pure homes. Not only working-class women but the poor in general are typified as filthy and immoral. It is enough to mention Engels' famous characterisation of Mancunian labourers; Disraeli's representation of the destitute in his famous trilogy; Arnold's remarks on the filthy anarchical populace; Mayhew's depiction of the poor, particularly of prostitutes in his *London Labour and the London Poor*; and Booth's later, but similar descriptions of East Enders.[104]

Public and political preoccupation with hygiene notwithstanding, this subject remained taboo in literature and the visual arts. Thus the ideal Victorian heroine is unblemished, but does not need to wash. The traditional discussion on the Orient and the exotic, on the other hand, presents a different attitude towards physical hygiene. And both the language of class and that of the exotic combined to shape the outlook of the women writers. Orientalists and even travellers who were not specialists on Islam had been aware that the believers were exhorted to cleanse their bodies. Muslim ablutions, before prayer and before and after the meals, were noted by virtually all tourists. Female hygiene, however, was a somewhat problematic subject, for it had become associated with sexuality. In the orientalist context *cleanliness* in women was a symbol of impurity and disorder. The *hammam*, as already mentioned, had been identified as the *locus sensualis* of the imaginary Orient. The public bath had become the *ne plus ultra* of luxury, indolence and sexual deviance. Recall Ingres', voyeuristic *Bain Turc*, or J. F. Lewis's Circassian bathers or Gérôme's nudes.[105]

Women writers on harems were placed in a unique and difficult position. A visit to the *hammam* was *de rigueur* to every female tourist. And, in the early decades of the nineteenth century, the baths were much more easily penetrable than the private household, where introductions had been required. The *hammam* was fairly early stereotyped, earlier than the *haremlik*. And the Victorian stereotype certainly differed from the eighteenth-century model. Washing, like eating, a private, natural function, was relegated from the *private* to the public sphere and was socialised.

Most writers realised that the public-bath had distinct social functions. It was the meeting-place of women of all classes; a beauty parlour, where the hair was dyed and braided, the hands tinted with henna and superfluous body-hair removed; a club where information had been exchanged, gossip passed on, financial transactions concluded, and marriages made.[106] The *hamman* seemed to the travellers a less formal place than the *haremlik*. In the bath, the rigid etiquette of the urban middle and high-class household was not observed and discipline was relaxed. The *hammam* is, in more than one sense, the opposite pole of the desexualised harem. All Westerners were shocked by the noise and heat in the baths, conventionally juxtaposed with the calmness and orderliness of the high harems. And, most significant, cleanliness in the home is admired and praised, while washing in 'public' is suspiciously looked upon. Travellers notice that Ottoman women, even in the remotest places, are fastidious. Fanny Janet Blunt remarks that personal and public hygiene in rural Anatolia are more advanced than in Europe's cities. She is particularly impressed by the high standards of personal hygiene amongst the Ottoman labouring classes, noting that private baths are installed even in the poor *konaks* (households). Private baths in Britain, at that time (the 1870s and 1880s) were a luxury even in middle-class houses, let alone in the dwellings of the poor. The baths, opines Blunt, are 'excellent institutions . . . as instruments of cleanliness. The constant and careful ablutions of the Turks are the principal preventives of many diseases, from which they are, comparatively speaking, freer than most nations'.[107]

What Blunt seems to merely imply, other writers state outright. The Ottoman poor are cleaner and more respectable than the English labouring classes. The former are sober, hard-working, fastidious and virtuous.[108] Arabs, on the other hand, are often stereotyped as unclean. But even those travellers who deplore lack of sanitary and the basic rules of hygiene, mark out the customary ablutions before and after meals and occasionally the cleanliness of the poorer dwellings.[109] Yet, as already mentioned, washing outside the protecting *haremlik* seemed dangerous. Lady Montagu, it has been noted before was criticised by many of her Victorian disciples for representing Ottoman women in the nude. Except in one case, that I shall discuss later, the nineteenth-century travellers did not 'expose' (Pardoe's term) bathers and 'covered' flesh.

To distance themselves from the overtly sensuous atmosphere of the public bath, the writers resort to elaborate stratagems. A few are altogether silent. Others mention a visit to the *hammam*, but do not actually describe its interior. Yet other travellers resort to pastiche and a deliberately facetious tone to cover their own uneasiness. Thus Rogers and Finn as well as Mary Mackintosh, an authority on Damascus in the 1870s and 1880s, never even mention the public baths, which they undoubtedly visited. Catherine Elwood, who did not dare enter a public *hammam*, refers her readers to Montagu.[110]

Mary Lucy Garnett, for once, substitutes a general and impersonal description for representation.[111] And Isabel Burton assumes, in those passages in *The Inner Life in Syria* devoted to the baths, the role of a facetious *Cicerone* and compares Damascene *hammams* to those near Regents Park.[112] The majority of writers, however, resort to excessive representation. They itemise architectural detail, the paraphernalia of the bathers and the stages of bathing. Yet when they fix on the bathers themselves, the tenor of the reporters changes and the descriptions become openly moralising. Take for example Sophia Lane Poole's picture of one of the women's baths in Cairo, in 1842, or 1843.

> On entering the chamber a scene presented itself which beggars description. My companions had prepared me for seeing many persons undressed; but imagine my astonishment on finding at least thirty women of all ages and many young girls and children perfectly unclothed. You will scarcely think it possible that no one but ourselves had a vestige of clothing. Persons of all colours, from the black and glossy shade of the negro to the fairest possible hue of complexion, were formed in groups, conversing as though full dressed, with perfect nonchalance . . . [113]

Lane Poole herself was anything but '*nonchalant*'. 'I cannot describe the bath as altogether a beautiful scene, in truth, in some respects it is disgusting.'[114] Her description is less clichéd than it may first appear. It is to be found in the 24th 'letter' (the *Englishwoman in Egypt* is written in epistolary form), and has an equivalent in chapter, or 'letter', XII. This letter is devoted to a description of the closed female ward at Cairo's mental hospital, which Lane Poole was the first Westerner to visit. The scene in the bath, and that in the closed ward, are almost interchangeable. In both of the scenes Lane Poole wanders, dressed in a riding-habit, amidst a crowd of naked females. In the hospital scene the patients occupy rows of cubicles ('cells'). The naked women – 'maniacs', in her expression – chained to their places, rave and scream. They are, or seem to be, totally oblivious to their surroundings and physical appearance. At the bottom of the central yard, Lane Poole finally sets eyes on the only person, beside herself, who is dressed. Significantly, that person also is articulate. It is an old hag who speaks, begging for five paras for tobacco.[115] The scene is evidently structured and designed to prefigure that of the *hammam*. The Englishwoman's sensibilities are offended; she feels threatened by the exposure of flesh and the lack of social and racial segregation affected in the *hammam*. Note how the sight of black and fair flesh, mixing together, disturbs her. The reader is made aware of the association between physicality and inarticulateness: the 'maniacs' rave, the bathers shout, none talk.

Like Lane Poole, Martineau is obsessed with the relation between cleanliness and sexuality. *Eastern Life* includes only one representation of the interior of a bath and oriental bathers. There are, however, quite a few examples of washing in open places and in natural surroundings like pools, lakes and rivers. It is evident that when bathing is dissociated from an oriental interior it becomes a purifying act, a symbolic baptism and, most important, a positive sensual experience. Take for example Martineau's passage on the famous thermal baths at Tiberias, in the Lower Galillee in Palestine:

> Through the dense steam, I saw a reservoir in the middle of the apartment, where, as I need not say, the water stands to cool for some time before it can be entered: – several women were standing in it; and those who had come out were sitting on a high shelf in a row, to steam themselves thoroughly . . . The crowd and the steam were oppressive, that I wondered how they could stay: but the noise was not to be endured for a moment. Everyone of them all seemed to be gabbling at the top of her voice, and we rushed out after a mere glance, stunned and breathless. To this moment, I find it difficult to think of these creatures as human beings and certainly I never saw anything, even in the lower slave district of the United States, which so impressed me with a sense of the impassable differences of race.[116]

This, one suspects, is the real Martineau. It is in representational passages like this (descriptions of the interiors of *harems* are comparable examples) that she discards the role of the rational, open-minded student of cultures and societies. The oppressive sensuality of the *hammam* is juxtaposed to bathing in the unpolluted Lake Tiberais: 'We sought refreshment, on our return, in a different sort of bathing. We were longing for coolness above everything; so Mrs Y. and I went into the Lake . . . the water was four feet deep; and through the wide vents, the moonlight broke the deep shadows on the waters, and rippled on the surface.'[117] The different sort of bathing is tirelessly pursued. Martineau paddles in every ravine, pond or reservoir she comes across. And she is quite explicit about her physical joy. Thus at the 'pagan' river Panias (Banias) 'the water was so warm that I was tempted to explore those delicious nooks by means of it. One dark recess or craven in which the water was not above three feet deep, looked very enticing . . . A gulf of light through a very low arch in the rock tempted me on. I stooped through it, and found myself in the shady core I had seen from the little beach, with the black duck beside me, still at anchor.'[118] Two pages later Martineau is in for another splash. 'I was tempted on and on by the sound of a waterfall, which, pouring down from the foundations of an old ruin, made a charming shower bath. What a luxury was our daily revel in cold water . . .'[119] Revel indeed. The picture of Martineau, that paragon of Victorian seriousness, in a 'bathing apparatus' (her words) waving her ear-trumpet is irresistible.

Martineau and Lane Poole's reactions seem to be quite typical. For the overwhelming majority of the writers connect fastidiousness and indulgence of the flesh with physical *and mental* degeneration. Ablutions after meals may be safe, as is the occasional bath, but ⸱egular washing, toiletting and the appliance of cosmetics endanger the female body. The bathers are made to appear unattractive and, sometimes, even repulsive. Washing and exposure to the 'sulphurous atmosphere' of the *hammam*, a metaphorical *inferno*, cause premature aging, deterioration of the nervous-system and debility. Unknowingly perhaps, the nineteenth-century 'moralists' echo the rationalist climatologists of the Enlightenment, who associated character and behaviour with climate, geography and physical environment. The effects of climate, especially heat – both 'natural' heat and the artificially created heat of the bath – on the physical constitution of oriental women and their *libido* were constantly commented on by eighteenth-century climatologists (the fifth book of Montesquieu's, *De l'espirit de lois* is, of course, the best-known example).[120]

Almost every description of the bath boasts of the figure of the old bather, or better, the bath-keeper, or, *hammamci*, a living lesson to all women. And the lesson is clear. Beauty is transient. And life is short. Indulgence of the flesh is sinful. Pardoe, Vane, Postans and Harvey, like Lane Poole and Craven before them, are disgusted by the sight of old flesh in the baths. Harvey's description of a pair of *hammamcis* is typical.

> [They] had been slowly boiling for so many years that they were shrivelled and parted out of the semblance even of 'womanity',

if such a word may be permitted. Strange to say that they had but few wrinkles, but their skin seemed tightly drawn over their faces, as over the bones of a skull, and hung loosely in great folds under their chins and around their throats . . . [they] had grown so much accustomed to the heated and sulphurous atmosphere in which they pass the greater portion of their days, that a purer and fresher air is quite painful to them.[121]

In final analysis, the representational parts of the women's narrative about harems seem to corroborate the rhetoric of freedom. Both discourses evince an attitude towards oriental women which is far more complex than that of either the Augustan women writers, or contemporary orientalists. The narrational language is middle-class language, encoding *bourgeois* sensibilities and *bourgeois* ethics of respectability and propriety. There appears to be a difference between the confident rhetoric of liberty, which idealises freedom of the married women, and representations of actual women. In rhetorical utterances the oriental woman is desexualised. In the excessively representational autobiographical parts there is room for female sexuality, both for that of the religious and cultural 'other' and the 'self' – that is, the writers' own. Of course elaborate codes are employed to convey to the audience what *bourgeois* sense of propriety made impossible to say in a more explicit manner. Indeed the very selection of topics and themes is innovative, if not radical. And that selection as well as the literary stratagems which the travellers use, seriously challenge the discourse of class they seem to draw on, and Victorian definitions of gender. Not only the boundaries between the genders are being reset. The distinctions between the private and the public, home and the world, these too are questioned. It is to representations of the private sphere that Chapter 5 is devoted.

5

The *Haremlik* as a *Bourgeois* Home: Autonomy, Community and Solidarity

THE RHETORIC OF DOMESTICITY: ATTITUDES TO SECLUSION, POLYGAMY AND CONCUBINAGE

Sometime in the Spring of 1847, Harriet Martineau, famous writer, Radical, populariser of Utilitarianism and the principles of Political Economy, feminist and Abolitionist, alighted in an harem in Cairo. She was fresh from a cruise down the Nile and on her way to Palestine, 'cradle of the monotheistic religions'.[1] And the one visit to the harem was her only meaningful encounter with life in 'modern' Egypt and – it later transpired – a fateful one. For Martineau saw very little of the life of Egyptian women and (without a translator and her celebrated ear-trumpet) understood even less about it. And the visit was to produce the most scathing attack, by a Victorian, on Middle Eastern polygamy and segregation:

> I declare that if we are to look for a hell upon earth, it is where polygamy exists; and that, as polygamy runs riot in Egypt, Egypt is the lowest depth of hell. I always before believed that every arrangement and prevalent practice had some fair side, some one redeeming quality; and diligently, did I look for this fair side in polygamy but, there is none. The longer one studies the subject, and the deeper one penetrates into it, the more is one'[s] mind confounded with the intricacy of its iniquity, and the more does one heart [sic] feels as if it would break.[2]

Martineau forgoes her own earlier advice to travellers, not to judge foreign societies by European standards, and to apply the prin-

137

ciples of 'scientific' inquiry to institutions, behaviours and systems of morals. The treatment of polygamy and domestic slavery
in *Eastern-Life* is neither historical nor scientific, drawing, as it
does, on Martineau's experience of the North-American system
of slavery and her commitment to Abolitionism.[3] Her outburst
– so uncharacteristic in harem literature – incensed some fellow-
travellers. One of them, Lucie Duff-Gordon, resented Martineau's
pity on Egyptian women, remarking that: 'Her attack upon harems
is outrageous: She implies that they are brothels.'[4]

Duff-Gordon's comment throws light on the more typical attitude
of women-travellers to polygamy and seclusion. These twin-systems
and their *locus*, the *haremlik*, are interpreted in *bourgeois* terms, are
divested of sexuality and de-politicised. Paradoxically, it is precisely
by ignoring, or playing down the more overtly sexual aspects of the
harems that the Victorians could interpret it in historical, rational
terms. The Victorians did not perceive the harem as a monolith,
but rather saw it as an historical phenomenon, that changed over
time and had many different social and economic functions in
different places and classes. Also, the *haremlik*, the actual *locus* of
non-monogamous sexuality is, in the women's writing, not merely
the uniform and changeless imaginary place that it had once been,
but an actual, particularised place. Differentiation and specificity,
then, are the keynotes of both the general discussion about the
harem-system and the eye-witness representation of everyday life.

First, the overtly rhetorical. Neutral and sympathetic travellers,
regardless of their sex, had, of course, always sought to dissociate the harem from the West's images of Islam as a sensual,
promiscuous religion. Tourists, as different as the Baron de Tott,
David Urquhart, Sir J. Malcolm, Pierre Loti, Richard Burton, and
Adolphus Slade, the famous Müşavir Pasha, had done much to
dispel the popular notion, so central to orientalist epistemology,
that polygamy and the seclusion of women had embodied the spirit
of a thisworldly religion which condoned promiscuity.[5] Throughout
the nineteenth century it had been argued that neither polygamy,
nor seclusion were Muslim in origin and that both practices existed
in societies outside the eastern Mediterranean.

The Byzantine origins of seclusion and the usage of eunuchs –
an historical example of the practice of seclusion by Christians –
was eagerly seized upon by art-historian Barnette Miller, the first
Westerner to have been allowed to survey Seraglio Point and the
(unoccupied) harem of Topkapi (her *Beyond the Sublime Porte*, was

researched before and during the First World War but appeared only in 1931).[6] Grace Ellison, a feminist with connections within the Turkish movement for women's suffrage, also insisted that the harem was not Muslim in origin: 'From that permission to marry [four wives] we have totally misinterpreted the words of the Great Prophet of the Desert. We have classed Islam as a religion deprived of spirituality, a religion which had degraded woman-hood.'[7] Ellison's *Englishwoman in a Turkish Harem,* published in 1915, was serialised in the *Daily Telegraph* and her views on Muslim attitudes to women reached large audiences. Four decades earlier, Ellen Chennels, referring to the harem of Khedive Ismail, argued that: 'It is no part of Mohametan religion to ordain polygamy and the shutting up of women. Such things existed before Mohamet [sic], who attempted to set some bound to the universal license which prevailed in his time'.[8]

Nor are these 'progressive' attitudes typical of the late writers. Some of the very early commentators on the harem-system refer to seclusion in glowing terms. Pardoe is one example, Catherine Elwood is another characteristic one. 'The seclusion of the Harem', she opines, 'appears to be no more than the natural wish of the husband to guard his beloved from even the knowledge of the ills and woes that mortal man betides . . . he wishes to protect "his lady bird" "the light of his Haram [sic]", from all trouble and anxiety . . . as we carefully enshrine a valuable gem or protect a sacred relic from the profane gaze of the multitude, so does he on the same principle hide from the vulgar kin his best . . . The Turks, in their gallantry, consider the person of a woman *sacred,* and the place of her *retreat,* her haram, is always respected' (my emphasis).[9] Elwood, somewhat vaguely, points at the familiar etymological connection between haram, that which is 'forbidden', 'unlawful' and, therefore, 'inviolable' (an, originally, *religious term*), and the secular application of especially the last of the three meanings to the *sacred,* an application that denotes that portion of a house which is occupied by the women and children.[10] But more significant is the characteristic juxtaposition of the 'sacred' and the 'profane'. Elwood typically identifies the first adjective with women and a female space; while the 'profane' is identified with man's world – 'vulgar', unsafe and ruled by the 'multitude'. Woman's enclosed place is a 'retreat', a 'shrine', the abode of the 'sacred' and her person or body 'respected', guarded and worshipped.

What is culturally meaningful about the discussion on the harem is not the women's tolerance towards oriental sexual and domestic politics, nor the naturalisation of the exotic, but the feminisation of a system, traditionally perceived as a patriarchal construct, designed to perpetuate male domination. The Victorian and Edwardian women saw the harem neither as a brothel nor merely as a gaol. To them it was first and foremost a 'home'. A 'home' was a *private*, feminine space. In harem literature the private and the public (that is, man's world) are sharply dichotomised. Travellers repeatedly apply to the harem-system and its *locus* words like: 'sphere', 'home', 'haven' and 'sanctuary' and combinations like: 'woman's sphere', 'sacred place', even *'sanctus sanctorum'*. And the key-words in the travellers' vocabulary of domesticity are the very terms of the broader discussion about woman's place and her social and cultural role. In mainstream Victorian thought and writing the relations between the sexes were formulised in terms of *space*, or 'spheres'. And that formula was particularly manifest in the notion of the male and the female as separate 'spheres', complementary opposites, biologically, mentally, intellectually and morally, poles apart. Gender differences according to that notion are nature- or God-ordained and are, therefore, essentially unalterable; they determine the 'spheres' that the man and the woman inhabit.[11]

The association between space and gender is a very well-known and well-studied characteristic of Victorian culture. The 'home' or 'hearth' is the aesthetic and socialised *locus* of the female and of the feminine experience of reality.[12] Most important, the idealised, that is *domestic* woman is a reversal of woman the temptress and sinner. The first archetype is divested of sex and incarnates the virtues inscribed in the home.

It is not surprising that the middle-class travellers projected Victorian values onto the Middle Eastern family and systems of marriage. What is astonishing is that the vocabulary of the 'spheres' was so resilient to social changes in Britain and outlived the late Victorian 'crisis of morals' of the 1870s and 1880s. Thus we can find John Ruskin's classical definition of the differences between the sexes and of the nature of 'true home'[13] echoed in texts as late as 1909. 'The term harem,' argues Mary Lucy Garnett, 'simply means a "sacred enclosure"' and, elsewhere, 'the *haremlik* is consequently the *sanctus sanctorum*, the place safe from all intrusion'.[14] And Elisabeth Goodnow, a year after the outbreak of the First World War, maintains that 'If woman is the conserver of the home in the West, guarding it strictly from innovation and change because it represents to her permanence, and is veritably her throne, the woman of Egypt is even more completely synonymous with her home-life, since it is her kingdom.'[15]

With the feminisation of the harem came the desexualisation of the system and its *locus*, the oriental household. According to the notion of the spheres woman is innately moral and morally superior to man. Her vocation is to save him from a carnal nature and 'uplift' him morally. The typical Victorian travel-writer would subscribe to Montagu's emphasis on the differences between the sexes, but not to her insistence that oriental women and men have the same sexual appetites. Indeed woman's morality is inscribed on the Victorian's harem. Given the right education any Muslim woman should be able to mitigate the corrupting influences of the world and elevate her children – and husband, or master – to a spiritually, generically feminine sphere. This view is shared by missionaries – who realised the educational potential in women – and by non-proselytising, 'secular' writers who objected to the missions. Mary Eliza Rogers advocates the education of Druse and Muslim women, commenting that in that way the true values of the home would be exported to the world.[16] Fanny Blunt, in a chapter on the Imperial Harem, argues that any woman in it, 'properly educated to [fit in] her true *sphere* could exercise her influence over high and noble object'.[17] Note that nowhere does she – or Rogers – argue for the statutory abolition of the harem (only for a reduction in numbers in the Imperial Harem). In fact, both these travellers emphatically object to interference from above, whether in the form of state legislation against polygamy, or in the form of proselytisation.[18]

About the same time as Rogers, Amelia Bythinia Hornby comments that the Ottoman women 'are far before the men in intelligence, far less prejudiced, and far more willing to know and adopt wiser and better ways'.[19] She marks out the Circassians and Georgians (the very sexual objects in the traditional discourse) whom she regards as ideal carriers of her pretentious educational project. Hornby's 'project', which she discusses in some detail in a letter addressed to Sarah Austin – a well-known blue-stocking and the mother of Lucie Duff-Gordon – involved the importation into Istanbul and the distribution there of Self-Help literature for married women of the commercial classes. Hornby had even approached the famous Müşavir Pasha (Adolphus Slade), who consented to inspect the translation of the books into Turkish.

Hornby's schemes were naïve and characteristically offensively paternalistic. But her conviction that change in the Ottoman Empire should proceed from the domestic to the political sphere rather than the other way around is revealing. The idea that women should be educated because they were the 'educators' of future generations is a logical conclusion of the ethos of spheres and 'women's vocation'. Seclusion, then, was acceptable, mainly because it could easily be fitted into the notion of the spheres, with the separation, in *bourgeois mentalité*, between the private and the public.

Attitudes to plural marriage and concubinage seem to be more equivocal. Polygamy, notwithstanding the permission in the Koran to marry more than one wife and the exhortations in the *Hadith* to espouse as many as four,[20] was uncharacteristic throughout the eighteenth and nineteenth centuries. Even before Lady Montagu, travellers to the Balkans and Asia Minor noted that plural marriages had been limited to the élite which had emulated the imperial model, and that society at large had been monogamous.[21] Throughout the nineteenth century, the travellers' overall impression was much the same; a polygamous urban élite and a monogamous majority.[22] In one hilarious passage, Anna Bowman Dodd ridicules the prevalent notions in the West about Ottoman polygamy in a (probably fictive) dialogue between a vulgar American tourist and a polite, yet exasperated, Ottoman official:

> To the casual visitor there is an unexpected embarrassment in finding almost all the Turks one meets, in society, married to one wife. The singularity of this singleness is as trying, apparently, to the Turk on certain occasions, as it is eminently disappointing to the European.
>   'I do so hope the Minister of —— may grant me the honour of visiting his harem, an American lady remarked with the charming aplomb characteristic of the American woman. ' . . . His excellency has no harem in the sense in which, I presume, most foreigners understand the word', was the corteous reply of the minor official to whom the remark was addressed. 'He has but one wife, as, indeed, we mostly all have'. 'Hasn't any one a harem?' The cry was almost tearful.[23]

Monogamy, however, was effectively modulated by unilateral divorce which, according to some writers, resulted in the substitution of 'serial' polygamy, or successive marriages for a 'simultaneous' one.[24] To this were, of course, added the effects of domestic slavery. In the second half of the century there were signs that even the élite was moving towards monogamy. Even 'the [Turkish] upper ten thousand', opines Dodd, who, in 1902, interviewed Sultan Abdulhamit I, 'practice, at least outwardly, monogamy.'[25] And there is scattered evidence that the Imperial and Viceregal Harems, the very bastions of custom and tradition, were slowly moving with the times. Hornby remarks that, but for the opposition of conservative circles, Abdulmecit, the reforming Sultan, would monogamise his house.[26] And Ellen Chennels argues that the Khedive Ismail, initiator of educational programmes for women, actually favoured the idea of a monogamous household and an hereditary dynasty.[27] This is probably pure conjecture (when the exiled Ismail left Cairo in 1911, there were thirty-three carriages packed with women in his retinue), but the wish-fulfillment of both writers is revealing.

The standard reason given for the practice of monogamy is the economic one. The *Hadith* stipulates that each wife receives a separate apartment, or household, and is properly maintained.[28] And this stipulation naturally made polygamy possible only to a few. Also, free-born women, especially Ottoman women, were thought to be more assertive than the propertyless and familyless Circassians and Georgians.[29] It is typically in the writings of casual visitors to harems, with only a superficial knowledge of the system, that we find generalisations about polygamy (Nightingale and Martineau are characteristic examples). Yet the fact that travellers saw polygamy in its real proportion did not prevent them from censuring it. And censure characterises both 'polygamists' – that is, the writers who did not condemn polygamy as such, but criticised its social and moral effects – and the 'anti-polygamists', typically missionaries, who objected *a priori* to all non-monogamous family relations which they regarded as deviations from the Pauline-Augustinian model. It is typically on the sexual aspect of polyga-mous arrangements that all censors fixed. The great Lane himself thought that plural marriage affected private and public morals, particularly the morals of women.[30] His nephew and literary execu-tor, Lane Poole (Sophia's son), himself a sympathiser with Islam, insisted that the polygamous house produced 'vapid, bigoted and sensual mothers'.[31]

Explicit reference to sensuality is quite unusual in the 'general' parts of the women's narrative on harems. And, usually, even those

women writers who condemn polygamy are aware of, and emphasise, the rights and customary privileges of the wife. These rights,
notes Bowman Dodd, as late as 1903, 'are many, so numerous,
indeed, that after a review of them it is the European rather than
the Osmanli women who seem to be still in bondage'. And, she
adds, 'even the woman suffragist [should know] that the laws of
Mohamet confer upon women a greater degree of legal protection
than any code of laws since the middle Roman Law'.[32] The attack
on suffragism, indeed on a *political* interpretation of women's rights,
echoes Garnett's diatribe against Mill a decade earlier. Like Dodd
and Garnett, most Victorian women-travellers de-politicised the
harem. Indeed, it was impossible for these writers to understate, or
ignore, the sexual aspects of the harem yet analyse it as a patriarchal
construct. Once the sexual *topos* was supplanted by the image of the
harem as a home, the traditional analogy between domestic and
political oppression had to be abandoned. The de-politicisation of
polygamy and seclusion constitutes a departure from eighteenth-
century models, both the model of the *philosophes* and that of
early feminists like Montagu and Craven. Analogy to the state is
pertinent to the orientalist writings of Montesquieu, Voltaire, Dr.
Johnson and Diderot. Usbeq in the *Lettres persanes* is a diminutive
Sultan. Admittedly Montagu severs the Ottoman household from
the Ottoman Empire, but her attitudes towards polygamy and
seclusion are inseparable from her anti-papism and her attack on
the Catholic monarchies. True, in the nineteenth century the reform
of the harem is seen as the key to reforms in the Ottoman Empire.
Nevertheless the *haremlik* is not a microcosmic state, or an image of
civil society, but its reverse. Like the Victorian home, the Ottoman
or Arab home seems to be cut out from the polity and the (male)
world.

   This domestic, a-political (or, rather, un-political) interpretation
of what is, undoubtedly, a patriarchal system made it possible for
the Victorians and Edwardians to perceive the harem as a society
within society, a female community, an autonomous sorority, little
affected by the world outside it. The purpose of the harem is
not the gratification of male *libido*. Rather, the former is represented as a self-sufficient, self-ruling and – sometimes – self-justified
community.

   The key to the whole structure was the combination of discipline
and self-rule copied from the imperial/viceregal model. In the
imperial household or *harem-i-hümayün* the *valide sultan*, or mother

of the Sultan, reigned supreme. After her ranked the *sultans*, or Sultan's daughters, who enjoyed considerable freedom and after them the *kadins*, official concubines, with the social though not legal status of wives. Then came the *ikbals*, or favorites, then the *gözdes* (literally 'those in the Sultan's eye'). Parallel to this reproductive pyramid was the pyramid of production, headed by the *kethüdâ* or *kâhya kadin* in charge of the entire harem service. The heads of special services were the *hazinedar usta* (treasurer) and the officials responsible for laundry, cuisine, baths, coffee-making and an army of clerks (*katibes*) and the cohorts of manual workers all, of course, female.[33]

Running an upper, certainly a middle-class harem was, naturally, a much simpler matter. But, as is often noted, the principles of hierarchy and autonomy, or self-rule, were respected and emulated regardless of the status or economic class of a household. The husband's mother was at the top of the domestic hierarchy. A few travellers went so far as to imply that the privileged position of sons' mothers was a relic of an archaic matriarchalism. Garnett included in most editions of her *Women of Turkey* a section on matriarchy. And Lady Ramsay notes that: 'How far the matriarchal system prevails I don't know, but . . . married sons [are] living with their parents or their widowed mothers. In such cases the mother is "boss" of the whole concern. The young wife, or each wife . . . has her own private apartment in the establishment, where she is mistress . . . ; but over-all the mother-in-law presides, often with an iron rule.'[34] Where there was no mother-in-law, position correlated with seniority and, many an observer insisted, seniority alone. The *büyük hanim* (literally great lady), or first wife, was undisputed ruler of the *haremlik* and entirely in control of the economy of the household. Certainly not all polygamous houses were peaceful. And life in many an harem was disrupted by jealousies and rivalries. But the fact that junior wives respected seniors struck most travellers. Needless to say that *odaliks* or slaves observed the etiquette religiously.[35]

Naturally, interest in slaves exceeded occasional observations on the hierarchical relations between *hanim* and *odalik*. Even those travellers oblivious to the political context of the harem could not separate between slavery and larger political (and humanitarian) issues. There had been in Britain a strong anti-slavery tradition from the late eighteenth century, in which women had played an important part. Moreover, there were organisational and ideological connec-

tions between the early reformist feminist and anti-slavery movements. The language of Abolitionists informed that of a-political or
pre-political feminists. Most significant, analogy between the slaves
and women was very common in public discourse. Notwithstanding, British travellers who encountered slavery in the Ottoman
Empire were aware that there was no basis for an analogy between
the Muslim and the Afro-American experience of slavery.[36] Harriet
Martineau's comparison between the South-Carolina planter and
the Cairene or Alexandrine slave-owner is not typical, and is to
be understood only in the context of her views and her commitment to Garrisonian Abolitionism (the abolitionist party demanding
immediate, complete and unconditional abolition). Martineau was
converted to the Garrisonian cause in 1835 and was to maintain
life-long relations with the Boston Garrisonians.[37] Typically even
zealous evangelical missionaries who vehemently criticised the
harem-system as such, recognised that slavery in Islam was a
particular case, and the experience of slavery of Middle Eastern
women was radically different from that of American blacks. Thus
Mary Louisa Whately agrees that slavery in Egypt cannot be compared with North-American gang slavery.[38]

Slavery in the Middle East, it is repeated time and again, was
not a permanent and changeless condition of bondage. It was,
rather, temporary and alterable, a transitory phase in the female
life-cycle. Concubinage, in particular, was a means to improvement
and upward mobility and therefore could not simply be regarded
as a form of sexual exploitation. To the Christian Circassians and
Georgians, enslavement spelt out emancipation. And concubinage
was sought after by the really ambitious and by their families.
For it meant an escape from the 'barbarous' (the travellers' own
term) conditions of life in Georgia and the Circassian areas around
the Black Sea (occupied in 1863 by Russia). As the Turkophile
Slade somewhat bluntly put it, the harem was to oriental women
what India had been to English men: a social ladder.[39]. Esmé
Scott-Stevenson who, in 1880, after official abolition of the slave
trade, interviewed expatriate Circassians resettled in Konia and
Cilicia reports: 'I asked him [her Circassian interviewee] which he
would prefer: his child to be the servant of a Russian or a slave in
a Turkish harem. He declared emphatically that all their women
would prefer the latter; for with the Turks they are kindly treated;
and [even if] their masters are tired of them, they are never turned
out to die of hunger.'[40] The interview is probably apocryphal. The

point is that it is there to confer Scott's own preconceived notions about Russian barbarism and Turkish humanitarianism. Exactly the same attitude is to be found in the writings of the reliable Blunt, Harvey and Hornby. Blunt, for instance, thinks that 'their first position [that of the 'enslaved' Christians] is one of extreme ignorance and barbarism.[41] Harvey, on a visit to (then) Russian Eupatoria, a watering place in the Crimea, is disgusted by the filth, ignorance and inborn 'slavishness' of Russian women, whom she compares with their Ottoman sisters.[42]

Slaves, it was noted, were not an exploited labour-force, nor merely degraded sexual objects. They had definite legal rights and, most important, they became integrated in the extended Muslim family and the Ottoman political system. The slave, whether the manual slave, or the concubine was, normally, an accepted member of the family, to be taken care of as long as she remained in the household and sometimes afterwards.[43] Her owner was responsible, by law, for her maintenance; she could claim liberty after seven years of servitude and custom demanded that she – especially a childless *odalik*, or an *odalik* who was not recognised as the mother of a child – be married off and provided with a dower and a trousseau by her master. 'There is', insists Ellen Chennels, 'no degradation implied here in the term [slave]. Those belonging to a great harem have generally been there since their early childhood; they have no recollection of their previous life; they have grown up with the family, and identify themselves with it. They are confined, it is true, within four walls, but they are allowed a degree of liberty within those walls, astonishing to our habits.'[44] And Chennels was referring to the (comparatively) disciplined and secluded slaves of Khedive Ismail.

Down the social ladder, the situation seemed to be even more favourable to the individual slave, and to the slaves as a group. Work was not arduous and, as is typical in a pre-industrial paternalistic community, leisure a recognised part of the worker's life: 'the lot of the slave girl in Turkey is in many aspects preferable to that of the domestic servant in the West. The duties of the slave are at no time arduous, be she housemaid, nursemaid, or *tchiboukdji* (*çubukcu*, the slave responsible for the pipes) and leave her plenty of leisure'.[45] The analogue with domestic service is as poignant as it is revealing and is a comment on the British class system. Unlike the servant in the *bourgeois* household, the Circassian, Georgian or Nubian is 'allowed in private considerable amount of freedom, both in speech and in action.'[46] More important, harem slavery is free of class-, race-, and gender-exploitation. And, rather than threatening the middle-class family, the slave, or *odalik*, is an integral part of the familial construct.

It is precisely this integration which could appeal to the Victorians and Edwardians. The harem-system succeeded to regulate and control male sexuality. And despite seclusion, despite inequalities between the sexes, the system seemed free of the notion of a double sexual standard. Bowman Dodd was blunt, but perceptive: 'a Moslem [sic] can practically have no sexual relations with any woman without assuming full responsibilities for such intimacy',[47] the implication being that the *bourgeois homme moyen sensuel* was free of such responsibilities, as indeed in class-conscious Victorian Britain he was. The double standard, with its emphasis upon female chastity, was reflected in the legal status of illegitimate children and that of unmarried mothers. The law did not recognise the issue even after the subsequent marriage of the parents and it remained *filius nulius*, which, of course, meant that he or she could not inherit. Indeed the law made the woman responsible for her 'transgression'.[48] The Muslim mediterranean system was, by comparison, far more humane. Travellers were impressed by the fact that the children of slaves were provided for and integrated into the polygamous family as was the slave herself. Once her issue was recognised by the father, it immediately became free and inherited equally with the children of the legal spouses. As for the mother, she could – as indeed often happened – marry her owner, or she would be married 'outside' and her dowry provided her. Most significant, the *odalik* became *ummüveled*, or 'mother of a child', a legal status that acquired for her freedom after her master's death.[49]

The inflated rhetoric of domesticity illustrates how acceptable seclusion was to the Victorians. Polygamy, concubinage and the physical segregation of women could be reconciled with the dominant ideology of the spheres. However, eyewitness descriptions of the *haremlik* reveal an equivocal attitude towards oriental domesticity.

THE PRIVATE AS PUBLIC: ORGANISATION OF SPACE IN THE *HAREMLIK*

During the nineteenth century the Middle Eastern house was transformed from the *locus* of the exotic to an actual place and was realistically reproduced by travellers and ethnographers. The Victorian reproductions or representations of the *haremlik* are important because the ordering and regulation of domestic life were central to the construction of Victorian class culture. Middle-class life was characterised by the organisation of space and time, according to the material needs of the *bourgeoisie* and the evolving idealogy of that class. The middle-class discovered privacy. And natural, 'private' functions of the body were separated from social 'respectable' activities and relegated to the 'back-stage', to specific parts of the house, invisible to the outside world. This modern segmentation of living was, as is well known, carried on in two stages. First, work had been separated from home. Even before industrialisation, the middle-class, urban family ceased to be an economic unit. The separation between the house and the work-place had far-reaching affects on the daily life of women and the ways in which women's time was ordered. Secondly, within the home, there occurred a separation between social activities and private ones as well as between age-groups and classes. Cooking, washing, dressing and sleeping – the 'natural' activities – were limited to private, specified rooms. Servants were confined to separate quarters and children were separated from adults and allocated places for eating, playing and sleeping.[50]

The *haremlik* presented to the Victorians an alternative ordering of life of individuals and the community. Oriental attitudes to privacy, to time and to work appeared to inscribe themselves on the architecture of the house, the layout of its parts, the furniture and the decor.

In contradistinction to the departmentalised life of people in the West, even within the home, domestic life in the Orient seemed homogenous and simple. The *haremlik* is represented as both a public and private place; the center of an organic community; an economic as well as a reproductive unit.

The first thing that struck newcomers was the spacious simplicity of the women's quarters. The sparsity of furniture and absence of creature comforts compensated for the sense of seclusion. To some visitors the simplicity of furniture and its functionality was a refreshing contrast to the cluttered Victorian drawing room with its display of wealth. Visitors, even to high-class harems on the Bosphorus and in Cairo, register their surprise at the lack of luxury.

The best inside information on the interior of the Royal and Vice-regal *haremlik* are to be found in the writings of Emmeline Lott and

Ellen Chennels, both of them governesses to the children of Khedive Ismail and both actually living inside the Khedive's palaces for long enough spells. Lott entered into contract with Ismail's agents in London in 1861 and was hired as an 'instructuress' to Ibrahim, his son from the second *kadin*. She was probably employed for one year only and may have been forced to leave her post. It is evident, from Lott's writing, that she had no real influence over the women of the harem, mainly because she found it hard to accommodate to her new surroundings. Her memoirs, entitled *Harem Life in Egypt and Constantinople*, appeared in 1866 and was immediately succeeded with the *Mohaddeyn in the Palace of Ghezire, or Nights in the Harem* (1867) and *The Grand Pasha's Cruise on the Nile in the Viceroy of Egypt's Yacht*. The three works are lugubrious jeremiads, itemising Lott's many petty grievances and real and imagined illnesses, and reveal as much about her own prejudices as about those of the Ottoman and Egyptian women she observed. Despite its obvious weaknesses, the trilogy abounds with detail on intimate life and social behaviour in the high-harems during a transitory period from a traditional pattern of life to a life exposed to Western, modern influences.

Ellen Chennels came to a less hostile environment and succeeded in accommodating herself to it. In 1871 she was appointed governess to Princess Zeynep (Ismail's only surviving daughter from the (same) second *kadin*, and took over the princess's education until Zeynep's death in childbirth in 1875. Zeynep's own history is doubly interesting. She was the first female member of the ruling dynasty to be educated outside the harem, and her education continued after her marriage. Chennels, much more sympathetic than Lott, documents the process of acculturation of the secluded *odaliks*, sensitively noting that, despite the increasing exposure to Western influences, consumer goods and styles, her pupils remained traditionalists and Eastern.

Despite the differences in their status within the hierarchy of the Viceregal household; their general attitude and their style of writing, both writers register similar reactions to their physical environment. Both effectively – albeit somewhat reluctantly – demolish the image of the rich and exotic harem. Lott openly challenges the authority of orientalists like Beckford and Moore and aristocratic travellers like Montagu. The part of the palace she lived in was simple and even ascetic. According to Lott's own middle-class standards the women's apartments were 'uncomfortable', 'unfurnished' and 'unornamented':

> . . . not any of the splendid rooms of the Enchanted palace of the
> Croesus of the Nineteenth Century [Ismail] contained anything,
> either for ornament or use, except the bare decorations . . . In
> fact, the whole of them seemed to me nothing more than places in
> which to lie down and in which to vegetate . . . They were often
> destitute of sofas, tables. Accustomed to the elegant manner in
> which drawing rooms of the nobility of my own country are
> set off with elegant fauteuils, superb occasional chairs, recherche
> nick-knacks, as well as a whole host of most costly things, they
> presented a most beggarly and empty appearance. The whole
> of the Harem looked like a house partially furnished; in short,
> like a dwelling either the poverty or the niggardliness of its
> proprietor had prevented from being properly furnished . . . I
> afterwards learned that it was *à la mode Turque,* for elegance is
> quite eschewed by all true Ottomans.[51]

Lott is still severer on the summer-palace of the Khedival family,
on the Bosphorus, not far from the Imperial Palace of Bebek. The
furnishing in some of the private apartments in both palaces was
simplicity itself. Each chamber 'was furnished with a plain iron
bedstead, with crimson mosquito-curtains, a large-mirror, and a
divan-cover of dark-brown chintz. The hangings of the door and
windows were of the same material, with the addition of white
muslin curtains; no other furnishing of any kind.'[52]
The austerity of the women's quarters, especially in the 'old-
fashioned', Ottoman-style mansions of the Khedive, is sharply contrasted with the shameless ostentation and glitter of the 'modernised' *selamlik* at the palace of Gezirah. Ismail's passion for the
'modern' and 'Western' (dubbed by the chauvinistic Chennels and
Lott 'French') was, of course, proverbial. His indiscriminate collector's mania is criticised. His unoccupied study is described as
something between a taxidermist's shop and a hall of curiosities,
packed as it was with the Khedive's stuffed game and mechanical
toys and automata.[53] Ismail's women, it is often implied, were more
discriminate in their acculturation, adopting only those Western
commodities which could be adapted to the traditional way of life.
A decade after Lott (that is in the 1870s) visitors to the Viceregal
Palaces were entertained *á la Franque.* Meals were served at a table
and the use of cutlery was *de rigueur.* But the older *kadins* and

odaliks preferred the *divans* and some were seen to squat on the Khedive's expensive Louis XVIII chairs and eat, nonchalantly, with their fingers.[54]

Items of furniture, even towards the First World War were, characteristically collapsible and easily movable from one place to another. Bedsteads were very rarely used outside the biggest urban establishments and the bedding piled up in built-in cupboards during the day-time. There were hardly any closets, chests or cabinets.[55] The interior of the *haremliks* was, then, one open homogenised unit of work and leisure. Moreover, the entire *haremlik* was visible to visitors. The homogenised space facilitated the regulation of the activities of the women and, at the same time, encouraged sociability. Western furniture may have been adopted by the rich, but the departmentalisation of the house into dining, sleeping and 'work' areas was resisted.

In *Turkey of the Ottomans*, Garnett describes a provincial *haremlik* of the Young Turk period. Her account of the women's quarters is probably the most detailed that we have. It is, also, remarkably impersonal. Having described the entrance and separate courtyard and garden of the *haremlik*, she notices the separate *kahve ocak* (coffee-hearth) and kitchen (in Turkish houses generally an outbuilding) then devotes her attention to the living quarters:

> A wide staircase leads from the entrance floor to the upper-hall, the centre of which is generally occupied by a spacious anteroom, on which other apartments open. In some of the older houses the *divanhane*, or principal reception room, contains a large alcove, the floor of which is raised above a foot above the level of the rest of the apartment. A low divan furnishes its three sides, and its most comfortable corner is the *hanum's* habitual seat. If the *divanhane* has not such a recess, one end and half the two adjoining wings of the room are usually occupied by a continuous sofa, and the fourth is furnished with a marbletopped console table surmounted by a mirror and candelabra, and flanked on either side by shelves in niches, containing rose-water sprinklers, sherbet goblets, and other ornamental objects . . . A few framed *yftas*, or texts from the Koran, may be seen on the walls, but pictures are, generally, conspicuous by their absence . . . Each room contains a large cupboard, built into the wall, in which the bedding is piled during the day, and at night the slaves come in, when summoned, to make up the beds on the floor.

Other bedroom furniture in the shape of washstands, dressing-tables, and wardrobes is dispensed with as superfluous [private *hammams* are common][56]

'Such a mansion', Garnett summarises, ' . . . may be found in every provincial town.'[57] In the 'modern' houses, especially in the suburbs of Istanbul, European furniture is usually adopted but 'the disposal of the rooms is naturally that best suited to Osmanli customs'.[58] Note the emphasis on the sparseness of the interior of the *haremlik*. The spaciousness and simplicity of the divan were the very opposite of the density of the crowded Edwardian drawing-room with its 'superfluity' of furniture and decorative items (and that 'superfluity' is, actually, implied in the last paragraph). For Garnett, as for a few other writers, the 'simplicity' and 'sparseness' of the women's material surroundings stood for inner, spiritual qualities. Duff-Gordon noted after a visit to a dilapidated house near Luxor that the interior of the Arab abode causes Europeans to change their notions of gentility and respectability.[59]

The women's quarters were a gregarious place. The group counted more than the individual. Despite seclusion, the private and public parts of women's lives were not as easily distinguishable as in the West. Every harem was connected with other harems in a close-knit net of social activities. The *divanhane*, or central reception hall, was open to all (female) comers. Relatives, neighbours, women vendors and artists (dancers and story-tellers were most popular in the *haremliks*) habitually dropped in for a free meal, a chat or for business. The sociability of harem life evinced itself in the architecture of the women's quarters. The *divanhane* opened up to smaller rooms, or apartments, officially belonging to certain individuals but, in fact, open to *all*. Rooms did not have specific and well-defined functions, but were all-purpose chambers.[60] The *divan* was a workshop, a dining-area, a reception-hall and a recreation room, all in one. In upper-class harems smaller sections of the house served as sleeping and storage quarters. In the poorer households women and children slept in the *divan*. A greater contrast to the Western middle-class abode can hardly be imagined.

Domesticity precluded privacy. Indeed the very notion of privacy was, to Middle Eastern women, incomprehensible and strange. The thing travellers resented most was the suffocating 'club-like' atmosphere of the *haremlik*. Lott and Chennels had difficulties in finding and adjusting keys to the doors of their rooms. Both locked themselves in their apartments to the amazement of the entire palace. The more discreet Anne Blunt had a servant wake her up whenever a member of the household of Ibn-Rashid, ruler of Jabal Shammar in Northern Arabia, in whose Ksar she and Blunt stayed, approached her door.[61] It is revealing that once 'safe' in the privacy of their rooms, the travellers devoted themselves to their journals. Journal-keeping was *de rigueur* to the serious Victorian traveller. And journal, or log-keeping is, of course, a private and highly individualised activity of the self. Writing a journal was a statement of the Western, middle-class identity.

The sociability of life in the *haremlik* had another and, to the Victorians, more 'positive' side: the mixing together of women of different classes, different age-groups and, usually, different races. For seclusion was not the only form of physical and social segregation known to middle-class Englishwomen. They were accustomed to the separation between children and adults and between masters and servants. The barriers of class and culture were typically crossed in those sections of the house where the two 'segregated' groups, middle-class children and the servants, met and interacted.[62]

Physical segregation ran counter to the very logic of the harem-system, based as it was on racial and social intermixture and upward mobility. Certainly etiquette was religiously observed in the urban harems. And hierarchy existed in most *haremliks*. But the class-conscious, nineteenth-century travellers could distinguish between class and temporary status, and they did see that the *haremlik* was typified by the second, not the first. The female community was 'democratic' in the sense that it offered opportunity to individuals regardless of class or colour. Indeed, Muslim society as a whole was not race or color conscious. Lucie Duff-Gordon reports, with evident relish, how Seleem Effendi, *mahon* (her term, or local magistrate) of Luxor, came one day into her house, begging for some olives craved by his pregnant slave girl.

I [said the Mahon] might have some and forgive the request, as I, of course, knew that a man must beg or even steal for a woman under these circumstances. I called Omar [her servant] and said, 'I trust there are olives for the honourable Hareem of Seleem Effendi – they are needed there'. Omar instantly understood the case, and 'praise be to God a few are left . . . ' And then we belaboured Seleem with compliments. 'Please God the child will be fortunate to thee', say I. Omar says, 'Sweeten my mouth, oh

Effendi, for did I not tell thee God would give thee good out of this affair when thou boughtest her?' *while we were thus rejoicing over the possible little mulatto,* I thought how shocked a white Christian gentleman of our Colonies would be at our conduct to make all this fuss about a black girl – 'he give her sixpence' 'he'd see her d——d first', and my heart warmed to the kind old Muslim sinner as he took his saucer of olives and walked with them openly in his hand along the street. (my emphasis)[63]

Gordon is unsurpassable. And she clearly enjoys shocking the Empire-loving audience. But what she so blatantly states, numerous other writers describe in a less direct manner, or merely imply at: in many senses the Muslim Middle East is more equal, certainly more humane, than the Christian West.

Slaves and children are visible in the representations of the *haremlik* – especially slaves. They are not confined to their dormitories 'downstairs', nor to the background. Georgian and Circassian slave girls, Nubians and – to the astonishment of many a Victorian – even black manual workers, mingle freely with their mistresses. Indeed, most visitors to the harems failed to distinguish between slaves and freewomen. The custom among Ottoman women in the high-harems was, on special occasions, to display their own jewels on their slaves appearing, themselves, very simply attired. Early travellers in particular mistook slaves for their mistresses and there are quite a few examples to this *trompe d'oeil* in the writings of Pardoe, Vane and, later in the century, Paine and Chennels.[64] Certainly, in the harems of the élite etiquette strictly forbade intercourse between menial workers (normally blacks) and the *odaliks* (Circassians and Georgians and, sometimes, Nubians). Sophia Lane Poole notices that black slaves were not allowed past their dormitories and the outer apartments.[65] During receptions they did not enter the *divan*, but stood at the hallway, separated from the *odaliks* and *kadins*. Lane Poole referred to Mehmet Ali's traditional house at Ksar ed-Dubarak, which she visited sometime in 1842. There is evidence from some of her successors that by the time of the reign of Ismail Pasha, etiquette was not at all as rigid as in the days of the Albanian founder of the dynasty. Indeed, 'white slaves and black were mingled indiscriminately', 'disgusting looking negresses' mixing with fair-skinned Circassians.[66] Yet, throughout the whole of the nineteenth century, travellers emphasise the symbolic meaning of the *physical* place occupied by individuals in the *haremlik*. In the high, Ottoman style harems the physical place of a person, the position and posture of the body (whether a woman receives guests reclining on a *divan*, or a sofa, or sitting upright, or standing up) and her propinquity to, or distance from, other women, signified status. The travellers painstakingly 'deciphered' the signs, faithfully transmitting them to their readers. It was quite conventional to describe women of the highest rank – usually actual members of the Imperial and Viceregal families – reclining or lying down in bed. And, often, an illness or an indisposition is attributed to them – apparently an outward sign of dignity and respectability. Esma Sultan lies down 'indisposed' when Pardoe pays her respects to her. Nazli Hanîm, notorious daughter of Mehmet Ali, rarely seen by visitors (but fictionalised by quite a few of them) is convalescing from an illness when Lane Poole sees her. Lott interviews the Khedive's mother and his *odaliks* who appear to be 'indisposed'.[67] As a rule, *immobility* is emphasised and, often, idealised. It is associated with an inner tranquility, good-breeding and harmony with one's surroundings. It is revealing that Ottoman women who are represented picturesquely while immobile, are ridiculed when they move, especially out of doors.

Anne Blunt, with an unfailing eye for the grotesque, indirectly criticises the European tendency to idealise inactivity. In *Pilgrimage to Nejd* she reports a real conversation (a version of an earlier transcript in her journal) between herself and the women of a branch of the family of Emir Ibn Rashid, at Ha'il. 'I should die if I did nothing. When I am at home I always walk round the first thing in the morning to look at my horses. How do you manage to spend your lives? Zeh: We sit. Thus supreme contentment in the harim [sic] here is to sit in absolute idleness.' 'It seems odd', adds the hyperactive Blunt, 'where the men are so active and adventurous, that the women should be satisfied to be bored; but such, I suppose, is the tyranny of fashion.' Her interviewees, it seems, pity the restless Blunt in the same way that a group of articulate *odaliks* pities the peripatetic, unveiled Caroline Paine. The lot of the mobile European, these *odaliks* observe, is not to be envied.[68]

Outside the high-harems slaves, regardless of race or colour, are conspicuous. They mingle freely with their mistresses and even with visitors. So much so, in fact, that quite a few tourists – instinctively making the analogue between the slave in the Muslim household and the British house-maid – thought the former too impertinent and her behaviour 'improper'. Slaves appear chattering, rudely inspecting newcomers, idling or playing. And references to strict discipline, exploitation and needless to say cruelty towards *domestic* slaves are so rare and far between that they do not signify.[69]

Children – new-born babies, infants and small children – of both sexes are ubiquitous. The very visibility of children is meaningful. For in contemporary descriptions of the British middle-class house, children are invisible. To be sure, the domestic novel is *about* the family, but typically it is about adult men and women. Children and infants, like servants, are confined to the back stage, or the nurseries 'upstairs'. The appearance of children in the common, public rooms is timed and regulated. Figuratively speaking, children were banished from the middle-class parlour, or the drawing room. In the *divan*, children are conspicuous and noticed by virtually *all* travellers. In the households of the great, the middling-classes and in those of the poor, children show up unexpectedly and are 'shown off'. They participate in public, ceremonial activities. More significant, children are taken care of in public. They are washed and dressed, spoken and sung to, played with and fed. And – to the horror of many a visitor – children eat with adults, 'adult' food. Infants, like the anoretic women, were not allowed to the Victorian dining-table.

Almost every writer from Montagu onwards was impressed by the warmth of Eastern mothers, especially Turkish women, to their children. On the whole, the Middle Eastern family is presented as a *child-oriented* family.[70] There are very many remarks about lack of discipline and indulgence towards children.[71] These remarks reveal a great deal about the commentators themselves, and their views regarding proper education. Yet even those writers who were openly hostile to the harem-system were affected and even moved by the kind of mother-and-child relationships they witnessed in the *haremlik*. Emmeline Lott is a good example, precisely because of her ambivalence towards the Muslim family and Muslim women. The following are extracts from a long description of a daily ritual in the Viceregal palace: putting the children to bed. Lott, uncharacteristically sensitively, captures the group of wives, *odaliks*, children and slaves, in their most intimate moments:

As soon as he [Ibrahim Pasha, her pupil and Ismail's son from the second kadin] was dressed in his night-clothes a silver brazier filled with charcoal, was brought into the room. In it was thrown a quantity of wood of aloes, aromatic gum and lumps of crystallised sugar. Then the head-nurse lifted up his Highness in her powerful arms, and swung him round her nine times, while she counted that number aloud in Turkish; but why that number was used I was unable to learn. After this she exclaimed, *Allah! Allah! Bismillah!* The same ceremony was performed by each of the other nurses with their Highnesses the little princesses; then they were laid down in their bed. The nurses then took it in turns to repeat stories, or else sang himself and his sisters to sleep; their everlasting monotonous chant consisting of Baba, Ni-na! Baba, Ni-Na! 'father, mother'; Ni-na Ni-na! . . . All the nurses sat at the side of the beds, or else at the door. Those who were not engaged in telling stories were employed at needle work, which they executed with their left hand, until they retired to rest . . .

She then movingly describes the crowd of sleeping adults and children:

Above the whole of that most motley group which was assembled together *in the Reception Hall*, hung suspended an enormous large coloured muslin mosquito-curtain, made in the form of a *canopy*, similar to that which is daily seen carried in *Catholic countries* over the head of the dignitary . . . when the *Host* is being carried to a dying person. Attached to the four corners of the square flat top piece were sewn four large gilt rings, through each was fastened to the large brass hooks that were driven into the walls . . . the long end hanging down to the floor and being tucked underneath the mattresses, left the whole group of children and nurses snugly ensconced within its ample folds. A larger silver-gilt lantern, containing two lighted transparent wax – candles, as long as those used by mourners in Catholic countries. (my emphasis)[72]

There is a very similar, almost exchangeable description in Rogers' *Domestic Life in Palestine*. Rogers actually shared the *divan* with entire harem of Mahmud Bey 'Abd al Hadi. She too is deeply moved by the warmth and intimacy of the scene she is describing and the feminine camaraderie of the harem.[73] Note that Lott refers, several times, to Catholic practices (the candles, religious processions, the Host). And at the end of the passage quoted above she mentions that at ten o'clock the outer doors of the *haremlik* are bolted by the eunuchs and that the whole household prepares for the 'Great Silence', until dawn.[74] Now the analogy with the convent is transparent. Indeed it is explicitly made by Lott herself in three other places and often appears in the writings of other travellers. The rule of silence in the high harems during meals is likened to the silence observed by the contemplative religious orders; the *yashmak* itself evokes the nun's veil; finally, the very régime of abstinence from sex, enforced on the majority of slaves (in the more populous households), is compared with the celibate lives of nuns.

If the *odalik* is likened to the *religieuse*, we have travelled a long way from the Augustan writers.

WOMEN AT WORK: THE *HAREMLIK* AS A WORK PLACE

The image of the harem as an organic community and a productive, self-sufficient unit, could not be complete without the representation of women at work, or the discussion of women's work. In eastern Mediterranean countries, especially outside the cities, working women were visible, even to the passing tourist. 'Visible' had two meanings. Women worked in public places: in markets, in the fields, in workshops and even in factories. Working women usually did not veil themselves and their faces were exposed to the public gaze. (In Muslim tradition the female face is the most seductive, hence the most covered part in a woman's body.) There is abundant evidence that the veil was donned in the urban centres and that *fallahin* and Bedouin women appeared in public unveiled. Examples of descriptions of women at work can be multiplied. Mary Mackintosh writes about peasants in Syria during harvest and grape-harvest and lists seven kinds of work, carried on by men and women or exclusively by women, like threshing and winnowing.[75] Charles Warren refers to women artisans in Jerusalem.[76] Elisabeth Ann Finn represents washerwomen 'wrangling and bargaining'.[77] Travellers sailing between Luxor and the First Cataract were regularly accosted by women vendors and by children, offering the local produce of villages and cheap souvenirs.[78] Pleasure-seeking travellers had contacts with dancing-women, the equivalent of prostitutes.[79] There is also scattered reference to factory-work, in the sugar refineries of the Khedive Ismail and in the Sultans' factories, in and around Istanbul. Pardoe opens her chapter on the 'progress of Turkish industry' with a description of women piece-workers employed by the Imperial Fez Manufactory at Ayoub, where fezs for the entire Ottoman army were made. The manufactory, probably the biggest in the Middle East, employed as early as 1836 some 3,500 workers, a little of one-seventh of them women. Significantly men were employed as wage labourers, on the factory's premises, while women did piece-work in their own homes. A coarse fez fetched the equivalent of a shilling and capes of fine quality brought seventeen pence the piece. Pardoe marvels at the sight of 500 piece workers awaiting in a separate women's hall the delivery of material.[80] Quite conventionally she singles out in the crowd a few national types:

> As we passed the threshold a most curious scene presented itself. About five hundred females were collected together in the vast hall, awaiting the delivery of wool which they were to knit, and a more extraordinary group could not perhaps be found in the world . . . the Turkess with her Yashmac folded closely over her face . . . the Greek woman . . . with a scarf . . . the Armenian, with her dark bright eyes flashing from under the jealous screen of her carefully arranged veil . . . [81]

Seclusion is extended from the home, to the factory. Note that Pardoe focuses on the veils of women workers, not on their bodies, describing degrees of segregation and concealment. Women enter the factory by a separate entrance. They are hired only to do piece-work and even the Christians don the veil.

There is nothing out of the ordinary in representations of the urban poor, or of *fallahin* at work. What may appear quite extraordinary is the image of upper-class women as workers. The Turkish-Circassian *hanim* and *odalik* are depicted not as the consumers of luxury goods, but as producers and the harem is elevated to an industrial community. Emmeline Lott itemises the daily chores of the inmates of the *haremlik* at Cezirah and even Lott, who was obsessed with cleanliness and order, devotes a few passages to the Khedive's laundry, operated by his *odaliks* and their slaves. The following is a typical description of a wash day.

> On the floor a square piece of matting was laid down, and a large piece of calico as big as two ordinary sheets was placed over it. Kneeling down on it were eight slaves with two rolling-pins, similar in length and thickness, not an inch larger than those used by cooks for making pastry. After having first damped the pieces of washing, they folded them, then rolled them right round of the rolling-pins, which they laid down upon the sheet, and with the

other rolling-pin in their hands, they kept rolling the end of it. For they held it straight up in their hands like a stick against the other one round which they twisted the linen. This process, which they called mangling, being finished, the German maid began ironing H. H. the Viceroy's and the Grand-Pasha's body linen. At eleven-o'clock the Lady Paramount (H. H. the first wife), [sic] under whose superintendence the whole of the household arrangements were carried on, entered the laundry . . . She was both sleeveless and stockingless; but her feet were encased in a pair of polished wooden clogs, standing as it were upon the two wooden bridges like the strings of a fiddle. The parts on which she rested her feet were lined in velvet, the ties were the same materials, and the clogs were studded with silver headed nails. Her hair hanging loosely about, was tucked under the handkerchief round her head.[82]

Lott's description of the Viceroy's first *kadin* at work is quite different from Pardoe's oblique representation of working-class piece-workers. The very choice of ritual washing is meaningful. For, as argued earlier, (see Chapter 4), the Victorians associated washing and cleanliness with the purity of the body. Washerwomen – invariably working-class women, sometimes reformed prostitutes – could be sexually threatening. Moreover, while Pardoe obliterates the body of the worker, Lott emphasises somatic detail. And she chooses to fix on exposed parts which in contemporary discourse symbolised sensuality: a stockingless, shoeless foot, an uncovered arm, etc. However, she tames the potentially sexual by reference to items of dress and the exasperatingly long description of the wooden clogs (they were used in the *hammam*). Lott, then, used work both as a metaphor for sexuality and a trope of domesticity.

Evidently work in the harems of the élite was not functional, but ritual. Other writers like Pardoe, Vane and Dawson-Damer refer to various domestic chores, from the tending to children, to patching, embroidering and sewing. Dawson-Damer describes the 'silk worms manufactory' in the palace of Shami Bey, secretary to Mehmet Ali. Shami Bey's *odaliks* tend the silk worms and specialise in manufacturing raw-silk.[83] I do not doubt that the representation of the *odalik* as a worker is rhetoric and ideological and that there was a great deal of idleness in the upper-class houses. The palaces of the Khedive Ismail were anything but houses of industry. Indeed, they may serve as examples to the uncontrolled consumption of Western goods in a pre-modern, pre-industrial society. The domestication of work and its association with the high-harems served the need to normalise Middle Eastern sexuality. The writers of the second half of the nineteenth century came from an industrial society in which the home and the work-place had long been separated and the middle-class woman had ceased to play a productive, economic role. Even more significant than the social, economic context is the ideological aspect of the dichotomy of the symbolic home and the work-place. The two symbolic *loci* of the home and the factory represented opposing poles of purity and sensuality. By introducing work to the harem Victorian writers domesticated sexuality and contributed towards the normalisation and humanisation of popular images. The busy *odaliks* who rise at five in the morning to say their prayers, before starting the round of household chores, are not unlike ordinary housewives. The 'Lady Paramount' is comparable to the *bourgeoise* who supervises the servants. Mary Lucy Garnett, writing in the early 1890s, reminded her readers that the *topos* of the indolent concubine 'reclining on a *divan*, eating sweets or playing with jewels' was obsolete.[84] It was erroneous to suppose that 'an Osmali woman of the better class has no duties or occupations beyond a certain amount of servile attendance to her blue-beard of a husband . . . the *hanim* is very domesticated and no accomplishments are so very much appreciated in a marriageable maiden as proficiency in domestic arts.'[85]

The *haremlik* of the Victorians is not merely a physical place, but an ideal and symbolic one. The realistically depicted Middle Eastern home is reconstructed in the image of the monogamous, middle-class abode. And there is no doubt that the writers understate, or prefer to ignore, altogether, the obvious political and sexual aspects of seclusion and polygamy. The few testimonies of upper-class Egyptian and Ottoman women that came down to us, represent an altogether different picture.[86] Notwithstanding, it was precisely the usage of Western gender ideology that made it possible for even a Turkophobe like Lott to appropriate the exotic and ultimately normalise it. For if the concubine is likened to a house-wife, or to a celibate *religieuse*, that concubine is the same as the middle-class lady – the image of the West rather than its 'other'.

Part III

Evangelising the Orient: Women's Work and the Evolution of Evangelical Ethnography

6

Evangelical Travel and the Evangelical Construction of Gender

How you'd exult if I could put you back
Six hundred years, blot out cosmogony,
Geology, ethnology, what not
(Greek endings, each the little passing bell
That signifies some faith's about to die),
And set you square with Genesis again.
Robert Browning, Bishop Blouram's Apology.

He has but to print his prophetic sermons and bind them in lilac and gold, and they will adorn the drawing-room table of all evangelical ladies, who will regard as a sort of pious 'light reading' the demonstration that the prophecy of the locusts whose sting in their tail is fulfilled in the fact of the Turkish commander's having taken a horse's tail for his standard, and that the French are the very frogs predicted in the Revelations.[1]
George Eliot on John Cumming, the premillenarian preacher.

The religious journey, the oldest and culturally most acceptable mode of travel for women was, also, the one to survive longest. It persisted down to the twentieth century. Indeed the concept and popular image of the pilgrimage, as well as actual travel to the Holy Places, had a revival during the second half of the nineteenth century. Of course, the concept of the religious journey still retained some of its original medieval associations. A pilgrimage was a physical journey to shrines and sepulchres where the sacred *relicia*,

165

or remains of Christ or the saints, were prayed to. 'Pilgrimage' still signified the *peregrinatio por christo* that is: a life in *this* world, which is devoted to Christ and which is appropriate to Christian men and women. In Britain after the Reformation, the progress of the pilgrim became a popular allegory to the spiritual development of man. And in a still wider and entirely secular sense, the pilgrimage came to be a metaphor for the quest of the individual for a truth, or a meaning in a godless and meaningless world. Among the most famous pilgrimages to the Orient, Burton's voyage to Meccah and Wilfrid Blunt's journey to Nejd in central Arabia present the best examples of the secular Romantic quest.[2]

Notwithstanding, Victorian religious travel and the religious travelogue depart from the early model in several ways. The changes in the Christian experience are related to the influence of evangelicalism on Victorian men and women, particularly to the so-called 'feminisation of religion' in the nineteenth century.[3] It is significant that the development of the new, non-academic orientalist sciences coincided with the feminisation of philanthropic work in the Middle East (see Chapter 1). Missionary work attracted women because it combined a gender-specific, Christian way of life with degrees of freedom denied to the Christian woman in the West. The Middle East was doubly attractive. Unlike Africa, or China, or the Indian sub-continent, the eastern Mediterranean was part of Western religious culture. Palestine and Syria, to repeat Raymond Schwab's expression, were 'inside the Western room'.[4] The Scriptures and the landscape of the two countries were rich with examples of Christian womanhood. In fact the Orient, as we shall see, more than any other part of the world, provided historical models of Christian feminine conduct and life.

In what follows I focus on the feminine aspects of evangelical travel and work, then discuss the evolution of evangelical ethnography devoted to the study of domestic life in Palestine and Syria and the description of Biblical landscapes. I do realise, however, that the women's experience cannot be separated from the general interest in the Judeo-Christian Mediterranean (as distinguished from the Muslim Orient). So the gender specific experience is considered in its relation to two cross-fertilising developments in Victorian religion: the evangelical construction of femininity and the revival of millenarian evangelicalism. A few more words concerning my (latitudinarian) usage of the key-word in this part of the book. 'Evangelical' and 'evangelicalism' – both spelt with a small 'e' –

are applied inclusively, rather than in an exclusive manner and denote forms of vital religion inside the established Church and outside it. When capitalised, the terms specifically denote people or organisations in the COE.[5]

Evangelical religion had profound and complex influences on the life and world-view of women. For evangelicalism sharply gendered society and distinguished 'femininity' from 'masculinity' and redefined the relations between a Christian home – identified as a feminine sphere – and the masculine world. The notion of the un-Christian or nominally Christian world was applied to groups outside the middle classes: the aristocracy, or the urban poor. But more important to us, the religious notion of difference or exteriority expanded during the age of colonial expansion. The empire was multi-racial and non-Christian. Indeed in the imperialist rhetoric religion was often used to justify domination over non-Europeans.[6] Christian Western culture was, it was argued, superior to non-Western, non-Christian ones. The heathens, the apostates (a category more appropriate to Muslims, or Jews) and the non-regenerate, that is non-protestant Christians, deserved to be reformed and converted, like the poor.

The ideology that stressed domesticity at the same time encouraged women to move away from the home and into the 'world'. A 'religion of the heart', a practical religion that placed service and manners before doctrine, evangelicalism exalted characteristics which were considered as naturally feminine. It stressed emotion, self-sacrifice and service to others. But as Leonore Davidoff and Catherine Hall argue, evangelical literature increasingly stressed the flexibility of the relations between the spheres, their 'negotiability'. Woman's moral superiority, her generic spirituality, the very qualities that had made her the custodian of the 'home', qualified her as a social and religious reformer.[7] The missions, as I later show, emphasised the role of women in the moral reform of the Middle East.[8] The key to the spiritual regeneration of the Ottoman Empire seemed to be in the harem.

But evangelical ideology alone does not explain the appeal of Palestine. It is precisely here that gender specific aspects and more general ones converge. Central to all brands of evangelicalism is the status of the Scriptures as a revealed text to be read and interpreted literally. Literal Biblism, as was recently argued, led to the emergence of a brand of millenarianism, commonly known as pre-millenarianism and characteristic of groups inside the COE.

Evangelicals, but particularly the pre-millenarists, read Biblical texts not as myths, or allegories, or merely stories, but as the living words of God. Equal emphasis was put on all parts of the Scriptures, on the historical parts as well as the richly symbolical texts of the prophecies. Indeed the very term *millennium* was interpreted literally.[9] The conversion of the Jews, prophesised in the book of Daniel and the Revelation, was perceived as a prerequisite to the universal spiritual awakening and the *millennium* which would precede the second Advent of Christ. Clearly the idea of the mission is central to pre-millenarianism. The regeneration of the Jews, or of oriental non-Protestant Christians, should occur before millennial times and precipitate the awakening of the Orient.[10]

Evangelicals had only a limited interest in Muslims. First because, as Albert Hourani pointed out, in the Christian cosmology and history there was no place for a third revealed religion.[11] Islam is not mentioned in the Scriptures, hence was easy to write out of the providential scheme of history. And the tendency to exclude the Muslim world and Muslim history from the Western *Weltanschauung* is particularly manifested in those branches of evangelicalism which emphasised the prophecy. The second reason for the lack of interest in Muslims is one of expediency. The proselytisation of Muslim Ottoman subjects was prohibited by law and punishable by death. Even the conversion of indigenous Christians (to protestantism) was made legal only in 1851. The main Evangelical missions directed their efforts at the Eastern churches and the Jews. The Church Missionary Society took over southern Syria and Palestine. And the London Jews Society (LJS), founded in 1809, worked exclusively for Jews. However, smaller organisations for the propagation of female education attracted Muslims and Christians alike. The middle-decades of the century were the heyday of philanthropic and proselytising activity. Small missions, like the Scottish Mission, the Baptist Mission and the Women's Society for Promoting Female Education in the East, together with a plethora of voluntary associations, also entered the field and competed with the larger organisations over the souls of the unregenerate.

Biblical literalism and the efforts to corroborate the status of Scriptures as revealed texts precipitated certain changes in the approach to Palestine as a geographical and historical place. The Holy Land came to be perceived as the actual *locus* of sacred events in the past and of prophesied millennial occurrences. The landscape itself was a sacred text[12] to be read and interpreted literally, rather than allegorically or symbolically. Nature – organic and inorganic, the *flora* and *fauna* of Palestine, customs and manners *and* the inhabitants of the country – were treated as illustrations to the veracity of the Scriptures. Travel itself, the pilgrimage to the Holy Places,[13] became a weapon with which to fight skepticism, the new Biblical criticism, Positivism and, from the 1870s, Darwinism. Travel, indeed, became a substitute for study or theoretical knowledge. To actually be in Palestine was to verify and authenticate the Word of God. Seeing the places where Christ had lived, was believing in him. Examples to the resistance to the new criticism and the dangers of science are legion and may be found in the works of men and women alike. The greatest Biblical archaeologists of the century, notably Edward Robinson, read the land and local place-names as Biblical texts unchanged from the times of the Patriarchs or the Prophets. But the access to the Scriptures and the licence to interpret them literally had special appeal to women, precisely because faith in the Word did not depend on formal education.

As is the case with harem literature, so with religious writing by women, experience has precedence over formal study and scientific authority. Take, for instance, the writings on the eastern Mediterranean of Frances Power Cobbe. Cobbe (1822–1908), an Evangelical turned agnostic, philanthropist, feminist and one of the first proponents in Britain of education and employment for women, first published her series of impressionistic vignettes on Mediterranean travel in the *Fortnightly Review* (1862) then in a book entitled *Cities of the Past*. According to Cobbe, travel is the only means to a comprehension of and identification with Christian history because travel diminishes the two hindrances that prevent an understanding of authentic (that is, early) Christianity: geographical distance and the distance in time.

> Hitherto, in especial between us and the prophets and apostles of the Bible, there has intervened both a natural and a fictitious distance: there has been the natural and inevitable distance of both place and time – a place remote from us by thousands of miles and a time composed by so many centuries, that we continually lose our consciousness of the perspective of the earlier ages . . . Infinite have been the mistakes, and woeful the mischief, which have been risen from this source both as regarding the men themselves and the books they have bequeathed to us; and few labours will tend more to hasten the progress

of religious thought than the removal of such misconceptions. Among the best means by which this may be accomplished is the nullifying of the perspective of space by familiarising to ourselves the actual scene of the Bible story, while we strive to neutralise that of Time . . . How much this familiarity with sacred localities will effect towards bringing closer to us the great souls who once inhabited them, may be seen by comparing works like those of Stanley with the sacred biographies common in the beginning of the century.[14]

What Cobbe is actually offering is a de-historicisation of Palestine and a diminishing of the perspective of time. To 'nullify' time and 'neutralise' it, to 'diminish distance' (her very words) practically is to mythologise the Middle East and recreate it as a changeless place outside history, the *locus* of peoples who had not developed since Biblical times, or the life-time of Christ. Learning by travel is, according to Cobbe, an individual and personal process, an experience accessible to all, but specifically beneficial to women. Significantly the paragraph quoted above follows an exhortation to 'ladies' to travel to Palestine on their own, 'unprotected' and untrammeled by social restrictions. Only in this way can they recover faith and study the land. Anyone, anywhere, regardless of sex, class or education

can for himself narrow the distance between him and the great souls of the past by visiting the land where they dwelt and so cutting off, at least the *perspective of place* which adds not a little to the effect of the perspective of time. Walking where they walked, living in the same kind of houses, with the same sort of flowers and trees and animals around us, the same food and wine, the same soft sky overhead by day, and southern stars and night, the same names of hill, and grove, and fountain echoing in our ear.[15]

About the same time as Cobbe's vignettes appeared Elizabeth Charles Rundle's *Wanderings over Bible Lands and Seas* (1862). Like Cobbe, Charles came from an Evangelical background though she was never the victim of doubt and skepticism. And like Cobbe she addressed large audiences. Charles was one of Britain's top-spelling Evangelical novelists and her *Chronicles of the Schönberg Cotta Family* (1863) – a historical tale about the Reformation in

Germany – was translated into all European languages, Arabic and a number of Indian dialects. Charles consciously seeks to authenticate the Scriptures and promote faith by travel to the Holy Land. 'This is', she notes complacently, 'the true undying interest of travelling in the Holy Land . . . we feel sure it was such a house and surrounding scene of plain and sea and rock [which] the apostles trod.'[16] The very progress through the familiar domesticated landscape is reassuring and comforting. The same point is taken in and hammered down by later writers like Augusta Cook, one of the CMS's most industrious hacks. The prolific Cook produced a barrage of 2d (two penny) tracts on the prophetic texts and guides to the Holy Land. Her works have characteristic emblematic titles like: *The Divine Calendar or Studies of the Revelation* or; *Light Ahoy: Prophecies on Daniel and Revelation With an Israelite Standpoint*, etc. *By Way of the East*, published in 1908, begins:

> One of the first questions I was asked on my return from the East was whether what I had seen and heard in the Holy Land . . . verified Scripture or otherwise.

Cook never even had the shadow of a doubt:

> I unhesitatingly replied that the fact which had struck me the most was the wonderful verification of God's word. All along our Eastern path we found it written whether in stone or monument – on hill or dale – in customs that have survived the passing ages.[17]

Cook's is a rather vulgarised version on the narratives of earlier millenarian travellers. Yet not only pre-millenarians, but critics of evangelical eschatology and Biblical literalism sometimes read the landscape and used their own experience of Palestine as a substitute for theoretical 'learning'. One revealing example is Harriet Martineau's attitude to 'Palestine and its Faith' (the title of the third part of her *Eastern Life*). Martineau was more qualified than most travellers to opinionate on the Bible and Biblical criticism. Coming from a Unitarian, Priestlian background, she was specially placed to look at the Scriptures as historical, rather than revealed texts. She was – by the time of her voyage to the East – acquainted with the more popular writings of the New-Hegelian Bible critics (it is certain that she had read Strauss's *Leben Jesu*) and the works of the better known Biblical archaeologists. But she regards the individual experience of the East as superior to theoretical – literary and philological – inquiry.

> the new and astonishing sense of the familiarity of his [Christ's] teachings – a thing which we declare and protest about at home, but can never adequately feel – brought me nearer to an insight and understanding of what I had known by heart from my infancy.[18]

Emphasis on the spiritual and educational value of travel and depreciation of academic (male) education were not mandates for feminine emotionalism. And even the evangelical religion of the heart does not licence enthusiasm. Indeed, most writers are careful not to be bracketed as 'enthusiasts'. They avoid emotional excesses and when they witness them, deplore the uncontrolled emotionalism of pilgrims or travellers. Emotional excesses in women pilgrims are singled out and, sometimes, condemned. Mary Eliza Rogers, Harriet Martineau and Adella Goodrich Freer lampoon the enthusiasm of Latin and Greek women in sacred places. Martineau ridicules the Russians. Even devout travellers like Charles and Egerton criticise the simplemindedness of those believers who sheepishly follow local *Ciceronii*, whose prejudice and ignorance were – to the informed tourists – proverbial. Excesses in English women are particularly lamented.[19] The writers must have been aware of the criticism on evangelicalism as a 'ladies' religion'. Women were thought to be specially susceptible to the allures of Bibliotary and eschatology. I particularly have in mind George Eliot's critique in her review on the works of the millenarian preacher Cumming: 'ladies [believing] that the prophecy of the locusts whose sting in their tail is fulfilled in the fact of the Turkish commander's having taken a horse's tail for his standard, and that the French are the very frogs predicted in the Revelations.'[20]

It is the stress on personal experience, an individual familiarity with the *locus realis* of Christian history (and eschatology), which explains why the new branches of amateur science connected with the Bible and Palestine attracted so many women. As the prosopography of travel shows, women were conspicuous in the fields of Biblical archaeology and 'scientific' field archaeology, the latter conventionally dated from 1901, the year of Sir Flinders Petrie's first scientific digging at Tel-el-Hesi, using stratigraphy and periodisation by classification of pottery. Women, it shall be recalled, are well represented on the contributors' lists of the Palestine and Egypt Exploration Funds, in both of which they average 30 per cent of the subscribers. The appeal of the new societies has to do with their religious character as well as with the ambiguity of status of the new sciences.[21] The PEF is a good example. Despite emphasis on its scientific character and the avoidance of religious controversy, the Fund, especially in its popular publications, left enough room for the travellers and amateur students of the Bible and Biblical history. Thus the Fund's first prospectus frankly states that: 'no country more urgently requires *illustration*. The face of the landscape, the climate, the productions, the manners, dress and modes of life of the inhabitants, differ in so many material respects from those of the western world, that without an accurate knowledge of them'[22] and, most significant, 'even to the more casual traveller in the Holy Land, the Bible becomes, in its form and therefore to some extent in its substance, a new book'.[23] The prospectus repeatedly mentions the writings of Mary Eliza Rogers, perhaps the best observer of customs and manners in mid-century Palestine, and Emily Beaufort, Viscountess Strangford. Beaufort's work on the area between Tyre and Tibnin, in her *Egyptian Sepulchres and Syrian Shrines*, is praised for its ethnographic accuracy.[24]

Women were ethnographers and Biblical archaeologists but not surveyors or (with the exception of Lewis and Gibson) Semitic philologists. They were amateur naturalists – botanists, naturalist painters and entomologists – but not zoologists.[25] Practically all long-time residents in Palestine engaged in 'naturalist' painting, or collected samples of Biblical *flora*. And Britain's two most prominent women naturalists, Marianne North and the entomologist Margaret Fountaine, produced valuable work on Palestine. Travelogues by women abound with verbal and pictorial descriptions of *flora*, whose sole function is to demonstrate knowledge in a generically feminine topic.

The new societies, on their part, were quick to realise the potential in women's work. Thus, Charles Warren, Biblical archaeologist and first surveyor of Jerusalem for the PEF, urges women contributors to help conserve the walls of Jerusalem and carry on the survey of the Holy Land, particularly dear to them.[26] And during the Society's worst financial crisis, in the mid-1870s, Walter Besant appealed to Elisabeth Anne Finn, the staunch millenarian, philosemite and philanthropist, to start a 'ladies' fund' for Palestine, to help out the parent organisation. The Ladies Auxiliary Fund, discussed in Chapter 1, could boast of numerous branches outside London.[27] It was, however, not on the women's auxiliary work in the metropolitan organisation, but on the decentralised, individualised work in the Middle East that the combined influence of evangelical eschatology and the new gender ideology had a decisive effect.

7

The Women of Christ Church: Work, Literature and Community in Nineteenth-Century Jerusalem

WOMEN'S WORK

The work of evangelical women in nineteenth-century Palestine was very much like their work at home: not easily definable; relative to men's work; unpaid and informal.[1] Women's labour in God's vineyard developed outside the metropolitan centres of evangelical politics and therefore was not directly controlled by the bigger missions. The first career missionaries arrived in the Middle East only in 1887, the second generation of proselytisers. Their predecessors, the millenarian evangelisers active in the middle decades of the century, had built the foundations for a 'professional' work. Missionary work, then, manifests the same characteristics as the new specialist work thriving in the new scientific organisations. But unlike these organisations, the British missions were reluctant to employ women. To be sure, there had always been a place for the missionaries' wives or daughters. Single men could easily be corrupted in exotic, permissive societies. So wives served not only as help-mates and home-makers but were bulwarks against temptation.[2] Single women, however, were an altogether different matter. Clearly the evangelical ideology of work in and for, the non-Christian 'world', clashed with the *bourgeois* sense of propriety.

There were women's missions before the 1880s in the Middle

175

East and the Indian sub-continent. The assault on *purdah* and plural marriages was led by the famous *zenana* missions and the missions devoted to female education. But characteristically the early organisations were separatist women's societies. The big metropolitan organisations remained hostile to the ideas of employing women. The CMS, the biggest missionary society, changed its policy only in 1887. The London Jews Society, the second largest organisation in the Middle East, did not have a definite policy. Confusingly the Society did not employ women officially. It appears however that a number of female missionaries were paid by it for work in Palestine in private philanthropic enterprises. A close look at the uneasy relations between the group of women proselytisers and the CMS may throw light on the nature of the female religious career.

Despite its policy not to employ single women, unofficially the CMS did hire female employees who appear on its pay-role as far back as the 1820s. Campaigns to formalise the anomalous position of women, in 1857, 1863 and 1867, failed.[3] The Society's committee repeatedly argued that women were more valuable as spouses and as daughters of missionaries than as independent field workers.[4] Significantly it was from Palestine, from a field-worker at Jaffa (Rev. Langley Hall) that the call came to send off to that country ten women, at their own expense.[5] At the Keswick convention in 1887, women were officially accepted as missionaries. Seventeen single women immediately started off for Palestine, thirteen of them paying their own expenses and one missionary part of the expenses. 'The Lord himself', confesses Eugene Stock, the Society's official historian, quite unashamedly, 'we cannot doubt, was leading the society step by step . . . and so he raised up Christian ladies with private means as pioneers of perhaps the most important development of the work which in recent years we have witnessed.'[6] Obviously. And 'private means' undoubtedly made the women particularly attractive to the committee. Stock, however, hastens to add that women of 'humbler origins' too were allowed to work in the Lord's vineyard. Actually the society even hired one mill-lass from Lancashire.[7]

The increase in the numbers of unmarried professional missionaries is indeed significant. The Handbook of the Society's missions in the East lists 75 single women employed in Palestine between 1887 and 1909.[8] If we look at the distribution of this total figure over decades, the overall trend is very clear. At any time between the two dates, there were more single women than men (married, or single) working for the CMS with a ratio of 20 to 11 in 1894, 29 to 12 in 1894 and 90 to 1 in 1902. For a comparison, the ratio in Persia is 27 to 24 and in Turkish Arabia 11 to 11. The figures do not include missionaries' wives, nor women working directly under the Female Education Society (FES), but on the pay-roll of the CMS.[9]

Even the cautious Stock has to admit that the feminisation of the missions was the most significant change in missionary policy in Palestine. Indeed, the decision to employ females was 'the most conspicuous development in the mission in the Middle East.'[10] The change was not merely one of quantity because the new missionaries were professionals, trained and schooled in the evangelical training centres for women, the 'Willows', or 'Olives', or the Mildmay Deaconesses Institute, founded by the Reverend Pennefather in 1860 and modeled after the famous deaconesses' institute at Kaiserswerth. Moreover, missionaries were now recruited from the new girls' boarding-schools and the women's colleges. Of the 72 missionaries, listed in the handbook on Palestine, 25 received training in the evangelical women's institutes, at Highbury, the 'Willows' and the 'Olives', 5 received training as nurses elsewhere and 5 attended a university.[11] Professionalisation, then, went hand in hand with a formal education of sorts. And that combination distinguishes the new type of missionaries from the earlier, mid-century evangelicals who are the main protagonists in this chapter. Yet despite the change, itself very significant, the case of the CMS is typical and manifests certain continuities. First, is the take-over of small enterprises by the big organisations and the institutionalisation of women's work. Before the take-over by these organisations, women worked individually (or collectively) alongside, rather than for, the missions.

Typically a privately-run institute was merged into the mission after the death, or retirement of the individual, voluntary worker. Thus, Mary Louisa Whately, founder, financier and for over 20 years only manager of the entire network of girls' schools in Egypt, handed over her life-work to the CMS in 1882.[12] In Jerusalem, the famous Jewesses Institute, founded by Caroline Cooper, at whose life and work we shall look later, passed on to the London Jews Society a little before her death. An article in the *Jewish Intelligence*, the official organ of the *LJS* exactly points at the relations between the women proselytisers' work and the metropolitan missions. As already mentioned, the LJS did not officially employed women. And

(like the CMs in Whately's case) grudgingly assisted those individual enterprises which proved economically successful. Cooper,
like Whately, raised funds in Britain, and herself financed the
Institute. 'A fellow labourer and sister in the Lord',[13] Caroline
Cooper certainly was. But 'she undertook her work and carried it
on there [in Palestine] independently, our Society [IJS] being in no
way concerned in it, beyond contributing a sum annually for the
last few years'.[14] There is, however, evidence that Cooper and her
volunteers were reinforced by paid missionaries sent by the LJS even
before the take-over. This of course makes the Society's reluctance to
publicly acknowledge its support of female philanthropic enterprise
all the more intriguing. Such caution, in an effusive obituary and
on a platform that specifically addresses prospective donors, is
revealing. Cooper's disciples in southern Syria, the sisters-in-law
Elisabeth Bowen Thompson and Augusta Mentor-Mott, founders of
the immensely successful Syrian Schools Mission (Girls' Mission),
present a case that is strikingly similar to Cooper and Whately's.
The schools were first subsidised by Thompson herself. Only after
her death was a Syrian fund of L9000 established (the largest
sum in the possession of single mission in the entire province
of Syria), to support Mentor-Mott's work. In Jaffa too, the two
most successful philanthropic ventures, started in the mid-decades,
Jane Walker-Arnott's Tabitha School for girls and Miss Newton's
hospital, founded at her own expense, were taken over by the
Scottish Mission and CMS respectively.[15] Louisa Proctor, founder
and sponsor of a number of boarding schools in Schweifat, south
of Beirut, as well as a medical mission, handed her life work to a
committee which was eventually merged into the CMS.[16] To turn
to the second continuity. The pattern of the organisation of work
is clear. Voluntary female work developed locally and sometimes
independently of the established missions. And this work was
never as successfully centralised as the work of men. Indeed the
centralisation in the 1890s was gradual and not always intentional.
Moreover, work before the last two decades of the nineteenth
century was, first and foremost, the effort of individuals. And
individualism and considerable autonomy particularly characterise
the first generation of proselytisers, who were to become models for
the cohorts of professional missionaries. To truly assess the effort of
these pioneers we have to penetrate beneath the surface of statistics
and discover the 'human' aspect of the picture. It is only by getting
to know the small, sometimes claustrophobic world of evangelical

women in the mid decades of the nineteenth century, that their *Weltanschauung* can be recovered. And it is appropriate to have Jerusalem for a background.

THE WOMEN OF CHRIST CHURCH, BY JAFFA GATE

Not surprisingly, Jerusalem attracted the largest numbers of evangelical tourists. It was not a typical oriental town. The holiest and most evocative place in the eastern Mediterranean, Jerusalem became the *locus* of eschatological hopes and the centre of millenarian activity.[17] Jerusalem also had the largest evangelical community in the Middle East. The Anglican (British-Prussian) Bishopric in Jerusalem was founded in 1841 and the first protestant church in the Levant, Christ Church, was consecrated in 1849 and prospered to a hub of a fervent – if not always successful – proselytising activity. Jerusalem also had a seasonal population of literary and artistic pilgrims, yearly migrating into the town and mingling with the local European community.

We may focus the close-up of the group of evangelicals by looking at the long and extraordinarily busy career of Elisabeth Ann Finn (née McCaul) who, literally and figuratively speaking, looms very large in the group portrait of the community of Christ Church. Finn's background is impeccably Evangelical. She was the daughter of the Reverend Alexander McCaul, a Hebrew scholar, one of Britain's first missionaries to the Jews in Eastern Europe, a founding member of the LJS and, most important, a staunch millenarist. In 1845 Elisabeth Ann married James Finn, socially her inferior but, like her father a Hebraist, philosemite and missionary to the Jews. Finn had been recently appointed Britain's Vice-Consul to Jerusalem and when his wife accompanied him there she was not yet twenty. She was to remain in Jerusalem for over eighteen years until 1863, when Finn's diplomatic career was abruptly ended.[18] As a consul's wife and pre-millenarian Evangelical Mrs Finn was particularly placed to influence the female British and local community in Jerusalem. She was also, specially and, for a woman unusually, equipped for a career as antiquary and ethnographer. She mastered Hebrew and Jewish (Yiddish) and acquired a smattering of Ladino, the medieval Castilian spoken by the Sepharadic Middle Eastern Jews, and Arabic and, most unusual, Syriac or Aramaic. Throughout her long stay in Jerusalem Mrs Finn was involved in, and pushed through, a number of charity projects for indigent Jews, notably a 'House of Industry' for inquirers, or prospective converts; an agricultural settlement, 'Abraham's Vineyard', outside the city walls; and a farm near Artas, not far from Bethlehem, the first attempt, in Palestine, at modern capitalist farming on a large scale. Mrs Finn saw to the business side of these philanthropic enterprises. She was involved in a number of complicated and shady land-transactions, buys and sales, which she could not possibly have entered in her native Britain (being, by law, a *femme couverte*). Under Ottoman law she was free to carry on business. Her work for local Jewish women and literary activity in the Jerusalem Literary Society (JLS) are not well-known and deserve our attention.

In January 1854, Mrs Finn, together with a few other female parishioners of Christ Church, started a visiting society, to aid indigent Jewesses in their *own* homes. The Sarah Society[19] or Benot Sara (literally Sara's daughters, after the verse in Peter's first epistle 3,6), was evidently modelled after the evangelical visiting societies in Britain's larger cities for the poor and destitute. Mrs Finn herself, and probably a number of her sister philanthropists, had been apprenticed in good works before coming to Palestine. Visiting was a familiar and socially acceptable form of charity. The very idea of 'visitation' is Christian, a manifestation of human *charitas*, humility and the ideal of service. Kept alive in rural paternalistic society, the tradition of 'visiting' had a revival, in the mid nineteenth century, in myriad charity organisations which mushroomed in the slums of the industrial cities.[20] Visiting came to be identified as a female charity. Contact with the poor in their homes was advocated in evangelical prescriptive literature. Obviously visiting combined charity with control on the life and behavior of the socially inferior. In the Middle Eastern context visitation, whether the visitation of harems or non-segregated Christian, or Jewish households, acquired new aspects. The regulated, ritual contact with the needy made possible cross-cultural communication yet, at the same time, preserved the hierarchy of culture and race and prevented the evolution of a solidarity of gender, of the kind which characterises relations between non-evangelical travellers and Muslim women.

Apart from the Sarah Society there were at least two other charitable organisations: the Benevolent Society, for the Relief of Poor Jewish Women in Child Birth, started after Finn's time (1865) and the Dorcas Society, begun in 1849, initiated by Dora Gobat, wife of Jerusalem's second Anglican Bishop, Samuel Gobat, but dominated by Mrs Finn. The Benevolent Society, inspired by the visitations of St. Anne, combined evangelisation (Bible reading, the distribution of suitable reading-matter, sermonising) with aid in money, or kind, to destitute women in child-birth.[21] Later, the society diversified its activities and catered for the entire indigent population of Jerusalem. In 1872, the year of the 'great famine', it fed some 1351 women, children and men.

The Dorcas Society is probably the earliest example in Palestine of a Christian women's organisation and was to become the model for the later visiting societies. It exemplifies the ways in which Mrs Finn and her circle of evangelical philanthropists internalised religious models of femininity and female-work, pragmatised gender ideology and applied it in everyday life in an alien, non-Christian environment. The Dorcas Society was a non-denominational body, an ecumenical one even, admitting non-Protestants (German deaconesses and even Catholics and Jews). The members devoted themselves to a work which they perceived as feminine and Christian: aiding needy women in childbirth. The monthly meetings were elaborate affairs, semi-religious rituals combining industry with studies and prayer, usefulness with piety. The purpose of the organisation and its regulated activities may be gleaned from the following extracts from the 'Rules':

1. ... a working Society is established, consisting of the ladies of the congregation of Christ's Church Jerusalem, to be called the Dorcas Society.
2. That the members of the Society meet on the morning of the first Thursday of each month at Mrs. Gobat's house.
3. That each meeting be closed by the reading of a portion of Scripture and prayers.
4. That each member contributes whatever she likes, either in money, or materials, the latter to be made up into baby linen and given to such poor Jewesses as come under the notice of the members.
5. ... better information respecting the state of the Jews here (especially of the females), or the reading of some useful books, to be carried on during the time appointed for work-ing.[22]

Almost everything about the work of the society is symbolical. The very name Dorcas is meaningful, commemorating Tabitha, or

Dorcas, the 'good woman of Joppa', arisen from the dead, a paragon of feminine humility, industry and piety. Indeed Dorcas was the patroness of the garments-industry, and her example was imitated in a plethora of ladies' sewing circles in Britain and the United States. Dorcas lent her name to girls' schools which offered practical Christian education to the poor at home and to the unregenerate abroad. The combination of prayer and work, manifested in the ritual Bible-reading, which concluded every meeting, is richly symbolic. Female industry is not for profit. Quite the contrary, it is an actual vocation. Prayer and the reading of the Bible emphasise the charitable and essentially pre-modern character of women's work.

There is, however, new stance to the gestures and rituals of the daughters of Dorcas. The last and, I think, most important rule of the Society, stipulates that books on the Jews of Palestine, particularly on Jewish women, be read to the members at every meeting.[23] Charity to the unconverted, it seems, is not enough. And the evangeliser cannot save the souls of the unregenerate without studying their customs and manners. Indeed, ethnographic knowledge is prerequisite to evangelisation. Mrs Finn was very conscious of the connection between work *for* women and writing *about* women and the family. After her return to Britain she produced two factional accounts on domestic life in Jerusalem, *Our Home in the Holy Land* and its sequel, *A Third Year in Jerusalem*. She also published a number of pamphlets on domestic life and domestic economy in the times of the Patriarchs and the Early Monarchy.

Of special significance is the connection between the charitable work of the evangelical Tabithas and their work as ethnographers in the Jerusalem Literary Society (JLS). The JLS, founded by Mr and Mrs Finn the same year as the Dorcas Society, was an antiquarian society of evangelical enthusiasts, devoted to the investigation of Palestine and its people. The Literary Society soon became the hub of literary and artistic activity of Europeans in Palestine and, through its Middle East branches and 'correspondents' (members), the focus of amateur learning and writing. Throughout the period for which the records survive (1849–1865), women outnumbered male members of the Society and the former were specially active as collectors of antiquities and curiosities (for the museum of the JLS) and as compilers of miscellaneous vignettes on Palestine.[24]

In theory, if not always in practice, the JLS was a non-denominational body. Like the Palestine Exploration Fund, which ultimately developed out of it, the older antiquarian society was frankly evangelical and unscientific. The sole purpose of its founders was the 'investigation and elucidation of any subject of interest, literary or, scientific of any period whatever with the Holy Land', the last being a loose term, covering the 'territory between the Mediterranean and the Euphrates and [between] the Nile and the Orontes'.[25] Consul Finn's address to the Society's meeting sometime during 1850, is very clear on the purposes of the antiquarians:

> In the elucidation of Biblical manners and customs, we have in our *daily walks and rides* or even *domestic scenes*, the advantage of *comparing actual life with Holy Scripture, more certainly than can be learned in Europe from such books as those of Burder and Harmer, where the habits of Jews in Palestine are explored by customs of Egypt, Morocco . . . and the South Sea Islands.* (my emphasis)[26]

That the Holy Land is to be interpreted as an 'illustration' to the revealed text of Scriptures is clear. Clearer still is the tendency to de-historicise places and peoples. Finn is openly contemptuous towards the emerging science of anthropology and proscribes the comparative study of cultures. Note his reference to Burder and Harmer. The stress on the individual, everyday experience of the amateur (acquired casually, in 'daily walks' and 'rides'), and an acquaintance with domestic life ('the domestic scene'), could be specially appealing to the women in Finn's audience. The JLS certainly recognised the potential in women's work and writing. They were admitted as members on the same basis as men, with the only stipulation that: 'ladies being members are permitted to appoint any gentleman present to read their contributions'[27] [the compulsory papers, delivered, at least, five times a year]. 'Permitted', however, is not 'required' and a few female members delivered their own papers themselves. In the 1840s, 'speaking in public' was regarded as 'unwomanly'. Thus the exhortation to women to avoid speech is rather conventional.

The names which appear most frequently on the records of the JLS are those of women active in philanthropic organisations. Three of the seven founding members of the Society were prominent female philanthropists: Mrs Finn herself, Caroline Cooper (the founder of the Jewesses Institute) and Lucy Harding, a schoolteacher and member of the Sarah Society. The records of the second meeting include the names of new recruits who, all of them, appear on the records of the Dorcas Society: Mrs Ewald (wife of the famous missionary to the Jews), Mrs Sanford, Mathilda Creasy, involved with the Dorcas Society and Caroline Cooper's school for Jewesses, and Sophia Hovendon, the more gullible of the two Misses Hovendon, loyal members of the literary society, do-gooders and staunch Evangelicals.[28] Of the 21 names on the fullest list of members in the records of the Dorcas Society, dated April 1857, twelve appear on those of the JLS. And, let us remember, philanthropists usually diversified their activities and tended to be involved in more than one kind of charity, Finn being the most salient example.[29]

Caroline Cooper may be taken as an example of the humble missionary, taken on by the Church and the evangelical metropolitan community and elevated – even during her lifetime – to a saint. Little is known about her life before 1848 when, following a long and painful conversion, she responded to a 'calling' to settle in Jerusalem. Immediately upon her arrival, spurred on by Mrs Finn, Cooper started on her own and at her own expense, the school for Jewesses that came to be known as the Jewesses Institute, probably the most successful evangelical enterprise in Jerusalem in the mid-century. Self-consciously perhaps, Cooper drew on the model of the industrial school for working-class youth, combining an apprenticeship in a 'useful' and honest occupation, with indoctrination in a simple practical religion, proper manners and morals. The difference between her institution and the evangelical model is that the former took in married women and girls (mothers and daughters) to be apprenticed in needle-work, millinery and weaving. Of course, apprentices were potential 'inquirers' or converts, and a dosage of religious instruction was administered to them daily. They were read to in Hebrew, Ladino and Arabic, from the prophetic parts of the Scriptures.[30] Inadvertently, perhaps, the practical education of Jewish women is historically more significant than the abortive attempts at their proselytisation. In the context of the Jewish Yishuv or settlement before the Zionist immigration to Palestine, merely separating women's work from the home and removing them from the patriarchal segregated household is quite revolutionary. Most Jews in the Holy Cities of Jerusalem, Hebron (Nablus), Tiberias and Safat, depended entirely on support from the diaspora, the 'Haluka' money, sent regularly from Eastern Europe and distributed in the communities in Palestine.

Cooper and, following her, other missionaries in Palestine and southern Syria, apprenticed women and girls in domestic female industries like weaving and millinery. Women's work, then, did not disrupt the Jewish patriarchal household and, indirectly, contributed to the modernisation of the domestic economy and the economy of the Yishuv. According to the very reliable Mathilda Cubley, the very first cloth woven in Jerusalem, on a mechanical loom, was by one of Cooper's apprentices. More significant even, the centralisation of work did not necessarily result in segregation and specialisation according to gender. In the Jewesses Institute, which separated between adults and children, women were employed in the early stages of the production which in the West had been typically carried on by men: washing the bales, picking and carding. A water-colour drawing, reproduced in Cubley's *Hills and Plains of Palestine*, features a group of Sepharadic women, in their traditional headdresses, busy spinning.[31]

Not surprisingly, the Jewesses Institute became a showcase of missionary work, a tourist attraction, on the map of every evangelical traveller. A few months before her death Cooper travelled to London, where she recruited superintendents and instructoresses for the Institute which she handed over to the Jews Society. Her death in 1859 gave the sign to the Society and to local evangelicals and travellers who between them, weaved the legend of Caroline Cooper, a humble servant in God's vineyard, a saint and a paragon of Christian womanhood. The different versions of Cooper's biography, as distinguished from her less important life, throw light on contemporary perceptions of the role of the female evangeliser in Palestine and women's place in the providential scheme of history and the millennium. The following versions are from the Evangelical *Jewish Intelligence* (1859); Elizabeth Charles' *Wanderings over Bible Lands and Seas*; Emily Beaufort's *Egyptian Sepulchres and Syrian Shrines* (1862) and Mrs Finn's *Home*. All the sources, with the exception of Beaufort, are Evangelical and millenarian. All capitalise on the enormous propaganda value of evangelical biography. But they each tell a different story. In the earliest *Intelligence* version, great emphasis is put on Cooper's conversion. It is not a *fiat* that could disqualify her as an 'enthusiast' and damage her serious image, but a protracted and painful process:

> long and patiently she did wait, often with little hope, but in unceasing prayer, till at last every hindrance was moved, and she was enabled, with a full conviction that the Lord was ordering her steps, to enter the work she loved.[32]

Throughout the obituary, Cooper's self-sacrifice, her patience and humility, but also her active practical faith are stressed, a combination that makes her a model of evangelical womanhood. Elsewhere, the *Intelligence* cites an effusive description, allegedly 'by a witness' of Cooper's last days in her tent, near the historic town of Bethlehem. Her last moments in a Biblical landscape associated with the life of Christ appropriately conclude a life of service and sacrifice. Charles repeats the version only with small alterations. But both she and Emily Beaufort shift the emphasis from the conventionalised Evangelical biography, which focuses on the motif of the conversion and the passive acceptance of the 'call' to Cooper's choice and action. In Beaufort's version Cooper is transformed from an *instrument*, a receptive and impressionable vessel, into a free and active agent. The theme of the 'call' is completely secularised:

> [Cooper] went to live at Jerusalem in order to devote herself in the improvement of poor Jewesses, her cherished purpose from her earliest years. Her income was *very* small, but by means of extraordinary self denial and frugality, she contrived to house and feed one or two poor girls, spending the whole of every day, not devoted to them, in visiting the Jewesses in their miserable homes, helping them with her own hands, working for them and teaching them to work for themselves, and though for several years she met with but little encouragement or assistance from others, the persevering earnest labours of this single-minded woman – working alone, in poverty and weak health – effected a real change in the idle, dirty, ignorant state in which she found the Jewesses of Jerusalem sunk.[33]

After years of toil and, eventually, with little help from various London societies (not specified), Cooper succeeded in 'providing a good house for her little family of orphans when her worn out figure sunk under a slight fever'.[34] Inaccuracies apart, Beaufort's Cooper comes out a forceful character – determined, compassionate and anything but humble. Most important, it is the individual, solitary work of a non-partisan that particularly impresses Beaufort and the modern reader.

Ironically, though not surprisingly, the most secular, most idiosyncratic version of Cooper's story is that of the devout Mrs Finn. Finn departs from evangelical role models and the conventions of evangelical hagiography. In their stead, she develops a secular narrative of a female *Bildung* and a truly independent *Bildungsheld*. In *A Third Year in Jerusalem*, Cooper is fictionalised as Miss Brandon, an enterprising do-gooder, newly arrived from England. Miss Brandon's voice, and words, are unmistakably those of Mrs Finn. The young missionary criticises the Middle Eastern policies of the LJS, particularly their neglect of indigent Jewish women. 'Christians', opines Brandon/ Cooper, 'owe a debt of gratitude to the Jews; and until it has been paid, every one who can ought to do something for them.'[35] And elsewhere: 'Nothing is being done for the Jewesses; this is an omission that ought not to be . . . the Jewesses as a body are quite uncared for.'[36] Nor is that all. The debate on the nature and trajectory of missionary work climaxes in a polemic about 'charity', with Brandon/Cooper representing the aggressive, individualistic approach to philanthropy and Mr Selwyn, an evangelical tourist, timidly defending Exeter Hall.

The philistinism and bathos of middle-class charity workers are lampooned. And the vocabulary used is almost Arnoldian:

'What would the subscribers say, Mr. Selwyn if, instead of preaching, or giving away tracts, the missionaries were to spend their time in secular employment.' 'As I happen to be a subscriber myself, Miss Russell, I can only say that I might consider teaching people to work for their living a useful part of missionary work. But you are right: possibly Exeter Hall might be of a different opinion'. 'Then Mr. Selwyn', remarked Miss Brandon in her positive way 'if Exeter Hall won't let the missionaries do it, some one else ought to come forth and supply the deficiency'.[37]

That someone else being, no doubt, Brandon/Cooper herself, or Miss Russell (another thinly disguised Mrs Finn) or any of the female parishioners of Christ Church in Jerusalem. Finn's version then is a far cry from the official biography of Caroline Cooper and the story of her conversion and modest labour in Palestine. And undoubtedly the former is more authentic. For it captures the spirit of women's work for women in the mid-nineteenth century and the meanings for middle-class philanthropists and missionaries, of a 'positive' activity and life abroad.

Jerusalem had a magnetic appeal to women like Finn or Cooper, both to the married part-timers, and to single, full-time workers. Examples can be multiplied. Jane Cook, a healthy philanthropist from Cheltenham, donated L700 for the purchase of the site of Mrs

Finn's Industrial Home and over L10.000 for a home for prospective converts, plus L2000 for the maintenance of inquirers. Mathilda Creasy, 'who preferred to live independently' in Jerusalem, became fluent in Ladino and Arabic and worked for Jewish women. Her unsolved murder in 1849, outside the Greek Convent of the Cross, stirred the placid local British community. And both the Finns darkly hint that there may have been more to Miss Creasy than meets the eye.[38] Lucy Harding, Creasy's intimate friend, opened a school which she herself ran until her departure to Britain in 1852. A few other single women were registered in the Consulate as teachers: Louisa Bank, Mathilda Dikenson, Lucy Mathilda Cubley, Frances James, Emma Heasell, etc. They were, in fact, missionaries, working for Bishop Gobat's diocesan schools, or the institutions of the LJS, and involved in charity work in the female philanthropic societies discussed earlier. The few paid workers did a work very similar to that of unpaid proselytisers like the Misses Hovendon, the devout Misses Crawford, the Misses Yarbough, Mrs Gobat, and Mrs Hampton, who frequently appear on the membership lists of the Dorcas Society and the Literary Society.

Fortunately the literary evidence may be supplemented with some numbers (see Table 2). The Registers of British-Born Subjects under the jurisdiction of the Consulate at Jerusalem may be used for information on the sexual and social composition of the evangelical community in this city, on familial patterns and the structure of occupation. A word of warning. We should be aware of the dangers of inflating the material because the information on the Register is rudimentary and limited.[39] Not all travellers and long-time residents were registered. And the records, kept by a succession of chancelliers, or secretaries (in the fifties by the ubiquitous Mrs Finn, acting as secretary to the Consul), are far from being complete. Usually only the sex of an individual, the duration of stay (the lag between registration – not to be confused with actual arrival – and departure) were recorded. Characteristically unmarried women are entered separately and the names of the married ones under the husbands' names. Furthermore the sample is small and includes only 130 people. But then in the mid-nineteenth century, the British population in Jerusalem was not much bigger. And British Jerusalem, because of its religious and cultural importance, was not a typical colonial outpost. In fact it was very untypical. These weaknesses notwithstanding, the Register may inform us on some structural characteristics of evangelical

Table 2 Evangelical travel, life and marriage in nineteenth-century Jerusalem.

	Males	Females
Duration of travel		
Unknown	10	14
Short (1–)	20	12
Middle (1–3)	13	12
Long (3+)	20	19
Occupation		
Unknown	7	9
Vocational Workers plus 'general'	24	24
Diplomatic	8	0
Professional incl. teaching	20	11
Service	4	14
Marital Status		
Unknown	1	1
Married	11	19
Single	51	37

Source: Israel State Archives; Register of British-born Subjects under the jurisdiction of the Jerusalem Consulate.

travel and work in the eastern Mediterranean. The first of these characteristics is the almost 'positive' sex ratio, that is an unusually high proportion of females, which is considerably higher than that in the community of travel-writers. Of 130 subjects, 63 or 48 per cent are males and 56 or 43 per cent females. So that unlike the typical colonial community the community in Jerusalem in the 1840s and 1850s was not male. Secondly the proportion of unmarried women is higher than that in the sample of travel-writers. 64.9 per cent (37) in the Register compared to 49 per cent in the other sample. Still there was in Jerusalem a surplus of single men, 51 or 81.8 per cent of the male population. The third and most interesting characteristic is that socially the female sector in the community is much more heterogeneous than the group of writers. In other words the community is *not* solidly middle-class. In fact 24.6 per cent of the women came to Palestine as servants, a few on their own, the majority together with their employers. And 19.3 per cent were registered as teachers or governesses. There is no information on the occupation of the other 56.1 per cent but evidence from other sources (the Finn journals, travel-literature, the records of the philanthropic and missionary societies) show that another 22.8 per cent were engaged in charity work. Only 6.3 per cent of the male population were employed as servants, or manual workers (builders and carpenters). But 12.7 per cent were diplomats, and 38.1 missionaries (see Table 2). Clearly the motives of working-class women and men seeking work in the Middle East were economic rather than religious or ideological. There is, however, some evidence, scattered in the records of the Consulate and in autobiographical writings, that servants were integrated into the local and European Christian communities. And women servants certainly took part, albeit not a major one, in benevolent work for indigent women.

It is, of course, difficult, even impossible, to separate spiritual from socio-economic motives. As with traditional religious travel, so with the modern, secularised pilgrimage and missionary work, material reasons combined with ideological and religious ones. In a final analysis, the changes in gender ideology within the dominating religious culture had a decisive influence on individual choices of career and life abroad. And the evangelical construction of gender, as I tried to show, certainly influenced the development of the organisation of work and its objectives. On the other hand, the new ideology would not have had material effects at the particular historical moment had there not been the apparatus of literal millenarian Biblism. In 1871, Ellen Miller, not an Anglican but a Quaker, addressing the Friends in Britain and the United States, summed up her tour of missions in Palestine with a plea to women to take part in the new spiritual experience: 'to be a missionary there' she pleaded, 'it may be given to advance even the literal fulfillment of the glorious promise made through the prophet Isaiah, – a promise spiritually fulfilled in peace, joy and blessing'.[40]

8

'Domestic Life in Palestine': Evangelical Ethnography – Faith and Prejudice

SOME CHARACTERISTICS

Sometime in May 1859, the Jerusalem Literary Society advertised a public lecture by Fredrika Bremer, the celebrated Swede novelist and travel-writer, a do-gooder, and, later, leader of Sweden's national Suffragist movement. Bremer, known by reputation to the members of the small literary and philanthropic community around Christ Church, was to speak twice: once, in the open-air, somewhere near Bethlehem and, a second time indoors, to a select audience of members of the JLS, in the English School.[1] The lectures were to be read by a gentleman member of the JLS. Bremer, it seems, acquiesced to the unwritten rule against public speaking by females. Her topic is somewhat hackneyed: Hebrew Women of the Bible and New Testament[2] – a popular theme with evangelical writers. But Bremer gives the familiar subject novel stance and one which is rather unorthodox. The entire post-Lapsarian history and the fulfillment of prophecy in the millennium are interpreted in terms of gender. Women, both 'real' Christians, that is Western, evangelical women, who are the true inheritors of the Hebrews and Jewish women, the unworthy descendants of the historical Hebrews, are assigned a special role in a universal, providential scheme.[3] Women are instrumental in the processes preceding Christ's Second Advent. Christians would appeal to the inner religiosity of their Jewish sisters, and their naturally feminine compassion and try to convert the latter to the 'faith'.[4]

191

The conversion of Jewish women would precipitate that of the entire people of Israel and its return to its historic land. In short, certain gender characteristics transcend religious and cultural differences. The maternal instincts of Jewesses and their capacity for suffering and self-sacrifice make them not only potentially good Christians, but agents of universal changes.

So far, there is nothing that is entirely novel in Bremer's cosmology,. What *is* quite unusual and may have shocked Mrs Finn Mrs Gobat, Caroline Cooper and the Misses Hovendon (all in the audience), is Bremer's reading of the Scriptures, particularly the story of the Fall. She abolishes the distinction between the two archetypes of Christian womanhood: Eve the sinner and temptress and Mary, the redeemer.[5] In fact, argues Bremer, 'Eve too is a saviour of mankind because she suffered. She is Mary's predecessor not her antithesis'.[6] Indeed, the entire 'women's history' (Bremer's epithet) is one of the evolution of the notion of suffering,[7] a suffering which is related to motherhood. This notion has evolved from an 'instinctual', 'biological' phase, characterising the ages of the Patriarchs and Judges, through the 'tribal' or 'national' phase (typical of the Early and Late Monarchy and Post Exilic times) to the selfless spirituality of motherhood which suffers for mankind, a spirituality described in the Gospels and Acts of the Apostles.[8] Hebrew Women, Bremer argues, have neglected their historic religious role. Blind to true 'faith', exiled from their land or, in it, subjected to foreign rule, degraded and degenerate, their redemption is in a cooperation with Christian women.[9]

The rehabilitation of Eve, by an evangelical, alive to the notion of the original sin, as well as Bremer's original interpretation of the Transgression and post-Lapsarian history, are audaciously heterodox. But Bremer does emphasise some aspects which are common to most religious writings on women in the Middle East. The first aspect is a focus on Jewish, or Christian women and a conscious exclusion of Muslims as objects of observation and representation. When Muslim women *are* noticed and described, this is done in a perfunctory way which demonstrates an uncertainty about the most basic facts regarding the harem-system. As Adella Goodrich-Freer, no lover of evangelicals, puts it:

> [the fact that] no one, at least . . . no English person, has collected information from the women [Muslim women of Palestine] is easily explained by the fact that the strict separation of the sexes

has prevented any man from taking advantage of the possibilities, and that the only women who have had the opportunity, the missionaries, have not been of a type to avail themselves of it, useful and valuable as it would be to the antiquarian, the anthropologist, the humanitarian, and, one would have imagined,the intelligent religious teacher.[10]

Goodrich-Freer, herself author of the now seminal *Inner Jerusalem* (1904) is, of course, mistaken. English women did collect information from women (she herself acknowledges the works of Mary Eliza Rogers and Isabel Burton).[11] Her proscription is adequate, however, in that 'missionaries' (her epithet for all evangelicals) did not avail themselves of information about Muslims. The thin references to and descriptions of, harems are in sharp contrast to the detailed accounts of 'secular' travellers, with the latter's obsession with accuracy.

To return to the second aspect. Evangelical tourists and proselytisers approach women's life in nineteenth-century Palestine unhistorically as illustrations to the past, as revealed in a canonical text, or to an unhistoric (millennial) time. Thus characteristically information on women, family life, customs and manners is not reckoned as important in itself but, as a means to the authentication of the Scriptures. Information could also facilitate evangelisation. Know the indigenous Arab or Hebrew, before you convert her. But, the acquisition of data and knowledge is selective, albeit not discriminate, and aimed primarily to validate *a priori* assumptions.

The third common feature is the attempt to domesticate Palestine and feminise its landscape. Not only the domestic sphere is described from a female angle, this is self-evident, but Nature itself is associated with religious experiences which are perceived as generically feminine as well as with women's history as it is revealed in the sacred texts. The fourth and last characteristic is the evolution of a notion of the social, historic role of women and their role in the providential scheme of history. Typically the writers define themselves and their work *vis-à-vis* the position of native women. This, as already mentioned, involves the evolution of a discourse which distinguishes evangelical ethnography from secular descriptions of the Orient. In what follows I shall touch on all four aspects, though, mainly for methodological reasons, treatment of landscapes is separated from that of the purely domestic.

CHRISTIAN AND MUSLIM WOMEM

In the eschatological *Weltanschauung* of devout travellers and philanthropists, there is very little place for Muslim women. Clearly not
pagans, but lacking the attraction of Jews, or local Christians, the
Muslims are seen as apostates. And as such, they do not fit well in the
evangelical notion of history, and the *millennium*. Indeed, domestic
Palestine is perceived as part of a Hebrew and Christian tradition,
from which the 'foreign' Muslim Orient is excluded. Local customs
and manners predate the Islamisation of the eastern Mediterranean
and are, essentially, Biblical. To be sure, Muslim (that is, Turkish)
rule is a political fact, but it too is perceived as a pre-ordained phenomenon, a part of a divine plan. The misery of Jews or Christians,
their persecution by Muslims and Turkish tyranny and misrule, all
these are interpreted as signs of the fulfillment of prophecy.[12]

The very framework of evangelical ethnography excludes the
idealisation of the harem and the position of women, that is so
typical of 'secular' writers. The bias against oriental familial systems
is religious rather than racial – that is, it is against Muslims but *not*
Arabs. For Christian Arabs, can be placed in the evangelical reading
of history. As already noted, the reasons for the writers' bias against
Muslims are pragmatic as well as ideological. Prejudice and the
policy of the missions seriously hindered any understanding of,
and tolerance towards, Muslims.

Thus serious discussion of the position of women is limited to
Jewish and Christian women. Mrs Finn is a characteristic example.
Both in her fictionalised accounts about life in Jerusalem in mid-
century and in her *Reminiscences* she emphasises that her interest
is limited to the domestic life of Europeans – Christians and Jews
– and does not extend this interest to orientals. Referring to Rogers'
Domestic Life in Palestine, written at the same time as her own *Home
in the Holy Land*, Finn remarks that: 'We [Rogers and herself] each
took a different point of view, and our sketches may be regarded as
distinct pictures of schemes which have only the chief features in
common.'[13] Domestic life, then, is life in the homes of Europeans
abroad, or in Jews' homes. In Finn's two works there is only a single
eyewitness description of a harem and it is perfunctory and thin. The
author, who prides herself on her knowledgeableness about Jews
is, self-consciously, and rather deliberately, ignorant about Arab
women.[14] Finn's fellow-worker at the Sarah and Dorcas Societies
and the JLS, Sophia Hovendon, refrains altogether from referring

to harems. In a confused paper given to the Literary Society (it is entitled 'floating atoms') she represents Muslim women in the open landscape. Reporting on Arab women she met on one of her walks around the city-walls, Hovendon indignantly bursts:

> [Muslim women] especially shock all our ideas, and it is diffi-
> cult sometimes to suppress the feelings of disgust which their
> offensive, unfeminine and foolish manners too often inspire; pity
> them as we may and ought, – but they are at once so silly and so
> familiar and so haughty, so very unlike that 'ministering angel'
> woman.[15]

Hovendon is repulsed by Muslim women because they are 'unfeminine'. Indeed they present the very opposite of the Vic-
torian 'ministering angel'. It is therefore possible to present them outside the home. About the same time as Hovendon, Mathilda Cubley includes in her *Hills and Plains of Palestine* a very general and not particularly specified description of Muslim women. The book is a collection of illustrations, annotated with mini-chapters. The verbal text is consciously used as sub-text to the pictures. Cubley is concerned about accuracy in her passage on the Jewish home and Jewish women. [16] The illustration (both the pictorial and verbal one) of the harem, on the other hand is general. Obligatory descriptions of harems are cursory and glaringly lacking in details. Take for example Harriet Catherine Egerton, countess Ellesmere's *Journal of a tour of the Holy Land, in 1840*, perhaps the earliest pre-millenarian text on Palestine by a woman. The journal includes one vague oblique description of a harem. The name of the household is not specified; not one of the women is named; there is very little reference to ethnographic detail like food and etiquette. There is no conversation. Indeed, the entire passage evolves around the writer's difficulty in communicating with the Arab women.

> I crumpled myself up to the best of my power, in company with
> the ladies, . . . and then began an attempt at communication
> between us; but the only medium we possessed in common
> were signs, and I found to my great despair that even that was
> a failure, for the code of signs in the East is totally different from
> that which is used in the West, so that we were quite baffled![17]

And, sometime later:

My condition in the harem was now growing somewhat irksome, and I began to think that I had had enough of sherbet, signs and squatting. Moreover, the sun was set, and much, I knew, remained for us to do before the return home; yet I despaired of ever getting away. My signs they did not, or would not understand, and I continued to be taken from one home to another.[18]

When finally Egerton is 'released' from her imprisonment she outbursts: 'Poor things, what a miserable existence is theirs . . . How intensely thankful I am to providence that my lot is cast in Europe and not in Asia.'[19]

Note that underneath her apparent *naïveté* Egerton is very perceptive. She describes the failure to communicate with Muslim women in an astonishingly modern vocabulary. They are speechless and are spoken for, by westerners. Moreover, the Muslim and Western woman, each use a system of signs, a language or a cultural 'code' (Egerton's word) that the other cannot, or would not, break and decipher. Signs and gestures are ignored. Mannerisms, behaviors and the etiquette of the harem are misinterpreted. Egerton's hosts, she feels, fail to realise her wish to be 'released', the implication being that they are oblivious to their own imprisonment. Significantly her difficulties are only with women. Eastern men interest her and she can appreciate the special traits of Arab male culture, or, for that matter, Jewish or Samaritan culture. She is impatient to finish the visit to the harem to interview, for the second time, members of the Samaritan community at Nablus which attracted evangelical ethnographers. The disregard for ethnographic detail and the scarcity of reference to manners and customs are the same as in the writings of Finn, Cubley and Hovendon. And Writers on the Lebanon and southern Syria (for example Mary Mackintosh and Augusta Mentor-Mott and Elisabeth Bowen Thompson) are also very stingy with detail and eyewitness descriptions. Or, typically these writers locate Muslim women *outside* their house. Hovendon's case, cited before, immediately comes to mind and a few other examples could be added to it. Augusta Mentor-Mott, founder with Elisabeth Thompson, of the Syrian Schools Mission, devotes ample space to Greek Orthodox and Maronite women of the Lebanon and southern Syria and represents Muslim and Druse women only in open landscapes.[20]

Apparent disinterestedness in the Muslim house and the Muslim family as historical and geographical variants of a social system precludes serious analogy between the harem and the Western *bourgeois* home. In contrast to the writers of harem literature, evangelicals approach the women's question from a *moralistic* stand. Thus they fall back on the traditionalist view of Islam as a thisworldly and sensual religion and of the harem as a patriarchal construct. The *haremlik* in evangelical writings is not a bastion of feminine values, but the ultimate *locus* of impurity. Take, for example, Mary Mackintosh's typology of the *haremlik* and Muslim women, in her chapter on 'The Mohamonedan Quarter' in Damascus. Mackintosh gives no specific details, and omits places and proper names that can identify the subject of her description. Her oblique presentation of the house of 'a pasha of European reputation' is followed with an admonition of travellers who idealise the position of Muslim women:

> Some writers are induced in the present day to look with a favourable eye on Mohammedanism, or at least strive to paint it in the fairest colours they can. I only wish such gentlemen could be admitted to the best conducted harem . . . We often are painfully reminded of the saying, 'Can anyone touch pitch and not be defiled?' Some of the women are very ready to own the pain of their degradation, and to wish they had the peace and happiness of a Christian marriage . . . The very arrangement of a Muslim house, professedly to protect women, shows the *impurity of thought* and mind that makes such arrangements necessary.[21]

Evidently there is no solution but to 'try to *purify* the minds of the people by the introduction of Christian teaching. When the fountain becomes pure the streams will be pure also'.[22] The entire passage abounds with epithets, denoting physical uncleanliness and, by implication, sexual impurity. Combinations like 'defilement', 'pitch degradation', 'impurity', 'a pure fountain' etc. conjure up the image of the Muslim house as a place of lasciviousness and sexuality. Mackintosh ignores the original etymological meaning of *harem*, as the 'sacred' and 'forbidden', and emphasises only the sexual aspect of plural marriage and concubinage. The obsession with impurity is revealing. The metaphor of the defiled spring for the Muslim woman is indeed a far cry from the secular presentations of the *haremlik* as the *bourgeois* hearth, the temple of feminine values.

Naturally the harem-system (segregation, concubinage and, in particular, polygamy) is condemned explicitly in the general, informative parts of the narrative and indirectly in physical representation. Polygamy brings forth horror, disgust and pity. But more important, the writers are complacent and self-congratulatory. They, fortunately for them, are not Muslim. Christianity is the emancipator of women, both as individuals and as a gender. Thus evangelical writers never proceed beyond gazing at the harem. They are onlookers rather than participating observers. And they certainly do not progress from representation to the comparison between cultures, nor, it is needless to say, to the self-criticism which is so pertinent in harem literature proper. The implications on the position of women in the West, of the subjection of Eastern women, are never discussed. On a personal level philanthropists take advantage of the freedoms offered by the new ideology of gender, but they fail to extend freedom beyond the individual level. Consequently their attitude towards the questions of oriental sexuality is conservative. 'How intensely thankful I am to Providence, that my lot is cast in Europe and not in Asia', remarks Egerton. And Mackintosh, citing self-pitying Muslims, 'Oh, how we wish we were like you, married once, married always, and not being subject to dismissal'.[23]

Their own cultural complacency notwithstanding, the position of the writers is awkward. Plural marriage is not typically Muslim, nor particularly characteristic of eastern Mediterranean societies. Sephardic or Eastern Jews with whom most philanthropists in Jerusalem worked and whom they found more open to Western influences than Ashkenazi, or Eastern-European Jews, were allowed by law to marry more than one wife. More important even, condemnation of polygamy was contrary to the letter of Scriptures and, according to evangelical rationale, could undermine the status of the canonised text. Nowhere in the Old Testament is plural marriage forbidden, let alone condemned. Indeed, the lives of the Patriarchs, which the writers regarded as unchanged models, persisting down to the present, abound with examples of polygamy, concubinage and the sequestration of women. As Goodrich-Freer shrewdly notes: 'This custom [e.g. polygamy], like much else in the Moslem faith, was probably borrowed from the Jews, among whom, Scriptural examples apart, the Mishneh [Mishnah] allowed an ordinary Jew four wives.'[24]

Yet the patriarchal household is idealised by the literalists and the sexual aspects of Scriptural polygamy are simply ignored. Even in the Gospels and Acts of Apostles, despite the Pauline negative attitude towards marriage, polygamy is not once explicitly forbidden

– except to bishops. Indeed, Protestant polygamist polemics, from the Reformation onwards, based the defence of plural marriage on the Patriarchal example. The literal interpretation of the Scriptures and the treatment of contemporary life in Palestine as an illustration to a revealed text, should logically bring about tolerance towards non-Christian mores. But this was not to be. The conflict between the evangelical sanctification of monogamy and the idealisation of the Patriarchal model perhaps explains why evangelical women are silent about Biblical polygamy. The Jewish connection of sexual mores that, in Muslims, are unequivocally condemned, is ignored, or played down.

Polygamy is described as exclusively and generically Muslim. It is presented as the exemplar to Muslim lasciviousness and promiscuity. Indeed the harem, like the *zenana* in India, becomes the pivot, both the strategic and ideological one, of evangelical propaganda and philanthropic activity. Upon a reform of the harem and, first the abolition of polygamy, hinges not only the emancipation of oriental women, but political regeneration of the Ottoman Empire.

CHRISTIAN AND JEWISH WOMEN: 'MOTHERS' AND 'DAUGHTERS'

Jewish and Christian women are central in evangelical writings. But the attitude of the devout travellers toward non-Muslims is equivocal. There was, as most writers were painfully aware, a meaningful discrepancy between Scriptural models of womanhood and real women in contemporary Palestine, between the text and the land, the illustration and the original. The women in the Bible and the New Testament are elevated to paragons of Christian femininity. The Matriarchs, Sarah, Rebecca and Rachel; the women in the times of the Judges – Deborah and Hannah in particular; the women surrounding Christ, 'last at the cross and first at the sepulchre', Anne and the Marys, Dorcas and Phoebe, are all models, internalised by evangelicals in their daily life. Contemporary Middle Eastern women presented a glaring contrast to the idealised models of the past. The position and low status of the contemporary Hebrews both as Jews and as women are constantly deplored. Indeed, the physical and spiritual poverty of Jews are purposefully stressed, being potent signs of the fulfillment of the prophecy. The lower the status of Jewish women the greater the prospects for the female evangeliser and, as we shall later see, the easier it is for the latter to reconstruct her own self-image. The relations between poverty and mental or spiritual degeneration are emphasised both in official reports in the missionary press and in the accounts of travellers. A typical report in the *JI*, dated August 1856, is worth quoting at length:

> the missionary in calling upon, and seeking their [the Jews'] spiritual welfare, not infrequently entails them trouble and affliction. The same argument, however, does not hold as regards the female members of the family, who, as society is constituted, and as education subsists among these people, take little head themselves of such matters, the male branches feeling indeed less concern about this sex in spiritual affairs. The ignorance in which they are brought up is considered a sufficient guarantee against any consequences their influence over society might produce. So different are the feelings as well as customs between the Easterners and ourselves, that even from the lips of these females, as if they gloried in the confession, we constantly hear the declaration that *all that regards the soul*, or their future welfare, concerns them not it being the business of the other sex . . . Hence the souls of the daughters of Israel being in such keeping, the Jew is little moved by the impression the missionary might ask to make upon his wife and daughter; if he should not laugh at the bare conception of the spirituality in woman. Who among the fairer half of the creation can pursue this without feelings of indignation?[25]

it is evident from the concluding remark that the anonymous writer particularly addresses women readers (and potential donors). But the juxtapositions of educated Christians with ignorant Jewesses and soulless orientals with spiritual westerners are not merely tactical. The symmetrical opposition between Christian and non-Christian is characteristic of evangelical epistemology. Yet the very comparison raises questions. If indeed the Jewish or oriental female is so worthless, why use her as means to moral reform? If she has sunk so low, why elevate her to a precipitator of the *millennium*? The answer is, it seems, simple. It is the degradation of Jewish/Christian women, their very marginality in their society, that makes them so appealing to Christians. A report on the activities of the Sarah Society, also from the *JI*, typically associates poverty and squalor with spiritual degeneracy:

so far as their resources [the resources of the members of the Sarah Society] will admit, [they undertake] to relieve the [Jewesses] temporal wants, seizing the opportunity thus afforded to converse upon topics, which concern their spiritual welfare.[26]

And over a decade later, in reference to the activities of the Benevolent Society for the Relief of Poor Jewish Women in Childbirth: 'words cannot paint the scenes of misery and wretchedness . . . at times a lonely sufferer is encumbered in some damp cellar, hardly large enough to hold the only article of furniture, a straw pallet upon which she lies sick, neglected and almost in despair . . . homeless, friendless, barely kept alive by the small pittance they [she] receive[s] from the rabbis.'[27] The passage is, of course, stiffly clichéd. It smacks of the vocabulary of prescriptive literature and journalist writing on urban poverty in industrial Britain. And as already noted, most philanthropists in the Middle East were acquainted with poverty in Britain, and they project their attitudes to the poor at home on indigient populations abroad. In travel and ethnographic literature, the plight of the Jewesses is even more dramatised than in the evangelical press. Poverty is, sometimes, regarded not as a social problem, but as the realisation of divine schemes, determined by an impersonal, super-human agency. Read Elizabeth Charles' description of Jewish women at prayer at the Wailing Wall:

Two white-veiled women stood and pressed their faces against the stones, weeping and wailing so that their whole frames quivered with sobs. How much of this is dramatic or ceremonial, I do not know. But it was an affecting scene, not so much from the thought of what they felt, as of what they are, in comparison with what they might have been; outcast, despised, and degraded, having exchanged the joyous music of their sanctuary for vain wailings by the outer wall, which, at peril of life [the wall borders the Haram-el-Saref, forbidden to Jews] they dare not pass.[28]

Charles herself regards the scene depicted above as typologically symbolical and characteristic, referring to the women as 'that strangely typical company'. The passage divides between two 'Biblical coincidences' that is descriptions of people and landscapes, illustrating the Old Testament. And this location of the Wall episode makes it particularly forceful. Mrs Finn too reads the mythical past and the millennial future in the present. Unlike

Charles, however, she does not explain the position of Jewish women only in eschatological, supra-natural terms. The politically and economically anomalous conditions of the Jews contribute to their spiritual degeneration. In *Third Year* the energetic philanthropist Miss Brandon delivers a harangue on the mission to the Jews, which she concludes with a Jeremiad on the state of the Jewish community in Jerusalem. 'It pains and grieves me to see, as I did the other day in the Jewish quarter, so many lovely children utterly neglected, and, still more, to see the meaningless expression which has kept over the faces of their mothers and elder sisters. I never in my life saw more intelligent-looking children, and am sure they were not made to grow up into such senseless women'.[29] Degeneration is related to pauperisation, early marriages and lack of education. As with the poor at home, so with needy women abroad, a combination of practical education and evangelical propaganda is prescribed. Evangelical education may help solve social and economic problems and ultimately to bring about spiritual regeneration (for the actual application of this formula, see Chapter 7).

Note Mrs Finn's interest in young girls and adolescents rather than adult women. Certainly most philanthropists and religious writers eulogised the Jewish mother, a model of self-sacrificing and suffering parenthood. But, as already mentioned, the actual life of women contrasted with Biblical/Christian images and myths. One way to narrow the gap between evangelical mythology and reality was to construct definable roles for both the evangelisers and the evangelised and relate those roles to new patterns of relations between the 'true' and 'nominal' or potential Christians. Girls, or adolescents, were naturally more exposed to the influences of evangelical education. There is ample evidence that Muslims sent their daughters to the Missionary schools in Syria and Palestine. Practical education for women which apprenticed them in the crafts and domestic economy was appreciated even by the hostile local population.[30]

But interest in Jewish or Christian youth cannot, I think, be explained away merely in terms of expediency and the pragmatic politics of the missions. Focus on girls and adolescent females certainly did not simply represent the actual work of missions. Evangelicals catered for both the married and unmarried, children and adults. This obviously is the case with Cooper's Jewesses Institute and Thompson and Mentor-Mott's Syrian Schools. Why then the shift in evangelical writing from the married woman, to the adolescent, or the child? In harem literature proper, it may be recalled, it is the *hanîm*, the wife and mother, who is the symbolic and real focus of the household. And why are children and adolescents idealised and stereotyped as ideal potential converts? The focus on a religious and sentimental relation between Christian women and inquirers, or potential converts, fulfills for the former certain emotional and mental needs and at the same time fits well in the writers' ideology of femininity as well as the ideology of class.

Characteristically evangelical writers perceive or describe their relations with Jewish or Christian women in familial terms. Typically the devout writer or traveller sees herself as a 'mother' and her pupil, or protegée as 'daughter'. Less commonly, the former is described as an elder sister (evidently a substitute mother) and the latter as a younger sibling. Both the mother-daughter relation and that between siblings make it possible for evangelical women to combine the idea of protective care with that of parental authority. Significantly authority derives from age difference as well as from the difference in religion and culture. Certainly hierarchy is emphasised, but is underscored by the metaphors of motherhood and sisterhood. Of course, familial metaphors, especially the metaphor of motherhood, are characteristically Victorian and typically applied to relations between middle-class reformers (notably feminist reformers) and philanthropists and working-class women. Outside Britain, in the Middle Eastern context, the mother-daughter metaphor acquires novel and poignant meanings. The female relationship of protection and deference replaces the patriarchal construct typical of the oriental family and oriental society in general. The English 'mother' disciplines her pupil-daughter, educates her and sometimes christianises her. The evangeliser thus replaces both the biological father and the religious mentor, whether the priest or the Rabbi. Unmarried and childless missionaries could derive great satisfaction from the constructed relations with local women. Cooper's Jewesses institute is described by Beaufort in familial terms. Cooper assembled girls in her own home, giving them lodging, instruction and care.[31] Miss Walker-Arnott, Jane's sister and, from 1879, a teacher at the Tabitha school at Jaffa, regards the Arab pupils as daughters. In the following, a description of Christmas Eve at the school, she particularly emphasises the family relations between pupils and teachers and the relationship with donors at home.

all these 60 children in their neat frocks and pinafores, singing their Christian hymn – the tree before them laden with presents, whilst the male native servants and teachers, in their Eastern dress, gave a picturesque touch to the scene. The children then sang: 'Hark the Herald Angels', in English . . . and then we began to despoil the tree. The dolls were given first . . . Each of the children who had some little gift from their English mothers were so pleased that they had been remembered.

The biological parents of the scholars (especially the mothers) are described in epithets like: 'not nice', 'miserable', 'not a nice woman'.[32] Augusta Mentor-Mott makes the most of the mother-daughter metaphor. The evangelised Maronites of southern Syria are elevated to symbols of purity and innocence. In a long and particularly detailed passage, Mentor-Mott describes a Sunday outing organised at Hasbaya by the Syrian Mission for school girls and for the widows and mothers of the victims of the Druse massacres of 1861–62. It was:

> Such a treat as Hasbaya certainly never saw. All the dear children were assembled at a most lovely romantic spot in the Hasbany [one of the sources of the Jordan] . . . these Eastern girls are so graceful in their movements; this is greatly owing to their long mandille, which prevents boisterous mirth. They played chiefly under the dry arch of the bridge such games as 'thread-the-needle'. One of their games consisted in each girl having in her hand a long branch of flowering oleander, first gracefully holding it aloft, waving in the air . . . then forming a double line, and each laying the oleander branch at the feet of one who was dear to them . . . Nor need I say that prayer was offered for those dear children, and the Scriptures read to them . . . I am sure the sacred Jordan never witnessed a happier group.[33]

Mott's sentimentalised representation of an Arcadian idyll is interrupted by the dramatic entrance of a group of Maronite widows, whose black dress is picturesquely contrasted with the children's white mandilles.

> What a sight of human misery some of them presented! To see them creeping down the opposite winding paths, and then toiling up to our tents. Some very aged; some quite blind; some lame;

1.   Women on the banks of the Nile

2.   Lepers in Jerusalem *c* 1885

3. Nubian woman with *marghile*, probably 1880

4. Arab woman in an outing dress *c* 1885

5. Bedouin encampment near Jericho *c* 1885

6. Courtyard of a Jewish house in Damascus, *c* 1875

7. Bedouin vegetable vendors *c* 1885

8. Arab woman on a donkey, 1880s

9.　A corner of the vegetable market, Jerusalem, 1908

10.　The mill, a 'primitive' [sic] method of grinding, 1908

11. Emmeline Lott *c* 1865

12. Moslem [sic] women attired in *mandril*s and *izzar*s

13. 'Mosque of Sultan Valide' [sic] featuring unveiled women, which is quite rare

14. (above left) Turkish lady in yashmak or feradjen

15. (top right) Stamboul Jewess and Jew in izzar

16. (left) Turkish lady

17. (below) Peasant women and children

18. (top) Jewesses at work

19. (centre left) Women making carpets
    c 1860

20. (left) A Bethlehem bride *c* 1904

21. Julia Pardo

22. Lucy Duff-Gordon
by Henry W. Phillips *c* 1851

23. Elizabeth Anne Finn

24. Isabel Burton in 1869

such faces of anguish, I never, never saw. We got them seated in rows, under a large tree; and the bright young girls, forming the other half of the circle, under another large tree; and after a little talk of kindly greeting and sympathy, the sweet hymn was sung by the girls, 'Just as I am without one plea', each verse being distinctly read first, and then . . . the parable of the ten virgins.[34]

She could not have staged the little school celebration better. Indeed, the entire scene is religiously and culturally meaningful. Evangelised girlhood epitomises feminine purity and chastity. Intriguingly, the mandille, or cover hiding the face, is transformed from a symbol of subordination and sexuality, into one of decorousness, modesty and virginity. However, unlike the veil metaphor in harem literature, the mandille in Mott's usage does not signify autonomy and freedom of movement. Actually it 'prevents boisterous mirth' and other freedoms. And she contrasts the innocence and modesty of evangelised Arabs with the boldness and audacity of the unreformed women of Hasbaya who had not the benefit of evangelical education. The contrast between adult and adolescent Christians is even more dramatic than that between Christians and Muslims. The black dresses of the widows, their slow movement (the do not walk but 'creep' and 'crawl'), are juxtaposed with the lightness of colour of the girls' clothes, their graceful movements and agility. Not only philanthropists, but travellers too, describe young women as 'children', thus endowing them with an aura of innocence and purity, which they themselves find difficult to associate with adults. Even Mary Eliza Rogers – an evangelical but not a millenarian – and outspoken opponent to organised proselytisation, refers to the women of Palestine as 'sisters', or 'daughters', or as 'children'. They usually address her as 'sister', a gesture which truly touches her, and which she regards as sincere and meaningful. She even 'claimed sisterhood with Bedouin girls'.[35] Significantly Rogers reverses the parent-child relationship, by allowing older Muslim women to address her as daughter.[36] Elisabeth Ann Finn uses the themes and metaphors of mother-daughter relations and those between siblings in a more conventional manner. Unlike Rogers, she is careful not to let sympathy with individual women to develop into a solidarity of gender. She identifies with the Jerusalem Jewesses, not because they are women, but because she is a philosemite, and they are Jews.

Finn's evangelical rhetoric is more typical than Rogers', and it is because of that, and because of Finn's position in the community, that we should look in detail at her artistic construction of the network of relations between natives and Englishwomen. Finn's fictionalisation of evangelical life in Jerusalem is valuable for yet another reason. It is the fullest, best-documented account we have on the attempts to christianise Middle Eastern women as well as on the indoctrination and re-education of women inquirers.

Home in the Holy Land and its sequel, *A Third Year in Jerusalem*, both based on Finn's private diary and the consular diaries kept by herself and the Consul are, literarily, a curious mixture. The novels are *romans-à-clef*, programmatic *romans-à-these* and rather crude versions on the evangelical *Bildungsroman*. The theme is that of evangelical education in Palestine. The two main strands of action which thread together a number of secondary episodes are: the education of Walter Russell, a traveller and orientalist painter and, parallel to it, the conversion and socialisation of a Jewish woman, Rachel, daughter of a Hebrew-Christian, Rabbi Abraham. Walter's own education is conventional enough. Finn provides a model of the inexperienced, formally educated and well meaning young *bourgeois* who, after a few false starts and with the help of well-disposed friends, builds himself a career and realises his purpose in life. As in every *Bildungsroman*, so in Finn's *oeuvres*, Middle Eastern travel, is a phase in male education. Walter arrives at Palestine after an unsuccessful artistic trip down the Nile, in search of the ideal subject for the definitive, most authoritative painting of a Middle Eastern scene and Middle Eastern life. Significantly for the story, the theme is a Biblical one – the return to Bethlehem of Naomi and Ruth. Walter's choice of a career is accompanied by that of a wife – naturally, Rachel the convert. Her own conversion and education are self-consciously related by Finn to the broader topics of conversion and female education.

Now both the *Bildung* stories are told by Emily, Walter's sister, Rachel's guide and substitute-mother and, structurally, the pivot around which the two histories evolve. It is significant that the male characters, Walter and the group of missionaries surrounding the Russells, are moved by the forceful female protagonists: Emily, Rachel herself and Mary Anderson (modelled on the philanthropist Miss Nicolayson, daughter of Reverend Nicolayson, the first and longest serving missionary to the Jews). Readers identified Emily Russell with Mrs Finn who emphatically denied any relation between herself and her replica, first in the 'preface' to *A Third Year*, then in the *Reminiscences*.[37]

Rachel's education and socialisation should particularly concern us. She is, undoubtedly, the ideal convert. She is technically motherless – her mother steadfastly holds to Judaism and rejects the advances of missionaries – young and inexperienced. She is, in short, the very stuff that makes a convert. Finn continuously stresses Rachel's simplicity – though not simple mindedness – and her innocence. She is charmingly 'naïve', 'bewitchingly simple', 'the shiest creature in the world'.[38] It is her *naïveté* and simplicity which, in the first place, attract both Walter and his sister to Rachel. Significantly the conversion itself and Rachel's catechising are achieved painlessly almost effortlessly. What is more problematic is the nature and purpose of the convert's education and her identity. Should she receive a practical education, that is a typical working-class course of studies that would prepare her to support herself and teach her basic domestic skills? Or should she be taught secular and aesthetic values, broader than the 'rudimentaries' of evangelical education? Does conversion transform a Jew into a Christian, or does she or he remain 'Hebrew' (Finn's term)? Is Rachel's Jewishness compatible with evangelical Christianity and culture? The didactic Finn anatomises these problematics in several written-in polemical conversations between Rachel and her Christian friends. The first, which concerns her religious and ethnic identity, is between Emily Russell and Mrs Wells, the Consul's wife (and another sketch of Finn).

'Listen to this child, Miss Russell. She says she does not wish she had been an English girl. Is not that what you said, Rachel?' 'Yes ma'am, at least – I mean' – 'That you don't want to belong to us. And had rather be a Russian'. 'Oh no, ma'am; I had much rather be English than Russian' 'I wonder why?' 'That's a difficult question, Mrs Wells; let me answer it for her. She has seen more of English people, and had more friends among them . . . ' 'Then why don't you want to be English? . . . England is such a beautiful country'.[39]

The respectful Rachel finally puts in a word:

'My country is beautiful . . . This is our country, ma'am. How beautiful it is! And when our nation comes back and have it

again, it will be much more beautiful. All the mountains will
be covered with vines and fig trees, and all the towns will be
full of people.' 'You don't mean to say that you had rather be
a Jewess than English?' 'Yes, certainly, I had rather be a Jewess.
Is not my father a Jew? . . . was not King Solomon a Jew, and all
the kings, and all the prophets? There is no other nation as great
as my nation.'[40]

Note that Rachel is allowed to speak standard English. Muslim and
Christian women are stereotyped in speech and use an archaic
idiom, Finn's notion of the Arab manner of speaking. Rachel
buttresses her argument with an 'It says so in the Bible', which
nonplusses her literal-minded guides.

Passages like this – and the two novels abound with them –
are straightforward missionary propaganda. The convert does not
automatically become a Christian, certainly not an Englishwoman.
Rather she retains her Jewishness and historical role as precipitator
of a global awakening and the *millennium*. The proselytisation of
the Jews and their restoration to Palestine fulfill the prophecy.
Note Rachel's confident: 'it says so in the Bible'. Yet despite the
emphasis on Rachel's Jewish identity, despite her refusal to eat
humble pie, her education is experimental and wide. Significantly,
Rachel studies English and Music. She becomes an accomplished
pianist and composer. Finn picks up music because it is so marginal
in Judaism and because the emphasis even in low-church liturgy, on
sound and instrumental music, are to an orthodox Jew, suspicious.
To liberate her disciple, Emily not only teaches her the catechism
but Handel's Messiah. And music becomes the dominant influence
in Rachel's life, as much as painting is in Walter's.

It should be noted that the efforts to proselytise the Jews
and indigenous Christians failed. The London Jews Society, and
the independent separatist female organisations and non-partisan
philanthropists affiliated to it, had minimal success in attracting
converts. Jewish women in particular seemed – even to enthusiasts
like Cooper – specially resilient to change. As virtually all students of
the history of the mission agree, the LJS's reports about successes are
utterly baseless and unreliable. Independent conservative estimates
(like Harriet Martineau's) and more generous ones (Tobler and
Frankl's) are between 60 and a little over 100 converts over a period
of half a century, during which the Jewish population of Jerusalem
soared from under 2000 to 10,000.[41] Moreover, all the evidence

points that converts came from the margins of the community – the destitute and unemployed. And the strongest inducement to conversion, it seems, was financial, a gift of 6000 piasters upon Baptism. Furthermore, baptism, as even Finn herself realises, was no guarantee to effective evangelisation. For a few baptised Jews carried on an un-Christian life. More significant even, the attempts at productivisation by practical education were vehemently criticised. Cooper's industrial school was a quixotic enterprise. As Martineau shrewdly notes in 1848, individual experiments in education could not succeed in a hostile environment which rejected modernisation and industrialisation.[42] The majority of converts were devoid of an economic basis. Severed off from their old community, they depended for their livelihood on the evangelical one and the Anglican Bishopric. The same year that Martineau published her account, Bishop Gobat ruled that no Jew was to be baptised unless he or she would earn a living. Finn herself was painfully aware of the hindrances to the missionary enterprise. It is ironic that her ideal convert, who receives a middle-class education, is dislocated from her environment and sent off to England, far from the turbulent social scene of Palestine.

It is in the writers' own religious *vision* and ideology that significant changes occur. Foremost among these changes is the transition from pilgrimage to mission or, put slightly differently, from the experience of the individual traveller, to a religious work which is socially and ideologically meaningful. Evangelical gender ideology and the development of the apparatus of literal interpretation of texts, together expanded the traditional mode of experience of the Middle East. However the evangelical vision of Middle Eastern women was as myopic as it was exclusive. As emphasised earlier, there was no place in it for Muslim women. And it was distorted by class as well as by religious bias. Mrs Finn's Rachel is an exception. Typically the model for the enlightenment of the unregenerate was that of working-class education, with the emphasis of the latter on discipline and an apprenticeship in an 'industry' or gainful manual occupation. Moreover, sympathetic as it is, the image of Jews and Christians too is distorted. For it is de-historicised. In contradistinction to secular literature on harems, evangelical ethnography dislocates the life of women out of its context and time. And as we shall see, writings on non-domestic topics, display the same weaknesses on an even larger scale.

9

Feminising the Landscape

Outside the domestic sphere, in the open landscape, even the confident Mrs Finn seems to lose her self assurance. She corroborates experience with authority. Women's work for women is one thing. Writing about it is another. Both are compatible with evangelical gender ideology and the policy of the metropolitan missions. But describing landscapes, relating the story of a journey, this is something altogether different. It involves a redefinition of the relationship between the pilgrim and historic places and a space traditionally perceived as public and identified as male. Of course, as already argued, evangelical gender ideology emphasised the negotiability of the domestic and public spheres. And vital religion made women's travel more acceptable than ever before. It appears, however, that once outside the *haremlik*, or the Jewish or Christian 'home', women writers tend to depend on external authority and draw on conventional or culturally dominant images of the Orient.

'Authority' comprises two kinds of popular discourse which converged and cross-fertilised in the middle decades of the nineteenth century. The first discourse is the semi-scientific language characteristic of the new non-academic orientalist fields of study, examined in detail in Chapter 1, notably Biblical geography and archaeology. Adjacent to this discourse is the visual imagery of paintings of Biblical, or Scriptural themes. Both kinds of discourse had a similar purpose: the authentication of the Scriptures. Devout geographers and painters sought to illustrate the historic and prophetic parts of the Bible and the New Testament and not to investigate the texts scientifically; to corroborate the status of the Word of God, not to doubt its veracity. Moreover, geographers and painters used comparable approaches and technical apparatus in their respective interpretation of texts and landscapes: literal Biblism and symbolical, or figurative visual typology. Each of these apparatuses, with their respective techniques, were utilised by travellers to authenticate their own experiences. Most significantly, in contradistinction to the higher criticism of the Bible and the science of philology, Biblical geography and painting were accessible to non-specialist and informally educated audiences, notably the female audience.

Averagely educated tourists were familiar with the major works on the geography of Palestine, its *flora* and *fauna* and the customs and manners of its people. Edward Robinson's *Biblical Researches* and its sequel *Later Biblical Researches in Palestine* (1842 and 1856) are reckoned practical guides to the contemporary Palestine, together with the Bible itself and Josephus' *Wars of the Jews*. *Flora* and natural life are observed with the help of Henry Baker Tristram's works. William Maclure Thompson's best-selling *The Land and the Bible* is known to virtually all evangelical tourists, even the despised 'Cookites'. From the early 1870s, the better informed tourists draw on the surveys of Palestine, issued by the PEF.[1] The wealth of geographical literature put at the disposal of travel-writers a pseudo-scientific vocabulary, a terminology that could render the amateur discussion an aura of authority. Picture images of Palestine too were acquiring a status comparable to that of the popular semi-scientific texts. By the 1850s, paintings of Biblical themes were mass-produced commodities, within the reach of heterogeneous audiences. The originals of Roberts, William Holman Hunt, Wilkie and Karl Haag fetched these artists large sums (Hunt's 'Scapegoat' brought him L5,500, the largest sum paid for the work of a living artist). Biblical themes were regularly exhibited at the Royal Academy, not to mention more popular (and down-market) platforms like the famous Leicester Panorama. Reproductions of the old masters and modern painters were available in the mass-circulated family Bibles and in the albums of Biblical portraits and scenes produced by the brothers Dalziel. As George Landau and Kenneth Bendiner have pointed out, the visual imagery of Victorian painters was shaped by evangelical writing.[2] I would argue that artists, specially landscape painters, in their turn had a formative influence on travellers who utilised pictorial symbolism and conventions. The travelogues of women in particular seem to draw on visual images. Before examining the relations between visual and verbal representations of exteriors, a few words on the dependence on textual authority are in order.

To reconcile between authority and actual experience, the women resort to the citationary technique which is quite common in travel-literature. As Percy G. Adams notes, a traveller cites earlier tourists to authenticate his or her own experience.[3] Characteristically men travellers or geographers are cited. Thus authority has obvious connections to gender. To the reference to authority may be added the apparent diffidence and self-depreciation of female writers. Apparent is the key-word, because the resort to masculine authority is rhetorical and is used as an artistic ploy. This stratagem already characterises the works of the early evangelical tourists. One typical example is Catherine Harriet Egerton, Lady Ellesmere, whose views on harems were discussed earlier. In the apologetic preface to her travelogue on Palestine, Egerton, in a rather diffident tone, states that she did not write for money. She is not a professional writer, nor an experienced traveller, but a pilgrim and philanthropist. The book, in fact, was commissioned by the Female Hibernian Society, a separatist women's organisation, devoted to the education in the 'rudimentaries' of poor Irishwomen and girls.[4] A philanthropic motive, then, legitimises Egerton's venture into a masculine genre. Indeed the stated purpose of publication is generically 'feminine' and Christian: charity to needy women. Moreover, throughout the book Egerton interchangeably uses two distinct voices. Her own voice is audible in the passages on domestic life in Palestine. In those passages which describe travel she resorts to the first person plural, which is the common voice of herself and Francis Egerton, first earl of Ellesmere, her husband and co-traveller and a fellow evangelist.

Two decades after the Egertons, Marthilda Cubley begins her *Hills and Plains of Palestine* humbly, with an *apologia* which echoes that of her predecessor. Cubley dutifully acknowledges her debt to learned authorities on the topography and history of Jerusalem, stressing her own ignorance and amateurism. 'Indeed, I wonder at my audacity in identifying my name with a description of Jerusalem – a subject that would certainly employ the noblest pen.'[5] Cubley is in fact a gifted sketcher and her illustrated album is still considered a classic and is sought by collectors. Significantly she is not apologetic in the parts on women and domestic life. Emily Ann Beaufort, Cubley's contemporary, is exceptionally well-read in classical authorities and in contemporary literature on the Scriptures. Yet she is not easy when writing on historical sites and their location. The chapter on Jerusalem in her *Egyptian Sepulchres* begins with the conventional, almost obligatory, self defense:

It would be very presumptuous and quite as useless for me, to attempt to a detailed description of Jerusalem: but as most of those who are anxious to glean a more distinct image of that one holiest place on all the earth, have derived from faint idea of the locality from the various accounts of travellers.[6]

Faint indeed. Her professed ignorance notwithstanding, Beaufort proceeds to a carefully annotated description of the city. And her reader is hectored with quotations from the Scriptures, Josephus, Robinson, Fergusson, the Italian topographer and surveyor Pierotti, Solomon Munk and August Salzmann. There is no doubt that Beaufort's citationary technique and seeming lack of confidence are designed to impress upon an informed audience her image as a knowledgeable and widely-read traveller. Still in the 1860s, Mary Eliza Rogers and Mrs Finn, both recognised as authorities on contemporary Palestine, adopt a male voice. Neither travels 'unprotected'. Rogers is always accompanied by her brother, the Vice Consul Edward Thomas Rogers. And she habitually uses a de-gendered first person plural. Finn's Emily Russell, the writer's replica and alter-ego, too, is never allowed to travel alone outside Jerusalem. She is protected by her brother Walter, or by a male missionary. When Emily/Finn discusses local religious traditions, or place names, she does not do so in her own voice, but in that of one of the male protagonists.[7]

The respect to authority and the rhetoric of citation create the impression that the religious experience of women is subsumed in the evangelical tradition of travel and Biblical inquiry. It is the intention of writers like Finn and Rogers to create such an impression. Underneath the rhetoric of deference, however, the women's works reveal a disillusionment with texts and with the power of words to represent landscapes and recapture the experience of sacred places which the writers underwent. The mistrust of textuality is, of course, generic and characterises travel-literature as such. Travellers from the seventeenth century onwards, had been aware that words do not 'translate' sights or sense-impressions satisfactorily. And travellers to the Middle East, as Van der Bilt argues, were no exception.[8] Women, it seems, were painfully aware of their own inadequacy as writers. Significantly they relate the poverty of verbal images and the degeneration of language to cliché, to gender. Thus women repeatedly argue that their power of observation and description is limited. They emphasise their lack of originality. And they sense that what they write is different from what they saw, in the way in which a reproduction is different from its original. Most significant, their own reproductions fall short of the standards of travel-literature. The self-depreciation of Egerton, or Cubley, may be juxtaposed with the self-confidence of writers on the harems like Pardoe, or Dawson-Damer, or Finn herself in the 'domestic' parts of her works on Palestine.

The mistrust of textuality leads writers to seek inspiration and authority in religious painting. And visual representation is increasingly perceived by these writers as more 'real', more true to the original and more emotive than words. As Disraeli shrewdly observed, devout Anglicans fueled their spirit not by mediating the images of a Catholic Christ, but by rapturously poring over reproductions of landscapes. In one steamy, though technically euphemistic passage in *Tancred*, he describes how Montacute hangs over Lady Bertie:

> with pious rapture, as they examined together Mr. Roberts' Syrian drawings, and she alike charmed and astonished him by her familiarity with every locality and each detail. She looked like a prophetess as she dilated with solemn enthusiasm on the sacred scene.[9]

Clearly the absence of figures in Roberts' landscapes made them acceptable not only to a Tractarian, like Montacute, but to Low Church Anglicans too. Thus during the Second Revival of the mid-century 'empty' landscapes, which did not feature figures, could move audiences in a way comparable to that of Catholic iconography.

A number of women tourists and missionaries drew in water-colours, or sketched. I already mentioned that Mrs Finn, a Low Church Evangelical, advocated a liberal artistic education to female converts. She illustrated her two books on Palestine with sketches of Biblical scenes and 'types'. Mary Eliza Rogers, a gifted engraver, contributed four illustrated chapters to Wilson's *Picturesque Palestine*, a lucrative quarto reproduction in three volumes (she was the only woman contributor). Cubley, Mackintosh, Egerton and Beaufort, all included sketches in their books. Non-evangelicals like Marianne North and Elisabeth Butler were even less inhibited in their treatment of picture images than the religious travellers. Note that there are numerous women sketchers and water-colourists, but not oil-painters. Sketching and water-colour painting were amateur occupations. Unlike the 'serious' arts they did not require formal training and could be studied inside the home. More important, sketching was reckoned feminine and was one of the 'accomplishments' of the middle-class woman.[10]

It is hardly surprising, then, that women who were insecure in their role as travellers and travel-narrators presented themselves to the reading-public not as scribes but as 'sketchers', or 'drawers' and, in the last decades of the century, 'photographers'. The 'sketch', or 'impression', whether pictorial, or in words, is an incomplete artefact, the work of the amateur. On the other hand, sketching may also be a metaphor for that kind of writing which seeks to imitate the immediacy of a painting done 'on the spot' (one of the writers' favoured expressions) or a photograph. Only visual images, or their reproduction in word images, it was felt, can capture the emotionally charged landscape of the East. Emily Beaufort, looking at water-colours of Tadmor (Palmyra), is affected by them as Montacute is affected by Roberts' lithographs of the Syrian landscape. The lethargic, weakly Beaufort is invigorated merely by looking at the pictures of the ruins of Tadmor. One of her co-travellers is none other than Karl Haag, one of Britain's foremost water-colour artists and a specialist in oriental and Biblical themes.

Beaufort's own description of Tadmor, the longest I have come across (covering, as it does, 50 pages) brings to the fore the Christian chapter in the history of Tadmor and celebrates the legendary Zenobia, Queen of the Syrian Desert, a paragon of womanly virtue, who had dared defy the power of Rome. The entire description swarms with references to colour, design and to painting techniques.[11] Mathilda Cubley declares that in her work:

> The descriptive letter-press is a subordinate part of the work, and I have nothing to advance in extenuation [sic] of its want of power, its prosaic sentences, and many other defects. I am sensible that it too much resembles the description that might be given by a showman in exhibiting a travelling panorama.[12]

As early as 1870, Ellen Miller, the Quaker missionary, notes that a photographic reproduction of a landscape, especially the emotionally charged landscape of Palestine, is more 'real' than the travel account: 'Would that a process of mental photography were invented, whereby the innumerable plates in the camera of memory, might be made to cut their impression on paper, with the atmosphere, colouring, and glow of the East'.[13] But how then, to reconcile art and evangelical religion? For surely Low Church Evangelicals *and* non-conformists regarded painting in the same way that they did the theatre (Arnold's denunciations of the views at Exeter Hall on the arts immediately spring to mind). The spectacle, the image and the icon were associated with the Catholic Church. And they smacked of Tractarian idolatry. As Landau and Bendiner note, there was no strong tradition of religious painting in Britain after the Reformation.[14]

Notwithstanding, in the middle decades of the nineteenth century, artists associated with the Pre-Raphaelite Brotherhood and drawing their inspiration from Ruskin's *Modern Painters*, attempted to combine realistic detail with spiritual content and a message, in a genre aptly described by Landau as *typological, or figurative symbolism*. Events in the Scriptures, or Biblical scenes were depicted in realistic detail and designed to be interpreted by the viewer as prefigurations, or anticipations of events in the life of Christ, in the history of the Church and in Christian cosmology. Thus Hunt's 'Scapegoat', featuring the *sair l'azazel*, or Talmudic penitential goat, is a 'type', prefiguring the *agnus dei*, the emblem of Christ's own sacrifice to humanity.

Now typological symbolism has certain affinities with Biblical literalism. In the same way that they read the Bible in search for Christian types, or gazed on the landscapes of Palestine in search of illustrations to the veracity of the prophetic texts, so did evangelicals look at the works of Hunt or Roberts. Thus Thomas Hartweel Thomas, in a standard work for divinity students, argues that a 'type' primarily denotes a 'draught' or a 'model', from which 'a perfect image is made out'. But in a theological sense:

> a type may be defined to be a symbol of something future and distant, or an example prepared and evidently designed by God to prefigure that future thing.[15]

The association between visual images and the vision of the prophet is particularly apt here. Interestingly Hunt, like Ruskin himself, saw the painter as a prophet and an interpreter of his own times, with a vision of the future.[16] Not only churchmen like Thomas, but unordained men and women of all denominations, were schooled in the protestant tradition that encouraged the pursuit of Biblical examples and types. Countless sermons and books preached a reading in search of the anticipations of Christ and the *millennium*.

And the evangelical millenarian propensity to a literal reading of the Scriptures, discussed in some detail in Chapter 6, made evangelists specially placed to utilise visual images.

By the 1860s, reference to painting is so common that a skeptic like Frances Power Cobbe, an evangelical recently turned agnostic, thinks it necessary to review the phenomenon critically. Cobbe questions the ability of painters to reproduce Biblical types and landscapes. Significantly the butt of her criticism are not the Old Masters, but 'modern painters' like Hunt whom she, unjustly, accuses of lack of realism. Cobbe begins her discussion rather casually by relating a simple, innocent episode. On her way to the Dead Sea, she passed a young Bedouin shepherd, with a lamb on his shoulder. Cobbe reads the scene in a rather literal manner. The two figures and the landscape in which they are framed are illustrations to a Biblical scene and, at the same time 'types', or prefigurations of future events. The scene enacts the parable of the lamb. Every detail, every 'particular was true to the story': the shepherd, the rescued lamb, the hills and plains of Judea and 'literally too, when he had found it, he laid it on his shoulders'.[17] The lesson too, is clear: 'no lost sheep is suffered to wander away from the true faith'. Cobbe turns from this rather disingenuous exercise in literal interpretation, to a disparaging criticism on contemporary representation of scenes similar to the one she just described:

> I longed for a painter's power to perpetuate that beautiful sight, a better and truer lesson than the scapegoat. Men wonder sometimes what is to be the future of art, when opinions change and creeds become purified, and we need Madonnas no more than Minervas for idols, and are finally wearied of efforts, ever fruitless, to galvanize with the sport of art, the corpses of dead religions. It seems to me as if modern painters and sculpturers have before them a field hitherto almost unworked, in giving the *real* colouring to the great scenes and parables of ancient story . . . and not repeating for ever the conventional types and costumes, and localities, which the old masters adopted of necessity . . . No oriental ever wore those pink and blue robes, or sat in those attitudes. The real dress of a peasant of Palestine is at once far more picturesque and more manly, the real attitudes of repose intimately more imposing and dignified. Look at the painted scenes in Palestine, the deep, dark, shadowy woods, and

Greek temples, and Roman houses. Are these like the bare grove
of Gethsemane, or the real edifices of Syria?[18]

The allusion to Hunt's 'Scapegoat', probably the most written
about contemporary painting, was not lost on Cobbe's readers.
More relevant here, not only the metropolitan audience, but the
evangelical community in Palestine, was quite familiar with the
story of the production of the 'Scapegoat'.

Instead of aping artistic conventions, Cobbe urges travel writers
to restore to the narrative arts ('history' and 'poetry') their status.
Only by a factual treatment of actual places and people, she argues,
a treatment that is clean of symbolism and ideology, can we capture
the character of a place. Palestine, 'its climate, *fauna, flora,* geography, and all the rest, have a right to be considered in illustrating its
history, or its poetry'.[19] Cobbe exemplifies the subversive reference
to authority. The passage is rounded off with a final allusion to the
failure of the 'Scapegoat' to illustrate a Biblical theme: 'As to the
goats, [of Palestine] they are awfully vicious-looking, with long
black hair, and an extremely diabolical cast of countenance.'[20] More
characteristically, writers are not as openly critical as Cobbe towards
authority. Yet even those among her female contemporaries who did
not abandon evangelical Christianity use the rhetoric of deference
discriminately and, sometimes, rather subversively, criticise authority and validate the female experience of travel.

EVANGELICAL FEMININE GEOGRAPHY

The main characteristic of the women's travelogue is an insistence
on the domestic aspects of Palestine. 'Domestic Palestine' – the title
of Mary Eliza Rogers' famous book – is a mobile term. It describes
the private, female space of the harem, but is also extended to public
spaces, traditionally identified as male and associated in evangelical
ideology with 'the world'. The modern version of the pilgrimage
becomes a statement on gender, on the historic role of Christian
women, and their role in evangelical eschatology. The Scriptures
and Scriptural landscapes are read complementarily, in search of
female types, or of examples of feminine behaviour, which may
serve as models for contemporary women. Special emphasis is
put on domestic themes and episodes in the Bible and the life of
Christ. And, as we shall see, typological symbolism and painting

techniques are utilised in the reading and representation of events and types which prefigure, or foreshadow, occurrences in history, or in the *millennium.*

Certainly, the gendering of geography is not typical of women writers. Indeed, the association between Nature and gender is central to modern travel-literature after the emergence of the scientific journey. As Barbara Maria Stafford notes, certain geographical features, notably mountains, had been used as metaphors for masculinity. Other features and landscapes – declivities, rivers and lakes – had become metaphors for femininity and female sexuality. Furthermore, as virtually all students of orientalist travel-literature agree, the geography of the Middle East in particular was subjected to the erotic fantasies of Westerners. Not only the harem, but oriental landscapes were eroticised and feminised, and elevated to symbols of fertility and sensuality.[21] Evangelicals, men and women divest the orient of its sexuality. They tame the exotically oriental, by locating landscapes and people in a conceptual and ideological framework familiar to the Christian West. Nature has its place in the providential scheme of history and thus is comprehensible and controllable. It is not the grandeur of a landscape, or its sublimity that attract religious tourists, rather the ordinary, domestic aspects of the Eastern panorama. To be sure, the grandeur of Nature, or of sacred places, is commented on in a rather conventional manner. And the sight of the Walls of Jerusalem, or Lake Tiberias, or Bethlehem, or the Cedars of Lebanon never fail to move tourists. But it is the familiarity of a place or a type which is singled out. Take for example Elizabeth Charles. Having dutifully noted the importance of Arabic nomenclature for the identification of Biblical sites, she proceeds to a personal statement:

> It is delightful to . . . go in and out among the sacred names, and acquire a kind of everyday familiarity with the sacred places by the associations of every day life . . . for the ordinary occupations of daily life there is nothing incongruous with the association of faith. The ties that bind us to our sacred histories are no flimsy gossamer of devotional sentiment . . . but heart ties which *familiarity* only strengthened; and what we feel more is, how the life and the men of the Bible times were how like our own life.[22]

'Sacred names' – and the allusion to Edward Robinson's writing on place-names is transparent – become real and meaningful only when we associate them with the familiar and ordinary. Charles is referring to the raging debate on the location of the last events in the life of Christ and the Crucifixion, whether they took place on the site of the Sepulchre, or nearer to Mount Temple, as Fergusson implausibly argued, or outside the Walls of Jerusalem. She realises that archaeology and the study of local nomenclature contribute to an understanding of the topography of Biblical and early Christian history. Nevertheless she points out that the debate is of very little use to an ordinary pilgrim, like herself:

> . . . the interest of the general landscape [is] so far greater than precise accuracy as to a few years of ground, that we took care not to confuse our recollections of the whole scene by entering into discussion as to the exact site of particular events . . . [23]

'Precise accuracy' and details may take over the scene or entire picture. About a decade after Charles, Agnes Smith, later to become one of Europe's foremost Hebrew and Syriac scholars, argues that the authorities on the geography of the Holy Land are of little use to female travellers. Smith's *Eastern Pilgrims: Travels of Three Ladies* is one of the most original and shrewdest accounts on Victorian religious travel. The book relates the actual journey to the Middle East, of the Lewis-Gibson twins (thinly disguised as 'Agnes' and 'Edith') with their chaperon Violet. Smith's litany of the difficulties of the three middle-aged spinsters, their ordinary joys and commonplace response to sights and people, is a burlesque on travel-literature. The following, picked up at random, is a pastiche on the literal Biblism of evangelical pilgrims:

> 'Is it not strange', said Edith, 'to think how this soil has been watered with the blood of Philistines, Midianites, Syrians, Israelites and Egyptians – that here Sisera was vanquished, and the city of mourning went up for good King Joshia [sic], as the mourning of Hadadrimmon in the Valley of Megidon? so shall be the repentance of Israel; and may not this valley yet be the scene of cruel slaughter when the world's armies shall be gathered to the battle of Armageddon?'
>
> 'I', said Agnes, 'have been studying the site of Naboth's vineyard, which was probably on the bare slope of the North East below this town. How can I fancy Jesabel looking out of her palace window, as Jehu drove furiously along that valley.'

'And I', said Violet 'have been wondering if these howling dogs of Zera'im are the descendants of Jesabel's devourers? Also if the Aible we passed is the same as Ibleem, where King Ahazia was smitten'.[24]

The sense of familiarity with the historically or geographically remote is enhanced by the nature of the relationship between geographical places and their parallels in the Scriptures, between contemporary orientals and Biblical types. The smallest episode gleaned by the traveller is interchangeable with a Biblical theme, or story. This relationship cannot be described simply as associative. And it is not allegorical or symbolical, because the allegorical or symbolic travelogue interprets things described as *in reality* signifying or symbolising others.[25] To give an example, what Bunyan's Christian and Apolyn signify, what the 'delectable mountains' stand for, is far more important than their allegorical personifications in the *Pilgrim's Progress*. Typological descriptions, such as the travellers', trace connections and similarities between two sets of unique events, one literal (or Scriptural) and the other *real*, each of which is equally concrete. What permits such reading and representation is the assumption that the Holy Land is changeless. Its landscape and people are immobile. The modern Arab or Jew are the very same as the Biblical or early Christian types. Similarly customs, costumes and manners are practically unchanged from the times of the Patriarchs. Charles and Finn see in a piece of land near Bethlehem the very place where Ruth met Boaz, an event which itself foreshadows the birth of David and the nativity. To the devout Augusta Mentor-Mott and Elisabeth Bowen, a storm in Lake Tiberias, is the very storm that rocked the boat of Jesus.[26]

Paradoxically, evangelical women need to de-historicise the landscape and people of Palestine, to locate themselves in the eschatological picture of history. The sights of historic places visually evoke 'types' or examples of a truly Christian feminine life. Examples abound. The village of Magdala (Biblical Migdal) near Lake Tiberias as well as the neighbouring hamlets of Bethsaida and Chorazin evoke the life of the Magdalene, an example of repentance, humility and conversion to the true faith.[27] Sarepta, or Biblical Zarepath, is home of the devoted widow, a paragon of Christian motherhood, awarded by the prophet Elijah, who revived her dead son.[28] The sight of Tyre makes Christ's commendation to the woman of Tyre

meaningful and real: 'O woman, great is thy faith; be it unto thee
even as thou wilt.'[29] The valley of Isdraelon invokes a multitude of
female characters which are public and political and are therefore
difficult to identify with. The prophetess Deborah; Jezebel, the
idolatrous, murderous queen; Jael, wife of Heber the Kenite, herself
slayer of Sisera are, all three of them, dangerously assertive. 'He
[Sisera]', notes Mott, 'craved shelter and a draught of water, but
the treacherous Kenite brought him *lebban* in a "lordly dish"; and
when the wearied fugitive, confiding in her hospitality, was fallen
asleep, she took nail . . . and fastened it into his temple. Treacherous
Jael . . .'[30] In Mott's opinion, Deborah's domesticity atones for
her political activity and qualifies her as one of the 'mothers of
Israel'. Jezebel and Jael, devoid of motherly instincts, cannot serve
as ideal feminine models. The village of Shunem is a reminder of yet
another paragon of womanhood, the Shunamite, whose offspring is
restored to life, as a reward for her faith in the prophet. Women
drawing water from a well near Schechem (Nablus), illustrate the
episode in which the woman of Samaria brings water to Christ.
The water is 'the holy spirit whose purifying stream shall raise her
[the Samaritan's] soul from earth to heaven'.[31]

Jerusalem presents a feminised space, rich with Scriptural types
of femininity and domestic episodes related to the life of Christ. The
stations of the Cross, along the Via Dolorosa; the Church of Holy
Sepulchre; Bethany, hometown of Mary, Martha and the restored
Lazarus; the Garden at Gethsemane, each and all of them exemplify
the innate religiosity of women, their capacity for a faith 'of the
heart' and their affinity to Christ. The presence of the pilgrims
themselves in those places where historical types had once lived
has remarkable effects on these pilgrims. Lady Herbert's neglected
account of religious travel, entitled *Cradle Lands* and probably published in 1865, swarms with references to the role of women in
the Life of Christ, to their devotion and, most important, to the
relevance, for Herbert's contemporaries, of historical types. Mary
Elizabeth Herbert, née A'Court, a spiritual child of Henry Manning
in his Tractarian period, who later followed him into the Roman
Catholic church, shrewdly compares the experience of Catholic
women to that of 'Protestants' (the latter being her euphemism for
Low Church evangelicals). Her heroine, an unnamed 'English Lady'
– obviously Herbert herself – tours the Holy Land unprotected,
together with a saintly Catholic philanthropist. The itinerary of the
two women resembles that of the medieval pilgrim. They enact the

experience of the women surrounding Christ during his last days. And that experience is not only emotionally fulfilling but socially significant:

> It is a blessed and comforting thought to women, wearied with the struggle and strife and misunderstandings of this hard world, that to them alone was granted the unspeakable privilege of ministering to this sacred Humanity, and that he never rejected their love or their sympathy. The last at the cross, the first at the sepulchre, it was to a woman that our master first showed himself after the Resurrection. Therefore, let them take heart, going forth, like Mary, to meet Him with his Cross, ministering to the suffering members of his sacred body, and keeping ever near to his sacred feet; and so will their love and fidelity meet with its reward.[32]

Herbert's corporeal imagery and her adoration of the body of Christ are anathema to evangelicals, who typically substitute places, or empty exteriors, the *loci* of sacred events, for figurative representation. Yet evangelicals, like High Church Anglicans, make typological connections, not only between types, or anticipations and their 'anti-types', or realisations, but between *situations* in the lives of Hebrew or Christian characters and similar ones in the lives of modern women. 'Last on the Cross and first at the Sepulchre' is not a trope. It becomes an historical reality which the evangelisers utilise in their propaganda. The Scriptural examples are the explanation and justification for the women's role as missionaries and reformers. In the interesting case of Low Church Amy Fullerton there is a situational parallel, between conversion and the Sin, both associated with the garden. Fullerton's own conversion occurred in *the* Garden, at Gethsemane, the scene of Christ's agony and betrayal. The very image of a garden is complex, conjuring up as it does pictures of domesticity and sexuality. For the original garden is the place of sin and the Transgression, brought on by a woman. Fullerton reverses the traditional image, associated with Eve. And significantly she combines a religious message with a realistic description, distinctly visual and rich in colour.

> I found myself in a small enclosed area, in the centre of which stood two olive trees of very great age, carefully surrounded by a small low palling, and the space within planted with

flowers. Plants also were arranged outside the railed space on stands, and a low seat, overshadowed with geraniums and other creepers of the wildest growth, seemed to offer a most desirable resting place. Many were the reminiscences which rose in connection with the scenes before me . . . It was a solemn moment for reflection on sin, on the great and dominant power over the human heart of that Great enemy of mankind – Satan – existing now in so many fearful forms, and causing at that time Divinity in humanity to experience a mortal agony, and sow forth drops of blood over the ground. Oh, what refuge is there in prayer . . . prayer that our heart may be opened more and more to the blessed truths left us in the teachings of our Divine master, who, having loved us, will love us to the end.

Note that Fullerton's moment of realisation – of the sin – is brought on by a visual experience. Seeing the pictorial scene of the Garden causes her to 'reflect' and convert.[33]

RUTH AND NAOMI: FIGURES IN A LANDSCAPE

Obviously certain landscapes and sites are more open to interpretation than others and invited over-reading for doctrinal purposes. Places which could not be easily classified as 'Jewish' or 'Christian' held special fascination for millenarians, who reproduced them in countless descriptions, in travelogues and prescriptive texts. Characteristically domestic plots from the Old Testament are mixed with episodes from the New, and Hebrew types typologically connected to Christian characters. Palestine, then, is perceived as a syncretic place. The geographical syncretism of the country is associated with the diversity of religions. Naturally, Christianity triumphs. Nevertheless the interrelations between Jewish and Christian history inscribe themselves in landscapes, as well as in the customs of the people. It is typical of evangelical geography that it writes out Arab (Muslim) landscapes. In a similar manner, Victorian Christian ethnography ignores the Muslim family and the harem (See Chapter 6).

As with descriptions of the domestic, indoor space, so with those of exteriors, the theme of the relationship between the Jewish past and contemporary evangelical Christianity is anatomised in stories of conversion. Typically the stories are about women and not men.

Scriptural models of conversions are related in a typological manner to the work of women missionaries with local Jewish and Christian women. The scene of the conversion is as important as the type, or character, of the convert. The landscape is subjected to evangelical ideology. Places like Magdala (Migdal), Bethlehem, Samaria or Jerusalem, associated with traditions of conversion, are reproduced in pictures and in countless verbal descriptions.

The ultimate place of conversion is Bethlehem. Descriptions of the town and its surrounding countryside are usually longer and more intense than most representations of Scriptural landscapes. It is important to note that the writers treat the town itself and the Church of the Nativity perfunctorily. The Nativity as a domestic episode and a concrete, historical event are located in the country-side. What attracts these writers is the combination in Bethlehem, of a Jewish tradition, the conversion of Ruth the Moabite, and the archetypal motif of the Nativity, coated in Christian terminology. The story of Ruth prefigures that of Mary. For David, born of Jesse, son of Oved, son of Ruth, foreshadows the real Messiah. Moreover the plot of the Biblical story is distinctly feminine. It evolves around the relations between an older and a younger woman. Ruth forsakes her country of origin, her family and religion to accompany her widowed mother-in-law, Naomi, on the latter's return journey to Judea. As already argued the friendship between an older woman and a younger one, the missionary 'mother' and her disciple and 'daughter', is an important theme in evangelical ethnography. The Biblical example of a solidarity between women is then incorporated in the propaganda of the missions. Moreover Ruth is a domestic character. She is not assertive, nor overtly sensual like Jezebel or Jael. She looms large in the landscape of Bethlehem but does not oust the patriarchal figure of Boaz. Thus she does not offend notions of hierarchy. Finally Ruth – rather than Mary, whom she prefigures – is the link between Jewish and Christian eschatology, being chosen as the matriarch of the clan from which David and Jesus came. Beaufort's representation of the countryside of Bethlehem is typical.

> the night was gone, the beautiful stars had vanished back into heaven, and the sunlight in vast tides of brightness had come in . . . it lit up the hill-tops and brightened the terraces and the little meadows, while all the distant mountains of the Dead-Sea deepened into hues of blood-red and deep purple. Then I looked

back at Bethlehem, all white and radiant like a peal of great price, as the bright beams shone on the convent walls where many hearts were then bowed in prayer; the vines and the corn around it soon lightened up, and I thought of Ruth, the gentle, brave-hearted girl, and half-fancied I saw her following after the broken spirited Naomi, as she turned back to the home of her childhood; I fancied I saw her treading the oak roads of Moab – descending those steep and rocky mountains yonder – crossing the rushing river and the wide, hot plain of Jericho – cheering and supporting her mother-in-law across the barren, desert hills and valleys of Judea with firm but tender words – herself strong in the unselfish, earnest purpose of her heart, until the instinct of her guileless purity had led her to her kinsman, Boas, and she went singing through the golden corn with her heart full of the glad promise . . . I thought of David, the beloved of God, chanting on those breezy hills his own sweet hymns . . . and of another meek and guileless virgin yet more pure and more lovely than even Ruth of old, who arose and went rejoicing in God her saviour into the hill-country of Judea, and bare [sic] a Babe in the little Bethlehem – the fertile, the city of Ruth and David, by whom she and all the world shall be blessed.[34]

Note the application of female images to the land and the town of Bethlehem itself. Both are 'fertile', yet pure, exactly like Ruth and the virgin Mary. A popular vulgarised late version of gendered Biblical geography may be found in Augusta Cook's guidebook, *Way of the East*. Cook's title is brazenly emblematic: 'Shepherd's Field'. And the text itself similarly revealing.

Christ! David! Boas! Ruth! these are the names for ever linked with Bethlehem. And it was there, in that same shepherd's plain, that Boas reaped and his maidens gleaned. The East changes rarely if it changes at all: where the corn grows today is just where Ruth followed the reapers. Far away, beyond the Judean hills appears the blue outline of the mountains of Moab. That is where Naomi, Ruth and Orpah climbed, and when they had reached a certain point stood and wept together.[35]

And so on and so forth. It says much for Mary Eliza Rogers that instead of repeating the Biblical episode she refers to it very subtly. Rogers visits the symbolic house of a Bethlehem carpenter whose wife – her name is, naturally, Miriam – has just delivered of a child. The child is put in the arms of the visitor who may vicariously experience motherhood. It is remarkable that the unmarried and childless Rogers does not let her intense feelings dim her observatory skills. She reproduces details like the swaddling of the baby, the apparel of Miriam and her mother (obviously a rustic St. Ann). She (Rogers) then fixes on the older woman's veil, expertly using synecdoche, to invoke the Biblical original of the miniature picture she represents: 'Her long linen veil fell from her head over her shoulders, in graceful folds to her feet, which were naked! In such a veil as this, Ruth, the young Moabitish widow, who three thousand years ago gleamed in the fertile fields of the broad valley below, may have carried away the six measures of barley, which her kinsman, Boas, the then mightily man of wealth of Bethlehem – Juda [sic] give to her'?[36]

Rogers' description should be read together with Finn's representation of Bethlehem. Written three years apart (in 1863 and 1866 respectively); drawing on diary and official consular materials and on contemporary religious painting, the two versions are only superficially similar. Finn is a pre-millenarian. Her whole approach to landscapes is, thus, influenced by the evangelical notion of prophecy and the centrality, for its fulfillment, of the conversion of the Jews. Of course, Rogers too is an evangelical, but – it may be recalled – she explicitly proscribes institutionalised proselytisation. She can, therefore, get through the Biblical story without explicitly mentioning conversion. As for Finn, she arranges the entire *Home in the Holy Land*, so that it evolves around the story of Ruth and Naomi. But most significant, Finn's *roman-à-cléf* is about the representation of the story of conversion in pictorial images. And her book is a comment on the relations between religion and authenticity in art.

Let us remember that the main strand of action in the book is the preparations of the Russells (Emily and Walter) for Walter's painting of the Biblical theme, in its historical place and from life models. Finn's evangelical *Bildungsroman*, then, is intertwined with a discussion about the problem of suitable representation of Biblical landscapes. The idea of a realistic painting, from Nature, of the story of female devotion and conversion, is introduced by Mr Russell, Walter and Emily's father, on the road from Jaffa to Jerusalem. It is his last wish – for he dramatically expires on that very road. His son Walter comes to Palestine to execute his father's last wish. The rest of the book is about the preparations for the actual painting.

It may appear that the female *Bildungsheld* is subsumed in a story
of symbiotic brother-and-sister relationship. It is Walter who paints
Bethlehem, not Emily. It is he who builds for himself a career. She
provides him with a home. But without Emily there can be no paint-
ing. Significantly she selects the female live models. She chooses
Jewish, rather than Christian or Bedouin ones. The choice is impor-
tant. It is, in itself, a statement. Evangelical ethnographers, indeed
Biblical ethnographers in general, must choose between Christians,
Jews and Muslims as the remnants of the historical people of
Israel. Whose life best illustrates Biblical customs and manners?
The Bedouins, the most obvious successors of the nomad Patriarchs,
were too 'oriental'. *Fallahin* and town-dwellers even more so. And
Muslim women would never pose for strangers. Evangelicals were
attracted to Jews. But what Jews? The dress of Ashkenazi, Eastern-
European Jews resembled that of eighteenth-century Polish nobles
more than the apparel of their Mediterranean ancestors. Sepharadic
Jews and local Christians seemed more suitable 'illustrations'. Both
fitted in the evangelical notion of pre-ordained history with its
emphasis on conversion and the restoration of the Jews to their
land. Emily/Finn, then, chooses two Sepharadic Jewesses as models
for Ruth and Naomi. Obviously without Emily there could be no
Ruth and Naomi. And it is naturally from her point-of-view that
the reader is presented with the picture.

Like Rogers, Finn utilises contemporary paintings and ideas about
the authentication of the Scriptures in religious art. There is evidence that Walter's original is the painter William Holman-Hunt.
Like his Pre-Raphaelite model Walter prefers landscape painting
to portraits. And this is by default and not by choice. As is well
known Hunt chose the Biblical penitential goat for a theme because
he failed to procure human models. The litany of his dealings
with his Jewish models was the talk of the protestant community
in Jerusalem and was known to both Finn and Rogers.[37] Pre-
Raphaelite ideas concerning representation from 'Nature'; concerning the importance of ethnographic accuracy in a picture; concerning
the inadequacy of academic norms – are discussed throughout the
book. Walter wants to paint a 'real picture', a picture that the
inhabitants of Palestine, not a European audience, will comprehend.
He emphasises local colour and detail. His artistic notions, are in
short, those of Hunt's, as expressed in the characteristic statement
of that painter: 'my idea was to paint the picture direct from the
nature found in Palestine and to learn, whilst living with the people,

their ways and thoughts.'[38] Add to all this the fact that Hunt himself began, in 1850, a pen and ink drawing, which he never completed of Ruth and Boaz. He soon realised that to be absolutely accurate, the picture would have to be done from nature: 'Hunt talks of going to Jerusalem when he can . . . set about the Ruth, and paint it on the spot'.[39] Hunt did go to Jerusalem, though only in June 1854, staying there until the autumn of 1855. It was during that time that the Finns and the other missionaries to the Jews came to know the painter. Rogers, possibly, even probably, the daughter of Hunt's teacher and her namesake (she is registered in the records of the consulate at Jerusalem as the daughter of a Mr Rogers, 'engraver'), knew Hunt. She mentions the painter in *Domestic Life* and is singled out in his memoirs as a *connoisseur* of painting. And it is she who brings him news on the pre-Raphaelite Brotherhood.[40] Neither Finn nor Rogers publicly acknowledge a debt to pre-Raphaelite ideas, but these ideas come across pretty clearly. Finn's *Home* concludes with a chapter entitled 'My Brother's Picture, Return of Naomi and Ruth', which includes a detailed description of the painting. The picture is dominated by the two female figures. Significantly Boaz is pushed to the background.

> The expression of Ruth's countenance was in the picture – subdued, chastened by sorrow, yet lighted up not more by the sunshine which fell full upon her by a glow of surprise and joy at the warm welcome which the people of Bethlehem were giving to her mother-in-law. She glances half shyly, yet with extreme delight, upon the crowd of kinsfolk, old and young, which are pouring from every door and gathering upon every roof and terrace to greet Naomi.[41]

Finn then moves on to a close-up of the figures, drawn from Sephardic models picked at the mission's 'house of industry' (Caroline Cooper's Jewesses Institute):

> Black eyes and raven tresses are generally associated with majesty, heroism, fire, but here they were the ornaments of a sweet, confiding, womanly woman. True, the lines of the face contributed in no small degree to this effect; and constancy, rather than firmness, was expressed by that gentle mouth . . . The graceful bend of the beautiful neck told of willing submission to her adopted mother.[42]

and Naomi:

> Naomi was a contrast to Ruth in most respects, not only in age but in fairness of complexion; in the marked and beautifully chiselled features for her face; in her firm step, and the decided expression of eyes, nose and mouth . . . There was dignity, but no longer pride in her carriage.[43]

Finn then moves away from the female figures at the center, to the Biblical landscape.

> The principal figures – Naomi and Ruth – were represented with their faces towards Bethlehem, which they were just entering. The houses, tier above tier, received the rays of the declining sun, which shone cheerfully from behind a clump of olive trees upon the faces of the travellers . . . Behind Naomi and Ruth . . . the landscape sloped downwards and stretched away, mountains and valleys in successive descent towards the Jordan Valley, now lit up by the evening sunshine, or varied by lengthening shares . . . Far in the background the Moab mountains closed the landscape: they reflected not now the glorious tins of their winter colouring, but were veiled by a mist of ethereal blue; their summer robe; vague, dreamy-looking, the very type of unchanged ground. But the town of Kerek (Kir in ancient days) gleamed and glittered as the rays of evening fell . . . Kir and Bethlehem, the two cradles of David's royal line, bathed in glorious sunlight . . . [44]

The reference to Hunt and to realistic orientalist painting is transparent. Finn (like Rogers) emphasises local colour, folkloric types and Biblical themes. There is, however, a novel stance in her usage of Biblical typology and Biblical literalism. Finn/Emily succeeds where Hunt and numerous other orientalist painters had failed. She produces a verbal-pictorial illustration of the feminised landscape of Palestine which is 'authentic'. Her illustration of the Scriptures draws on live female models and her own intimate knowledge of the life of Jewish and Christian women. Emily can paint women because she herself is a woman. She can domesticate the empty landscape and fill it in with figures.

The evangelical writers and illustrators may seem more qualified than most tourists to represent an ethnographically accurate picture of the people of Palestine. Missionaries were field workers, intensively experiencing the life of their object of study; they resided in the Middle East for long periods and they mastered local languages. Among the philanthropists and amateur ethnographers located in Jerusalem were a few polyglots, with a command not only of Arabic, but also Hebrew and Ladino (the Finns are salient examples). But the proselytisers were not, could not be, 'ethnographers' in the sense Clifford uses the term. For their vision of the 'other' is pre-determined by millenarian Christianity and a proselytising zeal. The ideological and religious bias, apparent in writing on women, particularly evinces itself in descriptions of landscapes. Feminised exteriors even more then domestic spaces are framed in the millennial, philosemite ideology and are utilised for missionary propaganda.

Part IV

A Secular Geography of the Orient: Authority, Gender and Travel

10

Harriet Martineau's Anti-Pilgrimage: Autobiography, History and Landscape

EASTERN LIFE AND MARTINEAU'S WESTERN LIFE: THE JOURNEY AS *BILDUNG*

In 1847, a righteously indignant John Murray the III turned down the manuscript of Harriet Martineau's account of her recent travels in the eastern Mediterranean. There must have been a good reason why Britain's leading publisher of travel-literature, known for his interest in that very region, rejected a book on it by Britain's leading female journalist and political writer. Murray, it later transpired, was put off by Martineau's 'unChristian' views.[1] He was also disturbed by her use of a book on travel as a medium for a study on religion. His proscription of *Eastern Life* echoes in the reviews which followed the publication of that book by Edward Moxon.

Periodicals as different as the Evangelical *Eclectic Review*, the latitudinarian Tory *Fraser's Magazine* and the liberal *British Quarterly Review* joined together in a chorus of disapproval: 'If she had confined herself to the proper object of a book of travel', opined the *Review* 'and not ventured beyond the sphere of her own knowledge and experience, she might have produced a work second to none in its class and value.'[2] The gender of the author, it seems, disqualified her from scientific observation and an analytical work on religion. The *Fraser*, in a review emblematically entitled 'Fuss in a Book-Club, as Related by a Copy of Miss Martineau's *Eastern Life*', is less restrained: 'I should have liked it better if all that Socinian trash had been extracted, to form a tit-bit, for such a delight in the monstrous crudities of the dim-sighted infidel.'[3] The general feeling summed up by Henry Crabb Robinson was that: 'It is not in a book of travel that Christianity is to be attacked.'⁴ Certainly not in a book on the 'cradle-lands' of modern faiths.⁵

The 'crude' and 'monstrous' mixing together of a personal narrative of travel and an impersonal general essay on the history of religion was very deliberate and carefully structured. Martineau, as most of her students agree, was neither a Biblical scholar, nor an expert on religion. Nor was she an original thinker. Like her other political works and popular 'philosophical' writings, *Eastern Life* is a synthesis, a *compendium* of second-hand ideas.⁶ But it is an original autobiographical account of one writer's Middle Eastern experience. And it is precisely the juncture between autobiography and Martineau's quintessentially Victorian notion of history that marks out the book from the usual kind of travelogue, and it is on that particular juncture that most of this chapter focuses.

The combination of autobiography (that is the story of a chunk of a life narrated by an authoritative I) and a historical essay, makes it possible for Martineau to document as well as to vindicate her own break away from evangelical Christianity *and* the religious model of the female voyage. Or, put differently, she substitutes a truly secular journey for the pilgrimage. I begin by looking at the way in which travel is used as metaphor for her *Bildung* as well as for history. The rest of the chapter is organised on lines similar to those of Chapter 3 on Mary Wortley Montagu. First I look at the genealogy of the central concepts and themes in *Eastern Life*, locating their origins in culturally dominant literary and critical traditions. Then I discuss Martineau's ambivalent position in relation to these traditions and the dominant specialist discourse on the Orient. Special attention is paid to representations of oriental landscapes, because it is in these representations that Martineau's complicity with and resistance to, tradition best evinces itself.

As the very title of Martineau's work implies, *Eastern Life* is not merely the account of a journey. It is really about Martineau's own *Bildung*, her development from a Christian, a Necessarian Unitarian to a non-believer. The book then is a part of an effort to write a religious autobiography and vindicate Martineau's abandonment of Christian practices and Christianity. According to the *Autobiography*, written seven years after her Middle Eastern experience and seventeen years before her death, that experience remodelled Martineau's character, reshaped her view of the world and entirely changed her intellectual and emotional life.

I had little idea . . . how the convictions and the action of the
remnant of my life would be shaped and determined by what
I saw and thought during those all-important months I spent
in the East. I need say nothing here of the scenery, and the
atmosphere, and the novelty and the associations with hallowed
regions of the earth. The book I wrote on my return gives a fresher
impression . . . but there are effects produced on my character or
mind which it would have been impertinent to offer here.[7]

This, of course, is a *post-mortem* analysis. And Martineau is honest
enough to admit that she had not realised at the time how important
the journey was. Nevertheless, the fact that her Middle Eastern
experience is causally related to her re-education is revealing. Like
many other Victorians, Martineau saw travel as part of middle-class
education and the *Bildung* of *bourgeois* men and women.

Yet *Eastern Life* is more than merely an individual story of
development. The Middle Eastern journey is a metaphor both for
Martineau's own intellectual and emotional life and for history, the
'present' and the 'past'. Physical contact with the landscapes of
Egypt, Syria or Palestine with their many associations enhances her
own historical consciousness, her sense of the relations between the
past and the present and the notion of continuity. The centrality of
landscapes for the historicisation of the Orient cannot be overstated.
Travel in an open space becomes a metaphor for history. The traveller's progress in a landscape is analogous to the progress in time of
mankind and the evolution of civilisation. Progress is the key-word.
And it is a quintessentially Victorian one. It expresses the characteristic contemporary notion of history as linear and ameliorative, a
notion which has its basis in Britain's economic and political power.[8]
Martineau, with all her radicalism and criticism on the Macaulian
interpretation of history and Whig complacency, reveals herself to
be a Whig. The story of mankind, according to *Eastern Life*, is one of
unarrested progress, an evolution from 'lower' to 'higher' societies
and civilisations, from 'childish' or 'infantile' structures and ideas
to 'mature' ones. Contemporary Western civilisation is superior to
earlier ones and, naturally, to non-European civilisations still in the
'infantile' stage.

In the following, taken from the *Autobiography*, the notion of
evolution is presented in spatial terms. Martineau explains to the
reader how she arrived at her concept of the evolution of religion
and, at the same time, hit on a plan for the book. The moment of

revelation occurred while she was on her way from Petra, capital of ancient Edom to Hebron, the town of the Patriarchs:

> Step by step as we proceeded, evidence arose of the true character of the faiths which ruled the world; and my observations issued in a view of their genealogy and its results which I certainly did not carry out with me, or invent by the wayside. It was not till we had long left the Nile and were leaving the desert, that the plan of my book occurred to me . . . It was evident to me in a way it could never have been if I had not wandered amidst the old monuments and scenes of the various faiths, that a passage through these latter faiths is natural to men, and was as necessary in those former periods of human progress, as fetishism is to the infant nations and individuals, without the notion being more true in the one case than in the other. Every child and every childish tribe of people, transfers its own consciousness, by a supposition . . . to all external objects, so as to conclude them all to be alive like himself; and passes through this stage of life to a more reasonable view; and in like manner, more advanced nations and individuals suppose a whole pantheon of gods first, and then a trinity, – and then a single deity . . . in proportion as this stage is passed through, the perceptions of deity and divine government become abstract and indefinite, till the indistinguishable line is reached which is supposed, and not seen to separate the highest order of Christian philosopher from the philosophical atheist.[9]

Evidently Martineau still sees herself as a Christian philosopher, not yet an 'atheist'. And she still adheres to some 'infantile' Unitarian notions; the idea of the 'unity of deity', the belief in a personal God and the after-life (I shall discuss her Unitarianism and its influence on her Orientalism later).

Martineau was never one to understate a case. Indeed the entire passage swarms with spatial images, associated with movement and mobility. The landscape of eastern Palestine becomes a mobile location, that changes and develops. The ideas are conceived 'on the wayside'; individuals, like peoples, 'progress', 'passing' from lower to higher stages in their development. And implied in all this is Martineau's own development, from a Christian (though a particularly 'advanced' kind of Christian, a Unitarian rejecting the Trinity) to a 'Christian philosopher' and ultimately to an 'atheist' –

a development associated with the ages of man: childhood, maturity and the age of wisdom.

The ameliorative concept of history and religion superimposes itself on the narrative of travel. *Eastern Life* is divided into four sections, each corresponding to an historical phase or 'age' and at the same time to parts of the genetic journey. The first and largest section, 'Egypt and its Faith', devoted to the evolution of Egyptian religion from local and tribal Animism to a national monotheistic faith, covers the Nile journey from Cairo to Nubia and the Second Cataract. 'Sinai and its Faith' reenacts the Exodus, discussing Mosaic monotheism. The third section, describing Martineau's tour of Palestine covers the rise of Christianity and the concluding section, the shortest in the book is about Syria, home of religious syncretism, characterised by a syncretism of landscapes which represent pagan polytheism and Christian and Muslim monotheism. The sequence of the genetic journey then is parallel to Martineau's chronology of the genetically related religions.

Martineau thought herself rather original. In one smug and rather self-opinionated letter to Atkinson, the charlatan mesmerist and amateur positivist who entered her life in 1846, she notes that: 'I do not know of anyone who has regarded the matter [of the progress of religion] thus; and it is an awful thing to stand alone in it'.[10] Yet despite the claim to originality, despite her self-dramatisation and that of the narrative of the journey, that very narrative betrays Martineau's allegiance to contemporary critical and literary traditions. As the perceptive Emerson tartly noted: 'The vice of the book is that of the position, namely, the running to Egypt because other people do, and then writing of it with the air of . . . Herodotus.'[11]

'A USEFUL AUXILIARY', THE ALLEGIANCE TO TRADITION[12]

Of the critical traditions three in particular deserve our attention: the Unitarian tradition of reconstructive Biblical interpretation and an historical approach to Scriptural texts; the higher mythological criticism which had originated in Germany, in the *Tübingen Staft* and which had certain impact on English Bible scholars from the late eighteenth century; and last, but by no means least, the literary tradition of the essentially antiquarian *description de l'Egypt*, the *récit-de-voyage* which developed after Napoleon's occupation of Egypt and which narrates a tour of Egypt's ancient monuments.

There is no doubt that in 1847–48 Martineau was still most comfortable in the Unitarian tradition of Biblical interpretation. Like many Unitarian women she was thoroughly read in the Scriptures and, for a woman, well educated.[13] At an early age she became acquainted with the writings of radical Unitarian divines like Carpenter and thinkers like Benjamin Priestley, not to mention those of her own brother James, later to become the leader of British Unitarianism and, until the early 1830s, the single most important person in Martineau's own life[14] (as is well known Martineau's own conversion to positivism damaged the relations irreparably).

The most rational kind of Christian belief, Unitarianism, rejects the concept of the Trinity and the Divinity of Christ, which it substitutes with that of the unity and impersonality of God. More importantly, Unitarians treat the Scriptures not as a revealed text, but as an historical document, and are particularly suspicious towards those parts of the Old and New Testament which deal with the supernatural or unnatural (notably with miracles).[15] The Bible itself has to yield evidence of the non-Trinitarian nature of the first, pristine Christianity. Contrary evidence is connected with the historic struggle against priestcraft and Catholic (later Anglican) obscurantism, against the authorities who conceal the true nature of the text. So despite her attack on Unitarian beliefs and ethics (or rather the lack of both), and the attempt in the *Autobiography* to date back her own disillusionment with Unitarianism as far as the early 1830s,[16] it is precisely her allegiance to Unitarianism which equipped Martineau for the role of the critical, rational pilgrim. And I should like to emphasise the word 'pilgrim'. For *Eastern Life*, though it departs from the narrative of religious travel is, essentially, the work of a Christian apologist, not an atheist and is within Christian tradition, not outside it.

Moreover, as mentioned earlier, Martineau was not just a Unitarian but a Necessarian. At an early age (when exactly is not clear)[17] she embraced Benjamin Priestley's doctrine of Necessity which rejects the idea of a free-will and free choice and attributes human acts and natural phenomena to causes which are outside human control. Implied in Priestlian Necessarianism is a determinism and a materialism which Martineau found increasingly difficult to reconcile with her own optimism and belief in progress and the educability of humans. Nevertheless, *Eastern Life* uses Necessarian terminology and as I later show the very interpretation of the causes for the rise of the great faiths of the past, notably Egyptian religion, is Necessarian.

With the higher Biblical criticism, Martineau was only superficially familiar. It is certain that she read David Friedrich Strauss' *Leben Jesu*, available in Mary Ann Evans' (George Eliot) enormously influential translation.[18] She was undoubtedly attracted by Strauss' application of the 'myth theory' to the life of Christ, which he (Strauss) saw as an unintentionally creative legend (myth) developed between the death of Jesus and the writing of the Gospels in the second century. Indeed Martineau applies the notion of the myth indiscriminately: to Egyptian religion, to the Old Testament and naturally to the Gospels. Yet she is, it seems, completely unaware of Strauss' use of Hegelian dialectics in his own criticism (she had never read Hegel), and of the development at Tübingen of philological techniques of text-criticism.[19] As both E. S. Shaffer and Mineka show, Unitarianism had a special affinity for Biblical criticism. And Necessarians in particular were the first in Britain to embrace the mythological approach to the Scriptures. So the two critical traditions are mutually complementary.

To turn now to the third tradition. The very choice of the itinerary; the place apportioned in *Eastern Life* to the Nile journey; the emphasis on Egypt's ancient history rather than on contemporary Egypt; the reliance on classical travel-literature – all these betray a connection to the more traditional kind of travel-writing on the Middle East, the *récit-de-voyage* which describes ancient monuments. As is well known westerners rediscovered Egypt in the second half of the eighteenth century. But until the publication in 1836 of Lane's *Manners and Customs of the Modern Egyptians*, interest was limited to the pre-Islamic era. Muslim civilisation and contemporary Muslim society are hardly ever touched.[20] The works of Pococke and Norden, Ibry and Mangles, James Bruce, William Hamilton and Giovanni Belzoni are, all of them, motivated by a fascination with Egypt as it had been known through the classical texts of authors like Herodotus or Manetho. Even Wilkinson's enormously influential *Manners and Customs of the Ancient Egyptians* (1837) and Lane's own unpublished volumes on Egypt's monuments are, despite their reliance on contemporary scholarly methods, steeped in that classical tradition. As Leila Ahmed has pointed out, the anciently charted voyage in Egypt was itself an enactment of an experience already mentally formalised.[21]

More significant even, the early Egyptological texts, written decades before the emergence of Egyptology as an academic discipline,
depended entirely upon detailed descriptions of monuments. The
study of hieroglyphs was still undeveloped. And field (that is modern) archaeology, with its methods of stratigraphy for the purpose
of periodisation (based largely on the classification of pottery) was a
thing of the future. Monuments and the classical texts were the only
sources of information. And these monuments and the landscapes
surrounding them were seen as texts, testimonies about life in a
bygone age.

Martineau's work is informed by this antiquary and un-systematic
approach to the past. The very title of this work reveals a bias
towards pre-Islamic history. The fact that in the title the 'present'
actually precedes 'the past' should not deceive us. Martineau is
interested in the present not for itself, but as a contrast to a greater
past. She is a 'genealogist' (her own term). Time and again she
discloses her total lack of interest in the Muslim Orient and in contemporary Egypt. Out of 24 chapters in the section on that country
five are devoted to the 'modern Egyptians': two to Cairo, two to the
effects on Egypt of the Khedive's experiment in modernisation and
one is the notorious twenty-second chapter – 'The Harem', discussed
earlier. With the exception of the last chapter, the parts on modern
Egypt draw on popular contemporary texts and not on Martineau's
own experience. Already in the second chapter she remarks that: 'I
shall say nothing here of the great Arabian city [Cairo]. With me it
stands last in interest as last in time, of the sights in Egypt.'[22] Later
she sums up a three weeks' cruise up the Nile which, in her opinion
did not include 'sightseeing', that is the sightseeing of monuments;
'and now begins our real Egyptian journey'.[23]

The antiquarian, traditionalist aspect of the *récit*, particularly in
the part on Egypt, may also be evinced from the position *vis-à-vis*
classical travel-literature. Classical authorities are a source of information and inspiration. They are cited as often as Martineau's own
contemporaries. The image of the traveller who is also an historian,
an image embodied in Herodotus, is constantly evoked. Thus sum-
ming her impressions of the monuments at Luxor, one of the cities
built by the Pharaohs of the Middle and Late Kingdoms, Martineau
invokes the legendary figure of Herodotus 'who here seems a
modern brother-traveller [and who] stood on this spot remembering
the Iliad, as we are now remembering it'.[24] 'Brother-traveller' is, one
suspects, both a generic and a literal combination. Martineau could

not affiliate herself to a female tradition of travel-writing. So she applies the familial imagery, characteristic of her representation of history and the genealogy of religion, to orientalist scholarship and the orientalist tradition, which has roots in the classical attitudes to the East. She is a member of a family as well as a professional community, a guild, as it were, of historians. Furthermore, her reverence of and reliance on the classical tradition outweigh her insistence on a commitment to science. Herodotus' own mythologising of customs and beliefs during the Middle Kingdom becomes the basis of her own speculations on the 'genealogy of religion'. She cites a number of Greek and Hellenic authorities known in the West fragmentarily or only at second hand: Hecataeus of Miletus, Hecataeus of Abdera, Diodorus Siculus, Strabo and Eratosthenes of Cyrene. For chronology and periodisation she relies on the historian Manetho. [25] Significantly the only 'oriental', that is Muslim, authority cited in *Eastern Life* is the twelfth-century traveller Abdallatif, favoured by Western scholars because of the wealth of information in his *Travels* on Egypt of the Ptolemies. And Martineau knew Abdallatif only through Silvestre de-Sacy's 1810 translation. A chapter entitled 'Famine in Egypt', ostensibly on contemporary Egypt, incorporates Abdallatif's own account on the famine in the twelfth century. Information on Egypt is inferred from a medieval text and that very same text is elevated to an authority on Egypt of the Ptolemies. [26]

Martineau's notion of history is at odds with her antiquarianism and unhistorical methods. On the one hand, she advocates belief in progress and a notion of history as an ameliorative process. On the other hand, her belief in progress does not seem to extend to non-European societies and countries. The very usage of Abdallatif implies that Martineau sees Egypt as changeless and unalterable. And antiquarianism and anachronism sometimes belie her image of herself as the scientific modern traveller.

IDEOLOGY AND LANDSCAPE

Two notions emerge from the welter of borrowed ideas. They are not original notions, nor particularly coherent ones. Often they are incompatible. But a coherence of thought or consistency are not characteristics that one looks for in a 'useful auxiliary' writer. Rather one should look at the way in which Martineau received culturally dominant notions, incorporated them in her writing and complied with, or resisted, these notions.

The first notion is that human history is the history of ideas. 'Ideas', Martineau argues, not entirely originally, 'are the highest subject of human cognisance, the history of Ideas is the only true history and a common holding of Ideas the only real relation of human beings to each other . . . this constellation of Ideas is one and the same to all the different people.'[27] Martineau's definition of the unified 'constellation of ideas' is not precise. But at various points in the discussion she argues that a belief in a unified deity, embodying universal and cross-cultural values, is a characteristic of the great Middle Eastern religions which shaped Western culture and civilisation. The unified idea gradually evolved from the Animism of the Egyptians before the Early Kingdom; through the apparently polytheistic Pharaonic state-religion; through primitive Mosaic monotheism, which localised the concept of a universal deity; through the universalism of the early Christian beliefs; through Islam; through the transitory phase of 'doubt' and the rise of 'religious philosophy', towards the imminent end of belief in a personal deity.[28]

The fulcrum of all this is that Egyptian religion was monotheistic. Indeed it was 'purer' in its notions of the deity than Trinitarian Christianity. 'The Egyptian priests', maintains Martineau, 'upheld the doctrine of the unity of God and of a 'divine moral government.'[29] The plurality of deities, the diversity of cults and practices should not confuse students of Egyptology. Necessity alone, compelled the ruling élite to compromise with the needs of the common people. The very vocabulary Martineau uses tallies with Necessarian terminology which politicises religion, and with the Victorian language of class

> to meet the needs of the comprehension of the populace [the priests] 'lowered their doctrine' by deifying the attributes of the gods and creating a multitude of local, tribal and national deities, incarnated in animals. They were the creatures of their time. It did not occur to them that knowledge is the birth-right of all.[30]

And elsewhere: 'The plurality of deities rose merely from the practice for popular use of deifying the attributes of the one Supreme God' [Osiris, the incarnation of benevolent powers and of the Good].[31] The passages, picked up at random and interchangeable with many others, are immensely revealing. For Martineau's vocabulary discloses her sensibilities as a middle-class radical and reformer, sensibilities which shaped and directed the discussion on religion and travel. The Victorian notions of class are projected onto the classless theocracy of the Pharaohs (note the derogatory use of 'common people' and the 'populace'). Also, Martineau's belief in the educability of the lower class comes through the criticism on the Egyptian élite.

Factually – as even the contemporary critics noted – the argument for monotheism is very precarious. Martineau, it seems, draws on one historical example of (what in her opinion was) monotheism. The example is the promotion during the reign of Amenohtep IV, better known as Ikhnaton (ruled 1379–1362 B.C.) of the cult of Aton (a form of the sun-god Re-Horakhth) to a state cult and the abolition of the cults of the other deities, notably the powerful Amon, worshipped in Heliopolis. Martineau depicts Ikhnaton as a great religious reformer of the calibre of a Luther. Later scholars saw his reforms as a heresy, which did not affect popular belief. The supremacy of Aton came to an abrupt end with Ikhnaton's death.[32]

Contemporaries were particularly incensed by Martineau's insistence on the genetic nature of the relations between Mosaic monotheism and the cult of Aton. As a matter of fact, belief in the common origin of and the sameness of all Western religions was quite conventional and may be traced back to Christian apologetics at the time of the Deist attack on revealed religion. Martineau particularly draws on William Warburton's notorious *The Divine Legation of Moses* (1737–41) in which he, rather eccentrically, argues that the Hebrew legislator's lack of belief in a future life is solid proof of divine inspiration. Martineau dismisses the argument, but she shares Warburton's views about the historic Moses. The 'real man was an Egyptian priest. And it was from the priests that he received the notion of a unified deity. He popularised this notion and made it "democratic"'. The Exodus and Israel's wanderings in the desert were experiments in an education to democracy.[33] The analogue with the education of the English people is transparent.

The notion of history as the evolution of an idea is at odds with another, that is the belief that it is material conditions that shape ideas and beliefs and that these conditions change according to place and time. This muddle may be attributed to the fact that when *Eastern Life* was written Martineau was still a Necessarian and a Unitarian. And she had to reconcile the idea of necessity, discussed earlier, with her own optimism and a belief in free-will and the scope of human action.[34] The second, materialist notion of history is evident in Martineau's emphasis on the impact of the environment on individuals, societies and civilisations. And it is that emphasis which dictates the treatment, in *Eastern Life*, of landscapes.

Very early in the narrative of the Nile journey, Martineau brings on the idea that civilisation is determined by geography and that religion and morals are formed by landscapes. The idea is introduced in the form of a digression from a thin, seemingly naïve description of the Necropolis of Siüt, or Asyoot (the ptolemaic Lycopolis), the chief town in the *Nome* that is, province of the wolf – hence 'Lycopolis' – and capital of Middle Egypt. Martineau and her party paid a short visit to the chief attraction of Asyoot, the so-called Stable Antar, a tomb dating from the reign of Usertesen I of the XII Dynasty and identified only in the late 1870s by F. Lewellyn Griffith. Significantly this is Martineau's first actual contact with Egyptian monuments and the landscape of the desert. And she uses that opportunity to state her views on travel in Egypt and define the functions of observation and representation. She begins by presenting herself as the ingenuous, inexperienced and rather ignorant tourist, only to make it clear later on that she is none of these. She admits that she has no knowledge of hieroglyphs and can therefore comprehend very little of the manners and morals of the ancient Egyptians. Then she 'speculates' (her term)[35] on the prospects of a science of Egyptology. The combination of scientific inquiry and the applied mechanical sciences would make it possible in the future to 'uncover' places like Asyoot and ultimately 'discover' more about the past. For the oriental landscape, or 'nature', is not only a key to the understanding of the history of civilisation. It is also the reason for the destruction of ancient civilisations, the obliteration of our past. Significantly Martineau fixes on the two most mobile, most shifting of the natural elements: the quicksands and the river, symbols of change. The dunes of the desert had covered the ancient monuments, thus concealing the past. However, the desert had preserved historical evidence:

> for many thousand years [the sand] shared equally with the Nile the function of determining the character and the destiny of a whole people, who have again operated powerfully on the

characters and destiny of other nations. Everywhere, the minds and fortunes of human races are mainly determined by the characteristics of the soil on which they are born and reared. In our own small island there are, as it were, three tribes of people, whose lives are much determined still . . . by the circumstance of their being born and reared on the mineral strip to the west, – the pastoral strip in the middle or the eastern agricultural portion. The Welsh and Cornwall miners are as widely different from the Lincolnshire or Kentish husbandmen.[36]

The diversity of geological conditions and local topography shapes manners and morals 'everywhere'. However, 'no where is the original constitution of their earth so strikingly influential on the character of its inhabitants as in Egypt. There everything depends – life itself, and all that it includes – on the state of the unintermitting conflict between the Nile and the desert' and elsewhere: 'It is of the formation of their ideas and habits, and the training of their desires [that she wishes to know].'[37]

Like most serious travellers to Egypt, Martineau is aware of the historical role of geography and the time-dimension of landscapes. Nature and natural phenomena, notably the increase and decrease of the tide of the Nile, are recognised as *records* and as testimonies to the past and the evolution, in time, of ideas and religion. The landscape of Egypt in particular and the Middle East in general is a system of signs, at the disposal of the traveller, who can read these signs, note them down and interpret them. Significantly Martineau refers to that landscape as 'picture language'. And the analogy to the pictorial language of the hieroglyphs is transparent enough.

The traveller, that is the 'scientific', or 'philosophical traveller', or the 'historian' – and Martineau uses the three terms interchangeably – is called upon to use his faculties of observation. The pictorial quality of oriental nature and art calls for a particular kind of knowledge and investigation. Thus travelling is, first and foremost, seeing. *Seeing* the sights and monuments is *knowing* about them. And the historian is, first and foremost, a sightseer. It is pretty clear that the notion that the only kind of knowledge about the Orient is that acquired by means of sense impressions is derived from Necessarian literature (mainly from Priestley) and possibly, even probably, from Locke, whose *Essay Concerning Human Understanding* (1690) and *Thoughts Concerning Education*, she had certainly read.[38] More important than the origin of her notion of knowledge as empirical and sensory is Martineau's conviction that that kind of knowledge is superior to others. It is important to note that she de-genders learning and the persona of the 'scientific', or 'philosophical' traveller. Sometimes, as in the following passages, she employs the pronoun 'he', hinting that her ideal is male:

> I can imagine no experience more suggestive to the thoughtful traveller, anywhere from pole to pole, than that of *looking with a clear eye* and *fresh mind* on the ecclesiastical sculptures of Egypt, perceiving, as much as one must do, how abstract and how lofty were the first ideas of Deity known to exist in the world. That he should go with clear eyes and a fresh mind is needful: for if he carries a head full of notions about idolatry, obscenity, folly and ignorance, he can no more judge what is before his eyes, – he can no more see what is before his face, – than a proud Mohammedan can apprehend Christianity in a Catholic chapel at Venice, or an arrogant Jew can judge of Quakerism or Quietism. – If the traveller be less with the clear eye and fresh eye and fresh mind . . . he may be startled by the evidence before him of the elevation and beauty of the first conceptions formed by men. (my emphasis)[39]

The repetitive, even compulsive use of the image of sight and of verbal expressions which denote 'seeing' is immensely revealing. Martineau herself was devoid of the other senses: she was almost deaf and her olfactory sense and sense of taste were damaged irreparably after an illness, in her late teens. Sense-perception for her is seeing. And the keen eye of the androgynous 'thoughtful traveller' is, in all her autobiographical writings, a metaphor for her own communication with the outside world. *Eastern Life* itself abounds with examples of that metaphor. 'Who cannot see what a stimulating and enlivening influence this [the Nile] must exercise on the character of a nation.'[40] Or 'none but those who have seen the contrasts of the region with their own eyes . . . can have any adequate notion how the mortuary ideas of the primitive Egyptians, and through them, of the civilised world at large, have been originated by the everlasting conflict of the Nile and the Desert [sic].'[41] And later on, in the prefacing chapter of the section on 'Sinai and its Faith': 'We were to see objects which he [Moses] saw, and as he saw them' and elsewhere she reveals that her sensory experience of the landscapes ('natural features') which shaped Moses'[42] beliefs and his monotheism made her realise the way history works, for 'only by its natural features could Moses himself now recognise the region where his mind was born and reared'.[43] And not only the traveller/historian, but the historical hero, the founder of a religion (naturally the prophet) too, is a 'seer'. The historical Moses could see that the Israelites were not yet ready to become a nation, therefore he re-educated them in the desert. Jesus could see that Egyptian/Mosaic monotheism was too rational. Therefore he introduced into it the doctrine of future life. Both these Coleridgean heroes (and Martineau is familiar with the dramatic visionary aspect of Coleridge's oriental heroes, notably Kubla Khan) saw the 'truth' even as they saw and merged with the landscape.[44]

The carefully cultivated image of the de-gendered traveller/historian who, objective and untrammelled by prejudice, gazes on an unknown landscape should not deceive us. The narrative of the journey in *Eastern Life* is subjected to Martineau's need to write her own history. And her representation of landscapes is determined by her muddled ideology of progress. Thus instead of the Evangelical geography that treats places and monuments as illustrations to a cosmogony, we get a geography whose purpose is to corroborate the secular materialistic myth of progress.

Yet there is no doubt that Martineau departs from the Biblical geography of the evangelical traveller and ethnographer. Her narrative may be appropriately described as an anti-pilgrimage and the *persona* of the traveller/narrator in *Eastern Life* is the very reverse of that of the pilgrim. To be sure, Martineau does not ignore the Biblical associations of oriental landscapes, of sepulchres and shrines. But she advocates a new kind of travel and a reading of landscapes that is radically different from the interpretation of the evangelical tourists. Throughout the whole of the book, but especially in the part on 'Palestine and its Faith', evangelical geography is trenchantly attacked. In its stead, Martineau proposes an historical understanding of the geography of the holy places. She criticises the 'literalists' who are so attentive to the word of the text that they forget its spirit and who, using the landscape as illustration to the Scriptures, dehistoricise places. 'Bibliotary', that is Biblical literalism, is tantamount to 'idolatry'. Taking her cue from Coleridge's condemnation of narrow-minded literalism Martineau charges on:

We hear much complaint from travellers of their pain from the superstition on the spot; but little or nothing of the perplexity or disturbance from the superstition they had left behind or brought with. The superstition I refer to is the worship of the letter of the Bible, to the sacrifice of the Spirit. As to the comfort and pleasure of the traveller in the Holy Land, it may truly be said that the 'letter killeth, but the spirit maketh alive'. I had opportunity to see the difference between those who were in bondage and those who were free. One of the best things that Coleridge ever said was that our idolatry would be succeeded by bibliotary. When I saw abroad, as I continually see at home, the curse of this bibliotary, I thought it hard to say which was the worst of the two. In idolatry, Christian or pagan, there is always some true idea involved, however much corruption may be associated with it; but in the awful error of mistaking the Records of the origin of Judaism and Christianity for the messages themselves, there seems no redeeming consideration. The error of bibliotary is the more gratuitous of the two. There is no declaration in the records themselves that they are anything more than records.[45]

And the corruption of bibliotary has so increased that the freedom of 'religious imagination' and 'reason' (both unmistakably Coleridgean terms) which had characterised the latitudinarian eighteenth century disappeared. Contemporary philosophers, scholars and historians in Britain have difficulty in publishing their studies (the last remark no doubt being an allusion to the rejection of Martineau's own manuscript).[46]

The invocation of Coleridge, indeed Martineau's affiliation to him, are immensely revealing. Coleridge, of course, had been a Unitarian like herself. And like Martineau he abandoned a form of belief which had initially equipped him with the critical tools necessary for a reconstructory historical interpretation of texts, and which had introduced him to the German higher criticism. More importantly, Coleridge had been the first influential disciple in Britain of the German mythologists Michaelis and Eichorn, founders of the Güttingen School. And as A. S. Shaffer has brilliantly argued, the German approach to the Scriptures as historical myths shaped Coleridge's literary imagination as well as his views on history.[47] Certainly, Martineau's own modest literary achievement should not be compared with his original genius. And she, unlike Coleridge, finally severed her relations with Christianity and opted for the 'religion of science' which he despised. However it is precisely because of Martineau's position as a 'useful auxiliary', the propagator of the beliefs and ideas of major Victorian writers and minds more original than her own, that her reference to and usage of an authority like Coleridge is interesting.

Although she had been always aware of the limits imposed on the true understanding of religion by bibliotary and superstition, it was travel through the historical landscape of the eastern Mediterranean which finally released Martineau from intellectual 'bondage'. The analogy to the Israelites and the Exodus is transparent. Most travellers, however, are still imprisoned in their unhistorical, prejudiced attitudes. In the following Martineau returns to the metaphor of the eye and to a pictorial, visual representation:

> Instead of 'looking before and after', and around them in the broad light of historical and philosophical knowledge, which would reveal to them the origin and sympathy and intermingling of the faiths of men . . . instead of having so familiarised themselves with the wants and tendencies of men as to recognise in successive faiths what is derived and what is original . . . instead of having the power of setting themselves back to the time when Christ lived and spoke, so as to see and hear him as if he lived and spoke at this day, our travellers may be seen, – even clergymen of the Church of England, – getting leave from the Bishop of Jerusalem to attend the ceremonies of Passion Week, joining in the processions in the Church of the Holy Sepulchre, wax candle in hand, and making obeisances to the priests. Travellers may be observed throughout doing one of two things; – overlooking . . . the incompatibilities of the Scriptural Narrative . . . or so fastening their whole attention upon one narration, to the exclusion of the parallel ones . . . I met with one devout pilgrim who was actually unaware of any incompatibilities in the different narratives of the birth and infancy of Jesus; and who declared, previous to inquiry, that there could be none, because – not the facts or doctrine – but the narrative was the Word of God! [48]

The passage is typical and interchangeable with a few other. Note the critic's emphasis on the Scripture as narrative, on the importance of a comparative reading and investigation of the text and on the status of the Gospels as historically constructed myths. Nor does Martineau's criticism stop here. Evangelical Palestine and its literally interpreted landscapes are presented as heathen places. The

Church of the Holy Sepulchre is a 'pagan temple'; the ceremonies performed in it are 'nunneries', lower than the lowest forms of fetishism; Jerusalem is the 'heathen Metropolis of Christiandom'.[49] In other words the Holy Places, the destination of the pilgrim, are to her abodes of profanity.

And not only the substance of what Martineau says, but the structure of the narrative, presents a departure from traditional or 'modernised' (that is contemporary evangelical) accounts of pilgrimage. In the first place the parts on the non-Christian (or pre-Christian) Orient – for example, Egypt or the geographically and religiously syncretist Syria – occupy more space than those parts devoted to the Judeo-Christian Mediterranean. Secondly, Martineau's voyage is not a journey of quest. There is no real conclusion, not on a personal autobiographical level, nor on an intellectual one. Certainly the earthly Jerusalem, symbol of the celestial city, is not her destination. And this is one important difference between her and the evangelical community of writers studied in Chapters 6–9. Moreover, travel in the Middle East taught Martineau that religion, even the most rational, historically oriented non-Trinitarian brand of Christianity is but a myth, shaped by geography and the material conditions of a society in a certain historic time. Yet she is not able to abandon her own irrational beliefs. She is in a transitory phase, parallel to the state of contemporary society, between 'Christian philosophy' and 'atheism' (her term) and belief in science. For instance, she still believes in the ideas of future life. And this is the reason why, time and again, she returns to attitudes of the ancient Egyptians to death, attitudes which may be evinced from the monuments and which, themselves, had been influenced by material conditions. Infantile, or childish societies, Martineau maintains, are 'by necessity' compelled to believe in the after life. Individuals too. She herself had been obsessed with the idea of death. The very act of writing an autobiography, twenty years before the end of her life, and of an autobiographical travelogue, is a proof of that obsession. As she wrote in a letter to Atkinson, dated 21 November 1874 and written when she was beginning the part on the Egyptian journey, in her own 'immature' phases Martineau found consolation in the belief in the hereafter.[50]

An *apologia pro vita sua, Eastern Life* is an attempt at a secular geography of the Orient, and a history that is not a cosmogony. It may be a blundering attempt, but still it is a culturally significant one. For despite her ethnocentrism, despite the cultural complacency and the firm belief, associated with it, in progress, despite the subordination of the discourse to ideology and autobiography, Martineau's is, I think, the first feminine travelogue proper that is not an account of a pilgrimage. It will take one generation and some changes in the position and opportunities of the educated middle-class woman for a non-autobiographical, ideology-free narrative to develop.

11

Queen Hatasu's Beard: Amelia Edwards, the Scientific Journey and the Emergence of the First Female 'Orientalists'

NEW CAREERS AND NEW ATTITUDES: THE BIRTH OF MODERN ARCHAEOLOGY

There is, apparently, a certain resemblance between the life and experience of the Orient of Martineau and those of Amelia Ann Blanford Edwards. Both women lived by the pen. Both had national reputations before their respective journeys. Both were unmarried and travelled in middle-age. Both seem to have embarked on their greatest adventure accidentally, almost thoughtlessly. For both women the *voyage-en-orient* would be the final stage in their *Bildung* as women, writers and feminists. Both travelled after long periods of illness, followed by depression and protracted convalescence, meticulously and obsessively recorded by Martineau, covered up by the more reticent Edwards.[1]

The similarities, however, end here. For in contrast to Martineau and the cohort of writers born after 1800 and active in the first half of the nineteenth century, Edwards, a generation younger, would benefit by the openings for women in journalism, the 'new sciences' and education. As a result of one fateful journey, in 1873, up the river Nile, she would move away from the traditional genres and a female literary occupation to traditionally masculine occupations: archaeology and Egyptology, the systematic study of Egyptian

254

antiquities and the history of Egypt that she, more than anyone in Britain and the United States, would promote.

Significantly Edwards carved a niche for herself in a male space which was not clearly defined and which had developed outside the orientalist establishment and the academe. As I argued earlier (see Chapter 1) the very ambiguity of status of the new oriental sciences of archaeology, Biblical topography and Egyptology, was what made them relatively open and particularly appealing to self-educated, self-made orientalists. Thus Edwards is doubly interesting. Her re-education in mid-life and move into a specialist career took place at the very same period when field archaeology and Egyptology were developing into disciplines. Also, her own *Bildung* and experience of travel may give us important clues to the experience and writing of women generally discussed in Chapter 1. These are the new orientalists, emerging in the 1870s and 1880s, on the periphery of the metropolitan sites of knowledge about the Middle East, apprenticed outside the universities in the last two decades of the nineteenth century and grudgingly accepted as members of the community of knowledge in the beginning of the twentieth. Warren Dawson lists some forty women Egyptologists in his *Who was Who in Egyptology*.[2] And 25 or 29 per cent of my own sample of travellers are professionals or semi-professionals, specialising in the 'new sciences'. Indeed the sample shows that the most significant shift after the decade 1881–90 is from work to a career and from pilgrimage, or literary travel to specialist travel.[3] Edwards combines elements of the old way of Mediterranean travel and the new. The 'queen of Egyptology',[4] founder of the Egypt Exploration Fund and writer of hundreds of works about Egypt, she was self-taught and self-made. And her work was informal and until about 1890 unpaid. To appreciate her relations (and those of the group she represents) to the orientalist community and the connection between the new experience of travel and the new kind of travelogue we must first look at the development of the new sciences which particularly attracted women.

It is not altogether surprising that women were attracted to the new orientalist sciences for the same reasons that had attracted them to the evangelical missions and proselytising work. The new sciences had a number of characteristics which could particularly appeal to an educated and enthusiastic amateur. To begin with these sciences – notably archaeology and Egyptology – emerged outside the universities and, until the very end of the period under discussion, were barely incorporated in the curriculum.[5] So no formal training existed either inside the universities or elsewhere. Oxford inaugurated a chair of classical archaeology in 1844, but of prehistoric archaeology only after the First World War. And at Cambridge the Anthropology and Archaeology Tripos, replacing the Anthropology Tripos, seemed worthy of a chair in 1924, 22 years before there was a chair of Egyptology. In the new secular University of London, more genial to women than the older sites of learning, a chair of Egyptology, the first in Britain, was founded in 1892 with Edwards' bequest.[6]

Thus the archaeologist or Egyptologist, like the evangelical ethnographer, culled his or her expertise from an informal individual experience, not from any formal training. Moreover, in a science particularly shunning theory and speculation and condemning deduction, that very experience was actually superior to theoretical *a priori* knowledge. The three great names in British archaeology may illustrate the characteristics of their trade. Sir Pitt-Rivers, Austin Layard, discoverer of Ninveh and, most important, Sir Flinders Petrie, the man who made the archaeology of the Middle East a discipline and a profession – none of them trained in a university.[7]

To females this individual and informal kind of work was doubly appealing. Edwards, for example, had never had any formal education. Travel was literally her *Bildung*, particularly travel to the eastern Mediterranean. As she was sailing up the Nile she was absorbing vast quantities of information about ancient Egypt and teaching herself the basics of hieroglyphic writing. The rest of her re-education as Egyptologist was completed in Britain, in the twenty years after her journey. The charismatic Scottish orientalists, the Giblews-twins, represent a comparable example from the adjacent field of Semitic languages. Admittedly linguistics – particularly the study of Hebrew and Greek – was a male profession and it flourished in conjunction with theology, probably the most misogynist of studies. But the twins, notably Agnes Lewis Smith, became experts on Syriac (Aramaic), which was neglected in the schools of divinity. Significantly despite their achievements, despite their international renown and despite their great wealth, the Giblews – figuratively and literally – hovered in the periphery of Cambridge, at a safe distance from the bachelor colleges.[8]

Unlike the first generation of writers, the cohort maturing at a time when the universities allowed in women was trained formally. Margaret Benson (1865–1914) was educated at Lady Margaret Hall at Oxford and acquired experience as excavator in fieldwork in Egypt, notably at the Temple of Nut at Thebes which became her major study.[9] Mary Brodrick, a student at the Sorbonne and *College de France*, under Maspero and Renan and later at University College, London, and was the first woman to be awarded a doctorate in archaeology (naturally not by a British university, women were awarded degrees only after 1919). And she successfully combined an active career as field archaeologist and Egyptologist with a teaching one. Only that happened after 1900.[10]

The informal, individualistic character of the new science un-doubtedly reflected and, at the same time stressed, a certain ambiguity concerning the purpose of archaeology, its methods and techniques, an ambiguity which had additional appeal. Broadly defined as 'the systematic study of antiquities as a means of reconstructing the past',[11] the new science superficially resembled the older evangelical archaeology of the Holy Land. What distin-guished the emerging discipline was its un-ideological nature and a stress on empirical study and field work, that is excavation, the systematic gathering of finds, their classification for the purpose of stratigraphy and periodisation. The 'dig', then, as Daniel put it, was the most salient feature of modern archaeology.[12] Moreover, the new students of oriental antiquities preferred artifacts to texts and material remains to literary ones. And increasingly the ordinary artifact for the daily use of ordinary men and women was becoming superior to the rare and extraordinary work of art.[13] Thus no primary knowledge was required of the excavator/classifier, only a great deal of work and meticulous care about detail (characteristics traditionally perceived as 'feminine').

The first generation of non-professional specialists, which Edwards represents, still remonstrated the antiquarian's 'promis-cuous' mixing of different kinds of material: artifacts and texts, great art and crafts, the rare and the ordinary, *colossi* and potsheds. Thus John Marsden, newly appointed to Britain's first chair of archaeology at Cambridge, writes of the 'close connection between the antiquary [archaeologist] and the poet'.[14] Both have great power on the imagination. And in 1866, Samuel Birch, Director of Egyptian Antiquities at the British Museum describes archaeology as 'the study of monuments of antiquity or the shape and meaning of sculpture, painting and symbolical representations'.[15] Sixteen years later Birch would obdurately oppose Edwards' plan to establish the EEF on the basis of her promotion of what he dubbed 'emotional

archaeology'.[16] Birch was expressing the fear of the orientalist establishment *vis-à-vis* outsiders like Edwards, Lewis Smith or Gibson.
His disgust at the imaginative and emotional aspects of the new
interest in Egypt undoubtedly has to do with the fact that the
founder of the Fund was a woman. Edwards herself, not known for
her admiration for Birch, echoes the views of the Fund's arch opponent. In a letter to the American antiquarian and Egyptologist, C.
Wm. Winslow, written after the publication of her work on Goshen
in the Delta area, she distinguishes between her own emotional
and 'romantic' brand of archaeology and the emotionless writing of her close associates, Flinders Petrie and Llewellyn Griffith.
Now Edwards' self-description is characteristically opinionated and
rather pompous. Yet it does point at precisely that appealing ambiguity of the new science, that mixture of the materials described and
the style in which they are represented.

> the Egyptologists do not write a picturesque and popular style
> like that of A. B. E. [Amelia Blanford Edwards], who had thirty
> years of literary work in the romantic school, and who has
> especially cultivated style – worked at it as if it was a science –
> and mastered it . . . style is an instrument which I have practised
> sedulously, and which I can plan upon. But our Egyptologists,
> etc., what do they know of that subtle harmony? They have
> never flung themselves into the life and love of imaginary men
> and women; they have never studied the landscape painting
> of scenery in words . . . It is not their vocation. I am the only
> romanticist in the world who is also an Egyptologist. We must
> not expect the owl of Athena to warble like the nightingale of
> Keats.[17]

Nightingale indeed. The very analogy with Keats is comic. And
one has an image of the formidable Edwards (whose childhood
ambition had been to be a vocalist) 'warbling' to the feebler 'owls',
Petrie and Griffith. But Edwards shrewdly compares herself not to
the traditionalist Egyptologists and antiquarians but to the young
generation of outsiders who within a decade or two would change
archaeology. She herself is in a middle-position, between a metaphoric writing, representing a romantic tradition and the stark style
of the professional. She had certainly moved away from 'romantic'
genres but did not quite become a 'scientist'. Her writing evinces
a tension between her literary inheritance and new experience.

Particularly this tension characterises the evolution of a new kind of *persona* of traveller/narrator.

THE MODERN EXPLORER: EGYPTOLOGY AS EXPLORATION

A Thousand Miles Up the Nile is not an 'Eastern life'. And although like Martineau's book, Edwards' book too is rich in autobiographical detail, the latter work is not an autobiography. It is in fact the nearest that we get to an impersonal, non-autobiographical *récit-de-voyage*. Furthermore, beyond commonplace utterances on the Scriptures and scriptural landscapes, there is very little religion in the book. And the narrator/traveller is definitely not a pilgrim. Nor is she a female *Bildungsheld*, developing and maturing after trials and tribulations. After 500 pages of the story we know very little about the real Edwards. The fictive one reveals a great deal about a woman experimenting with the genre of 'scientific', specialist travel-literature.

The narrator/traveller in *A Thousand Miles* is androgynous. Deliberately Edwards plays down gender and almost obliterates her female identity. She prefers to use the impersonal de-gendered third person 'author' or 'the author'. And on occasions she lapses to a narrative 'I'. As Dea Birkett notes, none of the European travellers in *A Thousand Miles* has a name. Instead these travellers are stereotyped as 'the author' (Edwards herself), 'the painter' (Edward McCalum, an experienced traveller and Orientalist artist), 'L' or 'the Lady' (Edwards' long-suffering companion). The large retinue of Egyptian sailors, cooks, servants and *dragomans* are known by their first names, a reversal of the conventional practice of travellers not to identify orientals by names. Significantly the sexless author has for a foil two other traditional female types: 'L', mentioned before and 'the young bride', part of 'the happy couple' on their honeymoon, also called 'the little lady', a rather denigrating epithet.[18] Both types are not really interested in the world but extend traditional domestic roles to their new surroundings. Edwards disassociates herself from the females in the group. In fact the only character she relates to is 'the painter', an artist and amateur Egyptologist like herself.

The de-feminisation of the traveller/narrator characterises Edwards' writing on Egypt. Her earlier fiction reveals an interest, an obsession even, with the theme of character development. Her most popular novels, notably *Barbara's History* (1864) feature young

Bildungshelds for whom travel abroad is truly a rite-of-passage. The only example of an androgynous traveller before *A Thousand Miles* is the very early *A Lady's Captivity Among Chinese Pirates in the Chinese Seas*, Edwards' first book-length publication, a translation of Fanny Laviot's adventure story. The reason for this change is, it seems, the ambiguity in Edwards' own position as Egyptologist and her status *vis-à-vis* orientalist authority, both the traditional, antiquarian authority (represented by Birch) and the authority of new professionals like Petrie, Brodrick and Benson.

The image of the professional, the genderless explorer, is further developed in the transcribed texts of a series of public lectures delivered during Edwards' American tour in 1890 and published a year later under the title *Pharaohs, Fellahs and Explorers*. Despite the attempt of Edwards herself and her American publisher Harper to represent *Pharaohs* as a popular history of Egypt, the collection is a meticulously researched work.[19] And it is anything but 'romantic' or 'picturesque'. The very title is misleading. It is taken from the first essay, which is apparently an account of nineteenth-century exploration in Egypt. Edwards departs from the everyday geographical notion of 'exploration', denoting travel in unknown places, and invests the former with an historical meaning. Her subject is the history of Egyptology from the pioneering work of Mariette, Egypt's first Director of Antiquities, appointed by Khedive Ismail, to Petrie's discoveries at Tel Nebesheh in the eastern Delta in 1886 and the uncovering, four years later, of the post-Ptolemaic city of Naukratis, celebrated by Greek travellers.[20]

An explorer, according to Edwards, is not a geographer. Indeed 'exploration' does not mean physical travel. It is rather the pursuit of knowledge about the past, by empirical field work, using induction and not received ideas and assumptions. The following, taken from *Pharaohs . . . and Explorers* is her most succinct yet most developed definition of orientalist exploration and an important typology of the explorer in Egypt.

> In the first place the explorer in Egypt must have a fair knowledge of colloquial Arabic, no small share of diplomatic tact, a strong will, an equal temper, and a good constitution. It is important that he should be well acquainted with Egyptian, Biblical, Babylonian, Assyrian, Greek and Roman history; for the annals of these nations continually overlap, or are dovetailed into one another, and the explorer is at any time likely to come upon cuneiform

tables . . . or upon relics of the Hebrews . . . the explorer must, of course, be a fairly competent Greek scholar. Still more, of course, he must be sufficiently conversant with the ancient Egyptian languages to translate any hieroglyphic inscriptions which he may discover. A knowledge of trigonometry, though not absolutely indispensable, is of value in surveying sites and determining ancient levels.[21]

But above all, this unbelievably versatile scholar must 'be a good "all round" archaeologist', Edwards then proceeds to define archaeology as a:

science or . . . rather the aggregate of sciences . . . that science which enables us to *register* and *classify* our knowledge of the sum of man's achievement in those *arts* and *handicrafts* whereby *he has*, in time past, signalised his passage from barbarism to civilisation. The first chapter of this science takes up the history of the human race at a date coeval with the mammoth and other extinct mammalia; and its last chapter, which must always be in a state of transition, may be said to end for the present with about a hundred or a hundred and fifty years ago. (my emphasis)[22]

'He', one suspects, is not only generic but literal. And Edwards' ideal traveller is a man. Mastery of the classical languages and ancient and modern oriental ones was a part of the education of a male élite, definitely not of the traditional female education. But it should be remembered that the text is from the early 1890s, when British universities had already admitted women and the first generation of formally educated females had completed the formal part of their studies. The informal part that is the archaeologist's work did not particularly require an academic training. Furthermore neither hieroglyphics, nor the Assyrian cuneiform, were part of the curriculum. They were studied privately. Edwards herself who in 1873 transcribed an impressive number of hieroglyphic inscriptions (which she could not then decipher), would later in her career be able to read them. The Gibson-Lewis-Smith sisters also learned Assyrian privately.

Like the characterisation of the explorer/archaeologist, the definition of archaeology itself reveals the equivocal status of the new phenomenon. Edwards' rather compulsive repetition of the word 'science' is telling. Archaeology is not an amateur field but a

'science' or rather the combination of 'sciences'. It is empirical
and pragmatic. And it involves a sense of history that distinguishes
it from mere antiquarianism. Very similar definitions can be found
in Petrie's own writings, notably in his *Inductive Metrology: or
the Recovery of Ancient Measures from the Monuments*, (1877). But
Edwards herself is far from being pragmatic. Indeed the study of
the material remains of civilisations of the past is motivated by
a belief in progress from 'barbarism' to 'civilisation'. It is that
very belief that defines the era of study. Her interest extends
from pre-historic societies to the eighteenth century, the age of
industrialisation and colonialism, the acme of human achievements.
Nor does the confusion between 'science' and belief end here.
Edwards characteristically includes art in the study of Egyptology
and draws both on the rare and beautiful and the mundane, a
tendency that is quite common among her contemporaries and
which was discussed earlier.

The very identification of exploration with archaeology and the
ideal explorer with the Egyptologist excludes interest in the contemporary Middle East. Archaeology is *per definitio* the study of
civilisations of the past. But Edwards' obliviousness to life and people in 'modern' Egypt is striking even in an archaeologist. She is not
even conventionally curious about customs, manners and morals,
society and politics. The very few obligatory passages in *A Thousand Miles* on everyday life in Egypt are stiffly clichéd and reveal
Edwards' cultural and racial prejudices. She is self-consciously
blatant and insensitive on subjects like poverty, disease and child
mortality which characteristically moved westerners and exuded
expressions of pity or sympathy even from the most prejudiced.
She is also callous. And this is very unusual in a woman traveller.
Take for example the following extracts describing (in that order)
the villages of Minieh and Siût in Middle Egypt and of Assuan.

I certainly never saw so many one-eyed human beings as that
morning at Minieh. There must have been present . . . from ten
to twelve thousand natives of all ages, and I believe it is no
exaggeration to say that at least every twentieth person . . . was
blind . . . this defect added the last touch of repulsiveness to faces
already sullen, ignorant and unfriendly. A more unprepossessing
population I would never wish to see – the men half stealthy, half
insolent; the women bold and fierce; the children filthy, sickly,
stunted, and stolid.[23]

Note that she lapses to the narrative 'I' and that for once she reveals her own feelings. Characteristically the 'scientific' parts of the narrative, on monuments and other remains of the past, are written in the genderless third person. In Siüt Edwards comments that:

> the thoroughfares are dusty, narrow, unpaved and crowded, as at Minieh. The people are one-eyed, dirty and unfragrant, as at Minieh. The children's eyes are full of flies and their heads are covered with lice, as at Minieh. In short it is Minieh all over again on a larger scale.[24]

And at Assuan: 'The streets of Assuan are just like the streets of every mud town on the Nile.'[25]

The urban landscape of modern Egypt is changeless. Minieh is interchangeable with Assuan or Luxor. And regional differences between the grain and cane-growing, partly industrialised areas of Middle Egypt and the isolated pre-modern area between the First and Second Cataracts of the Niles are ignored. Even more important is Edwards' lack of interest in domestic life and the material life of contemporary women and children, the very fabric of the ethnographic female literature on harems. In the whole of *A Thousand Miles* there is not a single description of the interior of a modern Egyptian house. There is a perfunctory half page on a *haremlik*. Children in particular are described in a denigrating manner that borders on the callous. There is one particularly shocking episode, describing an accident which occurred when one of Edwards' co-travellers misfired and wounded a four-year-old. That the wound was slight and the child in no real danger is beside the point. The point is that throughout her passionless detailed account of the episode, and the reaction to it of the villagers, there is not a single expression of sympathy with the wounded.

Edwards' prejudices and ethnocentric views should be related to the deliberate attempt to de-gender the account of travel. Hence the avoidance of utterances, gestures and behaviors which in her own society are identified as 'feminine' and which reveal sympathy and emotion. She is the only example of a woman traveller who shuns the traditional role of healer and does not administer to the sick and needy. The 'feminine' women travellers in the party distribute food and medicines. 'L', her companion, is called by the Arabs *Sitt-Hakim*, or 'Lady doctor'. To obliterate her own feminine identity Edwards not only avoids expressing sympathy but visual and physical contact with women and the domestic aspects of oriental life. 'I had not been many weeks on the Nile' she notes, 'before I began systematically to avoid going about the native towns . . . that I may so have lost an opportunity of now and then seeing more of the great life of the people is very probable; but such outside glimpses are of little real value, and I —— at all events escaped the sight of much poverty, sickness and squalor.'[26] It is perhaps the most self-revealing piece she wrote.

QUEEN HATASU'S BEARD: ANCIENT HISTORY AND WOMEN'S HISTORY

Lack of interest in the domestic, private aspects of life clearly does not extend to the pre-Islamic era. During eighteen years as Egyptologist Edwards wrote extensively on the material conditions of women in ancient Egypt. She showed particular interest in the legal and political status of women (those are her own terms) and their roles in society. *A Thousand Miles* is rich in domestic detail culled from monuments, funerary inscriptions, sculptures, bas-reliefs and the wall-paintings in tombs. *Pharaohs and . . . Explorers* includes a chapter on 'Queen Hatasu', a meticulously researched essay accompanied by Edwards' own transcriptions of hieroglyphic inscriptions and by her illustrations. The essay is a re-written and diluted version of a part of a public lecture delivered in Britain, probably in late 1889, then during the American tour. The one hundred page manuscript notes to the lecture, now in the possession of the EEF, presents us with important evidence concerning Edwards' views on sexual politics and the status of women in her own time and society.

The unedited, barely legible document bares the emblematic title 'The Social and Political Position of Women in Ancient Egypt' and may appear to resemble evangelical writings on the position of women in the Scriptures, or in the age of Patriarchs or in early Christianity. But the scientific explorer does not share the total world-view of her missionary sister travellers, nor the view of history as a divinely ordained process in which each of the sexes is destined to play specific roles. Indeed Edwards divests history of the notion of sin. And she describes a civilisation which is not characterised by sexual inequality and the separation between women and men. Last, but not least, unlike the evangelicals, she uses analogy between the past and the present, the East and the West, to criticise her own society. In other words, the 'Position of Women' is a popular scientific piece and, at the same time, a powerful feminist polemic, using an historic analogy between contemporary and ancient cultures to convey a political message.

The gist of the argument is that throughout the Pharaonic era, woman enjoyed equality with, sometimes superiority over, man. Her position was unique: '[a] vast gulf separates [her] history from the history of women in any other nation of the ancient east. We find her always free, respected and in the full experience of personal rights as extensive and widely recognised as the personal rights of man. She [is] his legal and social equal. In fact it is not too much to say that she is in some respects his superior'.[27]

Edwards' usage of different kinds of source-material and representation of the evidence to live-audiences are as important as the substance of what she has to say. She uses text and material remains, literary sources and artifacts, works of art and handicrafts and utensils for everyday use, the 'beautiful' and 'sublime' together with the ordinary and commonplace. Yet this mixture of materials is not as promiscuous as it may seem. In fact Edwards' approach to, and synthesis of, different information is truly historic and surprisingly modern. The first part of the presentation, dealing with the ruling élites, draws on hieroglyphic texts in inscriptions, funerary hymns and addresses, incantations and prayers as well as on the higher forms of the visual arts: wall paintings , bas-reliefs and sculptural monuments. The evidence used is pictorial rather than verbal and literal rather than symbolic. Egyptologists and linguists recognised in the hieroglyphs a system of signs that is not symbolic or metaphoric, but mimetic, involving the smallest possible gap between the object and its imitation. Unlike Martineau, who knew nothing about hieroglyphs, Edwards used this system as metaphor for a clean, faithful representation of the real world. And, as we shall see, she attributed the same mimetic quality to picture-images in general.

To return now to the second part of the presentation. In it Edwards moves away from élites to the common people, from queens to women of the middle and lower classes (her terms) and from monuments and works of art to texts (mainly legal documents) and artifacts. Significantly the bulk of the latter materials comes from papyri. It is noteworthy that the initial function of the manuscript was to illustrate the slides shown to the audiences, so that the superiority of visual over verbal images evinces itself in the very form of presentation. Edwards treats her audience to a pictorial history of the women of ancient Egypt between the Fourth Dynasty (the reigns of King Mena and the Pyramid Kings) and the Ptolemaic period. About a half of the manuscript is devoted to a history of the Egyptian queens and a section of that part to Queen Hatshesau or Hatasu, 'the greatest female figure in Egyptian history'.[28] The daughter of Thotmes I and a direct descendant of Ahmes I and Queen Ahmes Nefertari of the Seventeenth Dynasty (following the Hyksos' conquest of Egypt), Hatasu inherited the crown in virtue of her descent in the female line of the dynasty. Not surprisingly she is compared to Queen Elizabeth. Wedded in childhood to her brother, Thotmes II, and widowed in adolescence, Hatasu became Egypt's ruler, 'a female Pharaoh'.[29]

Now Edwards' treatment of Hatasu's reign has disturbing political meanings of which even the most innocent audience must have been aware. The female Pharaoh is an historical example of unlimited political power in the hands of a woman. She is an autocrat in an hierarchical system perceived by Edwards' contemporaries as patriarchal, a perception which she sets to refute. Moreover, Hatasu, a public figure, is the very opposite of the private, domestic female. Indeed her life is a spectacle, watched by her mortal subjects, and, after her death, by her equals, the Pharaoh-gods. Her action and achievements are outside the female sphere and are distinctly 'masculine'. She is the builder of monuments ('one of the sovereign builders')[30] an administrator, the supreme commander of a huge army. She is also the first explorer in history, the discoverer of an unknown land, who despatched 'the first exploring squadron known in the history of the world',[31] an inspiration and a model perhaps? Edwards is referring to the discovery and conquest of the legendary 'land of Punt', identified with Somali. Hatasu is elevated by the enthusiastic writer to a 'scientist', the Egyptian sailors and navigators to 'ethnographers' and 'naturalists'. And the association between exploration and travel on the one hand and political power on the other, is immensely revealing.

Edwards is fascinated by the iconography of political power. In a series of slides taken in the temples built to Amen (Amon) and the goddess Hathor, Queen Hatasu is represented with all the *insignia* of the oriental absolute ruler. She appears in male attire, wearing the pharaoh's short kilt, instead of the long cotton robe usually worn by Egyptian women. She is sandaled and helmeted, often crowned with the *kepersh*, or war helmet, worn on the battlefield. And most significant, she sometimes appears with a false beard, a sign not only of masculinity, but of seniority as well as of patriarchal power. Nevertheless the queen's status as Pharaoh does not desex her. The false beard, Edwards assures her audiences, was probably 'a touch of delicate flattery on the part of the artist'.[32] The slide showing the bearded queen is followed by three others (taken at the Berlin Museum) in which she is presented without her beard. Her dimpled face is described as 'feminine', 'animated', 'almost more European than oriental'[33] Thus Edwards, who in her writings on Egypt obliterates her own feminine identity and distances herself from domestic topics, now insists that power and femininity are not mutually exclusive. It is possible that by relegating the topics of domestic and sexual politics to a remote past, Edwards neutralises them. Identifying with contemporary oriental women is certainly different from writing about ancient Egyptian queens. The archaeologist's interest in the life of the latter women less easily renders itself to a classification based on gender.

The analogy between the status of Egyptian women and that of women in contemporary Britain becomes explicit in the second part of the manuscript. The reign of Hatasu, Edwards argues, was not a curious episode of female domination in a patriarchal era. For Egyptian women, regardless of class, enjoyed unparalleled degrees of freedom. Her interest in the material conditions of life of ordinary women marks her off from the antiquarian and, for that matter, from the contemporary historian. For history in the last decades of the nineteenth century was mainly political history and the 'common people' had not yet entered it. Like the modern student of *mentalité*, Edwards points out that 'up to this date we know nothing of Egyptian law, very little of Egyptian private life'.[34] She draws on the demotic papyri, dating probably from the Ptolmaic period (the latest documents she uses are from 260–270 BC) collected and translated by Revillont at the Louvre. She relies mainly on legal documents: deeds of sale, mortgages, transfer-leases, inventories, receipts, marriage contracts etc. And exactly like female ethnographers and writers about harems she is particularly interested in the position of the married woman, which was of course the focus of the debate on equal rights in the 1870s and 1880s.

Married women of all classes in ancient Egypt enjoyed great economic and legal freedom. They were 'traders and capitalists' in 'absolute control . . . over their own property'. The documents describe these women buying and selling lands and houses, lending money on usurious terms, foreclosing mortgages, even entering contracts with the state, with the smallest reference to their husbands. Furthermore married life in the age of the Pharaohs was subject to the 'rule of contract'.[35] And it is the contractual character of Egyptian marriage that distinguishes it from matrimony in contemporary Britain. Shrewdly Edwards refers to the Common Law notion of marriage as contract as 'pleasant fiction':

> So far is the British Bridegroom [sic] from caring to fulfil his vows, that it has cost us years of agitation and meters of petitions to obtain for the British bride a legal propriety right in *her own* property. But the ancient Egyp[tian] bride stood in no need of agitation and petitions. By the terms of her marriage contract, not only her own property but the husbands' was settled upon her and so settled as to be at her absolute disposal.[36]

The 'agitation' and 'petitions' Edwards is referring to are those preceding the Married Women's Property Act of 1882, which she supported. And the emphasis on contracts probably was not lost on British and American audiences. In modern liberal thought and in the liberal jargon of the 1880s and 1890s, the contracting, property-holding man is the symbol of civic and political liberties and the right to vote. The man who can enter into contracts and controls his property is also the citizen. Until 1882 wives were legally and economically subsumed in their husbands. And the married woman, unable to contract, logically could not become a citizen. So Edwards elevates the contracting Egyptian woman of the Late Kingdom to a symbol of equality between the sexes. Of course the very analogy between Victorian Britain and the classless Pharaonic despotic state is preposterous. Nevertheless rhetorically that analogy is quite effective. And for once Edwards feels secure enough to identify with a 'feminine' cause and feminist 'agitation' and 'petition'. She chooses to end the lecture with the wry comment that the history of the women in Egypt may

> have excited a sentiment of retrospectical envy in the hearts of the ladies here present. I should indeed be grieved if they went home lamenting they had not lived and died in the days of the

pharaohs [sic], that they are not at that moment occupying the proud position of mummies in the British museum.[37]

THE NON-METAPHORIC NILE JOURNEY

The Egyptologist's pre-occupation with ancient history naturally reflects on his or her imaginary geography. Thus unlike Martineau, Edwards is not interested in the Mediterranean Orient, but in Egypt alone. And Egypt is characteristically the Nile. The preface to the first edition of *A Thousand Miles* begins with Ampère's epigram: 'Un voyage en Égypte, c'est une partie d'ânes et une promenade en bateau entremêlées de ruines', freely translated by Edwards: 'A donkeyride and a boating trip intercepted with ruins.'[38] The narrative of the 'boating trip' appears to be within the traditional account on ancient monuments, known as the *description de l'Égypt*. Like contemporary orientals, contemporary urban spaces and rural areas are treated perfunctorily and only as a foil to the historical landscape of Egypt. Structurally, too, the book seems to follow the familiar tripartite pattern of the cyclical, secular journey. The traveller's departure from home, or civilisation and a journey are followed by the return voyage. *A Thousand Miles* begins with a description of the table d'hôtes at Shepheard's Hotel in Cairo, the 'base' of English travellers in Egypt and a symbol of commercial tourism. The boat-trip also is conventional enough: from Alexandria to Nubia and the Second Cataract then back to Alexandria and Cairo, the outposts of Western civilisation. But it is quite plain that Edwards is not a typical *habitué* of the Shepheard, that her journey is not conventional and that the notion of civilisation in *A Thousand Miles* is not entirely ethnocentric. For the book ends with a view from the Great Pyramid. And the narrator/traveller's gaze is directed to the South and the civilisation of the past, not to the West.

The order in which the sites are seen and the narrative of sightseeing arranged, are particularly important. Edwards is obsessed with chronology. She insists on seeing the monuments in exactly the same order in which they had been built. This, according to her, is the only way to historically grasp changes in the relations between a people and landscapes and between the latter and the development of art. Most travellers, starting in November (the beginning of the Season in Egypt) sailed up the Nile with the tide, taking advantage of the Northern wind until they reached their destination – usually the First or Second Cataract, then on the sail down river, visited the monuments. Thus the newer temples in Nubia and Upper Egypt were usually seen before the early ones, located in the Delta region and Lower Egypt. Martineau, it shall be recalled, had seen Greco-Roman Philae and the temples of the Late Kingdom before she saw the Pyramids and the site of Memphis. Edwards repeatedly urges travellers to 'see' Egypt historically and comprehensively:

> For the history of Egypt goes against the stream. The earliest monuments lie between Cairo and Siout, while the latest temples to the old gods are chiefly found in Nubia. Those travellers, there-fore, who hurry blindly forward with or without a wind, now sailing, now tracking, now punting, passing this place by night, that by day, and never resting till they have gained the farthest point of their journey, begin at the wrong end and see all the sights in precisely inverse order . . . [The oldest places] should be seen as they come, no matter at what trifling cost of present delay, and despite any amount of ignorant opposition. For in this way only is it possible to trace the progression and retrogression of the arts from the pyramid-builders to the Caesars.[39]

For her part, Edwards could not carry the whole of the programme into effect, but she *saw* most of the monuments in historical sequence. And at no trifling cost. For her insistence on that order caused delays and inconveniences and antagonised the hard-worked Egyptian crew and her co-travellers.

Insistence on 'programme' and 'order' does not mean, as in the case of Martineau's *Eastern Life*, ideological or metaphoric writing. Quite the contrary. Edwards emphasises the importance of accurate information gathered 'on the way' and verified in later study. *A Thousand Miles* took over five years to prepare (in comparison to the four months it had taken Martineau to write her own travelogue) because 'the writer who seeks to be accurate, has frequently to go for his facts'.[40] The 1882 edition incorporates all the archaeological work done between the first publication and the second. The ambition to describe phenomena and places as accurately as possible, to represent Nature and historical sites 'scientifically', impugn on style and language.

Edwards, like the evangelical writers, is aware of the weaknesses inherent in descriptions of landscapes. Language, she emphasises time and again, cannot adequately describe the physical world, nor the sensations of the observer of phenomena. Indeed verbal images are themselves translations of 'pictures' and not imitations of the real model. In standard descriptions of nature, or monuments, word images stand between the thing that is seen and the seer. To avoid bathos and repetition she resorts to two different techniques: the photographic description, absolutely bare of metaphor and comment and which simply enumerates details, and pictorial imagery borrowed from contemporary realist painting of oriental landscapes. The first technique characterises descriptions of monuments, especially of closed spaces like tombs, chambers, the inside of temples etc. Edwards often uses what Barbara Maria Stafford calls *parataxis*, that is the amassing of information that is then listed or 'spread' before the reader (horizontally as it were), with as little comment as possible. The best examples of the factual 'scientific' discourse are to be found in the descriptions of the temples of Osiris at Philae; the Colossi at Abu Simble; of a subterranean chamber discovered and cleaned by Edwards and her companions also at Abu-Simble near the southern buttress, a description in which literally every square inch of the walls of the chamber is 'shown' to the reader. To buttress the evidence there are numerous illustrations, sketched on the spot and later checked by specialist archaeologists and landscape painters. *A Thousand Miles* does not fall in the category of travel-album, or an illustrated travel account, in which the text is subjected to the sketches. The illustrations are only a sub-text, but the book has 81 drawings; *Pharaohs, Fellahs and Explorers* includes 150 illustrations, most of them Edwards' own.

As an adherent of the new science and scientific travel-writing, Edwards is particularly alive to the limits of texts and verbal images. Of course, what I called before the 'traveller's mistrust of textuality' is, by no means, typical to her, but characterises the evangelical and secular descriptions of the sacred geography of the Middle East. However, Edwards' own sense of the inadequacy of words is very poignant. On the sacred island of Philae, near the First Cataract, arguably the most photographed, most sketched and most widely described spot on the Nile, she becomes silent. Having described and sketched the boulders surrounding the Temple of Osiris she sums up her feelings:

Such, roughly summed up, are the fourfold surrounding of Philae
– the cataract, the river, the desert, the environing mountains. The

Holy Island – beautiful, lifeless, a thing of the far past, with all its
health of sculpture, painting, history, poetry, tradition – sleeps,
or seems to sleep in the midst. It is one of the world's famous
landscapes, and it deserves its fame. Every sketcher sketches it;
every traveller describes it. Yet it is just one of those places
of which the objective and subjective features are so equally
balanced that it bears putting neither into words nor colours. The
sketcher must perforce leave out the atmosphere of association
which informs his subject; and the writer's description is at best
no better than a *catalogue raisonée*.[41]

In the Second Cataract she feels that: 'words are useful instruments;
but like the etching needle, and burin, they stop short at form. They
cannot translate colour.'[42] *Catalogue raisonée* is a key-word. Edwards
herself consciously resorts to 'listing', to the guidebook technique,
thus writing out or playing down emotion or association in order
to avoid bathos and provide her readers with hard facts free of
encumbering metaphor. Note that her self-criticism and the attack
on the standard travel account or the illustrated travelogue is to
be found at the end of the chapter on one of the clichéd and
commercialised spots on the British tourist's map of the Nile. By the
1870s Philae was produced in numerous daguerreotypes, 'proper'
photographs and postcards and had its place in every Egyptian
'album'.[43] Edwards' own crude sketch of the 'inscribed monolithic
rock [in] Philae' which accompanies her comments (a sketch made
obsolete by the more 'advanced' representational techniques of
Orientalist landscape photography) is, then, in itself a statement.

But as noted before, the Egyptologist's *catalogue raisonée* is but
one possible technique. On quite a few occasions, Edwards uses
painterly metaphors, or the metaphor of the theatre, to describe
landscapes. The metaphor of nature as a theatre, or a drama, a
spectacle, is very appropriate. The Nile and the desert were habitually perceived as mobile, historically dynamic elements. Indeed, the
notion that nature was a static matter had disappeared with the
Newtonian revolution. And as Maria Barbara Stafford notes, the
visionary aspect of the mobile 'Nature' with its own life is one
of the most salient characteristics of the illustrated scientific travel
account. But note that Edwards conjures up images of mobility and
change in a way that is quite different from that of Martineau. The
following is a description of the Cataract and the surrounding
desert:

From the moment every turn of the tiller disclosed a fresh point of view, and we sat on deck [*of the dahabiah*], *spectators* of a moving *panorama*. The diversity of objects was endless. The *combinations of form* and *colour*, of *light* and *shadow*, of *foreground* and *distance*, were continually changing. A boat or a few figures alone were wanting to complete the *picturesqueness of the scene*; but in all those channels, and among all those islands, we saw no sign of any living creature.[44] (my emphasis)

And when a 'living creature' is admitted in the contrived, consciously organised scene he is immediately dehumanised and made into an actor. The dramatic effect is introduced in the description of the Sheik of the Cataract (responsible for the safe transportation of the travellers across the Falls) and his crew: 'The thing was *a coupe de théatre*, like the apparition of Clan Alpine's warriors, in the *Donna del Lago* – with backshish in the background. The chanting and movements of the crew are maliciously likened to those of a 'barbaric Sir Roger de Coverley Dance'[45] (a member of the fictional Spectator club, described in numerous issues of the *Spectator* and elaborated by Steele and Addison).

In this and quite a few interchangeable other passages, the traveller plays a passive role. In contrast to Martineau's 'seer' who is also an historian, able to read backwards into the past, Edwards' narrator is a spectator, watching the theatre of Egypt, the panoramic view of the Nile. There is abundant reference to the dramatic spectacular aspect of Oriental geography. Egypt is a panorama, a 'combination' of colour and form; it is characterised by a perspective of foreground and distance; it is altogether a *coup de théatre*. The 'creatures' appearing in the landscape are operatic figures or literary ones, bordering on the pastiche (I·have in mind Sir Roger de Coverely). Edwards does not control her landscapes, rather she passively and self-effacingly transcribes what she sees. Certainly the spectator or painter in *A Thousand Miles* is notably absent from the narrative, a thing that cannot be said about Martineau's ubiquitous traveller/historian.

Theatrical imagery and metaphor as well as the usage of the painterly picturesque and the evocation of particular painters (Turner, for instance) are particularly compatible with the archaeologist's attitudes towards artifact and Nature and the positional relations between them. One of the main characteristics of the new archaeological sciences – particularly typical of archaeology, it shall be recalled – was the mixing together of works of arts and simple artifacts or utensils, as sources of evidence about ancient civilisations. This is what separated the archaeologist of Edwards' generation from, on the one hand the amateur, the antiquarian orientalist particularly interested in monuments and sculptures, and on the other hand, from the professional archaeologist, drawing on pottery for stratigraphy, periodisation and the reconstruction of an historical context. Edwards is placed somewhere between Martineau, who had a bias towards the unique, the 'great' work of art, or grand landscapes and Petrie and his generation. Her own mixing of texts, materials, of monuments and ordinary utensils, of man-made 'mounds' or *tels* (the remains deposited by ancient societies and accumulated in layers that can be analysed and dated) and natural landscape, was discussed earlier. What should be added to this is the juxtaposition of Nature and art, a juxtaposition which, itself, reflects Edwards' dilemma as a 'scientific' traveller who has allegiance to the antiquary tradition.

The 'art' versus 'Nature' controversy, whether nature is inferior to art and should be 'improved', goes back to classical literature. More relevant to us here is the juxtaposition between natural phenomena and artistic representation from the Romantic movements onwards, relevant because it has particular bearing on the scientific travel account. As both Batten and Stafford have noted, towards the middle of the eighteenth century, art and Nature, that is *uncultivated* landscape, were becoming less dichotomised than they used to be. Artists and writers did not feel inclined to 'improve' landscape, to artificially organise and control it, but represented what they saw mimetically.[46] Indeed, sometimes Nature was seen as superior to art, more grand and sublime than man-made artifacts. Of course, the debate is more typical of classical travel-literature of the second part of the eighteenth century and the early part of the nineteenth (Burke, Gilpin, Addison immediately come to mind). Certainly in the second half of the century, with the emergence of substitute techniques of representation (like the guide-book and the photograph), the controversy was not very relevant. And realism in Orientalist painting stressed the importance of accuracy and fidelity to Nature. Notwithstanding, travel writers capitalised on the historical aesthetic debate, emulating conventions. Edwards herself repeatedly itemised the debate in descriptions of the Nile, the Egyptian desert and Pharaonic monuments. The landscape (that is 'Nature') cannot be distinguished from the monuments, being a 'work of art'. The terrain of the Nile Basin is likened to a piece of work produced by an Egyptian sculptor. And the colours of the desert are comparable with, even surpass, those of a painting. Thus, the beauty of the sand at Korosko (north of Philae) repays the fatigue of climbing it because it is:

> smooth, shiny, satiny; fine as diamond-dust, supple, undulating, luminous, it lies in the most exquisite curves and wreaths, like a snow-drift turned to gold. Remodelled by every breath that blows, its ever-varying surface presents an endless play of delicate lights and shadows. There lives not one sculptor who could render those curves; and I doubt whether Turner himself, in his tenderest and subtlest mood, could have done justice to those complex grays and ambers.[47]

At Assuan the rocky beds of the river are piled 'block upon block, column upon column, tower upon tower; as if moved by the hand of man'. And near Philae the mountains 'seem to lie . . . like stupendous cairns, the work of demigods and giants'.[48] And the colossi at Abou Simble , seem to have been created by Titans who 'left it for the feebler man of after ages to marvel at forever'.[49]

Whether as *catalogue reasonée*, or as a visual, pictorial narrative, Edwards' writing marks a move away from the autobiographical travelogue to an impersonal, apparently neutral, narrative. There is, however, one aspect in which she resembles both Martineau and the millenarian writers. Edwards' interest lies in the past, not in contemporary landscapes and people. Her panorama of Egypt is strangely devoid of human figures.

12

An 'Orientalist' Couple: Anne Blunt, Wilfrid Scawen Blunt and the Pilgrimage to Najd

WRITING COUPLES, A PRELIMINARY NOTE[1]

It is appropriate for at least two reasons to end this book with a chapter on couples travelling together in, and writing about, the Middle East. First, because of the tensions between orientalist authority and the individual gendered experience of the eastern Mediterranean; between canonicity and the writing against canonical texts; between feminine identity and the identity of the explorer; between the Victorian ethos of domesticity and travel, between the work of the professional orientalist and that of the amateur. These tensions emerge in accounts of travel, co-produced by pairs of explorers, married couples, but couples of siblings too. Which brings us to the second reason for the interest in the orientalist couple. I already argued that the single 'unprotected' female explorer is by no means the typical nineteenth-century woman traveller. For travel, emancipating as it was, reproduced certain familial constructs and conventional norms of appropriate 'feminine' behavior. Indeed the married traveller in a supportive and essentially domestic role seems to be as typical as the male explorer. Certainly travelling spouses outnumber spinsters. Sixty-three per cent of the female authors sampled in my own quantitative study of travel-literature were married (see Chapter 1). And over 50 per cent of these accompanied husbands (sometimes brothers) who were career-diplomats, soldiers and professional orientalists. Contemporary statistics of the Evangelical missions to the East (notably of the CMS) clearly show that although single female missionaries outnumbered male ones and missionaries' wives, the latter group constituted slightly over 30 per cent of the evangelical work force. The orientalist couple then is a phenomenon that cannot be ignored. It anatomises the relations between domestic economy and the economy of travel and travel-writing as well as connections, inside the metropolitan culture, between the orientalist and the educated classes.

But his chapter is not about life and work for Western couples in the Middle East, nor about the 'couple', that is the metaphysical notion of the 'pair' as 'intrinsic to the experience of symbolic systems in the West.'[2] My focus is on *a couple*, Wilfrid Scawen Blunt and Lady Anne King (Noel) Blunt, selected for various reasons which I later discuss in some detail. The travel and work of the Blunts on the Arabian peninsula are located in the context of the relations between Orientalism and domestic politics. I begin with a look at the politics of marriage of men and women with long-term interest in the Middle East. Orientalism has a domestic, familial aspect which is not widely known. And domestic politics shaped the rhetoric of domesticity which characterises the co-produced accounts of travel, notably the accounts of the Blunts. I survey the most common literary devices used by women to reconcile their role as wives with their status as travelers. Then the stratagems and rhetoric used by the Blunts during the production of Lady Anne's *Pilgrimage to Nejd* are examined in detail. Finally her attitudes to, and representation of, the landscape and people of the peninsula (notably the nomad tribes) are discussed in detail.

Significantly women who, throughout the nineteenth century, had been excluded from the places of knowledge and power, could and did marry into the groups which manipulated knowledge. So that scholarly or political interest in the Orient was further cemented by the gradual creation of an intellectual genealogy, which Noel Annan and, following him, Gertrude Himmelfarb called the 'intellectual aristocracy'.[3] Relations with the 'fathers of the Victorians' are difficult to trace. But both the old orientalist sciences and the new amateur ones share the propensity to endogamy and heredity that characterises the older Evangelical élites. Examples are legion. Sophia Lane Poole, sister of Edward William Lane, the greatest Victorian authority on 'modern' Egypt and herself an amateur ethnographer was, also, the mother of two orientalists, Stanley Lane Poole and Reginald Stuart Poole. Elisabeth Ann Finn, also an ethnographer, Hebrew scholar and missionary to the Jews, came from one Evangelical family and married into another. Her husband, James Finn, was Britain's longest serving Consul to Jerusalem in the nineteenth century. Like Finn the other female authority on Palestine, Mary Eliza Rogers, travelled with a male relative, her brother Edward Rogers, appointed in 1855 as Britain's Vice Consul to Haifa. Emily Ann Beaufort, a traveller and recognised authority on the Lebanon, became a specialist on the Christian Balkans only after her marriage to viscount Strangford, who was himself an authority on the 'Eastern Question.' Georgina Max-Müller was the wife and travel-companion of Friedrich Max-Müller, Britain's most prominent comparative philologist, translator of the *Rig-Veda*, Taylorian professor of modern European Languages at Oxford and world authority on Sanskrit. Emily Alston Beke married the less prominent, but more colourful Charles Tilstone Beke, traveller and Biblical topographer. And Agnes Dorothée Bensley helped Robert Bullock Bensley in his work, in the Sinai, on the Syriac gospels and later vindicated his memory in a travel book in which she waspishly criticised the Gibson-Lewis twins.

And even the newer, mobile and 'feminised' new sciences of archaeology and Egyptology, in which women became prominent show a tendency towards intermarriage. Thus F. Llewellyn Griffith's two cautious marriages to Egyptologists helped secure him financially and professionally. The settlement of his first wife Kate (née Bradbury), Edwards' companion and after the death of Edwards the first female on the Committee of the EEF, enabled Griffith to devote all his time to archaeology. Shortly after his first wife's death, he married his pupil at Oxford, Nora Christina Cobban, who also worked in Egypt.

But the most interesting, most intriguing example of an orientalist couple is that of Lady Annabella (Anne) King Noel King Blunt and Wilfrid Scawen Blunt. The Blunts are so intriguing precisely because they were so different from the professional middle-class academics or amateur scientists and, for that matter, from the Evangelical 'aristocracy.' Both the Blunts came from a traditional landed background, both – despite their espousal of a number of radical causes like Arab and Irish nationalism – and mistrusted Gladstonian liberalism. Blunt, as Albert Hourani aptly describes him, was a country squire.[4] Lady Anne was not exactly the 'squire's wife'. Her own background is impeccably aristocratic. She was daughter and heiress of Baron William King, later first earl of Lovelace and the eccentric mathematician Ada Augusta Milbanke, child of the unfortunate Lady Anna Isabella Milbanke and Lord Byron (whose only legitimate issue Lady Ada was). So that the Blunts' own brand of Orientalism was cemented not only by familial and social connections (Blunt was related to Lord Lytton, Viceroy of India between 1876–80 and was close to Curzon and Salisbury) but by the Byronic myth. Blunt himself would compare his own Arabophile sympathies to Byron's Philhellenism. In the *Secret History of the British Occupation of Egypt* he claims that Lady Anne's relationship to Byron makes her, and, by implication Blunt himself, filiated to the poet: 'the inheritor of the poet's admiration for the Orient'[5] and of Byron's attitude towards Eastern nationalism.

But the familial intimate nature of relations between orientalist institutions and social élites should not deceive us. And we should be careful not to interpret co-travel and co-writing merely as family partnerships that manifest and even enhance patriarchal constructs. In fact the position of 'auxiliary' travellers, wives (or sisters) in essentially supportive roles is far more complex than that of the single travellers, mainly because co-travellers took with them the familial pattern to the East. So how did women reconcile their self-image as travellers with their duties as wives? Was co-travel more prone than 'single' travel to the division of roles according to gender? And if this is so, did actual roles affect fictional ones, or put slightly differently, did the co-produced travelogue imitate the ideology and aesthetics of the separate spheres, or did it challenge that notion? A general description of the main forms of co-writing, preliminary to the discussion about the Blunts, may throw light on these questions.

THE CO-WRITTEN TRAVEL ACCOUNT

Co-writing satisfied real needs. It enabled individual travellers to co-opt a form of writing popularly identified as masculine and come to terms with a kind of experience hitherto perceived as male. Co-writing not only made the feminine travelogue an acceptable form but helped make travel compatible with *bourgeois* gender ideology and the ethos of domesticity. In other words the co-produced narrative enabled both the co-travellers and their putative audience to 'have it both ways', to preserve authority and hierarchy inside the 'couple' and within orientalist authority yet, at the same time, retain the newly gained freedom of the women and their new identity as explorers and writers.

The forms of co-writing are diverse and many. It may take the form of separate, female and male narratives, of a narrative by a feminine 'I' which is edited by a man, or, of a transcribed work with a male *amanuensis*, or scribe, mediating between the writer and her audience. Examples of each of these forms abound. Giovanni and Sarah Belzoni's *Narrative of the Operations and Recent Discoveries Within the Pyramids, Temples, Tombs* ..., describing their travels and work in Egypt between 1815–19 and published in 1820, comprises two separate accounts. Judith Montefiori's *Notes from a Private Journal*, circulated privately, then published in a limited edition in 1855, is a combination of her own *Notes* and the diaries of Sir Moses Montefiori, and the 'preface' acknowledges his (dominant) part in the experience. Isabel Burton's *The Inner Life of Syria, Palestine and the Holy Land* which saw publication in 1875 is a vindication of Burton's own life and his career as Consul to Damascus. And the entire text is heavily annotated by him. Anne Blunt, who would herself resort to co-writing, regarded Burton's influence on his wife as tyrannical and found Isabel's self-effacing narrative not only tasteless but impolitical. In a journal entry of 5 December 1878 she writes: 'it is all coloured by the constant fulsome praises of Captain Burton, his wisdom, courage, all of which must have done his prospects harm rather than good'.[6] Later examples include Agnes Dorothée Bensley's *Our Journey to Sinai: a Visit to the Convent of St. Catherine*, written after Bensley's death together with his pupil F. C. Burkitt and James Theodore and Mabel Virginia Bent's *Southern Arabia* appearing in 1896 and 1900 respectively. But undoubtedly the best, most complex examples of co-writing are Lady Anne Blunt's *Bedouin Tribes* and *Pilgrimage to Nejd*, issued by John Murray in 1878 and 1881.

Lady Anne's *Bedouin Tribes* is based entirely on her pocket diaries and journals. Blunt introduced the book and wrote its six concluding chapters. The final product seems to reproduce the well-known concept of separate spheres as well as his own patriarchal notions concerning women and the family. Two different narratives correspond to the distinction between the male and the female perception of reality, man and woman's experience and their respective modes of observation and organisation of information. Lady Anne's conclusion of the descriptive, linearly arranged part of the narrative, written by herself, is revealing:

All is finished but the last few serious chapters with which Wilfrid proposed to end this book for me. In them the information we picked up during our travels will be embodied, and though he says they will probably be dull, I trust they may not be without practical value.[7]

So she is the observer and, despite the self-effacing first-person plural, the sole collector of information. Blunt himself is presented in the preface and throughout the book as the analytical traveller, capable of abstract thought (juxtaposed with Lady Anne's passion for details). It is he who, allegedly, gives the narrative its form, producing a beginning and an end and thus shaping and 'embodying' the whole work. The *Pilgrimage* too is edited by Blunt who signs himself 'the editor'.[8]

In point of fact it was the self-deprecating Lady Anne, not her omniscient, authoritative editor who was the real mediator between the two co-travellers/writers and their audience. Before 1880 Blunt published only pseudonymously. And the first time that he allowed his name to appear in print was in his wife's book. Moreover, as I later show, the *Pilgrimage* is unmistakably Lady Anne's. The independence and originality of the narrative of her own odyssey belie the rhetoric and politics of the spheres. What should be stressed at this point, however, is the rhetoric itself which made it possible for the Blunts to reconcile their roles as husband and wife and their own unequal partnership with their new roles as explorers and the freedom experienced by Lady Anne during the Arabian journeys.

Similar partnerships and comparable stratagems of co-writing characterise the travel and writing careers of lesser authors. The early example of the Belzonis (probably the earliest one of a co-produced travelogue) is much cruder than the work of the Blunts. Yet the rhetoric of the spheres evinces itself even in the earlier pre-Victorian narratives. The pretentious *Narrative* is Belzoni's own. Mrs Belzoni is hardly allowed to appear in it (for example, when the exasperated Belzoni tartly remarks that unlike himself she had tolerable health all the time).[9] Her own narrative of the four years' work and travel is relegated to the end of the book and condensed to forty folios, about a tenth of the work. The title of that part is deceiving: 'Mrs Belzoni's Trifling Account of the Women of Egypt Nubia and Syria'. In fact there is very little on women and domesticity. The account is largely the narrative of Sarah Belzoni's solitary and adventurous journey across the Sinai Peninsula to south-western

Palestine then to Jerusalem. The separation between the masculine and apparently feminine narratives and the relegation of the exceptionally active Mrs Belzoni to the domestic sphere are immensely revealing. Almost as revealing as her own self-depreciation and the trivialisation of her work by Belzoni himself.

Clearly co-writing may easily degenerate to rhetoric, if not mere cant. Esmé Scott-Stevenson introduces her *Our Ride Through Syria and Asia Minor*, published in 1880, immediately after the Russian-Turkish War, with a stylised *apologia* which celebrates the part of her husband and co-traveller, Commissioner to Kyrenia (Cyprus) and which attributes Scott-Stevenson's political analysis of the war to him (she was an ardent Turkophile). At the same time, however, she pretends that her work was published surreptisiously and without the knowledge of her husband.[10]

AUTHORITY, AUTHORSHIP AND CENSORSHIP

It may well be argued that the Blunts were not an orientalist couple. Indeed that they do not typify the upper-class Victorian couple. They were not specialists on things oriental. Rather their expertise was acquired piecemeal, outside the orientalist institutions. And their political activity on behalf of Arab nationalism was informal, individual and sometimes quixotic. Indeed Blunt himself is conventionally described as an exception from an otherwise ethnocentric community of orientalists.[11] Yet the Blunts do seem to represent the ultimate orientalist couple with interest in the Orient. First of all because they made the Middle East not only an object of discourse, but a passion and a political cause. Secondly because their partnership was a long and fruitful one, lasting from their very first trip to the eastern Mediterranean in 1873 till their marriage broke up in 1906. The first trip was followed by five others: to Algeria in 1874; to Lower Egypt, the Sinai Peninsula and Palestine in 1875; to the Euphrates Valley and the highlands north of it, territory of the nomadic Shammar, then to the land of the Anayza and Sêba in the Syrian Hamad in 1877; to Najd in Central Arabia, then to Persia and India in 1878–79 and finally to the Hijaz and Egypt in 1881–82. From that year the Blunts became involved in a number of nationalist and pan-Islamic movements: for the overthrow of Turkish power; for a Caliphate under British protectorate then for greater autonomy for Egypt. And during the heyday of Gladstonian imperialism the couple came to be identified as enemies of the empire.

Blunt's own political activity is fairly well known and was documented by his many biographers as well as by students of early Egyptian nationalism.[12] So I shall be able to proceed to the third and, to us, most relevant reason why he and Lady Blunt seem to symbolise the orientalist couple. Their travels and writing appear to reproduce a marriage which struck even their contemporaries as an unequal partnership, a hierarchical relation, based on male domination and female deference. Even from my brief discussion of the formal prefaces to Lady Blunt's two travelogues it is quite clear that both the Blunts carefully cultivated a public image of themselves as a pair and as individuals. That public image was so convincing that neither critical contemporary commentators, nor Blunt's biographers, seriously questioned it.[13]

Blunt in particular is responsible for the invention of the public *personae* of travellers/orientalists, characterised by their gender. In his political diary and writing, in private records, letters, even in verbal utterances, he re-invents Lady Blunt as an utterly selfless, will-less, self-sacrificing spouse. She is almost too convincing a replica of the angelic custodian of the Victorian hearth and the Victorian family. But this fictive Lady Anne, like the real, historical Annabella Noel Blunt, is an incomplete woman. She failed in her biological role (she did not produce a male heir to the Blunt estates). Thus she is a wife, rather than a mother. She is also the classic help-mate, a travel-companion and a receptacle to Blunt's own ideas and views. Most significant, her writing is described by him (and by most of his biographers) as merely the transcription of these ideas and views.

Many examples illustrate the build-up of this suspiciously conventional image. But the most convincing one is to be found in an entry from Blunt's journal dated 23 April 1873. According to Blunt he gave up his journal on the eve of the first journey to the Middle East (he would resume it on the eve of the voyage to Najd, in November 1878). The daily record of events was entrusted to the faithful Lady Anne, because: 'I had no secrets to set down in one [journal]. What I thought she thought, what I felt she felt. These times were our true form of marriage.'[14] Blunt became so convinced of his own invention that when in 1880 he became aware of a secret, very private aspect of Lady Anne's spiritual life, he was shattered. One of the most important events in her life was her conversion to Catholicism in Persia and later baptism in the Catholic Church. What made this experience so painful to Blunt himself was not only Lady Anne's secrecy, but the fact that she chose the religion that he himself, after years of doubt and suffering had abandoned. In a letter to Lady Anne, written immediately after she had been accepted into the Church, Blunt bitterly complains that:

> For the first time . . . you had come under an influence not mine, which was leading you into regions of the future where I knew no part . . . . Your acceptance in so definite a form as the Catholic one . . . destroyed the sense I had up to that time of security and permanence in the devotion you gave me. I have felt ever since that you were, so to say, *serving another master, acknowledging another king, worshipping another.* (my emphasis) [15]

The language of submission and deference is adopted by Lady Anne, usually sincerely but sometimes rhetorically and rather subversively. Her letters to Blunt address him as 'master', 'my master', 'tyrant' and 'dear tyrant', and from the late 1880s as 'Head of Family' or 'H.F.' for short, a title which both she and their daughter Judith – later Baroness Wentworth – use alternately as a nickname and an epithet. Quite often the letters are signed 'your child'.[16]

Hierarchy and deference, like domination, are expressed not only verbally but in gestures, in dress, even by décor. From 1882 the Blunts lived in an oriental life-style. They divided their time between the family estate at Crabbat in Sussex where they bred Arabians (the Crabbat stud farm built and maintained with Lady Anne's money was the first of its kind in Britain) and Sheykh Ubayd, their Middle Eastern home, not far from Cairo. After the separation and until her death in 1917, Lady Anne practically lived in Egypt. In Sheykh Ubayd only Arabic was spoken. And it became Lady Anne's language of writing. Also significant is the symbolic use of dress. The Blunts travelled in the desert as Europeans. In fact they were the first Christians ever to have penetrated Wahabi Arabia undisguised probably because they felt secure enough, possibly because they were in a safe territory. Wallin, Palgrave, Burton even Doughty adopted an oriental cover and identity. Moreover, Lady Anne never donned the veil, a symbol of femininity so popular among women travellers. In its stead, she used to wear a male head-dress, the Bedouin *kaffiyeh* and an *abba* or *abaya* over her European riding-habit. Thus, without disguising herself as an Arab, she de-gendered her physical appearance. In their homes the Blunts adopted oriental dress, a symbol of their identification with Bedouin life-style and culture, but, no doubt, also an outward sign of the patriarchal life.

It is then not entirely surprising that Lady Anne's public image was accepted and perpetuated by Blunt's biographers and by historians. With one or two notable exceptions her achievements as explorer, diarist, writer, translator of pre-Islamic poetry and scholar are slighted. Significantly there is not one biography of her, not a single monographic study. And this is not because of a lack of materials (for the volume of her private records is impressive) but because it is so widely assumed that her Middle Eastern experience is subsumed in Blunt's. Sympathetic commentators appreciate her travel-books for their wealth of detail and even pay oblique tribute to Lady Anne's scholarship. Less benignly (and more characteristically) she is depicted as a tidy-minded, uninspired collector of facts, an 'artless' writer, and a 'snob' (Kathryn Tidrick's epithets), a 'second Lady Byron'. Her own life with Blunt, it is implied, duplicates that of her unfortunate grandmother, Lady Isabella Milbanke. And like grandmother like granddaughter: Lady Anne could not rise to her husband and master's expectations, to his political vision and compassion for a cultural 'other',[17] although, unlike the first Lady Byron, she did try very hard.

But there was another, less known Lady Anne. And her image of herself as an explorer and writer is different from the public, conventionalised role which, admittedly, she played quite willingly. The less familiar image can be gleaned from Lady Anne's journals, from her notes for a work on nomadic life in central Arabia (published posthumously under the title: *The Authentic Arabian Horse*) and, of course, from the published text of *Pilgrimage to Nejd*. To recover her experience of oriental landscapes and oriental society and reassess it, it is necessary to read Lady Anne's own writings together with those of Blunt himself and with comparable works on travel in the Arabian peninsula. But first a few words on the history of production of the *Pilgrimage*.

Clearly authority – both Blunt's own familial authority and orientalist scholarship and authority – played a central role in the reconstruction of the real, historic journey to Najd. The story of that reconstruction presents an intriguing example of the exercise of authority by censorship, or rather various forms of censorship exercised over different stretches of time; Lady Anne's self-censorship, evident both in the diaries and the published text:

Blunt's editorial control over both of the texts and last the attempt by Judith, Baroness Wentworth, to posthumously control her mother's private records, in order to create her own myth of her victimised mother. So Lady Anne's journals are not absolutely her own. They cannot be regarded as private. They never had been. Blunt was their putative and first actual reader. And this particularly applies to the records of the journeys to the Middle East. Her voice *and silences* reflect his dominating presence. A conscientious diarist from the age of ten (the 214 volumes at the British Library cover a period of a little over 70 years) Lady Blunt usually kept a daily record of her life even under the most difficult conditions. And the journals of the journeys to the Middle East are her most detailed and the ones most meticulously kept. The notes taken (in pencil) during the dangerous expedition to Najd are extraordinarily neat. They comprise ten *duodecimo* volumes: six volumes of the journals, one particularly revealing pocket-diary and a volume entitled 'Extracts from January 1879' which contains the plan of the book and, last, two sketch-books.

In contrast to Lady Anne's travel journals Blunt's own is, literally and figuratively speaking, rather thin. There are, it may be recalled, no records for the first four journeys. And although Blunt resumed the writing in November 1878 his record is erratic and rather irregular. There is no doubt that the *Pilgrimage* developed from Lady Anne's notes. More importantly, Blunt depended on her for information on the topography of Arabia, its *flora* and *fauna*, government, society and religion. Thus his report on the expedition to the RGS, on 8 December 1879, is based almost entirely on Lady Anne's observations and measurements. Similarly two of the appendixes he wrote to the book draw on her own notes on the morphology and topography of the *Nafud* or great red-sand desert, and on civil government among the Shammar Bedouins. There is no doubt at all that Blunt read through his wife's private journal at least twice, once in Simla, in May 1878, after he had proposed the publication of a volume of her notes and water-colours of Arabian horses, then in London sometime after their return.[18] Only a few sketches are included in the eventual two-volume book. And despite Blunt's influence, despite his part in the production and his editorialising, the *Pilgrimage* is Lady Anne's own.

Significantly the Najd journals are more repressed than the published account. Indeed for private records they are extraordinarily and uncharacteristically impersonal. The parts on Najd and

Jabal Shammar in particular are impersonal. They are work notes rather than an autobiography. They may be described as a *catalogue raisonée*, in which the traveller barely intervenes. Lady Anne's own voice, which is audible enough in other travel journals kept by her and in her travel books, is barely heard in the volumes known as additional manuscripts 53896–53902. She is silent about her own inner journey, about the quest which ended in the mystical experience, on 13 April near Shustar in Persia, and her subsequent conversion and acceptance to the Roman Catholic Church. Any evidence of a personal nature is eliminated (in the most literal sense of the word, it is cut out of the journal or blue pencilled). To fill in the gaps in the information, we have to read through the pocket diaries, to which presumably Blunt had no easy access and Lady Anne's letters, mainly the letters to her brother Ralph, later baron Lovelace, the person closest to her at that time, and to carefully look at the book itself. Because in the book, the spiritual aspect of the pilgrimage and its religious aspect are encoded in a narrative which is allegorical, and which although it idealises nomad culture in the Orient, departs from the romantic travelogue on Arabia.

THE UNROMANTIC TRAVELLER: REPRESENTATIONS OF THE DESERT

Arabia Deserta, that is the northern and central part of the Arabian Peninsula, was one of the most idealised, most widely romanticised places in the imaginary Orient. The attraction of that place often disturbed travellers and affected their judgment. This may seem the case with the Blunts. The *Pilgrimage* appears to be within the tradition of the romantic travelogue and the real, historical journey to the peninsula – a romantic journey. 'Romance', as virtually all of Blunt's biographers note, is the keynote of the famous 'Preface'.[19] And 'romance' is a keyword in the parts of the book which are written in a narrative 'I' (most of it is in the first person plural).

The two stated purposes of the expedition are 'romantic': the search for the origins of the authentic and primitive, that which is unadulterated by 'civilisation', both oriental urban civilisation and the civilisation of the West. The Blunts set out on a journey to find the 'pure' Bedouins and the authentic Arabian horse. Their second purpose was to acquire an *asil* (noble) bride for Mohammed Ibn Aruk, son of the sheik of Tadmor (Palmyra) in Syria, the Blunts' escort on the previous expedition to Mesopotamia, their ally and Blunt's own 'blood-brother'.[20] In the book the search for the bride is inflated to a theme and unifying plot which patches together the factual, descriptive, parts of the narrative. The 'romance of Mohammed Ibn Aruk', hardly a theme in the journals, is developed in Chapters 7 and 14 of the *Pilgrimage* which divide the book into three symmetrical parts.[21]

In fact Lady Anne's own approach to Arabia and to Arabian landscapes is at that stage (the late 1870s and the 1880s) unromantic. Her representation of nature is clean of metaphor. The landscapes described in the journals and the travel-book are not picturesque, artificially 'arranged' and structured ones. Nor is she the romantic, self-centred traveller. She is unemotional and self-effacing. This is in sharp contrast to the two former travellers to Arabia whose work influenced her most: Burton, whose *Personal Narrative of a Pilgrimage* lent the title to the *Pilgrimage to Najd* and Gifford Palgrave's *Narrative of a Year's Journey through Central and Eastern Arabia*, Lady Anne's text of reference and the butt of her criticism. The Najd journals set the basis of a factual, geographically and ethnographically authentic data, and on this data is erected a new edifice, a narrative that has allegiance not to the romantic travelogue on Arabia but to the allegorical, essentially pre-romantic journey, and to religious representations of landscapes. First the 'facts', the geography of the Blunts' Arabia and their actual, historical expedition.

The Blunts were not geographers, despite Blunt's own connections with the RGS. In fact their observations on the topography and geology of the Nafud and Jabal Shammar were very controversial. And, despite the interest in *flora* and wild-life in the desert they were not naturalists. But the Blunts can certainly be described as explorers and the discoverers of places and a civilisation barely known in the West. There were, of course, travellers to northern and central Arabia before them. The Finnish naturalist Wallin had reached Ha'il, capital of the Shammar in 1848 and even reported on his journey to the RGS. And in the early 1860s Guarmani and Gifford Palgrave crossed the Nafud and paid visits to Jabal Shammar. And Palgrave's *Narrative*, published by Macmillan in 1865 and re-issued seven times, had tremendous influence outside the select audience of geographers. It is evident that Lady Anne is greatly indebted to him.[22] However, Palgrave's maps were inadequate and had many gaps. More important even he, like the other travellers before the Blunts (including Charles Doughty who had visited Ha'il only a few months before the couple), was very restricted in his movements.[23]

In their land-journey of over 2000 miles, from Aleppo to the Persian Gulf (they were the first Europeans to have travelled by land from the Mediterranean to the Indian Ocean), the Blunts covered areas which differed widely in their climate, geography, *flora* and *fauna*. The couple crossed over the Syrian Hamad to the hilly Houran, cutting near the town of Bozra, in the direction of the Harra, a volcanic plain, north, north-east of latitude 32°. From the Harra they proceeded to Wadi-Sirhan, the declivity connecting the Hamad with the oases of Jawf and Meskakeh in the northern Arabian peninsula (29–30° west, north-west of the Wadi).

Between the oases and the fortress-town of Ha'il, capital of Jabal-Shammar – the authentic Arabia – and the site of the independent Emir Ibn Rashid, lies the great Nafud, mythologised by earlier travellers who had depicted it as a dangerous wilderness. The Blunts' short stay at Ha'il was followed by the Persian sequence of the journey, covering the Persian Pilgrims' road to Bagdad, then tracking the road parallel to the Bakhtiari mountains, down to Ram Hurmuz on the shore of the Gulf.

Rather conventionally, the Blunts use the citationary, 'reference' technique of the travelogue. Geographic and orientalist authorities on the desert and on nomad culture and society are cited, challenged and often refuted. Already in Blunt's 'preface' the accuracy and style of previous travellers is criticised and they are attacked directly and in an indirect manner, individually and collectively. Thus Henry Pely's maps of Southern Syria and Wadi Sirhan are found inadequate. Wallin's report to the RGS, on his own journey from the coast of the Red Sea to Ha'il proves unsatisfactory. Guarmani's account to the prestigious Société de Géographie in 1863 about his voyage to Jabal Shammar is dismissed.[24] Indeed Blunt's and Lady Anne's position on the geography and the very location of the *Jabal* is, as we shall see, rather unorthodox and clashed with authorities inside the Geographical Society. Lady Anne's harshest criticism, however, is reserved to Gifford Palgrave and through him to the Romantic tradition on Arabia. Indirectly, then, that criticism is a commentary on Blunt's own romantic attitude. The attack is two-pronged, aiming both at Palgrave's facts and at his representation of Nature, of himself as the egocentric traveller and his imagery of the desert.

Palgrave's Nafud is a *locus* of disorder, a disharmonious, chaotic place. It is a 'sea' of undulations, running from the North to the South, implausibly described as ' parallel to the axis of the earth' and attributed to the 'rotary' [sic] movement of the globe.[25] Occasionally the terrain is intersected by valleys and the whole mass of land between the oasis of Jawf and Ha'il is shifty. More significantly the Nafud is, according to the *Narrative*, destitute of vegetation and of wildlife, a permanently dry land and, consequently, an inhabitable place. His, then, is the *ne plus ultra* of the European notion of the desert. And to a stranger like himself this desert is perilous and even deadly.

In contrast, the Nafud described in Lady Anne's journals and the *Pilgrimage* is harmonious. It is characterised by 'order', a regularity of morphological and topographical features that gives it 'sense'. It is also a place full of life, agreeable to the traveller and hospitable to strangers. The key-words in Lady Anne's vocabulary are 'order' and 'reason'. Though her very first impressions are of an anarchical and senseless Nature – 'an absolute chaos, and heaped up here and hollowed up there, ridges and cross-ridges, and knots of hillocks all in utter confusion' – gradually there emerges a unity, a sense of the purpose and design in the wilderness: 'after some hours marching we began to detect a uniformity in the disorder, which we are occupied in trying to account for'.[26]

What orders the chaos is a certain regularity of the features of the terrain, undetected by the earlier travellers. The Nafud, it is noted, is intersected not by 'valleys' but by deep, horse-shoe shaped hollows locally known as *fulj* or *fulji*. The *fulji*, it seems, were identical in shape, though not in size (their depth averaged 100 feet, though according to Lady Anne's barometer measurements some were deeper than 200, and their width varied from 50 yards to nearly a quarter of a mile) and invariably ran north-west and south-east.[27] And this regularity of shape and direction gave the scene of disorder and purposelessness unity and symmetry. Moreover Lady Anne firmly maintained that the hollows were a permanent feature of the terrain, dated back by the Shammar to times immemorial and not a shifty element as Palgrave had thought.

The Blunts unravelled the skein without knitting the sock. Neither geologists nor geographers, they did not come up with a satisfactory explanation for the causes for the unusual phenomenon they had observed. Blunt's own hypothesis, that the *fulji* were the result of climate conditions and erosion, was as good a guess as Palgrave's.

And the now famous hollows were to become the subject of an acrimonious debate inside the RGS.[28] More relevant than the accuracy of Lady Anne's measurements is the significance she attaches to the uniformity and the design of the landscape of Central Arabia, to do with her spiritual experience in the peninsula (an experience which I later discuss in detail). At this point it is important to note another difference between the description of the desert in the journals and the *pilgrimage* and that in Palgrave's *Narrative*.

Lady Anne's Nafud, far from being sterile and lifeless is a fertile, luscious region. It is covered with vegetation. And it is literally crawling with living creatures: lizards and snakes, horses, sheep, gazelles and antelopes and ostriches. The variety of insects and birds is enormous – she particularly mentions, among other kinds, the houbaze, the hawk, the buzzard, the linnet, the wren, the desert lark, the wheat-ear and the crow. More significant even, the red sand desert is represented as the most fertile part of the Turkish and Arabian Orient. It is areas like the volcanic Harra and Wadi Sirhan that are referred to as wilderness.[29] And to the travellers they present greater danger than the hospitable Nafud.

But Lady Anne's most powerful critique on the authority of Palgrave is to be found in her rather subversive usage of his very idiom and imagery of the Arabian desert. It is by now clear that he was no lover of desert life and nomad society and culture. And the *Narrative* relates his forebodings about the voyage in the Nafud (spelt by him Nêfood). 'Much had we heard . . . from the Bedouins and countrymen, so that we had made up our minds to something very terrible and very impracticable.'[30] The reality proved more difficult than Palgrave's worse expectations. Read his description of the Nafud which Lady Anne uses as the motto for her classic Chapter 8:

> We are now traversing an *immense ocean* of loose reddish sand, unlimited to the eye and heaped up in *enormous ridges* . . . undulation after undulation, each swell two or three hundred feet in average height, with slant sides and rounded crests, furrowed in every direction by the *capricious gales* of the desert. In the *depths* between [the undulations] the traveller finds himself as if *imprisoned* in a *suffocating* sand pit, *hemmed in* by burning walls on every side; while at other times while labouring up the slope he overlooks what seems *a vast sea of fire* swelling under a heavy monsoon wind, and ruffled by a cross-blast into

little red-hot waves. *Neither shelter nor rest for eye or limb amid torrents of light and heat poured from above on an answering glare reflected below* . . . Add to this the weariness of long summer days of toiling. I might better say wading-through the loose and scorching soil, on drooping half stupefied beasts . . . and a veritable sun, such a sun, strikes blazing down till clothes, baggage and housing all take *the smell of burning* and scarce permit to touch. (my emphasis)[31]

'Were this eternal', concludes Palgrave, 'it were hell.'[32] The unfortunate Palgrave had crossed the Nafud in the summer whereas the Blunts travelled in early January and that did make a difference. But physical hardships alone do not explain away Palgrave's despair, nor the Dantesque idiom and images with which the entire lugubrious description abounds. Indeed Dante's *Inferno* and Palgrave's resort to the rather hackneyed romantic metaphor of 'sea' or 'ocean' are, neither of them, lost on Lady Anne. I already mentioned that the entire paragraph is quoted in the *Pilgrimage*. And there is in the book a significant addition to the journal description of the first encounter with the Nafud.

At half past three o'clock we saw a red streak on the horizon before us, which rose and gathered as we approached it, stretching out east and west in an unbroken line. It might at first have been taken for an effect of mirage, but on coming nearer we found it broken into *billows*, and but for its colour *not unlike the stormy sea from shore to shore*, for it *rose up* as the sea seems to rise, when the waters were high, above the level of the land. Somebody called out 'the Nefûd' and though for a while we were incredulous were soon convinced. What surprised us was its colour, that of *rhubarb* and *magnesia*, nothing at all like the sand we had hitherto seen, and nothing at all like what we had expected. Yet the Nefûd it was, the great red desert of Central Arabia. In a few minutes we had cantered up to it, and our mares were standing with their feet at its first waves. (my emphasis)[33]

There is apparent deference to convention and to Palgrave's inspiration and authority: in the citation of the *Narrative*; in the emphasis on colour (Lady Anne had been John Ruskin's pupil and a talented water-colourist); in the use of the metaphor of the sea and in the reference to the painterly picturesque. But conventional images and metaphors as well as their familiar meanings are reversed. Take for instance the red of the desert sand. It is not the colour of the eternal fire of hell, of Palgrave's burning pits. Rather it is the shade of the rhubarb and the magnesia so familiar to the reading-public. The latter was used by the Victorians medicinally. The Nafud, in other words, is tamed and domesticated. Evidently the need to organise and regulate inorganic nature, a need that is manifest in the insistence on topographic accuracy and morphological regularity and uniformity, also evinces itself in the more consciously dramatic paragraphs of the narrative, usually in additions to the journals. That which is 'ordered' and familiar is comprehensible and manageable. Thus instead of the romantic traveller merging with or being overwhelmed by a purposeless landscape (recall Palgrave's references to suffocation, burning and disappearance) we have him or her comprehend and control Nature.

The emphasis on 'order', 'sense' and design in the landscape of Central Arabia may be related to Lady Anne's spiritual crisis and regeneration during and immediately after the journey, more specifically to her conversion to a faith that stresses the personality of God and the divine purpose and design of the natural world.

The journey to Najd was a turning point in the spiritual and intellectual life of Lady Anne and took place at a moment of crisis in the life of Blunt himself. The pattern of Blunt's religious history – bouts of dissipation and disbelief, followed by (abortive) attempts to reconcile a need for an 'emotional' Catholicism with his materialism and evolutionary concepts – is well documented.[34] Lady Anne never rewrote her own life. And, as already pointed, the very narrative of the Najd journals and the travelogues is designed to conceal, rather than reveal, intimate details. But different kinds of evidence – from the pocket diaries kept in the winter and spring of 1879–80; from the letters to Ralph Wentworth and from utterances recorded by relatives – indicate that Lady Anne's pilgrimage was a real one and that it was, by no means, a romantic, metaphoric journey.

It is important to stress that at the time of the journey the Blunts were moving in opposite directions. Indeed the encounter with Arabia and authentic oriental civilisation influenced them in curiously reverse ways. Blunt's notions about Arabs and Islam, which would become better defined after he would meet the spiritual leaders of the Egyptian movement for the regeneration of Islam, Muhammad 'Abduh and Jamal al-Din (Aphghani), undoubtedly helped sever his allegiance with Christianity. Lady Anne's own conversion to the

Bedouin way of life and subsequently to Arab nationalism seems to coincide with a religious conversion, to a particularly immaterialist brand of Christianity that emphasised the personality of God.

The specificity and separateness of the experiences of the co-travellers, may be explained by the difference in their religious background. Blunt, converted to Roman Catholicism by his mother, at the age of 11, received a Jesuit education and found substitute fathers in his religious mentors. In 1862 he first read and almost immediately accepted Darwin's theory of evolution and natural selection, then adopted the materialist theories of Haeckel, concerning organic and inorganic Nature.[35] And it is pretty clear that even before the expedition to Arabia Blunt had despaired of reconciling evolutionism to Catholic dogma. Indeed he was to repudiate even 'modern' 'scientific' Catholicism in the anonymous debate between 'Amadeus and Proteus', published in 1876. The debate, in the form of letters exchanged between Blunt and the Jesuit Father Charles Meynell, is proof that he (Blunt) was unlikely to generate and insist upon the notion – so pertinent in the *Pilgrimage* – of a God-ordained Nature.

As for Lady Anne's early religious biography, she seems to have had none. At least according to Blunt himself. In his 'first impressions' of his wife, he emphasises the absolute lack of 'christianing' (sic) 'religious dogma' and 'a basis of supernatural teaching'.[36] And he saw her as a victim of the Feldenberg system of education, imposed on the young Lady Anne by her guardian, Lady Isabella Milbanke.[37] The public *persona* of Lady Anne, that *persona* invented by Blunt, is conspicuously lacking in spirituality, which is compensated for by a practical morality and rectitude. Blunt notes that she 'neither prayed nor needed prayer'.[38] But she did. And he resented that. On the night between the 12th and 13th of January 1879, on the road to Bushire (Persia) near Shustar, Lady Anne had a vision, converted to Christianity and vowed to become a Catholic. The instantaneous conversion was very different from the experience described by evangelicals. It was a *fiat*, not a long and torturous process of self-examination and doubt. And the convert seems rather passive. Significantly her experience in the Persian desert is related to her self-image as a failed mother and wife. In her vision Lady Anne saw the heavens open and three of her dead children 'in glory'.[39] Both the experience and the decision to seek formal conversion were concealed from Blunt, probably, even possibly, because of his own views on Roman Catholicism.

The convert was, of course, aware of Blunt's critique on Catholic dogma. Moreover, she was quite familiar with the currency of Darwinian evolutionism and anti-creationist theories. In a letter written from Simla to Ralph Wentworth and dated 19 May 1879, she refers to a discussion with Lord Lytton, the subject being Blunt's *Proteus and Amadeus*. Lytton's lack of sympathy for Proteus' need for a belief in a *personal* God upset her. (He thought faith 'not necessary'). What had attracted Lady Anne to the Catholic church was the premium it put on 'faith'. She was kept away not by doubt, but by her dislike of Catholic ritual. 'I, almost join the church though I am at once stopped dead in such an impulse by the vividness of my dislike and distrust to some (few) [sic] practices in it.'[40] She did join the Church. And this is, one suspects, not only an act of faith but a gesture. The espousal of the very religion fought against and rejected by Blunt is, itself, a statement. And that statement may be interpreted as a protest against his authority – the familial authority and the intellectual authority of a materialist. The conversion, in other words, is an exercise of choice that is condemned by Blunt himself. He refers to it as a rebellion against a beloved 'master'. And he dates the deterioration of the marriage to April 1879.[41]

So at the same time that she was undergoing a spiritual crisis Lady Anne was re-writing, from the journals, the experience of Arabia. A causal relation between the two developments, between the conversion from practical morality to a 'religion' and the conversion of the journals into a definitive text, may be assumed. The spiritual experience is encoded not only in the representation of Nature, but in allusions and messages, designed to create certain expectations in the contemporary reader. Lady Anne makes it clear that her literary *Pilgrimage* – if not the real one – is modelled after another older literary work, known to virtually every English-reading person: Bunyan's *Pilgrim's Progress*. As I point out in the Introduction, travellers to the Holy Places, during the nineteenth century, used the *Progress* as a text of reference. Indeed they recognised that it had kept the *idea* of the religious journey alive in a secularised society. Even agnostics like Harriet Martineau and Frances Power Cobbe emphasise the importance of Bunyan. Yet Lady Anne's usage of the allegory is different from that of the ordinary modern pilgrim. The narrative of the *Pilgrimage* climaxes in the ninth chapter, which describes the arrival of the Blunts at Jabal Shammar. The chapter is subtitled 'the delectable mountains' and the motto, taken from Bunyan's own description of Christian's journey is immensely revealing: 'which mountains belong to the Lord of the Hill'. Only the real 'Lord of the Hill' is the Emir Ibn Rashid, a fanatical Wahabi. Significantly, the Wahabis are referred to in the *Pilgrimage* as the modern Puritans.[42] Rather subversively, the allegory is used not in a Christian context (that of the Holy Places in Palestine, for example) but in a Muslim one. Both the Blunts and their readers identified central Arabia, as the 'cradle of Islam'. Not only is Ibn Rashid the 'Lord of the Hill', but Jabal Shammar is the 'delectable mountain'; Ha'il the city of Emmanuel, the earthly Jerusalem, symbolises the celestial city. And that city is located on the border of the country of Beullah, a reference to Persia not lost on the readers.[43]

The evocation of a household text, like the *Pilgrim's Progress*, also helps set limits to the exotic. By mentioning ordinary objects and familiar works, the writer and her audience are able to tame that which is unknown. The images of chaos and death, used by the earlier writers, give way to what is taken by Lady Blunt to be precise knowledge about the land of Arabia. Arabia is mapped and described. And most facets of it can be accounted for within the framework provided by the laws of a divinely ordained universe, or by a popular cultural and religious inheritance. Significantly not only Arabia, but the Arabs too, are relocated.

ETHNOGRAPHY AND EMPATHY: HUMANISING THE ARABS

The departure from the ethnocentric idiom and epistemology of mainstream orientalist traditions evinces itself in the treatment of nomad life and culture. It is in the writings on the Shammar people, regarded by the Blunts as the 'authentic' Arabs, that Lady Anne's most significant contribution to a humanised perspective of the Orient is to be found. A word of caution is necessary. Both Wilfrid and Lady Anne admired the Bedouins and nomad culture. And Blunt's own interest in the Arabian Peninsula was very early politicised. In the 1880s he penned his hopes for the spiritual and political regeneration of the Arab world on the Hijaz and central Arabia. A Turkophobe, Blunt advocated the severance of the Arabs from Turkish rule and the re-establishment of an Arab Caliphate. His unorthodox views appeared in 1880 in the famous series of radical articles in the *Fortnightly Review* (later to reappear as *The Future of Islam*).[44] There is no doubt that his political views influenced Lady Anne. And I do not propose to de-politicise her own writings or interest in the peninsula. But I think it necessary in this context to try to separate her own notions about the 'authentic' Orient from Blunt's own notions. In the remainder of this chapter I discuss her writings on the Bedouins in two kinds of text, the journal notes on the Syrian Shammar and those of Central Arabia and the posthumously published notes on Arabian horses. *The Authentic Arabian Horse*, edited and published by Lady Wentworth almost three decades after her mother's death, is usually dismissed as a book on horses. Yet Lady Anne herself regarded the notes for the book as her *magnum opus*, the *summa* of a life work on Arabic literature and culture.[45] Lady Wentworth's editorialising notwithstanding, the *Authentic Arabian Horse* contains some of Lady Anne's most articulate writings on the Arabs. More important even, this book is about the exchanges between Western and Eastern cultures and cross-cultural representations.

Westerners who knew so little about the geography of the Arabian Peninsula, had known even less about its people outside the urban centers of the Hijaz, Yemen and Jabal Shammar. Indeed the territories of the Bedouins had been *terra incognita* even to explorers and specialists like Burton, Palgrave and Doughty. As Thomas Assad and Kathryn Tidrik point out eighteenth- and nineteenth-century descriptions of nomads draw not on participant observation, but derive from second-hand information acquired from Western travel literature, written sources in Arabic and contemporary evidence gathered in the towns. Early descriptions like that of Laurent d'Arvieux, discussed by Tidrik, idealise nomad society and perceive it as an example of the exotic and authentically primitive.[46] Exoticism characterises eighteenth- more than nineteenth-century representation. And in the Victorian and Edwardian eras concepts of and attitudes to the 'primitive' underwent significant changes. 'Primitive' now came to stand for the undeveloped or incomplete, not an ideal but a culturally inferior society. Thus Gifford Palgrave who had idealised the townspeople of Jabal Shammar depicted the Bedouins in negative terms.[47] The great Burton, acquiring most of his information from literary authorities or in the towns of Hijaz, had no intimate knowledge on Bedouin life and society. And Doughty, who had visited Ha'il only a short time before the Blunts, characteristically stereotyped nomads.[48]

What marks out the notes on the Shammar from the reports of other travellers is that Lady Anne does not only represent Arabs but allows them to present themselves. They are not only 'spoken for' but speak. Speech in her writing is a metaphor for cross-cultural communication. The observation and description of the different, she emphasises, should not degenerate to a one-sided process, in which an articulate West represents a speechless, expressionless Middle East. Rather the traveller or ethnographer must be attentive to the 'authentic voice' of the Arab world. Thus instead of an ethnocentric discourse *on* the Orient, Lady Anne suggests an exchange of information between active, equally articulate participants.

The word 'authentic', even in the limited context of her writing, may cover three different meanings: historical, geographical and biological. Historically the authentic Arabs, or Bedouins are the descendants of the inhabitants of the Arabian peninsula in the pre-Islamic era, before the *hajra* and the islamisation of the Middle East. Turks obviously are not 'authentic' people, nor are the populations of the coastal areas, or the bigger towns. So 'authentic' in her usage is also a geographical designation. The authentic East, the prototypical oriental place is the desert, not the typical oriental city, essentialised and traditionally associated in the West with Eastern life. In fact Lady Anne was not really interested in urban spaces. Compare her economical and rather perfunctory description of Damascus to that of Rogers, or Beaufort, or to Mary Mackintosh's work. 'Authentic' may also be a biological notion. 'True' or 'real' Arabs are nobles (*asil*), whose status is not based on property or military prowess but on racial purity. Sheik Medjuel el-Mezrab, chieftain of the smallest clan of the Sêba, themselves a tributary of the Anayza (and also husband of the legendary Jane el-Mezrab, divorcée of Lord Ellenborough) exemplifies the authentic, noble Bedouin. Faris, young Sheik of the northern Shammar of the upper Euphrates Valley, is another example.[49] As Albert Hourani notes, the aristocratic Blunts could identify with the codes of a nomad, or pastoral, pre-modern society.[50] The chivalrous Bedouin warrior is admired precisely because, to the Blunts, he is the very opposite of the Western middle-class man whom they despise.

Other ethnic groups in the Middle-East, are compared with the Shammar. The latter become a criterion, the yardstick for values, manners and behaviours. The central juxtaposition in the notes and in the *Bedouin Tribes* and the *Pilgrimage* is not between orientals and occidentals, but between the Arabs (that is the 'authentic' tribes) and other Middle Eastern peoples. As already noted the Turks and the Ottoman Empire are the ultimate examples of the 'unauthentic' and corrupted. The differences between the Turks and the Bedouins, between the town and the country are anatomised as comical types, some of them celebrities known in the West. Lady Anne's Turkophobe views come across her malicious description of Midhat Pasha, the reformist Ottoman bureaucrat, governor of Damascus. Midhat is criticised for the very reason that so endeared him to Western politicians: his reformatory zeal. In the notes and the *Pilgrimage* he is accused of destroying the *fallahs* and Bedouins and for modernising the towns of Syria and Iraq. The published version is mild in comparison to the following extracts taken from Lady Anne's notes, dated 12 December 1879: 'he belongs to the good portion of mankind. But, I am sure, not to the wise'.[51] Elsewhere: 'Midhat must be a man of energy but he looks like an old fogey'.[52] He is also 'an ass' and 'totally unfit for his place. He is said to be completely in the hands of the Mufti . . . I am very surprised that Midhat should have so wide a reputation as he has. He has every appearance of a man given to drink, a real bottle nose'.[53] Compare these extracts or the disparaging remarks on the exiled Abd el-Kadr, vanquished leader of the Algerian uprising of 1847, to the descriptions of Faris, or of Medjuel el-Mezrab.

Even the bloodthirsty Emir Ibn Rashid, Lord of the Shammar and independent ruler of the central peninsula, is noted for his values and spectacular appearance (sometimes compared with that of Richard the III).[54] The detailed notes on the journey through Iran are rich with examples of comparisons between Arabs and orientals. For in contrast to the Arabian peninsula and the Bedouins, Iran and the Iranians are essentialised. The Iranian desert is inhospitable, dangerous and infested with marauders and brigands (the notorious Beni Laam, incidentally nomads and *not* Iranian). The Iranians are parsimonious; excessively religious (Shiites do not fare well in Lady Anne's works); ridiculously superstitious; cowardly and dishonest. They are moreover filthy. Their speech is affected. And, the worse sin in her book, they cannot ride. To quote a few examples, picked up at random:

> The Persian pilgrims, though not very agreeable in person or in habits (for they are without the sense of propriety which is so characteristic of the Arabs), are friendly enough . . . but on a superficial comparison with the Arabs seem coarse and boorish . . . their features are heavy, and there is much the same difference between them and the Shammar . . . as there is between

a Dutch cat-horse and one of Ibn Rashid's mares. In spite of their
washings, which are performed in season and out of season all
day long, they look unalterably dirty in their greasy felt dresses,
as no unwashed Arab ever does.[55]

Such racist remarks may not be found in the discussions on Arabs.
More significantly, not only individuals but forms of social organisation, government and familial structures which are tolerated (and
even admired) in Arab society are vehemently criticised in the
notes on Iran. Take for example polygamy and the sequestration of females. Bedouin society was polygamous. And Bedouin
women, Lady Anne observes, were segregated (most travellers
assumed that females in nomad societies were free). But they
had property rights, actual power and status. Sexual segregation,
of course, characterised Iranian society. In fact harem or *purdah* had
their origins in pre-Islamic Persia. And 'harem' may be a Persian
word. Lady Anne who tolerates the Arab harem or the Bedouin
familial construct vehemently attacks the Iranian ones. Bedouin
women are represented in positive terms, but their sisters in Iran
are stereotyped and essentialised. The latter become a crude version
of the 'oriental woman'. In one particular paragraph – too strong to
be printed – a group of wives and concubines at Dollahm Beshire
at the Gulf coast is lampooned:

> The maids to my surprise were all dressed like ballet dancers,
> with short petticoats that the Lord Chamberlain would certainly
> add a foot to, and above these petticoats instead of skirts or
> other articles of dress these women wore nothing but loose
> jackets next to the skin. Presently a bold-faced, vulgar and
> loud voice[d] young woman came in and the fat lady who had
> been entertaining me . . . rose hastily saying what I understood
> to mean this to be the wife of the *wakil* (vakil) . . . she wore the
> ballet dress still more flagrantly then the servants . . . The fat
> lady without ceremony began fumbling among her drawers and
> pulled off her trousers. It then transpired that these trousers are
> only worn out of doors.[56]

The narrator's voice, her openness, the obvious delight in describing
the vulgar and lewd (I have in mind the drawers of the *vakil*'s
wife) are incompatible with the public image of the pure but
humourless Lady Anne. Such passages as the one quoted above

obviously had no place in a popular travel book published by John Murray.

The treatment of Iranian and Arab women is comparable with Lady Montagu's attitude towards Catholics and Turks respectively. The tolerance of the Victorian writer, exactly like the latitudinarianism of her Augustan predecessor, are limited and influenced by politics and ideology. Thus Montagu's Turkophilism may be related to Whig anti-Catholicism. Similarly Lady Anne's Turkophobia and the bias against orientals who are not Arab reflect her criticism on the Ottoman Empire and on modern imperialism.

In the *Authentic Arabian Horse* she 'graduates' or progresses from the hyperbole which characterises the early writings to a more balanced attitude and critical observation. More significant even, the book suggests that between the early encounters with nomad life and her death, Lady Blunt had conceptualised her impressions of and views on, 'authenticity' and cross-cultural relations. We should not be misled by the title of the book. The history of the thoroughbred Arabian is also a history of the authentic Arab. Analogy between an aboriginal group, preserving the notion of a 'primitive' life and a 'pure' species, both representing Nature, rather than civilisation, is transparent and runs through the book. The Arabian is a standard among horses as the Arab is an ideal type among oriental people. But more importantly even, the *Authentic Arabian Horse* is about the exchange of information between cultures; about the ways in which knowledge in the West about the Middle East is processed and about the relation between cross-cultural observation and power. We seem, Lady Anne argues, to know a lot about Arabians (and Arabs) but our knowledge is in fact limited and derives from outside sources, in the West and the Middle East itself:

In the Western *outside world* the origin of the horse of Arabia has been and remains a subject of controversy, both as to where he came from and as to how he got his type. No such doubt exists in the *inside world*, which considers its possession of the Arabian horse is as ancient as the creation. Now the views of both outside worlds, Eastern and Western – and therefore the views of the great majority – have been expressed freely and abundantly, in countless volumes, in many languages, at first in manuscripts and later in print, while the *unwritten views of the restricted world* have remained almost inaccessible. For apart from the fact that the Nomad [sic] world is unable to produce a written record of its mood and thought, the chances of intimate intercourse with it by word of mouth are made difficult not for outsiders, even for those of the neighbouring Arabic-speaking regions.[57]

The passage deserves attention for three reasons. First is the location or relative position of the ethnographer/historian and his or her subject or interest. At the centre of the optical field is not the metropolitan society, nor even the familiar urbanised Orient, but the desert. The West is relegated to the periphery of the vision: it is the 'outside', a remarkable departure from the ethnocentric discourse on the Middle East. The second trait that marks off the text from standard writing is the distinction between literate and non-literate societies with an oral culture. The spoken word, both the conversation of contemporary Bedouins and the ancient lore preserved in Arabic poetry from before the *hajra* (notably in the Qasida or formal Arabic odes), is as important as written authorities.[58] Third and last is the association between political power and the collection of information. Nomad societies are 'minorities'. They are pressed by the politically superior West and those parts of the Middle East which had already been westernised, and were now exposed to processes of modernisation. And there is not a shadow of a doubt where the sympathies of the writer lie, nor where is the place and task of the ethnographer:

> my object is to present the case of the minority after giving a short survey of that of the majority; showing the gulf between the outer and inner circles, for it has been my good fortune to spend many years in intimate converse with members of those very horse-breeding tribes.[59]

'Converse' is the key-word. It denotes a system of communication in which two reciprocating parties exchange information. The nomad is not merely an object, but an active participant in a dialogue between cultures. Elsewhere, in a reference to Charles Doughty's remarks on the dangers to a nomadic culture in the urbanised and westernised Hijaz, Blunt again emphasises the need for faithful documentation of a disappearing minority. The duty of the sympathetic Westerner is to

> present the case of the seldom-heard voice from within before it shall have been finally stifled by the growing pressure from

without, as might well happen even as a more or less immediate consequence of the appalling upheaval of 1914.[60]

This was, I guess, written in 1916, certainly after the outbreak of the First World War, possibly, even probably, towards the end of Lady Anne's life (the extracts are titled 'Lady Anne Blunt's Last Words'), before the outbreak of the Arab Rebellion. And in the jingoist atmosphere of 1915 and 1916 criticism, even in the private, on the purpose and nature of the war, was daring and certainly not very common.

As with the writings on the landscape of the Nafud and Jabal Shammar, so with the notes on the Shammar themselves, Lady Blunt self-consciously adopts an approach that may best be described as unromantic. She is at pains to de-romanticise *Western and Oriental* notions about Arabians and Arabs. Her criticism then is directed both at the Western audience and unauthentic Eastern people. Romance, she argues, is alien to the nature of the Arabs and their view of the world and life. The Bedouins are materialists. Spiritualism, pietism and a propensity to fantasy and 'romance' characterise the Islamised towns of the peninsula and of the Middle East at large. And spiritualism and romantic escapism also characterise the modern West. The gist of the distinction between, on the one hand a materialist nomad people and on the other a romantic urban culture, means the disseverance of the former from Islam. Lady Blunt, it seems, admires the Shammar not because they are Muslims but because they have preserved the pagan culture of the era before the *hajra* and the Islamisation of the Middle East. Unlike Blunt she was not attracted to Muslim religion. And in contradistinction to him she does not seem to appreciate the materialist aspects of that religion which appealed to the Darwinist in Blunt.

Fantasy and romance are connected to the discussion on cross-cultural representation and the exchange of information, in the fifth chapter of the *Authentic Arabian Horse*. The chapter, unedited and, according to Lady Wentworth, quoted in Lady Anne's own words, elaborates on the metaphor of the 'Voice'. In discussion on the Arabian horse and, it is implied, in the discourse on the nomads, three voices are audible. First is the 'Nomad voice of Nejd', 'independent, original, local'.[61] It has been transmitted orally from the pre-Islamic past down to the present. Central to that lore is the tradition that a wild 'authentic' Arabian had always lived in the peninsula. The second voice of the 'outside' oriental world grafts on the pagan myths the fabric of fantasy and romance of Islam. Last and least in significance is 'the voice from our own outside world of the West'.[62] The reversal of the Europocentric geography of the Middle East and the Mediterranean is noteworthy. In Anne Blunt's imaginary map, which, curiously, resembles the 'map of the world' before the age of discovery and the scientific revolution, the margins are relocated in the centre. And the centre, that is the West, is relegated to the periphery. Clearly the question of location: of the Middle East *vis-à-vis* the West; of nomad *vis-à-vis* urban society; of oral tradition *vis-à-vis* the authority of texts – that question impinges on the position of Anne Blunt as the wife of an Arabist and as a woman Arabist and critic of the imperialist culture. Let there be no misunderstanding, I do not doubt that Blunt had an enormous influence on her work and ideas. Throughout this chapter I attempted to show the scope of that influence. Nor do I suggest that the rhetoric of Victorian gender ideology was imposed on a passive help-mate by the 'patriarchal' Blunt. To argue this would be ludicrous and would corroborate the standard image of the Blunts. Her writing combines domestic rhetoric (noted in her usage of Bunyan's popular text) with tolerance towards the different and a value-free, relativist approach to culture. Furthermore, Lady Blunt's views on Arabs and the Middle East were subject to changes. The ideological religious framework which imposed itself on attitudes to Nature and the desert, disappear in the later writing. The *Arabian Horse*, a summary of years of research and writing, represents a sense of the comparativeness of Western *and* Eastern values. It is clear that, in contradistinction to Blunt himself, she is not primarily interested in political institutions and the *political* future of the Muslim Middle East. Lady Blunt's interest lies in the predicament of a culture, threatened by modernisation and 'alien' influences – oriental *and* occidental.

The inseparable Eastern careers of the Blunts demonstrate that within 'authority' and alongside traditional discourse on the Orient, there was room for a dissenting feminine voice. Lady Blunt's vocal metaphor seems apt here. For her work, read together with that of other travellers, like Edwards and Martineau, also demonstrates the multivocal, heteroglot quality of the alternative discussion on the Middle East.

Each of the three writers represents a different facet of the secularisation of the feminine experience of oriental people and landscapes. The two earlier writers severed themselves from religious gender ideology and the evangelical tradition of travel, opting for 'science' or 'history'. In Martineau's case, the section proved traumatic. Hence the belligerent tone in *Eastern life*. Edwards moved further from the older model, yet her move was not as dramatic. The religionless Lady Blunt converted and returned to the model of the pilgrimage. But she secularised the *peregrinatio*, interpreted it in thisworldly terms, applying the theme of the Christian man's quest in a context that was outside Christian culture and society. Thus Blunt's work is more innovative and 'liberated' than that of her predecessors. Furthermore, the scientific travellers homogenised the Orient and de-historicised it. Martineau and Edwards assume a changelessness in Oriental landscapes and people. Edwards' analogy between women in ancient Egypt and Victorian women is historically as groundless as Martineau's comparison between Circassian slaves and Afro-American ones. The scientific framework and view of the Middle East could be as limiting as religious dogma. And as liberal middle-class feminists, Edwards and Martineau measured the society that they encountered according to their own Western standards, approaching the 'women's problem' primarily in political terms and connecting it to the 'Eastern question'. Neither of the writers could develop that empathy with another culture so characteristic of Lady Blunt.

Conclusion

I wish to convey an idea of the life that an English woman can make for herself in the East.[1]

So wrote in 1875 Isabel Burton, née Arundell, in a deceptively modest prefatory note to a work on the *Inner Life in Syria*. Her own life in the Middle East seems to have evolved around the perturbed life of Captain Sir Richard Francis Burton, sometime soldier, diplomat, explorer and geographer, defender of the Empire, scholar, amateur pornographer and expert on oriental sexuality. Isabel Burton was his indispensable companion, a help-mate, an *amanuensis*, the mediator between the renegade Burton and respectable society and, finally, his biographer. She made the mythical Burton by un-making the real one. As his literary executor she had unlimited power on his bequest. And she exercised this power mercilessly: bowdlerising editions of Burton's *magnum opus*, the literal translation of the *Thousand and One Nights* and destroying his notes and diaries in an effort to gain that respectability which had always eluded him. For Isabel Burton the East *was* a vocation, a Holy Place, the *locus* of freedoms denied her as the marriageable, self-educated spinster in a socially ambitious but impoverished, devout Catholic family.

A generation, class, religion and education separate between the 'Eastern life' of Burton and that of Gertrude Lowthian Bell. But the following passage, taken from the first chapter in Bell's *Desert and the Sown*, elaborates the utterance of her predecessor.

To those bred under an elaborate social order few such moments of exhilaration can come as that which stands at the threshold of wild travel. The gates of the enclosed garden are thrown open, the chain of the entrance of the sanctuary is lowered, with a wary glance to right and left you step forth, and behold! the immeasurable world. The world of adventure and of enterprise, dark with hurrying storms, glittering in raw sunlight. . . So you leave the sheltered close, and, like the man in the fairy story, you feel the bonds break that were riveted about your heart as you enter the path that stretches across the rounded shoulder of the earth.[2]

Bell appears to speak in a de-gendered, impersonal voice. And at one time she invokes the obviously fictional masculine *persona* of a traveller: 'the man from the fairy tale'. But she speaks of her own emancipation from an 'elaborate social order' and of her identity as a woman *and* a traveller. For the entire passage is structured around the rather banal juxtaposition of a feminine and masculine sphere, conventionally expressed in two sets of spatial images. The domestic life, sedate and protected yet imprisoning, is likened to 'an enclosed garden', a 'sanctuary', 'a sheltered close', secured by 'gates and chains'. The East, on the other hand, is a place of 'adventure' and 'enterprise', dangerous, but untrammelled. Travel is an emancipatory activity.

Gertrude Bell and Isabel Burton each made a life *for* herself in the Middle East. Their entirely different experiences and idioms reflect the diversity of the wider cultural experience with which this book has dealt. For both the writers, as for numerous other middle- and upper-class women, the East was not merely a physical place, but an ideal and imaginary one: a symbolic *locus* sometimes romanticised, sometimes 'expurgated' or 'cleaned' (as is the case with Isabel Burton's bowdlerised version on Burton's own imaginary Orient) but always intensely experienced.

The women's vision of the Middle East undoubtedly reflects their prejudices, as well as hegemonic notions on the exotic and 'oriental'. However, the vision was shaped primarily by gender and class. Isabel Burton's remark that an Englishwoman can make a 'life for herself' in the East was a poignant reminder, to her contemporary readers, of the position of women in the West. Like Burton herself, most of the 63 per cent of the married travellers in my sample of writers could not make a living and a life 'for themselves' in Britain. Travel opened up career opportunities and offered degrees of freedom, unknown in the travellers' own middle-class *milieu*. This certainly applies to unmarried, 'unprotected' explorers like Bell or Edwards, who made careers in the newer orientalist 'sciences' which burgeoned alongside academic Orientalism. More significant culturally is the encounter with a family structure and constructs of sexuality and gender, traditionally perceived as entirely different from the Western, Christian constructs.

The encounter was self-revealing. Observation of women's life in another culture brought on a re-evaluation, by the Western women, of their own position as individuals *and* as a marginalised group in a patriarchal culture. Burton, like her predecessors Montagu, Craven and Pardoe, and later writers like Garnett and Bowman-Dodd, was painfully aware of the predicament of the Englishwoman and criticised middle-class gender ideology, the double standard and a monogamy in name only which condoned sin in men, but commanded virtue in women. The sensitivity to similarities between Western and Middle Eastern societies made many writers gloss over the sexual aspects of the harem-system and understate, or ignore altogether, the relationship between domestic and social politics. To be sure, polygamy and the segregation of women *are not* approved of. Even the ardent Turkophiles among the writers would agree with Amelia Bythinia Hornby and Annie Harvey that degrees of freedom inside the *haremlik* and outside it '[do] not compensate for the slavery of the mind which they would have to endure. [The] mental imprisonment is worse even than bodily imprisonment'.[3] Notwithstanding, plural marriage and seclusion were not regarded as necessarily subordinating practices. Within the domestic sphere women exercised powers and enjoyed degrees of autonomies comparable to if not actually greater than, those of middle-class women in the West. Moreover, hierarchical Middle Eastern society in general and the pyramid inside the harem in particular, seemed more open and mobile than Victorian class society. Indeed, the harem seemed freer of most forms of exploitation of sex and class which characterised nineteenth-century Britain. It is significant that observers compare the slave in the Muslim household to the domestic female servant in the *bourgeois* abode and not the Afro-American slave (Martineau's analogy with the American experience of slavery and sexual exploitation is, as already noted, uncharacteristic).

I do not doubt that the Western women did not represent life in the Middle East as it was, but described what they had seen. And seeing is a pre-programmed activity. Middle-class gender ideology and the ethos of domesticity and feminine solidarity determined views on the culturally different. The few memoirs that we have by Middle Eastern women conjure up another image of harem-life. Huda Sha'rawi (1879–1947), Malek Hifni Nasif (1886–1918), Nabawiya Musa (1890–1951), Warda al-Yazji (1838–1925) and Zaynab Fawaz (1860–1919), to mention only a few examples, depict a grim reality, an experience of exploitation, oppression and claustrophobic isolation. These witnesses do not de-sexualise the *haremlik*, but openly refer to promiscuity and the violence of women towards other women. I particularly have in mind one macabre anecdote, in which Malik Hanîm relates how the infamous Nazli Hanîm served her own husband a dish of a baked head, stuffed with rice, of one of his concubines.[4]

As with domestic life and the private sphere, so with representations of landscapes and historical places, the writers' geography of the Middle East reflected beliefs and ideologies. Vital religion and active millenarianism shaped the evangelical narratives on Palestine and Syria studied in Part Three. And the secular, sometimes anti-clerical approach to the Orient, associated with the evolution of the 'new' amateur 'sciences' could be as limiting as the older, religious approach. Martineau's case, discussed in Chapter 12, demonstrates the limits of a historiography and 'science' determined by an evolutionary, ameliorative view of history and politics.

In a final, critical analysis, the elements of change in the alternative discourse outweigh those of continuity, the allegiances to the religious and literary traditions on the Orient. Three related processes – albeit not necessarily consecutive ones – may be discerned in the evolving experience and its reconstruction as text. First came actual contact with an alien world and alien people. Outside the framework of evangelical religion or that of the new sciences, the very presence of the writers on the scene to be understood and described, matured to what Clifford calls 'participant observation', a process which involves sensitive *rapport* of a kind with the other. This phase of observation, based on a shared experience, characterises writing on women but may be found elsewhere (in the work of Lady Blunt on the Shammar).[5] Second came the comparison between cultures, between systems of behaviors and morals. It is important to note that analogy did not necessarily result in an awareness of the diversity of mankind, of institutions and of *mores*. A tolerance towards the different – particularly the sexually different – characterises Augustans like Lady Montagu as well as the later Enlightenment writers. The Victorians, on the other hand, tended to emphasise the similarities between Western and exotic familial structures, rather than their differences. More important, throughout the nineteenth century, female observers note the sameness of womankind, regardless of culture, class or ethnicity. Innate and indelible feminine characteristics and aptitudes are emphasised by virtually all writers. The domesticity, the readiness to serve others and the maternal instincts of Muslim women are repeatedly referred to and commended, because these are values which *bourgeois* culture idealised. Similarly, the Jewish women in the 'Yishuv', or old 'settlement' in Palestine, are elevated to personifications of womanly suffering, common to them and the models of Christian womanhood. Third, and related to the second process, is the emergence of an empathy with the other and a solidarity of gender which undercuts the differences of religion or race. Solidarity arises from the sheer fact of a co-existence as women in a shared world. It is the sense of a common though by no means static, or changeless, condition of subjection that helps build the ideal of a sorority referred to by Anna Bowman-Dodd, at the end of a passage on the relationship between free women and slaves in the high-class harems: 'This love and attachment [between women]', she writes, 'is sometimes as touching as it is sublime. For women must everywhere cling to women at certain moments, whether they be within or without harem walls. In the long life struggle there are times and crises when only a woman can be turned to for full and complete sympathy.'[6] Indeed the awareness of a common experience, common generic characteristics and of the solidarity of women of different creeds, are recognised as major factors in any proposed reform in the harem. In Evangelical propaganda literature women's work *for* women and *with* women is a recurrent theme. In the writing of a sensitive religious woman (but an anti-missionary), like Mary Eliza Rogers, the prescribed changes in Middle Eastern society are expected to begin in the harem and to be precipitated by the contacts between English and Muslim women: 'It seems to me,' she argues, 'that all that we can do is to enter into sympathy with the Moslem [sic] women, and try to awaken and develop the highest feelings of their nature, and to help them to understand and feel the power which they have for governing and elevating themselves.'[7] Naturally attitudes and sensibilities do not evolve linearly or simply progress in time. Observation and comparison not always resulted in sensitive understanding and empathy, but could lead to cultural smugness and ethnocentrism that in the writing of Martineau, Nightingale and Edwards borders on racism. Similarly the work of avowed Turkophiles like Pardoe, Fanny Blunt, Scott-Stevenson and Bowman-Dodd is not the outcome of Montagu's earlier model. For each and every one of these writers challenged the Augustan prototype of the Ottoman harem.

It is tempting to describe the change from the eighteenth-century model to the Victorian one in dialectical terms. As aristocratic culture slowly gave way to the *bourgeois* attack on corruption and sensuality, the cosmopolitan, hedonistic appreciation of the exotic and oriental was supplanted by a preoccupation with 'propriety', accompanied by intolerance. Montagu and Craven's latitudinarian attitude towards feminine sexuality was succeeded by Pardoe and Lady Burton's concern about morality and propriety. Yet as Chapters 4 and 5 demonstrate, nineteenth-century attitudes to sexuality were more complex than those of female writers during the Enlightenment. The Victorians developed elaborate techniques of physical description which enabled them to discuss problematic topics like feminine sexuality, the female body and women's work. Ethnographic material on eating and food, costume and hygiene, as well as folklore, were collected, then translated into a descriptive narrative which was used as a code in the larger discourse on manners and morals, gender and the private and the public.

Linear or dialectic explanations of the changes which the book traces are inadequate for another reason. As the nineteenth century progresses, the experience of the *real*, geographical Orient, outlined in detail in Chapters 1, 6 and 7, became more complex and diverse. Consequently, the discourse based on this experience presents a wide variety of idioms and notions, and a multiplicity of literary forms and artefacts. Thus at the end of the century, popular Biblical geography co-existed with the 'secular' scientific archaeology and topography. And the feminine travelogue, relating a history of independent exploration, flourished together with the co-produced account of travel, reflecting the emergence of orientalist couples like the Blunts, the Bents and the Burtons, studied in the last chapter.

The most serious challenge to hegemonic notions about the 'other' and the 'elsewhere' and to cultural authority is to be found in the genres where it is least expected: harem literature and the co-written travelogue, which appears to duplicate familial structures and the ideal of domesticity. Harem literature *was* women's literature. And it was – as shrewd publishers acknowledged – a generically feminine artefact. Its authority derived from a generic experience, shared by European and Middle Eastern women and, vicariously, by Western audiences. It is precisely the legitimacy of the experience in middle-class culture that rendered the new genre its ethnographic authority and, at the same time, made possible the break away from the ideology and aesthetics of the dominant culture. The writers were able to de-homogenise the Orient and, by domesticating the harem, humanise the exotic. The condition of Muslim women was not perceived as a static state of bondage. And the Orient ceased to be a changeless *locus* of sensuality and was transformed to a dynamic place. The *orientale*, as a fixed category of promiscuous feminine sensuality, was supplanted by 'oriental women', whose *sameness* to the middle-class Western women was repeatedly emphasised. In other words, the exotic was transformed from the 'alien', or the entirely different, to that of a recognisable image of *Western femininity*.

Ironically, the observers who are the least capable of developing empathy and solidarity with Middle Eastern women, indeed with Middle Eastern culture as such, are liberal feminists like Martineau and Edwards and reformers with special interest in the 'women's question' in the West, like Power-Cobbe and Nightingale. Martineau's analogy between the master of the Turkish-Circassian harem and the slave-owner in South Carolina, between the *haremlik* and the plantation, is but one example of the myopic vision of a progressive liberal. As Chandra Talpade Mohanty shrewdly remarks, Western feminists always have had the propensity to homogenise 'colonial' (or 'third world') women to a rather reductionist category of the 'oppressed'.[8] Not entirely surprisingly, opponents to emancipation in Britain idealise the informal liberties of women in the Middle East guaranteed by custom, rather than statutory law. We should be aware, however, not to inflate the political dimension of the discourse. There are enough examples to contradict the association between ethnocentrism and liberalism, or between conservatism and defense of traditional Muslim practices like seclusion. Few writers had greater sympathy with Middle Eastern people than the radical Duff-Gordon. Few idealised the Ottoman harem more than the suffragist Grace Ellison. Fewer still, despised Muslim women more intensely than the Tory and Evangelical Mary Louisa Whately. The gist of all this is that the women's discourse was not political and that it cannot and should not be reduced to a reflection of contemporary imperialist discourse on the 'Eastern Question'.

Outside the generic experience of domestic life and 'feminine' genres, the position of the writers is somewhat ambiguous. The sense of this ambiguity, of the precariousness of feminine authority, is articulated by the dying Lucie Duff-Gordon, in one of her last letters, dated 25 January 1869, to her husband: 'Now that I am too ill to write I feel sorry that I did not persist and write on the beliefs of Egypt in spite of your fear that the learned would cut me up, for I honestly believe that knowledge will die with me that few others possess.'⁹ Duff-Gordon produced informal letters, instead of a formal, authoritative closed text on manners and customs, or on the standard Nile voyage. More characteristically travellers *did* describe beliefs, people and historic places (which Duff-Gordon, in a typical aversion of bathos, avoided writing about). But the fear of being 'cut up' by the 'learned' evinces itself in diverse ways. The tendency of the women to belittle the significance of their experience; the resort to citation; the repetitive reference to traditional sources; the self-depreciating tone – all of these testify to a lack of self-confidence that is foreign to the literature on harems. Thus the self-important, self-admiring Martineau, who never had had Gordon's modesty and sense of proportion, filiates herself with a long succession of men travellers and historians, among them Herodotus. Yet *Eastern Life* abounds with addresses to 'lady travellers', including even exhortation to Englishwomen to iron and starch their linen in the Egyptian desert (the versatile Martineau, it seems, was an accomplished seamstress)! The usage of a masculine, or a de-gendered voice in the 'serious', scholarly parts of the *Life*, and of a feminine one in personal passages, is immensely revealing. And Chapters 8–11 show that Martineau's stratagem was a common one.

Of the two patterns of travel and travel writing proper, one – the pilgrimage – provided neutral or feminine role models. During the evangelical revival of the mid nineteenth-century the traditional experience of the *peregrinatio* expanded and acquired new social and cultural meanings. Evangelical gender ideology, with its emphasis on an active life for women *in* the world, enhanced the development of a sense of Christian feminine identity. At the same time the spread of popular, amateur interest in the Scriptures and in Biblical studies made the Bible accessible to all English readers. That particular combination of ideology and a popular, un-scientific apparatus of inquiry, such as Biblical literalism, explains the enormous religious appeal of the Middle East to women.

In contradistinction to writing on manners and customs, the women's religious geography of Palestine and Syria reveals the same lack of self-confidence discussed earlier. Writers develop a rich rhetoric of deference: to the sacred texts themselves; to traditional evangelical writing and even to religious iconography and landscape paintings. Yet the availability of the apparatus of literal Biblism, together with changes in the status of the sacred text and its readers, validated interpretations of the Scriptures which emphasised gender. For if the text was 'open' to all Christians, then, potentially, all interpretations (provided that they were literal and not mythical, or allegorical) were equally valid. Thus evangelical women, notably feminists like Frederika Bremer and Power Cobbe, could develop a feminine version of the geography *and history* of the Near East. The sacred 'women's history' (Bremer's term) exalted feminine models of Christian behaviour and allocated contemporary women a special place in the evangelical cosmogony.

The emergence of an entirely new mode of travel, outside the religious experience, is the most significant development in the late Victorian and Edwardian era. The new model *did not* supplant the older one. Rather the two co-existed and interacted. Note that the dramatic rise in specialist work, by women, on the Middle East coincided with the surge in missionary activity and popular evangelical tourism in the 1880s and 1890s. Nor is the contiguity between the 'religious' and a 'scientific', semi-professional trend merely one of time. Both trends have in common a few structural features. First is the dominating presence of a doctrine, or an ideology, which predetermines inquiry and observation and which organises the view of the different. A belief in the progressive evolution of civilisation and in history as an ameliorative process, whose pinnacle is the present, or in a moral-free, positivist utopian future, could be as limiting as the evangelical cosmogony. The Middle East was invariably associated with the beginning of civilisation, or mankind, the West with their maturity. The second common feature is an interest in the historical ancient Orient and a disinterestedness in the contemporary Middle East. Third, and related to the second, is a strong bias against the Muslim Orient, which assumes various manifestations, in different genres. Evangelicals focus on Jews and on Judaic-Christian landscapes. Historians, archaeologists and philologists limit their interest to the pre-Islamic past. Even an Arabophile like Lady Blunt is attracted to nomadic cultures in Najd and the northern parts of the Euphrates Valley not for their Muslim heritage, but for the pagan traditions. Fourth and last, is the ambivalent attitude of the writers to traditional authority on the Orient. The position of the new, non-evangelical explorers and tourists is particularly difficult. Precisely because they have no feminine role-models, or patterns of travel and travel-writing, to fall back on. The 'unprotected female' touring the Middle East on her own was a challenge to the ethos of the spheres. And this challenge, unlike the more openly iconoclastic domestic ethnography (or evangelical travel) could not be integrated in the hegemonic middle-class ethos of femininity. Gertrude Bell's apposition of a 'secluded garden' and 'wild travel', along the open desert road, is very revealing. In the Victorian context 'wild travel' was a statement on society and the restrictions it put on women. The novelty of the experience may explain why so many of the travellers dissociated themselves from feminine topics; why they could not develop the ethnographer's sympathy with Muslim women and, even, why they became explicitly hostile towards orientals.

To conclude. The discourse on the Orient described in this book may be characterised by a plurality of voices and idioms, reflecting the proliferation, in the eighteenth and nineteenth centuries, of experiences of individuals and groups, of gender and class. There is not one authority ordering the experience, reconstructing the information gathered and shaping the discourse, but a few, equally significant models of perception *and action*, which moulded actual encounter with alien people and places and, in turn, were modulated by that encounter. There is not one literary canon, nor a 'monoglot' authorial voice, but diverse texts and a 'heteroglot' language, richly manifesting the shifts and changes in sensibilities. There is not *one focus* of power and knowledge about 'things oriental', but diverse *focii*, which, characteristically, are located outside the places identified with political domination, or economic expansion overseas. The voluntary philanthropic organisation; the smaller missionary enterprise; the struggling 'new' scientific society, these are the typical places where the feminine interest in the orient emerged.

Already in the introduction I raised a set of related questions, which may be relevant in a discussion on cross-cultural representation and the construction of the 'other', or different, and that of the identity of a group. Are social and economic categories more important than politics, or race or religion? Can marginalised groups, traditionally perceived as the 'other within', that which is different inside the hegemonic society, develop their own experience and notion of the 'other without'? And, implied in these questions is another: is the notion of a distinct (and unified) culture like 'the West', or 'Europe', always workable in historical analyses of the relations between Western European (and North American) societies and non-European ones?

Most of my answers to these questions have been made clear in the foregoing. But I should like to be more explicit and succinct about some points. My chief argument, which is by no means original, has been that 'Europe' and the 'West' are not unified categories, to be applied indiscriminately in studies of Orientalism, exoticism and cultural exchange in the colonial era. Apart from the national and regional varieties taken into account by most students of these phenomena there are varieties of class and gender which are much less readily recognised. Notwithstanding the political context of these cultural attitudes, they cannot be comprehended as solely political. Indeed, my reading of the material illustrates that social differences and gender could weigh more than political or cultural unities. Images of foreign or exotic cultures it is conventionally argued were, invariably, constructs of the Western Man's 'other'. 'Man', capitalised and elevated to a category and a standard was not merely a generic but a literal term (Clifford Geertz and Porter and Rousseau's argument).[10] The Orient came to be the opposite of a rational and rationalising West, superior and identified as 'masculine'. The oriental female apothosised that Orient's 'otherness'. But, as I hope I have shown, particularly in the first half of this book, the image of the different was never monolithic and, certainly, not androcentric. Women travellers, missionaries and writers did not perceive the oriental *woman* as the absolutely alien, the ultimate 'other'. Rather oriental *women* became the feminine West's recognisable image in the mirror. The *haremlik* was not the *ne plus ultra* of an exotic décor, but a place comparable to the *bourgeois* home. And even alien landscapes were domesticated and feminised, by evangelicals and non-evangelicals alike. Of course, the reconstruction of the Orient cannot and *should not* be separated from the construction of the notion of Empire and from modern Imperialism. Nonetheless the processes outlined in this book should be related primarily to the *Bildung* of individuals, the evolution of class culture and to concepts of gender and feminine sexuality. In a paraphrase on Peter Gay, the encounter with an 'other' was a part of the development of *bourgeois* sensibilities, as well as of 'the education of the senses'.[11]

A few last words. Representations of the different do not easily yield themselves to binary models, favoured by students of orientalism and other forms of 'cultural domination'. The symmetrical oppositions 'West' 'East', 'Man' and 'Woman', 'metropolis' and 'periphery', 'coloniser' and 'colonised' may become confusingly blurred. Especially when we shift our focus from hegemonic traditions and canonised texts to the wealth of materials which, like

Hester Stanhope's remains, lies buried outside national pantheons. If my limited study has any use, it will be as a small and modest contribution to an open-minded historical study of the European interest in the 'other', as well as in the intricate relations among human experience, culture and society.

Appendix A: Biographies of Travellers and Travel Writers

The biographical notes are a supplement to the prosopography of travellers in Chapter 1. There are, however, additional biographies of authors not included in the sample or in Bevis' list. An asterisk indicates authors in the sample.

***Amherst, Baroness Mary Rothes Margaret Cecil** (1857–1919), traveller, amateur archaeologist and collector of Egyptian antiquities. Eldest daughter of Lord Amherst and Margaret Susan Mitford; married Lord William Cecil. Margaret Cecil occasionally published in the *Annales du Service des Antiquitiés*. She is best known for her travel-book, *Birds Notes from the Nile* (1904).

***Arbuthnot, Lady Ann** (n.d., 1882), traveller, daughter of Field-marshal Sir John Fitzgerald; married Sir Robert Arbuthnot; lived intermittently in Egypt. 'Lady Arbuthnot chamber' inside the Great Pyramid, at Gizah, is named after her.

***Baillie, E. L. C.** (n.d.), traveller and writer of religious tracts and prescriptive books, toured the Middle East in the 1870s and published *A Sale to Smyrna, or an Englishwoman's Journal*, based on her travels (1873).

Baker, Florence (n.d.), explorer, wife of Samuel Baker – discoverer of the Nile's sources, and gold medalist of the Royal Geographical Society. Born in Hungary as Florence Ninian Von Sass; married Baker in 1865 (legend has it that he bought her at a slave-market, somewhere in the Balkans). Joined him on the voyage to Albert Nyanza, which they discovered together.

***Beaufort, Emily Anne, Lady Strangford** (n.d., 1887), traveller, philanthropist, nurse and hospital reformer, wife of Percy E. F. W. Sydney Smythe, eighth viscount of Strangford, oriental scholar, and expert on the Balkans. Emily Beaufort was the youngest child of

Admiral Sir Francis Beaufort and, according to legend, a descendant of the Beauforts of the Crusades. In 1860 she travelled to the eastern Mediterranean, residing in the neighbourhood of Beirut during the civil war between Druses and maronites, which she documented in *Egyptian Sepulchres and Syrian Shrines* (1862). A favourable review by Strangford in the *Athenaeum* started a friendship and Beaufort's eventual marriage to him. The two collaborated in the *Eastern Shores of the Adriatic* which concludes with a chapter by Strangford on the political situation in the Balkans. After his death in 1869, she embarked on her second career as a nurse, hospital administrator, philanthropist and social reformer. In 1873 she organised the National Society for Providing Trained Nurses for the poor. In 1877 she co-founded the Relief for the Bulgarian Peasants and during the Russo-Turkish War superintended a hospital for wounded Turks. In 1882 Beaufort founded and opened at Cairo the St. John's Ambulance Association and the Victoria Hospital, the first'modern' hospital in Egypt. She later founded a medical school in Beirut. Beaufort was literary executor and editor of her husband's works, as well as of the works of his brother, the politician George Augustus Fredrick Smythe, Disraeli's 'Coningsby'.

*Bell, Gertrude, Margaret Lowthian (1868–1926), explorer, archaeologist, specialising in the Early Christian era; linguist and translator from Persian; diplomat and founder member of the Anti-Suffragist League. Daughter of Sir Hugh Bell, an ironmaster baronet; born at the Hall, Washington, County Durham; educated at Lady Margaret Hall, Oxford and the first woman to gain First-Class Honours in Modern History at that university. Bell's early career as mountaineer, was followed by her work as field archaeologist, in co-operation with Sir William Ramsay. Her travels included journeys through Mesopotamia, a voyage, in 1913 to Ha'il, in Najd (in Northern Arabia) and Asia Minor. Before the First World War, she became involved in intelligence work and in 1916 was appointed political secretary to Sir Percy Cox in Basra. Later she was intimately involved in the negotiations over the dismantling of the British mandate in Iraq and supported Faisal in his claim to the throne. Became Government Director of Antiquities in Iraq and founded the National Museum at Baghdad. Died of a drug-overdose. Among her best-known books are: *Safar Nameh: Persian Pictures* (1894), *The Desert and the Sown* (1907); *Amurath to Amurath* (1911) and *Palace and Mosque at Ukhaidir* (1914).

*Belzoni, Sarah (1783–1870), explorer and collector of antiquities; wife of Giovanni B. Belzoni, the famous antiquarian and discoverer of Egypt's monuments. She accompanied Belzoni, on his voyage along the Nile and to Nubia, and in 1818 crossed the Sinai peninsula alone and travelled through Palestine. She probably was the first European to penetrate Haram al-Sharif in Jerusalem. Contributed an essay on her travels to Belzoni's *Narrative of the Operations and Recent Discoveries . . . in Egypt* (1820).

Bensley, Agnes Dorothée (n.d.), daughter of Baron Edward von Blomberg; married Robert Bullock Bensley, orientalist and Syria philologist, the decipherer of the Syriac palimpsest of the gospels and Biblical scholar. She accompanied Bensley and Agnes Smith Lewis on the expedition to Mount Sinai, where the palimpsest was discovered and copied, describing the journey in *Our Journey to Sinai; A Visit to the Convent of St. Catherine* (1890).

*Benson, Margaret (1865–1916), excavator and archaeologist. Daughter of Edward White Benson, Archbishop of Canterbury; educated at Lady Margaret Hall, Oxford. She visited Egypt several times between 1894 and 1900 and excavated, under P. E. Newberry, the Temple of Nut at Thebes. Her *Temple of Nut in Asher* appeared in 1899.

*Bent, Mable Virginia (n.d.), explorer and travel-writer, member of the Royal Geographical Society. Daughter of Robert Westley Hall-Date; married, in 1877, James Theodore Bent, the explorer, linguist and archaeologist whom she joined on seven journeys to the Arabian peninsula, which, from 1893, Bent made his special field of interest. She completed and edited the seminal *Southern Arabia*, often attributed to Bent himself (1900).

*Bishop, Isabella Lucy Bird (1831–1904), explorer, writer and missionary. Born in Yorkshire to a clerical family, started her literary career in 1847. Her first journey, recommended for health, was to Canada and the United States and produced *The Englishwoman in America* (1856). Later travels included Australia, New Zealand, the Sandwich Islands, Japan, China, the Hawaiian Archipalgo, and Tibet. In 1888 Bird Bishop embarked on a missionary career in the Far East. She was a fellow of the Royal Geographical Society. Among her works are: *A Lady's Life in the Rocky Mountains* (1879) and *The Yangtze Valley and Beyond* (1899).

*Blunt, Lady Annabella King-Noel (1837–1917), explorer, travel-writer, Arabic scholar, and supporter of Egyptian nationalism. Daughter of the first earl of Lovelace and Ada, only legitimate daughter of Lord Byron; married in 1869 Wilfrid Scawen Blunt, diplomat, poet and an exponent, in Britain, of pan-Islamism and Egyptian nationalism. Between 1875 and 1882, the Blunts travelled extensively through the Middle East. Their journey to Mesopotamia and pioneering voyage to Najd, in central Arabia and then to Persia produced Lady Blunt's two famous travelogues: *Bedouin Tribes of the Euphrates* (1878) and *A Pilgrimage to Nejd* (1879). Among her other works are: *The Authentic Arabian Horse* (published posthumously) and translations of pre-Islamic poetry. She separated from Blunt in 1896 and, until her death, lived in Sheykh *Ubayd*, near Cairo.

*Blunt, Fanny Janet (1840–n.d.), amateur ethnographer, married Britain's Consul General to Constantinople, known for her *People of Turkey* (1878), one of the most reliable accounts of everyday life in that country.

*Bodichon, Barbara Leigh-Smith (1827–1891), feminist activist and writer on the women's question. Born in Yorkshire, daughter of a radical MP; campaigner for the Married Women's Property Act and writer of a number of works on Women and the law. Founded the *Englishwoman's Journal*, married Ernest Bodichon in 1857 and afterwards lived in Algiers.

Beke, Emily Alston (n.d.), traveller, wife of Charles Tilstone Beke, famous Bible critic; accompanied him on his voyages and wrote *Jacob's Flight*; or *A Pilgrimage to Harran* (1865), a popular companion to Beke's Biblical studies and travelogue.

*Bowman, Anne (n.d.), a popular novelist, specialising in children's stories, published *The Young Nile Voyagers* (1868) and *Travels of Orlando, or a Tour Round the World* (1877).

*Brassey, Anna (Annie), baroness (1839–87), traveller and popular travel-writer, first wife of Thomas Brassey, the railway tycoon. She is famous for her yachting trips in the Mediterranean and around the world which she described in a series of best-sellers. Among them are: *A Cruise in the Eothen* (1872); *The Voyage in the Sunbeam* (1878) which went into nineteen editions and *Sunshine and Storms in the East* (1880).

*Brocklehurst, Marianne** (n.d., 1898), traveller and collector of Egyptiana. The Hieratic funerary papyrus is named after her.

Brodrick Mary (May) (n.d., 1933), archaeologist, Egyptologist, philologist, specialising in semitic languages. Brodrick studied at the Sorbonne and Collège de France with Maspero and Renan and later at University College, London and Kansas, where she was awarded her Ph.D. She combined an active career as field archaeologist (working under Maspero) with an academic career. Compiled the *Concise Dictionary of Egyptian Archeology* (1902) and edited Murray's handbooks for Egypt.

*Burton Isabel, née Arundel** (1831–96), traveller, travel-writer and journalist. Educated in a convent; married, in 1861, Richard Francis Burton, the explorer, linguist and travel-writer and accompanied him on his journeys. Wrote *The Inner Life of Syria, Palestine and the Holy Land* (1875) and *A.E.I., Arabia, Egypt, India* (1879). After Burton's death she expurgated his translation of the *Arabian Nights* and destroyed his diaries.

*Butler, Lady Elisabeth Southernden** (1846–1933), painter and traveller. Born in Laussane, daughter of Th. J. Thompson and sister of the poet Alice Meynell. Educated at the South Kensington School of Art. Famous for her painting 'The Roll Call', bought by Queen Victoria. Published *Letters from the Holy Land* (1903) and *Preludes with Illustrations* (1875).

*Corbaux, Marie Françoise Catherine Doetter** (1812–83), known as Fanny Corbaux, painter and Biblical critic. Studied at the British Institution and elected honorary member of the Society of British Artists and, from 1871, received a Civil List Pension. Wrote on the physical archaeology of Exodus and introduced Heath's *Exodus Papiri* (1855).

*Charles, Elizabeth (née Rundle 1828–96)** an Evangelical novelist and propagandist, traveller. Daughter of John Rundle, MP for

Tavistock; privately educated, married Andrew Charles, a manufacturer and widowed in 1868. Charles supported herself by her writing from an early age and travelled extensively. She was intimate both with the Oxford Movement and the Evangelical leadership at Clapham. Her novels, however, are decidedly Low Church. Her best known work is *The Chronicles of the Schönberg Cotta Family* (1863), on the domestic lives of Luther and Melanchthon; a revivalist novel *Against the Stream* (1873) and *Joan the Maid* (1879). She also wrote outright Evangelical propaganda which appeared under the imprint of the SPCK. A journey in 1861 to Palestine produced *Wanderings over Bible Lands and Seas* (1862).

*Chennels, Ellen (n.d.), instructress to the children of Khediv Ismail between 1871–6. Wrote *Recollections of an Egyptian Princess . . . by her English Governess*, the fullest inside account of life in the viceregal harems.

*Clark, Harriet (n.d.), evangelical writer, wife of Reverend E. Clark, founder of the Y.P.S.C.E. Her travels are described in *Our Journey Around the World* (1894).

*Cobbe, Frances Power (1822–1908), philanthropist and social reformer, Evangelical turned atheist, miscellaneous writer, feminist and prominent anti-vivisectionist. Her travels in the Middle East are described in *Cities of the Past* (1865). Among her numerous works are: *The Theory of Intuitive Morals* (1855–7); *Darwinism and Morals* (1872) and *The Duties of Women* (1881). Her *Autobiography*, published in 1904 is a classic of its kind.

*Craven, Elisabeth, margravine Anspach (1750–1828), playwright and traveller. Youngest daughter of the fourth earl of Berkeley; married William Craven, afterwards sixth earl of Craven, by whom she had six children. After a legal separation she travelled through Europe to Russia and Turkey, a journey which produced the classic *Journey through the Crimea to Constantinople* (1789). She wrote and translated numerous plays, some of which had a run on the London stage and in Germany. Particularly important are *Silver Tankrad* (1781); *The Yorkshire Ghost* and *Modern Anecdotes of the Family of Kinrerrankotspakengatchdern* (1779).

*Crowfoot, Grace Mary (1878–1957), naturalist, archaeologist and expert in ancient crafts and textiles. Born in Lincolnshire, lived in the Sudan, where she played considerable part in starting the government maternity service. Wrote *Flora of the Sudan* and *Some Desert Flowers*.

Cumming, Constance Frederika Gordon (1837–1924), explorer, travel-writer, water-colourist and sometime missionary. Starting in 1868, she travelled extensively to Ceylon, the island of Fiji, Tonga, Samoa, Tahiti, Japan and China. She wrote a number of books about her travels, including *At Home in Fiji* (1886) and *Wanderings in China* (1881). She is the author of two travelogues on the Middle East.

*Dawson-Damer, Mary Georgina Emma (n.d., 1848), traveller, Daughter of Lord Hugh Seymour and granddaughter of the first marquis of Hartford, married George L. Damer-Dawson. Travelled through Asia Minor and in Palestine and Egypt. Published *Diary of a Tour in Greece, Turkey, Egypt and the Holy Land* (1891).

*Digby, Jane, Lady Ellenborough (1807–1881) known as Jane Digby el-Mezrab, adventurer, water-colourist and linguist. Daughter of Rear-Admiral Henry Digby, second wife of Edward Law, Earl of Ellenborough, divorced by Act of Parliament in 1830, on the grounds of adultery. Lived in Damascus and in the Syrian desert, with the Mezrab, her fourth husband's tribe.

*Duff-Gordon, Janet. *See* Ross, Janet.

Durham, Mary Edith (1864–1944), traveller, expert on the Balkans (specialising on Albanian politics) and naturalist painter. Born to a medical family; trained as artist in Bedford College and the Royal Academy of Arts. From 1903 to the outbreak of the First World War she travelled yearly in the Balkans, including the passage from Montenegro to North Albania recorded in *High Albania* (1909). Elected Honorary Secretary of the Anglo-Albanian Society and the leading advocate in Britain of Albanian nationalism. She published more than ten books about her travels and on Balkan politics, among them *High Albania* (1909); *Through the Lands of the Serb* (1904) and *The Burden of the Balkans* (1905).

*Edwards, Amelia Ann Blanford (1831–92), popular novelist, journalist, Egyptologist and founder of the Egypt Exploration Fund and the Department of Egyptology at University College, London. Born in London to a banking family; educated privately. At an early age, Edwards started a prolific career as miscellaneous writer and novelist, contributing regularly to *Household Words*; *Saturday Review*; *Morning Post* and the *Academy*. A journey to Egypt and up the Nile in 1873, described in the classic *A Thousand Miles Up the Nile* (1877) changed her life. She became the chief exponent in Britain of Egyptology, co-founded the Egypt Exploration Fund (EEF) and became its Honorary Secretary and later Vice-President. Organised the Fund's first excavations in Egypt and published the work of Sir Flinders Petrie and Neville. Wrote on subjects related to Egyptology for the *Academy*, *Harper's Monthly* and *The Times*. Identified the Cypriote Phoenician signs on potsherds found by Petrie in the Faiyum.

*Egerton, Lady Harriet Catherine, baroness Ellesmere (1800–66), traveller, millenarian Evangelical and philanthropist. Daughter of Charles Granville; married Francis Egerton, first earl of Ellesmere, her companion in travel through the Middle East. Wrote *Journal of a Tour in the Holy Land in 1840*; *Egyptian and Eastern Scenery and Ruins* (1853) and *Egypt: a Familiar Description of the Land, People and Produce* (1839).

*Ellison, Grace (n.d.), traveller, feminist. Became entangled with the Young Turks Movement and Turkey's struggling feminist movement. Wrote a number of books on the position of Turkish women, notably *An Englishwoman in a Turkish Harem* (1915); collaborated with Malik Hanim, Abdulhamit's daughter in an autobiography of the latter: *Abdulhamid's Daughter* (1913) and edited *Zeyneb Khanim [sic]/A Turkish Woman's European Impressions* (1913).

*Fay, Eliza (1756–1816), adventurer, India merchant, ship owner, sometime writer. Born in Blackheath to a maidservant and a sailor; married up, Anthony Fay, barrister and advocate at the Supreme Court at Calcutta and joined him there. Her *Original Letters from India*, published posthumously in 1817, includes a section on Egypt.

*Floyer, Edith Louisa Butcher (n.d.) traveller, writer on Egypt under her own name and religious novelist under the pen-name Fleur de lys. Wrote popular histories of the church in Egypt and also a chronicle of the events in that country, between 1878–1908, *Egypt as We Knew It* (1911).

*Fountaine, Margaret (1868–1940), entomologist and collector of butterflies, traveller. Daughter of the Reverend John Fountaine, Rector of South Acre, near Norwich. Privately educated, initiated herself slowly into travel, first in Europe, then in the Middle East, the United States, Africa and India. In 1901 she met Khalil Neimy, a Syrian dragoman who became her travel-companion for over 28 years. She contributed regularly to entomological journals.

*Gibson, Margaret Dunlop. *See* Lewis, Agnes Smith.

*Gordon, Lucie Duff, née Austin (1821–69), a woman-of-letters, traveller and arabophile. The daughter of a literary couple, the feminist essayist Sarah Austin and John Austin, a jurist and professor of law, Lucie Duff-Gordon was close, from an early age to the Philosophical Radicals and London's literary circles. In 1840 she married Baronet Alexander Duff-Gordon, an impecunious Treasury official and court officer and had three children. She became the centre of an adoring circle of *literati*, including Thackeray, Kinglake, Tennyson (who modelled his *Princess* after her) and Meredith (who portrayed her as Lady Jocelyn in *Evan Harrington*). Ill health drove her first to the Cape of Good Hope and then to Egypt, where between 1860–69 she lived in Luxor, adopting local manner and immensely popular with the local *fallahin*. Her *Letters from Egypt* (1865) and *Last Letters from Egypt* (published posthumously in 1875) are the best documented and most sympathetic accounts of everyday life of the peasantry of Egypt during Khediv Ismail's experiment in modernisation and westernisation.

Gourlay, Janet A. (n.d., d. 1912), excavator, collaborated with Margaret Benson in *The Temple of Nut in Asher* (1899).

*Grenfell, Alice (n.d., d. 1917), collector of Egyptiana and scarab specialist, wife of Sir John Granville, master of Clifton College. Contributed to the *Recueil d'études egyptologiques* and the *Journal of Egyptian Archaeology*.

*Griffith, Kate (n.d., d. 1902), archaeologist, one of the very few women on the committee of the EEF. Born to a wealthy business family; a friend and companion of Amelia Edwards; excavated with Petrie in Egypt and married Griffith in 1896. Works: a translation of Wiedemann's work on Egyptian religion (1896) and various publications in the *EEF Archaeological Reports*.

*Griffith, Nora Christina Cobban (1837–1937), Griffith's second wife. Daughter of a Scottish surgeon, studied Egyptology under Griffith at Oxford and excavated with him in Egypt and Nubia.

Harvey, Annie Jane (n.d.), traveller and writer of historical novels. Wrote: *Turkish Harems and Circassian Homes* (1871).

Hornby, Emilia Bithynia (n.d.), traveller, wife of Sir Edmund (Marconi) Hornby. Her epistolary travelogue, *In and Around Constantinople* (1858–63) has chapters on the life of foreigners in Turkey, during the Crimean War.

*Hutton, Catherine (1756–1846), miscellaneous writer, antiquarian and armchair traveller. Only daughter of local historian and antiquarian William Hutton who describes her in the *History of the Hutton Family*. She wrote 12 books and 60 periodical articles (notably to the *Gentleman's Magazine*) and corresponded with a large number of celebrities (about 3000 of the letters survive). Among her publications are local histories of Birmingham, *The History of Birmingham*, in 8 volumes (1819) and *A Narrative of the Riots in Birmingham* (July 1795). She described the southern Mediterranean, which she never actually saw, in her three-decker *Tour of Africa* (1819–21).

Johns, Agnes Sophia (1859–1949), writer and translator. Sister of F. L. Griffith, the known Egyptologist; married Claude H. W. Johns the Assyriologist. Translated Erman and Maspero. Wrote *Egyptian Archaeology* (1914), *A Handbook of Egyptian Religion* (1907) and *Popular Stories of Ancient Egypt* (1915).

*Lewis, Agnes Smith (1843–1926), philologist, Biblical scholar and traveller, discoverer of the Sinai Palimpsest. Daughter of a Scottish solicitor, John Smith and elder twin sister of Margaret Dunlop Gibson, Lewis's travel-companion and fellow researcher. Educated at the Irvine Academy and privately. Lewis, unusual for a woman, was proficient in the classical languages and in Hebrew and Syriac. In 1887 she married the antiquarian Samuel Savage Lewis, librarian at Corpus Christi, Cambridge and, after his death, embarked on a career as traveller, philologist and Bible-scholar. In 1892 she discovered with her sister, at the monastery of St. Catherine in the Sinai, the Syriac version of the Gospels, known as the Sinai Palimpsest, underneath an eighth century script. In subsequent trips to the monastery, the work of deciphering was completed. Lewis and Gibson published a great deal of Syriac and Christian Arabic texts and a number of travel books. She was a gold medalist of the Royal Asiatic Society and obtained honorary doctor's degrees from the universities of Halle, St. Andrews, Dublin and Heidelberg. Notable works are: *The Forty Masters of the Sinai Desert and the Story of Eulogius* and *The Mythological Acts of the Apostles* (1904), both translations from manuscripts found at St. Catherine's.

*Martineau, Harriet (1802–76), miscellaneous writer, novelist, populariser of the principles of Political Economy, Comte's first translator into English, feminist and well-known abolitionist. Martineau was born to a Unitarian manufacturing family in Norwich. A precocious writer, she started living by her pen in her twenties, after the financial ruin of her family. She contributed to the Unitarian *Monthly Repository* and then regularly to the *Daily News* (some 1000 articles) and the *Edinburgh Review*. Her breakthrough came with the *Illustrations of Political Economy*, serialised by Ch. Fox (1832–4) and followed in the less successful *Illustrations of the Poor Laws and Taxation* (1834). Travelled to the United States, which she described in the classic *Society in America* (1837) and the Middle East, a journey which changed her life and beliefs and which is documented in *Eastern Life, Present and Past* (1848). Martineau's versatility is reflected in the range of topics she studied and wrote about. Among her works are: *The Hour and the Man*, a biographical novel on the life of Toussain L'Overture (1841); *Deerbrook* (1839), considered her best novel; *A History of England During the Thirty Years' Peace (1849); The Philosophy of Comte* (1853); numerous religious tracts, most notably *Traditions of Palestine* (1830) and *Essential Faith in the Universal Church* (1831). Her religious biography and move from Unitarianism via rational Necessarianism to Theism and finally Positivism is documented in her *Autobiography*, published posthumously in 1877.

*Max-Müller, Georgina Adelaide Grenfell (n.d.), traveller, wife of Friedrich Max-Müller, the comparative philologist and mythologist and Sanskrit scholar, sister-in-law of Charles Kingsley and J. A. Froude. Accompanied her husband on his Middle Eastern journeys and wrote *Letters from Constantinople* (1897).

*Menzies, Sutherland. *See* Stone, Elisabeth.

*Montagu, Lady Mary Wortley, née Pierrepont (1689–1762), woman-of-letters, poet and advocate of women's education, the first modern woman traveller to the Middle East. Montagu was the daughter of the fifth earl and first duke of Kingston and became acquainted early with the political (Whig) and literary life. Unusually educated for a woman, she was proficient in Latin and widely read in the classics. In 1712 she secretly married Edward Wortley Montagu, and accompanied him in 1717 to Istanbul, where he was sent as ambassador of the Levant Company and the Court of St. James. She wrote what later came to be known as the 'Turkish Letters', published posthumously in 1763. On her return to England in 1718, Montagu introduced into that country the practice of inoculation against smallpox. She became a leading member of society, famed for her talent, wit and writing. She wrote poetry and contributed anonymously to the Whig press, editing, at one time, her own periodical, *The Nonsense of Common Sense*, sponsored by Walpole (1737). In 1739 she separated from her husband and left England, never to return. Among her works are: *Town Eclogues* (1747); *Court Poems* (1747); *Verses Addressed to the Imitator of Horace* (1733), a satire on Pope, her intimate friend and correspondent, now turned an enemy.

*Montefiore, Judith (n.d., 1862), philanthropist and traveller, wife of Sir Moses Montefiore. Born in London, the second daughter of Levi Barnet Cohen, who was related to the Rothschild family. Lady Montefiore was her husband's inseparable companion in his wanderings in the Middle East. Their first expedition to the eastern Mediterranean is described in her *Private Journal of a Visit to Egypt and Palestine*, printed for private circulation in 1855.

Morton, Alice Anderson (n.d., 1902), Egyptologist. Studied at University College, London. Translated Maspero's *Au Temps de Ramsès* (1890) and collaborated with Mary Brodrick on a *Concise Dictionary of Egyptian Archaeology* (1902).

Murray, Margaret Alice (1863–1963), Egyptologist. Born in Calcutta, the daughter of an English businessman living in India. Educated at University College, London and became the first fulltime professional woman Egyptologist. Worked with Petrie and Griffith and became a fellow at the college in 1922. Among her many publications are: *Ancient Egyptian Legends* (1904); *Elementary Egyptian Grammar* (1905) and *Elementary Coptic Grammar* (1911).

Nightingale, Florence (1820–1910), founder of modern nursing, reformer of the health services and cult-figure. Born in Florence to a landed family of Hampshire, she shunned society and marriage. Trained in nursing at Pastor Flinders's Institute for Deaconesses at Kaiserswerth in Prussia and later in Paris with the Sisters of St. Vincent de Paul. Back in England, she reorganised the Governesses Sanatorium. In 1854, she was sent by Sir Sidney Herbert, Secretary of War, to the Crimea, to reorganise the appallingly mismanaged army hospitals at Scutari. She soon supervised all the hospitals on the Bosphorus, vigorously applying hitherto unrecognised standards of hygiene and medical care, and causing the rate of death to drop by 42 per cent. After her return to England, she became an invalid, but remained active, carrying on more general reforms in nursing and civil and military hospitals. The principles of her system are succinctly presented in *Notes on Nursing*. She travelled in the eastern Mediterranean and her Egyptian voyage produced *Letters from Egypt* (1854).

Oliphant, Alice Lestrange (1846–1887), traveller, utopist, disciple of Thomas Lake Harris. An heiress, Alice Lestrange married in 1872 Lawrence Oliphant, novelist, politician, utopist and Zionist and, immediately joined the utopian commune of Thomas Lake Harris at Brockton, New York State, known as the Brotherhood of the New Life. She became Harris' fanatical disciple, handing over her considerable fortune to the brotherhood, became estranged from her husband and almost induced to help Harris declare Oliphant – by then disillusioned with his mentor – insane. In 1882 she severed off her connection with the brotherhood, settling with Oliphant in Palestine, at the Templar colony at Haifa and subsequently at the Druse village of Dalia. She became an advocate of the doctrine of universal sympathy and equality between the sexes in a sexless utopia. Her somewhat eclectic doctrines drawing on Harris', are publicised in *Sympneumata*, introduced by Oliphant (1884).

Oliphant, Margaret, née Wilson (1828–97), one of the most prolific Victorian novelists, combining industry and mass-production with a degree of artistry. Came from a Scottish, *petit-bourgeois* background and married her cousin Francis W. Oliphant, an impecunious stain-glass artist working with Pugin, in 1852. She was compelled to support her increasing family by the pen, dogged, for the rest of her life by financial crisis. She wrote biographies (including the standard lives of Edward Irving and Lawrence Oliphant, not a relative), numerous reviews, literary histories and novels, notably, *The Chronicles of Carlingford* series, comprising *Salem Chapel* (1863); *The Perpetual Curate* (1864); *Miss Marjoribanks* (1866) and *Phoebe Junior* (1876) in which religious themes predominate. Oliphant also wrote a popular history of Jerusalem (1891).

Paterson, Emily (1860–1947), private secretary to Amelia Edwards and her associate, succeeded Edwards as general secretary of the EEF.

Paget, Rosalind (n.d., 1925), copyist and Egyptologist. Educated at University College, excavated in Egypt where she copied the scenes in the tomb of Ptah-hotep at Saqqara. Wrote *The Ramsesseum* (1896).

*Pardoe, Julia Sophia (1806–1862), historical novelist, traveller and travel-writer. Born in Yorkshire, the daughter of an army officer, Julia Pardoe distinguished herself as a child author, having a vol-ume of her poems published at fourteen. She travelled extensively abroad during her adolescence and youth and in 1835, accompanied with her father, reached Istanbul. Her stay there produced the *City of the Sultan and Domestic Manners of the Turks*, a classic of its kind and exemplar of harem literature. She also wrote *The Beauties of the Bosphorus* and *Romance of the Harem* (1839) and a number of historical novels featuring France of the *ancien régime* and Italy during the Renaissance. She was granted a Civil List pension of £100 before her death.

Petrie, Hilda Mary Isabel, Lady Petrie (1871–1950), Egyptologist. Once model for pre-Raphaelite painting, Petrie settled down to marriage with Sir Flinders Petrie, the 'father' of modern field archaeology and collaborated with him in a number of publications (all postdating the period covered in this book). She was Honorary Secretary of the British School of Archaeology at Egypt.

*Poole, Sophia Lane (1804–91), traveller, writer of *The English-woman in Egypt* (1844), one of the earliest examples of harem literature and a companion volume to Edward W. Lane's *Customs and Manners of the Modern Egyptians*. Lane Poole was the daughter of the Reverend Theophilius Lane, sister of Edward W. Lane and, in 1829, married the bibliographer and book-collector Richard Poole. Her son, Stanley A. Poole, became a well-known Arabic scholar. She lived in Cairo for seven years, collecting material on the harems of Mehmet Ali's family, information which was the basis of her book. In 1860–61 she collaborated with her younger son, Reginald Stuart Poole, in *Photographic Views of Egypt, Sinai and Palestine*.

*Quibbel, Annie Abernethie (1862–1927), excavator and draughts-man, assistant to Petrie, drew hieroglyphs. Her publications post-date the period covered in this book.

*Ramsay, Lady (first name not certain) (n.d.), traveller. Wife of Sir William Mitchell Ramsay, the distinguished archaeologist and rec-ognised authority on the parts of Asia Minor associated with early Christianity. Accompanied her husband on most of his journeys. Wrote *Everyday Life in Turkey* (1897) and tried her hand at fiction.

*Rogers, Mary Eliza (n.d.), traveller, ethnographer, a recognised authority on contemporary Palestine, the only woman contributor to Charles Wilson's *Picturesque Palestine* (1880). The daughter of an engraver and, most probably, unmarried. Rogers joined her brother, Edward Thomas Rogers, Vice Consul to Haifa and then Consul to Damascus and lived in Palestine and Syria at least four years (she arrived in July 1855). Based in Haifa, she accompanied Rogers on his numerous expeditions in Palestine, sometimes acting as his aide and as informer of the Consul to Jerusalem, James Finn. She was an accomplished water-colourist and amateur naturalist. Rogers is unsurpassable on women's life in mid nineteenth-century Palestine, described in *Domestic Life in Palestine* (1863).

*Romer, Isabella Frances (d. 1852), miscellaneous writer, travel-ler and fanatical believer in mesmerism and animal magnetism. Married 1818, separated 1827. Travelled alone through the eastern

Mediterranean. Romer published *A Pilgrimage to the Temples and Tombs of Egypt, Nubia and Palestine* (1852) and *The Bird of Passage* (1849) and, among her novels is one on mesmerism, *Sturmer, A Tale of Mesmerism* (1841).

*Ross, Janet née Duff-Gordon (1842–1927), traveller and biographer. Daughter of Alexander and Lucie Duff-Gordon. Married Henry Ross, manager of Briggs's Bank in Alexandria, and, after the financial crisis of 1866, which ruined the Bank, lived as an expatriate in Italy. She was Lucie Duff-Gordon's literary executor and biographer.

Shaw, Flora, Lady Luggard (n.d., 1852), journalist, *Times* correspondent and Colonial Editor, staunch imperialist. Daughter of a professional soldier and granddaughter of the Irish politician, Sir Frederik Shaw, Flora Shaw embarked on a literary and journalistic career in her early twenties. She travelled extensively, in North Africa and the eastern Mediterranean, sending articles to the *Times* and *Pall Mall Gazette*. In 1888 she became the *Gazette*'s accredited correspondent in Egypt. She was the only woman journalist attending the International Congress on the Suppression of Slave Trade at Brussels. After spells in South Africa, Australia and Canada, she was appointed Colonial Editor of the *Times*, and in 1895 became entangled with the notorious Jameson's affair, in South Africa. In 1898 she married Captain Frederik Luggard, retired from her work as journalist and joined him in Nigeria, where he was High Commissioner and Governor, respectively.

*Stanhope, Lady Hester Lucy (1776–1839), traveller, amateur excavator and a celebrated eccentric. The eldest daughter of the third earl of Stanhope and niece of the famous Pitt, Lady Stanhope left her father's house in 1880 and, from 1883, acted as Pitt's chief of household and private secretary, enjoying a considerable amount of influence in society. After Pitt's death in 1806, she received a handsome yearly pension of £1200. In 1810 she abandoned England and eventually settled among the Druse of Mount Lebanon, for the rest of her life. Her wealth, personality, and authority on the population of southern Syria were sufficiently commanding to induce Ibrahim Pasha, when about to invade Syria in 1832, to solicit her neutrality. Her *Travels* and *memoirs* were transcribed by her physician and *amanuensis*, Dr Charles Lewis Meyron.

*Talbot (initials uncertain), Countess** (n.d.), adventuress and traveller, chanoinesse of the order of St. Anne in Münich. Travelled alone from Egypt, via the Sinai desert to Palestine. Known for her stunts and feats of physical prowess (most famous among them the writing of a letter from the top of Pompey's Pillar, at Alexandria, which she climbed by a rope-ladder).

*Thomas, Margaret** (n.d.), painter, sculptor and traveller. She was educated at the Royal Academy and in Paris and Melbourne. Travelled extensively through the Mediterranean and between 1895 and 1897 resided in Palestine and Syria.

*Tinné, Alexandrine Petronella Francina** (1839–69), a Dutch and naturalised British, explorer, naturalist, explorer of the White Nile, the first woman to cross the Sahara Desert. The daughter of Philip Tinné, a merchant who made his fortune in the Napoleonic Wars and of baroness van Steengracht-Capellen, Alexandrine Tinné was left the richest heiress in the Netherlands. After travelling in Norway, Italy and the Middle East she set out, in January 1862 on her most ambitious journey, tracing the Nile to Bahr-al-Ghazal, then crossing overland, from Meshra-er-Rek, to Jabal Kosango, on the borders of the Niam-Niam country. During the last detour her enormous retinue of 300 considerably shrank. In 1863, she started from Tripoli on an expedition to Lake Chad but was murdered by Tuaregs in August that year. The geographic and botanical discoveries made during the Nile expedition were immediately recognised and were edited and published posthumously in Heuglin's *Die Tinnésche Expedition im westlichen Nilgebiet 1863–4* (1865), *Reise in das Gebiedest Weissen Nils* (1869) and *Plantes Tinnéennes*, a description of the plants discovered by her (1867).

Tirard, Lady Helen Mary** (1854–1943), Egyptologist and translator, a member of the Egypt Exploration Fund and Committee member. Translated Erman's *Aegypted und aegyptisches Leben* (1893). married.

*Vane Frances, marchioness of Londonderry** (n.d), traveller. The heiress of Sir Henry Vane Tempest, Frances Vane married Charles William Stewart, third marquis of Londonderry, a diplomat and soldier and Britain's ambassador to Vienna and later Saint Petersburg, who assumed the name of Vane. She accompanied her husband on his extensive travels and produced one book, *A Narrative of a Visit to the Courst of Vienna* (1844).

Wilkins, Louisa Jebb (n.d.), miscellaneous writer, particularly interested in the 'women's question', compiler of a number of popular texts on small-holdings. Wrote *By Desert Ways to Baghdad* (1908).

Appendix B: Evangelical Travel and Work in Mid Nineteenth-Century Palestine

The source for Figures 4, 5 and 6 on the following pages is the ISA, register of British-born subjects, British Consulate.

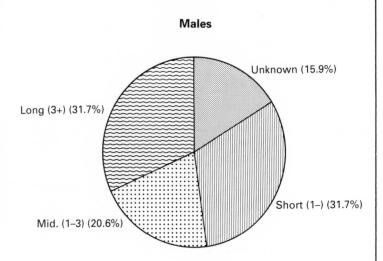

Males

Unknown (15.9%)

Long (3+) (31.7%)

Short (1–) (31.7%)

Mid. (1–3) (20.6%)

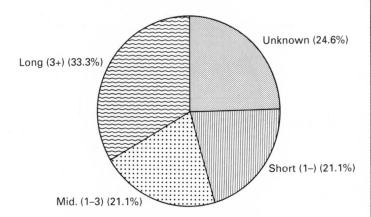

Females

Unknown (24.6%)

Long (3+) (33.3%)

Short (1–) (21.1%)

Mid. (1–3) (21.1%)

Figure 4 Evangelical travel to Palestine, duration

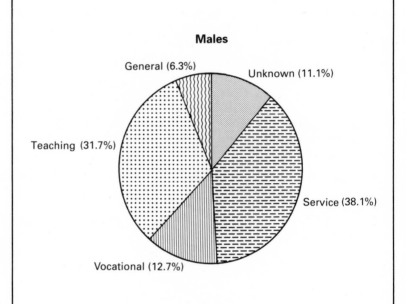

Males

General (6.3%)

Unknown (11.1%)

Teaching (31.7%)

Service (38.1%)

Vocational (12.7%)

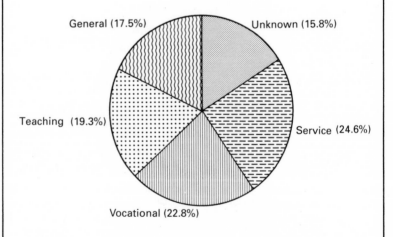

Females

General (17.5%)

Unknown (15.8%)

Teaching (19.3%)

Service (24.6%)

Vocational (22.8%)

Figure 5 The congregation of Christ Church, Jerusalem: occupation

Males

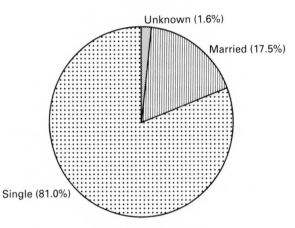

Unknown (1.6%)

Married (17.5%)

Single (81.0%)

Females

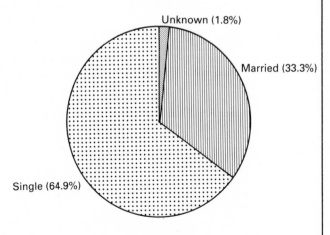

Unknown (1.8%)

Married (33.3%)

Single (64.9%)

Figure 6 The congregation of Christ Church, Jerusalem: marital status

Notes

INTRODUCTION

1. Claude Lévi-Strauss, *Tristes Tropiques,* trans. John and Doreen Weightman (Harmondsworth, repr. 1984) p. 531.
2. 'Journey's End for Lady Hester Stanhope', *Manchester Guardian,* 13 February 1989.
3. For a short survey of the relevant literature see notes 12; 17 and 19 below.
4. A short-list of classics on the woman as the 'other' should include the following: Simone de Beauvoir, *The Second Sex* trans. H. M. Parshley (New York, 1961); Claude Lévi-Strauss, *Mythologiques,* vol. III *L'Origine de maniéres de table* (Paris, 1968); Shirley Ardener (ed.), *Perceiving Women* (London, 1975); *Defining Females: the Nature of Women in Society* (London, 1978).
5. G. M. Trevelyan, *The Social History of England* (London, 1946), p. 7.
6. The complete title is: *Letters of the Right Honourable Lady Mary Wortley Montagu: Written During her Travels in Europe, Asia and Africa to Persons of Distinction, Men of Letters . . . in Different Parts of Europe, which Contain Among other Curious Relations, Accounts of the Policy and Manners of the Turks Drawn from Sources that Have Been Inaccessible to Other Travellers in Three Volumes.* For the early piratical editions see Robert Halsband, *The Life of Lady Mary Wortley Montagu* (Oxford, 1960).
7. Paul Fussell, *Abroad: British Literary Travellers between the Wars* (Oxford, 1980).
8. For the argument against a merely geographical and neutralised usage see Edward Said, *Orientalism* (London, 1978) and his 'Orientalism Reconsidered' in Francis Baker (ed.), *Essex Conference on the Sociology of Literature: Europe and its Others* (Colchester, 1985), vol. I, pp. 14–28. See also Rana Kabbani, *Europe's Myth of the Orient, Devise and Rule* (London, 1986).
9. On the etymological origins of the terms 'Near East' and 'Middle East' and the early usages consult Bernard Lewis, *The Middle East and the West* (New York, repr. 1966) pp. 9–10.
10. Said's own usage of 'imaginary geography' is influenced by the work of Gaston Bachelard, especially by the latter's *Poetics of Space,* trans. Maria Jolas (New York, 1964).
11. For some of the uses, misuses and abuses of 'orientalism' see Said's own work; Asaf Hussain, Robert Olson, Jamil Qureshi (eds), *Orientalism Islam and Islamists* (Vermont, 1984) especially Hussain's Introduction. See also Maryam Jammeelah, *Islam and Orientalism* (Lahore, Pakistan, 1981). The most powerful critique on Said's work

is to be found in James Clifford, 'Edward Said, "Orientalism"', a Review Article, *History and Theory*, vol. 19 (1980) pp. 204–24. See also Clifford's *The Predicament of Culture, Twentieth-Century Ethnography, Literature and Art* (Cambridge, Mass., 1988).

12. A phrase that is writ large on the works of post-colonial historians and in feminist historiography. Examples are Hussain and Joana de Groot '"Sex" and "Race": The Construction of Language and Image in the Nineteenth Century', in Susan Mendus and Jane Rendall (eds), *Sexuality and Subordination, Interdisciplinary Studies of Gender in the Nineteenth Century* (London, 1989).

13. For relations between the discourse on sexuality and that on race and class see de Groot and Lenore Davidoff, 'Class and Gender in Victorian England; the diaries of Arthur J. Munby and Hannah Cullick', *Feminist Studies*, vol. 5, 1979 repr. in J. Newton, Mary Ryan and Judith Walkowitz (eds), *Sex and Class in Women's History* (London, 1983). For the associations between Victorian gender ideology and attitudes to race see N. Stephan, *The Idea of Race in Science: Great Britain 1800–60* (London, 1982); Christine Bolt, *Victorian Attitudes to Race* (London 1971); V. Kiernan, *The Lords of Human Kind* (Harmondsworth, 1972), and R. Meek, *Social Science and the Ignoble Savage* (Cambridge, 1976).

14. Said, 'Orientalism Reconsidered' in Barber, *Essex Conference*, p. 23.

15. Norman Daniel, *Islam and the West: the Making of an Image* (Edinburgh, 1960); Dorothee Meltitzki, *the Matter of Araby in Medieval England* (New Haven, 1977); R. W. Southern, *Western Ideas of Islam in the Middle Ages* (Cambridge, Mass., 1980). See also Ron Barkai, *Cristianos y musulmanes en la Espana medieval (El enemigo en el espejo)* (Madrid, 1984) and C. F. Beckingham, *Between Islam and Christiandom, Travellers, Facts and Legends in the Middle Ages and the Renaissance* (London, 1983). For the Renaissance and Reformation consult S. C. Chew, *The Crescent and the Rose: Islam and England during the Renaissance* (New York, 1965). For the Enlightenment and the 'Oriental Renaissance' see Raymond Schwab's classic *The Oriental Renaissance, Europe's Rediscovery of India and the East 1680–1880*, trans. Gene Patterson-Black and Victor Reinking (New York, 1984) and Albert Hourani, *Europe and the Middle East* (London, 1980). The de-historicisation of the European notion of the 'other' particularly characterises the 'post-colonial' analysis of West-Eastern relations.

16. James Clifford, 'Edward Said'.

17. See Kabbani, pp. 7–8. See also Dea Birkett, *Spinsters Abroad, Victorian Lady Explorers* (Oxford, 1989), pp. 111–41, especially pp. 121–5.

18. Clifford, for the term 'monoglot', see 'On Ethnographic Authority,' *The Predicament of Culture*, pp. 22–3; Chandra Talpade Mohanty, 'Under Western Eyes: Feminist Scholarship and Colonial Discourses', *Boundary*, 2, 12 (Fall 1984): 333–58, for a critique on post-colonial and feminist historiography.

19. Helen Callaway, *Gender Ideology and Empire, European Women in Colonial Nigeria* (Oxford, 1987); Nona Etienne and Eleanor Leacock (eds), *Women and Colonisation: Anthropological Perspectives* (New York,

1980); Shirley Ardener, and Hilary Callan (eds), *The Incorporated Wife* (London, 1984); Catherine Barnes Stevenson, *Victorian Women Travel Writers in Africa* (Boston, 1982) and 'Female Anger and African Politics: The Case of Two Victorian "Lady Travellers"', *Turn of the Century Women*, vol. 2 (1985) pp. 7–17. See also *de Groot* and *Birkett*. Among the few historical works are: Margaret Macmillan, *Women of the Raj* (London, 1988). See also Jane Mackay and Pat Thane, 'The Englishwoman' in Roger Colls and Philip Dodd (eds), *Englishness, Politics and Culture 1880–1920* (London, 1986) pp. 191–230.

20. Richard Bevis, *Bibliotheca Cisorientalia: An Annotated Checklist of Early English Travel Books on the Near and Middle East* (Boston, 1973). See also E. G. Cox, *A Reference Guide to the Literature of Travel*, vol. I. *The Old World* (Washinton, 1935) and Malcolm Hamilton, *Travel Index: a Guide to Books and Articles* (Phoenix 1988). The most reliable among the nineteenth-century bibliographers and antiquaries are Reinhold Röhricht, *Bibliotheca Geographica Palestinae Chronologisches Verzeichniss der von 333 bis 1878. verfasten Literatur uber das Heilige Land mit dem versuch einer Kartographie* (repr. Jerusalem, 1963) and Julius Richter, *A History of the Protestant Mission in the Near East* (New York, 1910).

21. Royal Geographical Society, papers Related to the Admission of Women; *Royal Geographical Society, Proceedings and Monthly Record of Geography*, New Series, vol. I, 1888, no. 11, pp. 78–80; vol. XIV 1892, p. 553; *Geographical Journal* 1913, vol. 41 (Jan.), pp. 181–5. See also H. R. Mill, *The Record of the Royal Geographical Society* (London, 1882) pp. 107–12 and Birkett, *Spinsters Abroad*, pp. 214–27.

22. *Birkett*, pp. 229–30.

23. A. Wigham Price, *The Ladies of Castlebrae, A Story of Nineteenth-Century Travel and Research* (Gloucester, 1985) pp. 184–211.

24. There is no full-scale biography of Edwards. For her activity in the Egypt Exploration Fund and relations with the orientalist establishment see Margaret S. Dower, 'The Early Years' in T. G. H. James (ed.), *Excavating in Egypt, the Egypt Exploration Society 1882–1982* (London, 1983).

25. Claude Lévi-Strauss, *Tristes Tropiques*, p. 102. The human 'gaze' and the realisation of relativeness of European values and norms are also emphasised by Schwab.

26. On the pilgrimage movement of the Late Roman Empire and the role of women in it see David Hunt, *Holy Land Pilgrimage in the Late Roman Empire 312–460* (Oxford, 1982) and Ora Limor, 'Christian Traditions on Mount Olives in the Byzantine and Arab Eras', MA Thesis (Jerusalem, 1978) (Hebrew). On medieval pilgrimages consult Jonathan Sumption, *Pilgrimage, an Image of Medieval Religion* (London, 1975). On Huceburg see Marjorie Bonsnes, 'The Pilgrimage to Jerusalem: a Typological Metaphor for Women in Early Medieval Religious Orders' Ph.D. Thesis (New York, 1982). see: G. W. Atkinson, *Mystic and Pilgrim: The Book and World of Margery Kempe* (Ithaca, 1983); S. Dickman 'Margery Kempe and the English Devotional Tradition in England' (Exeter 1980) and Dickman's 'Margery Kempe and the Continental Tradition of the Pious Woman' in Glasscoe (ed.), *The*

Medieval Mystical Tradition in England (Cambridge, 1984).

27. John Pemble, *The Mediterranean Passion, Victorians and Edwardians in the South* (Oxford, 1987).

28. The move away from grand-tourism to commercialised tourism is discussed by Pemble and Naomi Shepherd. *The Zealous Intruders: the Western Rediscovery of Palestine* (London, 1978) pp. 170–93. See also Edmund Singlehurst, *Cook's Tours, the Story of Popular Travel* (London, 1982).

29. See Stratford Shaw and Ezel Kural, *History of the Ottoman Empire and Modern Turkey* (Cambridge, 1976–7), 2 vols; A. L. Tibawi, *British Interest in Palestine, A Study of Religious and Educational Enterprise* (Oxford, 1961) and, most important, Bernard Lewis, *The Muslim Discovery of Europe* (New York, 1982).

30. See above, *Tibawi*.

31. Giovanni Belzoni, *Narrative of the Operations and Recent Discoveries within the Pyramids, Temples, Tombs and Excavations in Egypt* (London, 1820).

32. Hester Lucy Stanhope, *Travels of Lady Hester Stanhope; Forming the Completion of her Memoirs* (ed.), Charles Meyron (London, 1846), vol. 1, p. 193.

33. Julia Sophia Pardoe, *The City of the Sultan and the Domestic Manners of the Turks in 1836*, 2 vols (London, 1837) pp. 373–8.

34. Mary Georgina Anna Dawson-Damer, *Diary of a Tour in Greece, Turkey, Egypt and the Holy Land*, 2 vols (London, 1841) p. 130.

35. See Shaw and Kural, *History of the Ottoman Empire*; Shepherd, *Zealous Intruders*, pp. 107–41.

36. Christian Zacher, *Curiosity and Pilgrimage, the Literature of Discovery in 14th Century England* (1976). See also Sumption, *Pilgrimage*.

37. See Marjorie P. Bonsnes, 'The Pilgrimage to Jerusalem: A Typological Metaphor for Women in Early Medieval Religious Orders'.

38. On the tension between pilgrimage and the secular notion of 'curiositas' see Zacher and Donald R. Howard, *Writers and Pilgrims, Medieval Pilgrimage Narratives and their Posterity* (Los Angeles, 1980).

39. On the pilgrimage as image and metaphor see for example George Roppen, *Strangers and Pilgrims: An Essay on the Metaphor of Journey* (New York, 1964); Frances Power Cobb *Cities of the past* (London, 1863) pp. 135–6; Harriet Martineau, *Eastern Life Present and Past* (London, 1848), pp. 431–2.

40. Percy G. Adams, *Travel Literature and the Evolution of the Novel* (Kentucky, 1983) particularly Two: 'Travel Literature before 1800 – Its History, Its Types, Its Influences', pp. 38–81 and Five: 'Structure: The Hero and His Journey', pp. 148–61. See also Northrop Frye, *The Secular Scripture* p. 53. See also Manfred Kusch, 'The River and the Garden: Basic Spatial Models in Candide and the Nouvelle Heloise', *ECS* vol. 12 (1978) pp. 1–15; Dan Vogel 'A Lexicon Rhetorical for Journey Literature', *College English*, 36 (1974), pp. 185–89; Billie Melman, 'The Widening Spheres, the Journey as Fact and Metaphor in Women's Writing on the Middle East', *Zmanim* vol. 16 (1986) (Hebrew).

41.   Raymond Williams, *The Long Revolution* (Harmondsworth, repr. 1980) pp. 83–5.
42.   Arnaldo Momigliano, 'Ancient History and the Antiquarian', *Studies in Histiography* (London, 1966), 1–39, pp. 3; 25.

CHAPTER 1:   A PROSOPOGRAPHY OF TRAVEL, 1763–1914

1.   Anthony Trollope, *An Unprotected Female at the Pyramides and Other Stories* (Harmondsworth, repr. 1984), p. 1.
2.   For the independent traveller see Dorothee Middleton, *Victorian Lady Travellers* (London, 1965) and Katherine Barnes Stevenson's *Victorian Women Travel-Writers* and 'Female Anger and African Politics'. For a thoughtful description of the relationship between individual explorers and the scientific and political establishment in Britain and the Empire see Dea Birkett, *Spinsters Abroad*. For a more popular account see Joana Trollope's *Britannia's Daughters, Women of the British Empire* (London, 1982).
3.   See Birkett, *Spinsters Abroad*, pp. 110–41 for a discussion of the women's emulation of a male tradition of travel and male modes of behaviour. Students of Orientalism, notably Said and Kabbani emphasise the subsumption of even the most original travellers in a patriarchal, imperialist heritage. Said, *Orientalism*; Kabbani, *Europe's Myths of Orient*, pp. 7–8.
4.   John Pemble, *The Mediterranean Passion*.
5.   A select list of monographs should include H. V. F. Winstone's *Gertrude Bell* (New York, 1978); Pat Barr, *A Curious Life for a Lady: The Story of Isabella Bird* (London, 1970); E. Moberlly Bell, *Flora Shaw (Lady Lugard DBE)* (London, 1947); Whigham A. Price, *The Ladies of Castlebrae* and Margaret Schmidt Fox's *Passion's Child; The Extraordinary Life of Jane Digby* (1978), Said, *Orientalism*; Kabbani, *Europe's Myths*; Percy G. Adams, *Travel Literature and the Evolution of the Novel* and, for inter-war literary travel, Paul Fussell, *Abroad*.
6.   The following are journalistic representations: Leslie Blanche, *The Wilder Shores of Love* (London, 1954) Mary Russell, *The Blessings of a Good Thick Skirt* (London, 1986); Julia Keay, *With Passport and Parasol, the Adventures of Seven Victorian Ladies*, based on a series of talks on Radio 4 and Anthony Sattin, *Lifting the Veil, British Society in Egypt 1768–1956* (London, 1988).
7.   Raymond Williams, *The Long Revolution*, See particularly the classical chapter on 'The Social History of English Writers', pp. 254–71; Richard Altick, 'The Sociology of Authorship: The Social Origins, Education and Occupations of 1100 British Writers, 1800–1935', *Bulletin of the New York Public Library*, no. 66 (1962) pp. 389–404 and *The Common Reader* (Chicago, 1957); For the relations between gender and the sociology of the novel consult Gaye Tuchman and Nina Fortin, *Edging Women Out* (New Haven, 1989).
8.   James Olney (ed.), *Autobiography: Essays Theoretical and Critical* (Princeton, 1980) and particularly Georges Gusdof, 'Conditions

and Limits of Autobiography' in *Olney*, pp. 28–48. A recent example of the feminist critique on Olney's 'individualist' model is Shari Benstock (ed.), *The Private Self, Theory and Practice of Women's Autobiographical Writings* (London, 1988) particularly Susan Stanford Friedman's essay on 'Women's Autobiographical Selves: Theory and Practice', pp. 34–63.

9. For the journey as *Bildung* see Elisabeth Abel, Marianne Hirsh and Elisabeth Langland (eds), *The Voyage in: Fictions of Female Development* (New Hampshire, 1983).

10. Elisabeth Craven, *Memoirs of the Margravine of Anspach* (London, 1826); Harriet Martineau, *Autobiography*, 2 vols (London, reprinted 1983); Julia Pardoe's 'Autobiography' is in manuscript among the Bentley Papers, BL, add. mss 28.511; Elisabeth Ann Finn, *Reminiscences* (London, 1926); Isabel Burton's autobiography is subsumed in her *Life of Captain Sir Richard F. Burton*, 2 vols (London, 1893); Fanny Janet Blunt, *My Reminiscences* (London, 1918); Marianne North, *Recollections of a Happy Life Being the Autobiography of Marianne North Edited by her Sister Mrs. J. Addington* (London, 1892).

11. Exemplary collections of biographies are Frank Maundrell, *Heroines of Travel* (London, 1897); *Heroines of the Cross* (London, 1897) and *Heroines of the Faith* (1989). See also Jennie Chappell's *Women of Worth* (London, 1908). There are quite a few popular monographs of Middle Eastern missionaries. To mention a few: Susette Harriet Lloyd, *The Daughters of Syria. A Narrative of the Efforts of the Late Mrs. Brown Thompson for the Evangelisation of the Syrian Females* (London, 1872), Julia Whately, *Life and Work of Mary Louisa Whately* (London, 1878).

12. On power and authority see Michel Foucault, *The History of Sexuality*, vol. I: *An Introduction*, trans. Robert Huxley (Harmondsworth, 1981); Jeoffry Weeks, 'Foucault for Historians, *History Workshop*, no. 14 (1982) pp. 107–19.

13. For the history of the *RGS* see Ian Cameron, *To the Farthest End of the Earth, the History of the Royal Geographical Society* (R.G.S. 1980) and the older but more useful works by Clement Markham, *The Fifty Years' Work by the R.G.S.* (R.G.S.) and H. R. Mill, *The Record of the R.G.S.* (R.G.S. 1930). The printed material consulted is the Society's official publication, *Proceedings of the Royal Geographical Society and Monthly Record of Geography*, and from 1888 onwards, *The Geographical Journal, Including the Proceedings of the Royal Geographical Society*.

14. There is a wealth of material in the Society's archives on the controversy relating to the admission of women as fellows, on the same grounds as men. Conveniently for the researcher the material is in a file entitled 'Admission of Ladies'.

15. Nineteenth and early twentieth-century histories of the PEF are useful. See for instance, *30 years' work in the Holy Land, a Record and Summary, 1865–95* (New Revised Edition 1896) and C. M. Watson, *50 Years' Work in the Holy Land: A Record and Summary 1865–1915*. Subscription lists can be found in the Society's *Annual Reports*, which also contain the minutes of the General Meetings. In later years the

reports are combined with the *Palestine Exploration Quarterly*. A recent history of the EEF is T. G. James's *Excavating in Egypt, the Egypt Exploration Society 1882–1982* (London, 1983). Subscription and membership lists are to be found in the *Reports of General Meetings* which include annual subscription lists and the society's Balance Sheet.

16. Thomas William Davies, 'A History of Biblical Archaeology', Ph.D. Thesis, (Arizona, 1987).

17. *Jerusalem Literary Society, Minutes*, PEF (JER) 6.

18. Richard Bevis, *Bibliotheca Cisorientalia*.

19. Only two books appeared between 1763 and the second decade of the nineteenth century, Montagu's posthumous *Letters* and Elisabeth Craven's, *Journal of a Tour Through the Crimea and Constantinople in a series of letters written in the year 1789 to a Noble Lord*. One book appeared before the eighteenth century, Katherine Evans and Sarah Cheevers', *This is a Short Reflection on Some of the Cruel Sufferings for the Truth's Sake by K. E. and S. Ch. in the Inquisition in the Isle of Malta*. Bevis mentions the 1717 edition. The earliest edition at the BL is from 1662. Bevis omits the popular religious autobiography of Margery Kempe of Lynn.

20. Tuchman and Fortin, *Edging Women Out*, pp. 5–9; 'Edging Women Out: The Structure of Opportunity and the Victorian Novel', *Signs*, Winter, 1980, pp. 308–25; 'Fame and Misfortune, Edging Women out of the Great Literary Tradition', *American Journal of Sociology*, July 1984, pp. 308–25.

21. Reinhold Röhricht, *Bibliotheca Geographica Palestinae*.

22. The general – as opposed to the women's – interest in the Middle East has received ample attention in recent years. On the orientalist travellers see Said's *Orientalism* and, in similar vein, *Kabbani*. See also Rashad Rashdy, *The Lure of Egypt for English Writers and Travellers During the 19th Century* (Cairo, 1955); Wallace C. Brown, 'English Travel Books and Minor Poetry about the Near East 1775–1825', *Philological Quarterly*, vol. XVI, 1937, pp. 249–71; Mohamad Ali Hachicho, 'English Travel Books about the Arab Near East in the 18th Century', *die Welt Des Islam*, vol. XI, ms 1–4 (Leiden, 1964) pp. 1.27; Reinhold Schieffer, 'Turkey Romanticised, Images of the Turks in Early 19th Century English Travel Literature', *Materialia Turcia*, 1982; For the Arabian Peninsula see Kathryn Tidrick, *Heart Beguiling Araby* (Cambridge, 1981). For Palestine see Yehoshua Ben Arieh, *The Rediscovery of the Holy Land in the 19th Century* (Jerusalem, 1979) and Naomi Shepherd, *Zealous Intruders*.

23. Ivy Pinchbeck, *Women Workers and the Industrial Revolution 1750–1850* (1930, reprinted London, 1930); For the problem of the definition and conceptualisation of women's work after industrialisation, Sally Alexander Anna Davin and Eve Hostetler's reply to Marxist labour historians 'Labouring Women: A Reply to Eric Hobsbawm', *History Workshop*, no. 8, 1979, and Sally Alexander, 'Women's Work in Nineteenth Century London', in Juliet Mitchell and Ann Oakley (eds), *The Rights and Wrongs of Women* (Harmondsworth, 1976).

24. F. K. Prochaska, *Women and Philanthropy in 19th century England* (Oxford, 1980) and 'Women in English Philanthropy 1790–1830', *International Review of Social History*, vol. XIX, 1974, pp. 426–45; Anne Summers, 'Home from Home – Women's Philanthropic Work in the 19th Century', in Sandra Barnum (ed.), *Fit Work for Women* (London, 1979) pp. 33–64.

25. Eugene Stock, *History of the Church Missionary Society* (C.M.S. 1899) vol. 3, p. 369.

26. For the distinction between 'travel' and 'tourism', see Paul Fussell, *Abroad*.

27. Elisabeth Longford, *A Pilgrimage of Passion, The Life of Wilfrid Scawen Blunt* (London, 1982) p. 71.

28. The term 'intellectual aristocracy' is Noel Annan's. See 'Intellectual Aristocracy', in J. H. Plumb (ed.), *Studies in Social History: A Tribute to G. M. Trevelyan* (London, 1955).

29. The professions and 'Professionalisation' are discussed in Magali Sarfati Larson's seminal *The Rise of Professionalism* (Berkeley, 1977). See also W. J. Reader, *Professional Men. The rise of the Professional Classes in 19th Century England* (London, 1966).

30. Eliza Fay, *Original Letters from India (1779–1815)* introduced by E. M. Forster (London, 1925) p. 28.

31. Ibid., pp. 28–9.

32. For women and the amateur sciences see D. E. Allen, *The Naturalist in Britain: A Social History* (London, 1978) and Birkett, *Spinsters Abroad*.

33. Davies, *A History of Biblical Archaeology*; Warren R. Dawson, *Who Was Who in Egyptology* (London, 1951).

34. Harriet Martineau, *Eastern Life Present and Past*. For her elaborate account see her *Autobiography* (reprinted London 1983), vol. 2, pp. 230–97; Amelia Edwards's *A Thousand Miles up the Nile* (London, repr. 1982), preface.

35. *PEF Quarterly Statement*, 1865, 1868, 1877, 1888, 1895, 1901.

36. Ibid., 1877, p. IX.

37. *EEF, Reports of the Annual General Meetings and Balance Sheets*, July 1884; August 1885–July 1886; August 1886–July 1887; August 1888–July 1889; August 1905–July 1906 and August 1910–July 1911.

38. For contemporary typology of gender and the notion of 'separate spheres' see Walter Houghton's classical *Victorian Frame of Mind 1830–70* (New Haven, 1975) pp. 341–72; Peter L. Cominos, 'Late Victorian Social Respectabilty and the Social System', *International Review of Social History*, vol. VIII, no. 8 (1963) pp. 8–48 and Leonore Davidoff and Catherine Hall, *Family Fortunes, Men and Women of the English Middle-Class 1780–1850* (London, 1988). For the association between gender and types of literature consult Elaine Showalter, *A Literature of their own: British Women Novelists from Brontë to Lessing* (London, 1978), Gaye Tuchman and Nina Fortin, *Edging Women Out* and Patricia Spacks, *The Female Imagination*.

39. Frances Power Cobbe, *Cities of the Past* p. 144.

40. Davidoff and Hall, *Family Fortunes*, pp. 114–18.
41. Ibid., ibid. and F. K. Prochaska, *Women and Philanthropy*, pp. 1–17.
42. See Emily Ann Beaufort, *Egyptian Sepulchres and Syrian Shrines, Including Some Stay in the Lebanon at Palmyra and in Western Turkey* (London, 1861), vol. 1, pp. 243–4; Elisabeth Ann Finn, *Reminiscences*; Susette Lloyd, *The Daughters of Syria* (for Bowen-Thompson and Mentor-Mott); Mathilda Cubley, *The Plains and Hills of Palestine* (London, 1860) preface; Julia Whately, *Life and Work of Mary Louisa Whately*; Lucie Duff-Gordon, *Letters from Egypt* (London, 1870) p. 101.
43. Julius Richter, *A History of the Protestant Missions in the Middle East* particularly pp. 222–3, 416, 418–19.
44. Ibid., ibid.
45. *Cobbe, Cities of the Past*, 111–12, 135–6.
46. Quoted by Prochaska, 'Women and Philanthropy', p. 28.
47. Elisabeth of Anspach, *DNB*, vol. 1, pp. 508–9.
48. Julia Pardoe's 'Autobiography', Bentley Papers, BL, add. mss. 28.511, p. 265.
49. BL, add. mss 466 14, f. 308; 46615, f. 172, f.174.
50. For Martineau's life and travel see R. K. Webb, *Harriet Martineau, A Radical Victorian* (London, 1960) and Valerie Kossew Pichanick, *Harriet Martineau, The Woman and Her Work* (Ann Arbor, 1980). For *Eastern Life* and her journey to the Middle East see *Autobiography*, vol. II (London, repr. 1983) pp. 270–96.
51. There is no full scale biography of Edwards. For biographical details see Margaret S. Drower, 'The Early Years' in T. G. H. James (ed.), *Excavating in Egypt* and W. C. Winslow's hagiographic, 'Amelia Edwards, The Queen of Egyptology', *The American Antiquarian*, November 1892.
52. E. J. Whately, *The Life and Work of Mary Louisa Whatley*.
53. I am particularly indebted to my student Marie-Noël Karpik, who drew my attention to Walker-Arnott's Work.
54. Richter, *A History of the Protestant Missions*, pp. 416–19.

CHAPTER 2:   HAREM LITERATURE, 1763–1914:
TRADITION AND INNOVATION

1. Claude Lévi-Strauss, *Tristes Tropiques*, p. 102.
2. Richard Francis Burton, *Personal Narrative of a Pilgrimage to Al Madimah and Meccah*, 2 vols (1856, Memorial Edition London, 1893), vol. II p. 85.
3. I follow modern Turkish spelling. The combinations 'harem system', 'harem structure', are used to denote the structures of polygamy and the seclusion of females. *Haremlik* is applied to the space in the house allocated to women. Since the model of the Imperial Harem was emulated throughout the Ottoman Empire, the Turkish terms are applied, on a few occassions, to non-Ottoman households. Exceptions are the quotations where the writers' own spelling is preserved.

4. For the relation between voyeurism and Orientalism see Susan Robin Pucci, 'The Discrete Charms of the Exotic: Fictions of the Harem in Eighteenth-Century France' in G. S. Rousseau and Roy Porter (eds), *Exoticism in the Eighteenth Century* (Manchester, 1990) pp. 145–75.

5. For the age of geographic discoveries and the emergence of scientific travel see Percy G. Adams, *Travellers and Travel Liars* and *Travel Literature and the Evolution of the Novel*, especially Chapter 2. See also Barbara Maria Stafford, *Voyage into Substance: Art, Science, Nature and the Illustrated Travel Account 1760–1890* (Cambridge, Mass., 1984).

6. *Porter and Rousseau*; Daniel, *Islam and the West* and *Islam, Europe and Empire* (Edinburgh, 1966); U. G. Kiernan, *The Lords of Human Kind: European Attitudes towards the Outside World in the Imperial Age* (London, 1969). On the *topos* of the harem during the Enlightenment see Alan Grosrichard *Structure de serail* (Paris, 1979) and M. L. Shanley and P. G. Shillman, 'Political and Marital Despotism'; Montesquieu's *Persian Letters* in J. B. Elshtain (ed.), *The Family in Political Thought* (Amherst, 1982) pp. 66–80.

7. Barbara Maria Stowasser, 'The Status of Women in Early Islam', in Freda Hussain (ed.), *Muslim Women* (London, 1984) pp. 11–14.

8. Alan Macfarlane, *Marriage and Love in England, 1300–1840* (Oxford, repr. 1987) pp. 217–23.

9. Ibid.

10. *Stowasser*, op. cit.; Norman N. Penzer, *The Harem* (Philadelphia, 1937).

11. Roy Porter, 'The Exotic as Erotic: Captain Cook at Tahiti', in Rousseau and Porter, *Exoticism in the Enlightenment*, pp. 117–45.

12. Albert Hourani, 'Western Attitudes Towards Islam' in *Europe and the Middle East*, pp. 1–19, especially pp. 7–10. See also 'Muslims and Christians' in ibid., pp. 74, 81. Assaf Houssain, 'The Ideology of Orientalism' in Houssain, Olson and Qureshi, *Orientalism, Islam and Islamists*, pp. 5–23.

13. Pucci's term, see Pucci, 'The Discrete Charms of the Exotic', *Rousseau and Porter*, p. 150.

14. Joana de Groot, 'Sex and Race', in Mendus and Rendall, *Sexuality and Subordination*, p. 104.

15. James Clifford, 'On Ethnographic Authority', *The Predicament of Culture*, pp. 20–5. See particularly note 1, p. 22.

16. On the Arabic editions see Mia J. Gerhardt, *The Art of Story-Telling, A Literary Study of the Thousand and One Nights* (Leiden, 1963). For the history of Galland's version and its reception see A. Abdullah, 'The Arabian Nights in English Literature to 1900', Ph.D. Dissertation (Cambridge, 1961); Thomas J. Assad, *Three Victorian Travellers: Burton, Blunt, Doughty* (London, 1964); M. Ali Jassim, *Scheherazade in England* (Washington, 1981); Marie de Meester, *Oriental Influences in the English Literature of the Nineteenth Century* (1915). For Edward William Lane's transcription see *Assad*, Kabbani, *Europe's Myth*, pp. 37–67 and Leilah Ahmed, *Edward W. Lane: A Study of his Life and Works and of British Ideas of the Middle East in the Nineteenth Century* (London, 1978).

17. Stanley Lane Poole, 'Preface', Edward W. Lane *The Arabian Nights Entertainment* (London, 1838), vol. I, pp. xviii–xix.
18. William Makepeace Thackeray, *Vanity Fair*, (New York, repr. 1981), p. 36.
19. I draw mainly on Kabbani and Gerhardt's discussion of the female models. See Gerhardt's *The Art of Story-Telling*, pp. 110–11, 121–5; and *Kabbani*, pp. 48–51.
20. *Kabbani*, pp. 50–51; Lisa Jardine, *Still Harping on Daughters* (London, 1983) p. 169; *Pucci*, pp. 169–70.
21. Richard Francis Burton, *The Book of Thousand and One Nights* (London, 1885–8), 17 vols, vol. I, pp. 71–2.
22. Lane, *The Thousand and One Nights*, vol. I., p. 4.
23. Frances Mannsaker, 'Elegancy in the Wilderness: Reflectins of the East in the Eighteenth-Century Imagination', *Rousseau and Porter*, p. 180.
24. Lane, *Nights*, vol. III, p. 686.
25. This and all following quotations of Lady Mary Wortley Montagu are from Robert Halsband's edition of her complete letters. LM to Lady Mar, 10 March 1718. Robert Halsband (ed.), *Lady Montagu: The Complete Letters* (Oxford, 1965–7), vol. 1, p. 385.
26. Julia Pardoe, *The City of the Sultan*, vol. 1, p. 89.
27. de Meester, *Oriental Influences*; Martha Pike Connant, *The Oriental Tale in England in the Eighteenth Century* (New York, 1908).
28. For the philosophical tale and the *philosoph* as ethnographer see Pierre Martin, *L'orient dans la literature française* (Génève, 1970), ch. 3.
29. For the expansion of the market see *Martin* and *Manansker*.
30. William Beckford, *Vathek* (1783, repr. Harmondsworth, 1983) p. 1.
31. Ibid., pp. 2–3.
32. On the use of travel literature in the oriental tale see Wallace C. Brown, 'English Travel Books and Minor Poetry about the Near East'; Rashad Rashdy, *The Lure of Egypt for English Writers and Travellers* and Mohamad Ali Hachicho, 'English Travel Books about the Arab Near East'.
33. *Pucci*, op. cit.; *Martin*.
34. Quoted in Alan Macfarlane, *Marriage and Love*, pp. 217–23.
35. John Cairncross, *After Polygamy was Made a Sin, the Social History of Christian Polygamy* (London, 1974) pp. 7–9.
36. Ibid.
37. Quoted in Daniel, *Islam Europe and Empire*, p. 20.
38. Ibid., pp. 20–1.
39. Percy, G. Adams, *Travellers and Travel-Liars*.
40. For the problematics of the evidence on the Imperial Harem see N. M. Penzer, *The Harem* and A. M. Moulin and P. Chuvin, 'Des Occidentaux a la cour du Sultan', *L'Histoire* 45 (1982) pp. 62–71.
41. On the tour of Domenico Hierosolimitano see *Penzer*.
42. Thomas Dallaway, *Diary (1599–1600) of a Voyage to Constantinople* quoted in *Kabbani*, p. 19.
43. Sir George Courthope, *Memoirs (1616–1685)*, ed. S. C. Lomas (London, 1907) p. 123.

44. Quoted in R. Schiffer, 'Turkey Romanticised', p. 97.
45. Dallaway, ibid.
46. From *Travel Through France, Italy, and Hungary*, quoted in Schiffer, 'Turkey Romanticised', p. 104.
47. Lane, *An Account of the Manners and Customs of the Modern Egyptians Written in Egypt during the Years 1833–35* (London, 1890) p. 152.
48. James Silk Buckingham, *Travels in Mesopotamia, Including a Journey from Aleppo, across the Euphrates to Urfah through the plains of the Turcomans, to Diarbakr in Asia Minor, from thence to Mardin, on the Borders of the Great Desert, and by the Tigris to Mosul and Bagdad with Researches on the Ruins of Babylon* (London, 1827) pp. 550–1.
49. Richard Francis Burton, *Narrative of a Pilgrimage*, vol. I.
50. Claude Lévi-Strauss, *Tristes Tropiques*, p. 102. See also Clifford, 'On Ethnographic Authority'.
51. Lady Mary Wortley Montagu to Lady Mar, Adrianople 1 April 1717, *The Complete Letters*, vol. 1, p. 327.
52. Pardoe, *The City of the Sultan*, vol. 1, Preface, pp. viii–x.
53. Sophia Lane-Poole, *The Englishwoman in Egypt: Letters from Cairo during Residence there in 1842, 3 and 4 with E. W. Lane, by his Sister* (London, 1884), Preface.
54. Annie Harvey, *Turkish Harems and Circassian Homes* (London, 1871) pp. 8–9.
55. Anna Bowman Dodd, *The Palaces of the Sultan* (New York, 1903) pp. 96–7.
56. John Murray, *A Handbook for Travellers in the Ionian Islands, Greece, Turkey, Asia Minor and Constantinople, Being a Guide to the Principle Routes in those Countries, Including a Description of Malta with Maxims and Hints for Travellers in the East* (1847).
57. John Murray, *A Handbook for Travellers in Turkey, Describing Constantinople, the Dardanelles, Bursa and the Plains of Troy with General Hints for Travellers* (1871).
58. Douglas W. Freshfild and W. J. L. Warthon, *Hints for Travellers, Scientific and General, Edited for the Council of the Royal Geographic Society* (3rd edn, 1893) pp. 432–3.

CHAPTER 3:   THE EIGHTEENTH-CENTURY HAREM (1717–89), LADY MONTAGU, LADY CRAVEN AND THE GENEALOGY OF COMPARATIVE 'MORALS'

1. Montesquieu, *Persian Letters*, trans. C. J. Betts (reprinted Harmondsworth, 1987) p. 92.
2. Quoted in Norman Daniel, *Islam Europe and Empire*, Introduction.
3. Robert Halsband (ed.), *The Complete Letters of Lady Mary Wortley Montagu, vol. I, 1708–1720* p. 327. Quotations, unless otherwise stated are from Halsband's edition.
4. The full title is: *Letters of the Right Honourable Lady M-y W-y M-e; Written during her Travels to Europe, Asia and Africa, to persons of Distinction, men of Letters &c. in Different parts of Europe, which Contain,*

Among Other Curious Relations, Accounts of the Policy and Manners of the Turks; Drawn from the Sources that Have Been Inaccessible to Other Travellers. For the different editions see Robert Halsband, *Letters,* vol. I, Introduction, pp. xvii–xx.

5.   For the reconstruction of the production of the 'Embassy Letters' I particularly rely on Robert Halsband. See his *Life of Lady Mary Wortley Montagu* (Oxford, 1960). See also 'A New Lady Mary Letter', *Philological Quarterly,* vol. 44, January 1966, pp. 180–4. Consult also Patricia Meyer Spacks, 'Borderline: Letters and Gossip', *The Georgia Review,* vol.37, no. II (1983) pp. 791–813 and Michele Plaisaint, 'Les Lettres turques de Lady Mary Wortley Montagu', *Bulletin de la Société d'Etudes Anglo-Americaines de xviie et xviiie siecles,* vol. 16 (June 1983) pp. 53–75.

6.   For Edward Wortley Montagu's embassy see Halsband, *Life,* pp. 55–9.

7.   For example 'Lady Mary to Lady —', 16 March 1718; 17 June 1717, Halsband, *Letters,* vol. I, pp. 387–91, 367–70.

8.   Lady Mary to Lady Mar, 18 April 1717, *Letters,* ibid. pp. 347–52; 10 March 1718; ibid. pp. 379–87.

9.   Lady, Mary to Alexander Pope, 1 April 1717, ibid. p. 330. Lady Mary to Abbé Conti, 1 April 1717; 17 May 1717; 29 May 1717, ibid. pp. 315; 353; 360.

10.   For Mary Astell see Joan K. Kinniard's impressionistic 'Mary Astell, Inspired by Ideas', in Dale Spender (ed.), *Feminist Theories, Three Centuries of Key Feminist Thinkers* (New York, 1983) pp. 28–40. See also Ruth Perry, 'The Veil of Chastity; Mary Astell's Feminism', in Paul Gabriel Boucé (ed.), *Sexuality in Eighteen Century Britain* (Manchester, 1982) pp. 120–41. For Astell's influence on Montagu see *Perry,* ibid.

11.   Quoted in Halsband, *Letters,* vol. I, p. 467.

12.   Ibid. p. 400, plate-1.

13.   Walter Benjamin, 'The Work of Art in the Age of Mechanical Reproduction', *Illuminations,* trans. Harry Zohn (London, 1970).

14.   My usage of the terms 'reception' and 'predisposition' is informed by Hans Robert Jaus's work on 'reception', particularly his 'Toward an Aesthetic of Reception', *Theory and History of Literature,* vol. 2, 1983, trans. Timothy Bathi, pp. 3–110.

15.   Paul Rycaut, *The History of the Turks from the Year 1678 to the year 1699* (1700); Richard Knolles, *The Turkish History from the Original of the Nation to the Growth of the Ottoman Empire with the Lives and Conquests of their Princes and Emperors (1687);* George Sandys, *A Relation of a Journey Begun An. Dom. 1610* (London, 1615); Aaron Hill, *A full and Just Account of the Present State of the Ottoman Empire in all its Branches of Government, Policy, Religion, Customs and Way of Living of the Turks in General (1709).*

16.   *Letters,* vol. I, p. 335.

17.   Lady Mary, To the 'Countess of ——', May 1718, *Letters,* vol. I, p. 405.

18.   Lady Mary to 'Lady ——', 17 January 1717 *Letters,* vol. I, p. 36.

19. Lady Mary to Lady Mar, 1 April 1717, *Letters*, vol. I, p. 328.
20. Lady Mary to Abbé Conti, 31 July 1718. This is the best exemplar of the neo-classical style and abounds with analogies to the classics. The Koran is referred to in the famous letter dated February 1718. Ibid., pp. 415–27, 454–5.
21. The harem of Armant Khalil Pasha is described in a letter to Lady Mar dated 18 April 1717; the 'Kahya's harem' is described in the same letter; the household of Sultan Hafise is presented in another letter to Lady Mar dated 10 March 1718. Ibid., pp. 347–52, 379–81.
22. Lady Mary to Lady Mar, 1 April 1717, ibid., pp. 325–7.
23. Lady Mary to Lady Bristol, 10 April 1718, ibid., p. 397.
24. Lady Mary to the 'Countess of ——', May 1718, ibid., p. 405.
25. Mia Gerhardt, *The Art of Story Telling, A Literary Study of the Thousand and One Nights* (London, 1963).
26. Lady Mary to Lady Mar, 1 April 1717, *op. cit.*, p. 328.
27. Halsband, *Life*, p. 67.
28. Withers treats the veil in *A Description of the Grand Signor's Seraglio or Turkish Emperour's Court* (1651) and Du Loir in his *Voyages du Siueur du Lole; ensemble de ce qui se passe a la mort du feu Sultan Mourat* (1659). Another example is to be found in Joseph de Journefort's *Relation d'un Voyage du Levant* (1717).
29. Elisabeth Craven, *A Journey through the Crimea to Constantinople in a Series of Letters from the Right Honourable Elisabeth Lady Craven to his Serene Highness the Margravene of Brandenburg, Anspach and Bareith Written in the year MDCCLXXXVI*, p. 205.
30. Ibid., ibid.
31. Lady Mary to Lady Mar, 1 April 1717, *Letters*, vol. I, p. 329.
32. Craven, *A Journey through the Crimea*, p. 232.
33. For Craven see her own 'Introduction' to the *Journey*, for Montagu, see Halsband, *Life*, pp. 13–17.
34. *Craven*, Introduction.
35. Roy Porter, 'Mixed Feelings: the Enlightenment and Sexuality in Eighteenth-Century Britain', in Boucé (ed.), *Sexuality in Britain*, p. 9.
36. Lady Mary to Lady ——, 1 April 1717 pp. 314–15.
37. Lady Mary to Alexander Pope, 12 February 1717, *Letters*, vol. I, p. 308.
38. Ibid., ibid.
39. Ibid., p. 455.
40. Lady Mary to Abbé Conti, 29 May 1717, Ibid., p. 364.
41. Lady May to Abbé Conti, ibid., ibid.
42. For the Enlightenment in Britain see M. de Gates, 'The Cult of womanhood in 18th Century Thought', *Eighteenth Century Studies*, vol. X (1976) pp. 21–40; K.B. Klinton, 'Femme et philosophe: Enlightenment Origins of Feminism', Ibid., vol. VII (1975) pp. 283–300 and P. M. Spacks, 'Ev'ry woman is at Heart a Rake', ibid., vol. VIII (1974–5) pp. 27–46. For a more general analysis of the notion of freedom and its relation to sex see Susan Moller Okin, *Women in Western Political Thought* (Amherst, 1982) and *Porter and Boucé*

43. *Okin,* ibid.
44. Lady Mary to Anne Thistlethwayte, 4 January 1718, *Letters,* vol. I, p. 372.
45. John Cairncross, *After Polygamy Was Made a Sin, the Social History of Christian Polygamy* (London, 1974).
46. Lady Mary to Lady Mar, 1 April 1717, *Letters,* vol. I, p. 329.
47. Ibid., pp. 329–30.

CHAPTER 4: EXORCISING SHEHEREZAD: THE VICTORIANS AND THE HAREM

1. William Makepeace Thackeray, *Vanity Fair* (Penguin edn) p. 216.
2. Julia Pardoe, *The City of the Sultan.* vol. I, p. 89.
3. For example, Byron who borrowed from her the rose-and-nightingale motif, used in his oriental poems and Ingres the painter. The motif is introduced in a letter to Pope, dated 1 April 1717. See Halsband, *The Letters,* vol. I, pp. 334–7.
4. *Pardoe,* vol. I, p. 136–7; Georgina Anna Dawson-Damer, *Diary of a Tour in Greece, Turkey, Egypt and the Holy Land* (London, 1891), vol. I, p. 154. Dawson-Damer's husband was Montagu's great grandson; Anna Bowman Dodd, *The Palaces of the Sultan* (New York, 1903), 'Two Old Travellers', pp. 413–21. For the men travellers see above.
5. Pardoe, *The City of the Sultan,* vol. I, pp. 136–7.
6. Emmeline Lott, *The English Governess in Egypt, Harem Life in Egypt and Constantinople,* 2 vols (London, 1866) vol. I, 'preface', p. v.
7. My approach to and definition of, 'representation' and 'rhetoric' is informed by W. C. Booth's work on the rhetoric of fiction. I am aware, of course, that descriptions, particularly physical representation, may be 'rhetoric'. But I limit my usage of the term and apply it to the general informative sections of the narrative. See W. C. Booth, *The Rhetoric of Fiction* (Chicago, repr. 1983). See also Rhetoric and Poetics, *The Princeton Encyclopedia of Poetry and Poetics* (Princeton, 1974), pp. 702–5.
8. See Clifford 'On Ethnographic Authority', pp. 31–2.
9. On etiquette in the harem, consult Fanny Davis, *The Ottoman Lady;* Barnette Miller, *Beyond the Sublime Porte,* pp. 162–70. She is very useful on costumes, See also Alev Lytle Croutier, *The World Behind the Veil* (London, 1990), pp. 41–71 and 145–71. For etiquette in the Imperial Harem, consult Croutier and *Penzer.*
10. Helena Michie, *The Flesh Made Word, Female Figures and Women's Bodies* (Oxford, 1987). See also Jeanne Fahnestock 'The Heroine of Irregular Features: Physiognomy and Conventions in Heroine Description', *Victorian Studies* (1980) pp. 325–50.
11. Michie, *The Flesh Made Word*: Barbara Ehrenreich and Diedre English *'For Her Own Good'; 150 Years of Experts' Advice to Women* (New York, 1979).
12. Fahnestock, 'The Heroine of Irregular Features'.

13. Florence Nightingale, *Letters from Egypt* (London, 1854) p. 13.
14. Ibid., p. 14.
15. Ibid., ibid.
16. Katherine Elwood, *Narrative of a Journey Overland from England by the Continent of Europe, Egypt and the Red Sea to India, Including a Residence There and Voyage Home in the Year 1825, 26, 27 and 28,* 2 vols (London, 1830), vol. I, p. 153.
17. Ibid., p. 340, on the women in Hodeida.
18. Pardoe, *City of the Sultan,* vol. I, pp. 100–1. She goes on to invoke the metaphor of the slippers.
19. Sophia Lane Poole, *The Englishwoman in Egypt,* p. 97.
20. Lucie Duff-Gordon, *Letters from Egypt with a memoir by her daughter, Janet Ross* (London, 1865, repr. 1983) pp. 135–6
21. Ibid., p. 136.
22. Duff-Gordon, *Letters,* quoted in Peter Gay, *The Bourgeois Experience,* vol. I: *Victoria to Freud* (Oxford, 1984) p. 350.
23. For legislation on divorce and the married women's property rights see Jeffrey Weeks, *Sex, Politics and Society: The Regulation of Sexuality Since 1800* (London, 1981); see Lee Holcombe, 'Victorian Wives and Property: Reform of the Married Women's Property Law, 1857–72' in Martha Vicinus (ed.), *A Widening Sphere: Changing Roles of Victorian Women* (London, repr. 1980) and *Wives and Property, Reform of the Married Women's Property Law in 19th Century England* (Toronto, 1983).
24. Among her other works are: *Mysticism and Magic in Turkey* (1912); *Turkish Life in Town and Country* (1909); *The Turkish People; their Social Life, Religious Beliefs and Institutions and Domestic Life* (1900).
25. Mary Lucy Garnett, *Home Life in Turkey* (London, 1909) p. 282.
26. Garnett, *The Women of Turkey and their Folk-Lore,* cheap edn, 2 vols in one (London, 1893) p. 546.
27. Ibid., and *Home Life,* p. 280; p. 282.
28. See Leila Ahmed, *Edward William Lane,* p. 117.
29. A short list of the important accounts on divorce should include Mary Lucy Garnett, *Home Life,* pp. 216–17; Fanny Janet Blunt, *The People of Turkey, Twenty Years' Residence among Bulgarians, Greeks, Albanians, Turks and Armenians* (London, 1878) p. 84. *Dodd* and *Pardoe.*
30. See note 29 above and for the legal status of wives and divorcees: Judith Tucker, *Women in Nineteenth-Century Egypt* (Cambridge, 1984) and Nadia Tomiche 'The Situation of Egyptian Women in the First Half of the Nineteenth Century' in W. R. Polk and R. L. Chambers (eds), *Beginnings of Modernisation in the Middle East* (Chicago, 1984) pp. 177–84. Also consult Louis Beck and Nikki Keddie (eds) *Women in the Muslim World* (Cambridge, Mass., 1979).
31. Elisabeth of Anspach, *DNB,* vol. 1, pp. 508–9.
32. See note 29 above and Tucker, *Women in Nineteenth Century Egypt.*
33. For legislation in Britain on divorce see J. Bryce 'Marriage and Divorce under Roman and English Law', in *Studies in History and Jurisprudence* (Oxford, 1901); O. S. Stone, 'The Status of Women

in Great Britain', *American Journal of Comparative Law*, 20 (1972) pp. 596–612 and Lee Holcombe, *Victorian Wives and Property*.

34. See *Tucker*; *Tomiche* and *Beck* and *Keddie*.

35. Ibid., *Tucker*.

36. On 'couverture' see William Blackstone, *Commentaries on the Laws of England* ch. 15., Tucker edn, 1903, 'Of Husband and Wife' and also *Holcombe*.

37. Fanny Janet Blunt, *The People of Turkey*, p. 78.

38. Lucy Garnett, *Home Life in Turkey*, p. 217 and compare to Richard Francis Burton, 'Terminal Essay', in *A Plain and Literal Translation of the Arabian Nights Entertainment*, vol. 7, p. 199.

39. Pardoe, *the City of the Sultan*, vol. I, pp. 103–6; on slavery and pp. 306–9. Mrs Harvey, *Turkish Harems and Circassian Homes*, p. 10; Garnett, *Home Life*; *Women of Turkey* vol. I, p. 40.

40. On domestic slavery, see G. Baer, 'Slavery and its abolition', in *Studies in the Social History of Modern Egypt* (Chicago, 1969) pp. 161–90; Ehud R. Toledano, *The Ottoman Slave Trade and its Suppression, 1840–1890* (Princeton, 1982). For more details see note 43, Chapter 5 below.

41. Pardoe, *City of the Sultan*, vol. I, pp. 306–9.

42. Ibid., 101.

43. Susan Kingsley, *Sex and Suffrage in Britain, 1860–1919* (Princeton, 1989), pp. 15–16, 35–59.

44. Mrs W. M. Ramsay, *Everyday Life in Turkey: Seventeen Years of Residence* (London, 1879) p. 108.

45. Pardoe, *City of the Sultan*, vol I, p. 126. See also, pp. 376–81.

46. Elizabeth Craven, *A Journey through the Crimea*, Letter LVI, undated, p. 264.

47. Ibid., p. 264: 'such a disgusting sight as this would have put me in an ill humour with my sex in bath for ages – hardly any – and Madame Gaspari [the consul's wife] tells me, that the encomiums and flattery a fine young woman would meet in the bath would be astonishing'.

48. Lavater, quoted in Julie F. Codell 'Expression Over Beauty: Facial Expression, Body Language, and Circumstantiality in the Paintings of the Pre-Raphaelite Brotherhood, *Victorian Studies*, vol. 29, no. 2 (Winter 1986) p. 275.

49. Helena Michie, *The Flesh Made Word*; Jeanne Fahnestock, 'The Heroine of Irregular Features'; Julie E. Codell, 'Expression Over Beauty'.

50. Quoted in Codell, 'Expression Over Beauty', p. 283.

51. *Fahnestock*, op. cit.

52. See, for example, *DNB*, vol. 15, p. 201.

53. *City of the Sultan* vol. 1, p. 9.

54. Ibid., 'The Fair Heyminé', p. 234.

55. Ibid., vol. II, pp. 98–99.

56. On eyes see: Caroline Paine, *Tent and Harem: Notes on an Oriental Trip* (New York, 1859) p. 259. She refers to 'large, hazel, beautifully languishing [eyes]; Pardoe, *City of the Sultan*, vol. I, p. 19; p. 29. See note 59 below.

57. *Paine*, op. cit.

58. Dawson-Damer, *Diary of a Tour*, vol. II, p. 204; Beaufort *Egyptian Sepulchres*, p. 121, for a very elaborate description.
59. Hornby, *In and Around Constantinople*, vol. I, p. 65.
60. Marianne Young Postans, *Facts and Fictions, Illustrative of Oriental Character*, 3 vols (London, 1844) vol. I, p. 135.
61. Mary Eliza Rogers, *Domestic Life in Palestine*, p. 222.
62. Ibid., ibid.
63. Emmeline Lott, *The English Governess in Egypt*, vol. I, pp. 74–5; p. 77.
64. *Rogers, op.cit.*, p. 92
65. For example: Chennels, *Recollections*, p. 25; p. 327.
66. Pardoe, *City of the Sultan*, vol. I, p. 33.
67. Hornby, *In and Around Constantinople*, vol. I, p. 62.
68. Harvey, *Turkish Harems*, p. 33,
69. On the Egyptian outdoor cover see, Lane, *Modern Egyptians*, pp. 45–50; Martineau, *Eastern Life Present and Past*, p. 6.
70. Mrs Ramsay, *Every-Day Life*, p. 102; *Martineau*, p. 6.
71. Elisabeth Goodnow Cooper, *The Women of Egypt* (London, 1914) p. 29.
72. See above, note 44.
73. See Chapter 8, pp. 194–5.
74. Nightingale, *Letters from Egypt*, p. 13.
75. On commercial photography and the mass-production oriental postcard see Louis Vazek and Gail Buckland, *Travellers in Ancient Lands: A Portrait of the Middle East 1839–1919* (New York, 1981), Nisan Peres, *Focus East, Early Photography in the Near-East 1839–1885* (New York, 1988); Engin Vizeer, *Photography in the Ottoman Empire* (Paris, 1988); for commercial pornographic representations see Mallek Allaila, *The Colonial Harem* (Minneapolis, 1986). I am grateful to David Prochaska for letting me read his analysis of commercial postcards, 'the Archive of L'Algerie Imaginaire' before publication.
76. Beckford *Vathek*, pp. 1–2.
77. On the 'Seven Deadly Sins' see *The Oxford Dictionary of the Christian Church*, 2nd edn, pp. 1264–5.
78. Daniel, *Islam and the West*, p. 148; Kabbani, *Europe's Myth*, p. 16.
79. *Vathek*, p. 1.
80. Alev Lytle Croutier, *The Harem*, see for example p. 95.
81. Isabel Burton, *The Inner Life of Syria, Palestine and the Holy Land from my private Journal*, 2 vols (London repr. 1884), vol. I p. 312; vol. II, p. 268.
82. *Blunt*, vol. I, Ch. XII. The chapter on 'food' includes information on kitchens; Turkish coffee and gourmet food; Greek and Bulgarian food and Jewish food.
83. *Hornby*, vol. II, pp. 154–6.
84. Garnett, *Home Life*, p. 269.
85. Claude Lévi-Strauss, *The Origins of Table Manners*, trans. J. and D. Weightman (London, 1978) pp. 496–508.
86. Michie, *The Flesh Made Word*, especially chapter 1: 'Ladylike Ano-rexia: Hunger, Sexuality and Etiquette', pp. 12–30. For a more

general discussion on food and gender in middle-class culture consult: Joan Jacobs Brumberg, *Fasting Girls: The Emergence of Anorexia Nervosa as a Modern Disease* (Cambridge, Mass., 1988).

87. Pardoe, *City of the Sultan*, vol. I, pp. 22–5.
88. *Michie*, pp. 12–13; Brumberg, *Fasting Girls*. On women as food-preparers see Lévi-Strauss, *Origins*.
89. See for example, *Brumberg,* Caroline Walker Bynum, *Holy Fast and Holy Feast Religious Significance of Food to Medieval Women* (Los Angeles, 1987).
90. Lévi-Strauss, *Origins*, pp. 498–9.
91. Penzer, 'The Second Court,' *The Harem*.
92. Thackeray, *Vanity Fair*, pp. 39–40.
93. Walker Bynum, *op. cit.*
94. *Pardoe*, vol. I, p. 24.
95. Emmeline Lott, *The English Governess in Egypt*, vol. I, pp. 91–2.
96. *Dawson-Damer, Diary of a Tour*, vol. II, pp. 207–8, Anne Blunt, *A Pilgrimage to Nejd, the Cradle of the Arab Race, A Visit to the Court of the Emir and our Persian Campaign* (London, 1819, repr. 1985), pp. 330–2.
97. Lott, p. 92.
98. Ibid., p. 153; p. 156.
99. Fanny Davies, *The Ottoman Lady*, p. 143.
100. Anne Blunt, Diary, January 4, 1878, BL, add. mass. 538987.
101. Mary Eliza Rogers, *Domestic Life in Palestine*, 233–4.
102. Mary Douglas, *Purity and Danger, An Analysis of the Concepts of Pollution and Taboo* (London and New York 1966, repr. 1988). For the Victorian associations between 'purity' and class and between 'purity' and gender see Leonore Davidoff, 'Class and Gender in Victorian England: The Diaries of Arthur J. Munby and Hannah Cullick'.
103. Lackey, *History of European Morals* (London, 1869), vol. 2, pp. 299–300.
104. On the social aspects of body-hygiene and the class association of impurity see Judith R. Walkwitz, *Prostitution and Victorian Society, Women, Class and State* (Cambridge, 1980) p. 4; Susan Kingsly Kent, *Sex and Suffrage in Britain 1860–1919* (Princeton, 1989), especially pp. 62–6. On the relations between instability and impurity see Eric Trudgill, *Madonnas and Magdalenes, the Origins and Development of Victorian Sexual Attitudes* (London, 1976).
105. For a discussion of visual representations of the *hamman* see: Thornton, *The Orientalists*; de Groot's '"Sex and Race" and Kabbani', *Europe's Myth of Orient*, pp. 73–4.
106. Fanny Davies, *The Ottoman Lady*, pp. 131–9.
107. Fanny Blunt, *The People of Turkey*, p. 234.
108. Ibid.; Pardoe, *The City of the Sultan*, vol. I, pp. 90–1.
109. A typical example is Amelia Edwards. See *A Thousand Miles up the Nile*, p. 101; p. 183; p. 86 for the filthiness of the *fallahin*. On ablutions see Rogers, *Domestic Life*, pp. 180 and 224.
110. Katherine Elwood, *Narrative of a Journey Overland*, vol. I, p. 120.
111. Garnett, *Home Life*, Chapter 15.

112. Isabel Burton, *The Inner Life in Syria*, vol. I, p. 144. In a similar vein is Dawson-Damer's description. See *Diary of a Tour*, vol. II, p. 200.
113. Sophia Lane Poole, *The Englishwoman in Egypt*, Letter XXIX, 'The Bath', vol. II, pp. 173–4.
114. Ibid., vol. II, p. 174.
115. Ibid., Letter XII, vol. I, p. 170.
116. Martineau, *Eastern Life*, p. 544.
117. Ibid., ibid.
118. Ibid., p. 554.
119. Ibid., p. 556.
120. See Cairncross, *After Polygamy*, pp. 106–7.
121. Annie Harvey, *Turkish Harems*, p. 75.

CHAPTER 5: THE *HAREMLIK* AS A *BOURGEOIS* HOME:
AUTONOMY, COMMUNITY AND SOLIDARITY

1. Harriet Martineau, *Eastern Life*, Part II 'Sinai and its Faith' and see below, Chapter 10, for her study of the genealogy of religion.
2. *Eastern Life*, p. 293.
3. '. . . . the Carolina planter, who knows as well as any Egyptian that polygamy is a natural concomitant of slavery, may see in the state of Egypt and the Egyptians what his country and his children must come to'. Ibid., p. 299. For her sympathy with Garrisonian Abolitionism see *Autobiography* (1877, repr. London, 1983), vol. 2, pp. 1–93; R. K. Webb, *Harriet Martineau, A Radical Victorian* (London, 1960), Chapter V.
4. Lucie Duff-Gordon, *Letters from Egypt with a Memoir by her Daughter Jannet Ross* (London, 1865 repr. London, 1983) p. 112.
5. See Norman Daniel, *Islam, Europe and Empire* pp. 36–8; Adolphus Slade, *Records of Travels in Turkey, Greece and of a Cruise in the Black Sea with the Captain Pasha in the Years 1823, 1830, and 1831* (London, 1833) pp. 314–32. Slade thought the Ottoman women 'happier than half the women in the world'; Burton, 'Terminal Essay', *Arabian Nights Entertainment*, vol. 7, p. 196. In the same passage Burton criticises Martineau.
6. Barnett Miller, *Behind the Sublime Porte: The Grand Seraglio of Istanbul* (New Haven, 1931), especially pp. 91–2.
7. Grace Ellison, *An Englishwoman in a Turkish Harem* (London 1915) p. 120.
8. Ellen Chennels, *Recollections of an Egyptian Princess*, vol. I, pp. 72–3.
9. Katherine Ellwood, *Narrative of a Journey Overland*, vol. I, pp. 153–4.
10. 'Harem', *Encyclopedia of Islam*, new edn (Leiden, 1967) vol. III, pp. 209–10.
11. There is a wealth of literature about the notion of the spheres. The following are particularly important: Walter H. Hougton, *The Victorian Frame of Mind 1830–70* (New Haven, 1975) pp. 341–72; Brian Harrison, *Separate Spheres: The Opposition to Women's Suffrage in Britain* (London, 1975) pp. 56–61; Nancy F. Cott, *The Bonds*

of Womanhood: Women's Sphere in New England, 1780–1835 (New Haven, 1977). For a different approach see Leonore Davidoff and Catherine Hall, *Family Fortunes*. See also Martha Vicinus (ed.), *A Widening Sphere, Changing Roles of Victorian Women* (London, repr. 1980).

12. See note 11 above and for the association between space and gender also Alexander Welsh, *The City of Dickens* (Oxford, 1971) pp. 149–61 and *Davidoff and Hall*. See also J. Habermas' inspiring 'The public sphere; Encylopedia Article', *New German Critique*, vol. 1, no. 3 (1971).

13. In his public lecture, 'Off Queen's Gardens', published in *Sesame and Lilies*. This is considered the most important single document for a characteristic idealisation of woman and home in Victorian writing.

14. Mary Lucy Garnett, *The Women in Turkey*, p. 441.

15. Elisabeth Goodnow Cooper, *The Women of Egypt*, p. 185.

16. Mary Eliza Rogers, *Domestic Life*, p. 372; also Burton, *The Inner Life of Syria*, vol. I, p. 165.

17. Fanny Blunt, *The People of Turkey*, p. 261.

18. Rogers, *op. cit.*

19. Amelia Bythinia Hornby, *In and Around Constantinople*, vol. II, p. 156.

20. Stowasser, 'The Status of Women in Early Islam'.

21. Daniel, *Islam, Europe and Empire*, p. 19; p. 37.

22. For example Dawson-Damer, *Diary of a Tour*, vol. I, p. 209; Ellison, *An Englishwoman in a Turkish Harem*, p. 57. See Daniel, *Islam, Europe*, pp. 36–8.

23. Bowman Dodd, *The Palaces of the Sultan*, p. 435.

24. Macfarlane, *Love and Marriage*, pp. 222–3, for serial polygamy.

25. Bowman Dodd, *The Palace*, p. 433.

26. Hornby, *In and Around Constantinople*, vol. I, p. 236.

27. Chennels, *Recollections*, vol. I, pp. 72–3.

28. Stowasser, 'The Status of Women'.

29. Ibid., pp. 15–16. And for assertive Ottoman women see *Dodd* and Garnett, *The Women of Turkey*, pp. 408–9.

30. Lane, *Modern Egyptians*, p. 296.

31. Stanley Lane Poole, quoted in Daniel, *Islam, Europe*, p. 38.

32. Bowman Dodd, *The Palaces of the Sultan*, pp. 435, 448.

33. For the structure of the Imperial Harem see: Miller, *Beyond the Sublime Porte* Chs. 5 and 12; Penzer, *The Harem*, Chapters 6–10 (particularly useful on the female hierarchy are Chapters 7 and 8); Ehud R. Toledano, *The Ottoman Slave Trade*; Bernard Lewis, *Istanbul and the Civilisation of the Ottoman Empire* (Oklahoma, 1963) and Alev Lytle Courtier, *Harem*.

34. Ramsay, *Every Day Life*, pp. 105–6.

35. Chennels, *Recollections*, p. 194; Lott, *Harem Life*, vol. I, p. 73; Pardoe, *City of the Sultan*, vol. I, p. 111. For the lower classes see Gordon, *Letters from Egypt*, p. 60.

36. See Adolphus Slade, *Records of Travel in Turkey* pp. 239, 241–2.

37. For Martineau's Abolitionism see *Autobiography*, vol. 2, pp. 1–93; R.

K. Webb, *Harriet Martineau*, chapter 5. For her views on slavery in the harems see *Eastern Life*, p. 241.

38. Whately, quoted in Elisabeth J. Whately, *The Life and Work of Mary Louisa Whately* (London, 1891) p. 126.
39. *Slade*, vol. II, p. 187 (1837 edn).
40. Esmé Scott-Stevenson, *Our Ride through Asia Minor* (London, 1881) p. 104.
41. Fanny Blunt, *The People of Turkey*, vol. I, p. 250.
42. Mrs Harvey, *Turkish Harems and Circassian Homes* pp. 245–51, especially p. 245.
43. On the legal status of slaves, domestic slavery and social mobility see Gabriel Baer, 'Slavery and its Abolition', in *Studies in the Social History of Modern Egypt* (Chicago, 1969) pp. 161–90; Toledano, 'Slave Dealers, Women, Pregnancy, and Abortion: The Story of a Circassian Slave Girl in Mid-Nineteenth-Century Cairo', *Slavery and Abolition*, 2 (May 1981) pp. 53–69 and his *The Ottoman Slave Trade*. For the travellers see Pardoe, *City of the Sultan*, vol. I, p. 103; Harvey, *Turkish Harems*, p. 10; Garnett, *Home Life*, pp. 211–13, 215–16 and her *Women in Turkey and Their Folklore* (London, repr. 1893) vol. I, pp. 382–3; Duff-Gordon, *Letters from Egypt*, pp. 180–1.
44. Chennels, *Recollections of an Egyptian Princess*.
45. Garnett, *The Women of Turkey*, p. 411.
46. Ibid., ibid.
47. Dodd, *The Palaces*, p. 449.
48. Thane, 'Women and the New Poor Law', *History Workshop*, 6 (1979) pp. 29–59.
49. For the legal status of the *ummuveled* see Tucker, *Women in Nineteenth-Century Egypt*.
50. Davidoff and Hall, *Family Fortunes*, pp. 357–70, especially pp. 359–60.
51. Emmeline Lott, *Harem Life*, vol. I, pp. 69–70.
52. Ibid.
53. Ibid., vol. I, pp. 84–5.
54. Chennels, *Recollections*, pp. 163–4.
55. Ibid., p. 24; Rogers, *Domestic Life*, pp. 231–2.
56. Garnett, *Turkey of the Ottomans* (New York, 1914), 'Home Life', pp. 202–5
57. Ibid. pp. 204–5.
58. Ibid. p. 205.
59. Duff-Gordon, *Letters from Egypt*, p. 110.
60. Philip Ariés' term. See *Century of Childhood: a Social History of Family Life* (trans. Robert Balbick) (New York, 1962) pp. 393–4.
61. Chennels, *Recollections*, p. 141; Anne Blunt, BL Wentworth Collection, add. mss. 53899 (16 Jan.–7 Feb. 1879), probably 23 Jan. 'We ate and wrote our journals a matter of some management as one has to be continually on the look out not to be surprised by visitors. Our door is kept shut by a wooden bolt.'
62. Davidoff, 'Class and Gender in Victorian England' 'Mastered for Wife in Victorian and Edwardian England', in A. Sutcliff and P. Thane (eds), *Essays in Social History* (Oxford, 1984).

63. Duff-Gordon, *Letters from Egypt*, pp. 180–1.
64. Lott, *The English Governess*, p. 73; p. 137; Paine, *Tent and Harem*, p. 55; Pardoe, *City of the Sulton*, vol. I, p. 113.
65. Lane Poole, *The Englishwoman in Egypt*, especially Letters XXI; XXX.
66. Paine, *op. cit.*; Lott, *op. cit.*, p. 73.
67. Lane Poole, *The Englishwoman*; Pardoe, *The City of the Sultan*, vol. I, pp. 334–15; Lott, *The English Governess*, pp. 146–7.
68. Blunt, *Pilgrimage to Nejd*, p. 248; Paine, *Tent and Harem*, p. 51.
69. Paine, *Tent and Harem*. She remarks on 'the good nature [of Turkish mistresses] that permits the slaves and visitors to enjoy visits.' p. 55. Pardoe remarks on the happiness of slaves of all ages, races and ranks. *City of the Sultan*, vol. I, p. 115. *Pardoe*, vol. I, p. 86.
70. Pardoe, *City of the Sultan*, vol. I, pp. 261–2, 97–8; Mary Mackintosh 'children', *Damascus and its People* (London, 1883). The theme can be traced back to *Montagu*.
71. See above and Fanny Blunt. See also Isabel Burton, *Inner Life*, vol. I, p. 260. *Mackintosh*; Rogers, *Domestic Life*.
72. Lott, *The English Governess*, vol. I, pp. 95–7.
73. Rogers, *Domestic Life*, pp. 231–2.
74. *Ibid.*, p. 97. Dawson-Damer compares the inside of a *haremlik* to a Catholic chapel. *Diary of a Tour*, vol. I, p. 209.
75. Mary Mackintosh, *Damascus and Its People*, Chapters 7–8.
76. Charles Warren, *Underground Jerusalem* (London, 1876), pp. 490–7.
77. Elizabeth Ann Finn, *Home in the Holy Land*, p. 65.
78. Edwards, *A Thousand Miles up the Nile*, pp. 158, 175, 182–4.
79. Gustav Flaubert, quoted in *Said*, pp. 167–8.
80. Pardoe, *City of the Sultans*, vol. II, pp. 348–51.
81. *Ibid*, p. 348.
82. Lott, *The English Governess*, vol. II, p. 238.
83. Dawson-Damer, *Diary of a Tour*.
84. Garnett, *Home Life in Turkey*, p. 269.
85. *Ibid*.
86. See for example Mervat Hatem, 'Through Each Other's Eyes, Egyptian, Leventine-Egyptian and European Women's Images of Themselves and of Each Other (1862–1900)', *Women's Studies International Forum*, vol. 12, no. 2 (1989) pp. 183–98. See also Huda Shaarawi, *Harem Years, The Memoirs of an Egyptian Feminist*, trans. Margot Badran (London, 1986).

CHAPTER 6:   EVANGELICAL TRAVEL AND THE EVANGELICAL
CONSTRUCTION OF GENDER

1. Quoted in Shepherd, *The Zealous Intruders*, p. 76; Sarah Kochav, 'Biblical Prophecy, The Evangelical Movement and the Restoration of the Jews to Palestine, Britain and the Holy Land 1800–1914'.

Papers given at a Conference at University College London (February, 1989).

2. In addition to the works on the traditional pilgrimage cited in notes, pp. 36–9, see George Roppen, *Strangers and Pilgrims: an Essay on the Metaphor of Journey* (New York, 1964).

3. For the 'feminisation' of middle-class culture and religion see the work of Carroll Smith Rosenberg and Barbara Welter, especially: Welter, 'The Feminisation of American Religion 1800–1860', in Mary J. Hartman and Louis Banner (eds), *Clio's Consciousness Raised; New Perspectives on the History of Women* (New York, 1974).

4. Raymond Schwab, *The Oriental Renaissance*.

5. On the semantic problem see particularly Ian Bradley, *The Call to Seriousness: The Evangelical Impact on the Victorians* (London, 1976) and Elisabeth Jay, *The Religion of the Heart, Angelican Evangelicalism and the 19th Century Novel* (Oxford, 1979), especially pp. 17–22.

6. For the evangelical ideology of gender see Leonore Davidoff and Catherine Hall's *Family Fortunes* particularly Part One 'Religion and Ideology'. See also the chapter on 'Evangelicalism and the Power of Women' in Jane Rendall, *The Origins of Modern Feminism: Women in Britain, France and the United States* (London, 1985), pp. 73–103 and Catherine Hall, 'The Early Formation of Victorian Domestic Ideology', in Susan Burman (ed.), *Fit Work for Women* (Canberra, 1979) and *Bradley*, Chapter 10, 'Home and Family'. On religion and Imperialism see Christine Bolt, *Victorian Attitudes to Race* (London, 1971).

7. *Davidoff and Hall*. For the moral superiority of women and their spirituality see Nancy Cott, 'Passionlessness: An Interpretation of Victorian Sexual Ideology 1790–1850', quoted in Susan Kingley Kent, *Sex and Suffrage*, pp. 36, 16.

8. *Davidoff and Hall*, pp. 429–36; F. K. Prochasca, *Women and Philanthropy* (Oxford, 1980) and 'Women in English Philanthropy, 1790–1830', *International Review of Social History*, 19 (1974), pp. 426–45. For the ideology of female missions see J. Jacobs Brumberg, 'Zenanas and wifeless villages, the Ethnography of American Evangelical women, 1870–1910', *American Quarterly Review*; Barbara Welter, '"She Hath done What she Could" Protestant Women's Missionary Careers in 19th Century America', *American Quarterly*, vol. 30, no. 5 (1978) pp. 624–39.

9. Mayir, Vereté, 'The Idea of the Restoration of the Jews in English Protestant Thought 1790–1840', *Middle Eastern Studies* vol. 8, no. 1 (1972) pp. 3–50. See also Sarah Kochav, 'Biblical Prophecy'; 'The evangelical Movement and the Mission to the Jews', paper given at the Weiner Seminar on Secularisation in the Modern World (Tel Aviv, Dec. 1988).

10. Kochav, 'Biblical Prophecy'.

11. Hourani, *Western Attitudes Towards Islam* (Southhampton, 1974). *Europe and the Middle East*.

12. Kochav; S. H. Levine, *Changing Aspects of Palestine in American Literature to 1867* (Ann Arbor, 1953).

13. See especially Th. William David, 'A History of Biblical Archaeology', unpublished Ph.D Thesis (Arizona 1987).
14. Frances Power Cobbe, *Cities of the Past*, pp. 173–4.
15. Ibid., p. 175.
16. Elizabeth Charles, *Wanderings in Bible Lands and Seas* (London, 1862), p. 54.
17. Augusta Cook, *By Way of the East, General Impressions of Palestine and Egypt, Smyrna and Ephesus* (London, 1908), 'preface'.
18. Harriet Martineau, *Eastern Life*, pp. 431–2, 441.
19. Goodrich-Freer, *Inner Jerusalem* pp. 35–46. Cobbe, *Cities of the Past*, pp. 183, 185–6 and for a sympathetic description of naïve piety see ibid., pp. 133–4.
20. George Eliot, *Westminster Review* (1855) a Review of John Cumming's prophetical writings, quoted in Kochav, *Biblical Prophecy*, p. 19.
21. For the correlation between gender and professional status see Dea Birkett, *Spinsters Abroad*, pp. 169–73 and Gaye Tuchman, *Edging Women Out* and Philippa Levine, *The Amateur and the Professional*.
22. PEF, Report, 1865, p. 1.
23. Ibid., ibid.
24. Ibid., p. 16, p. 18.
25. Elisabeth Fee, 'The Sexual Politics of Victorian Social Anthropology', *Femininst Studies*, no. 2 (1973) pp. 23–40; 'Science and the Woman Problem: Historical Perspectives', in Michael S. Teitelbaum (ed.), *Sex Differences: Social and Biological Perspectives* (New York, 1976).
26. Charles Warren, *Underground Jerusalem*, p. 20.
27. Elisabeth Ann Finn, *Reminiscences* (London, 1929), pp. 252–3.

CHAPTER 7:   THE WOMEN OF CHRIST CHURCH:
WORK, LITERATURE AND COMMUNITY IN NINETEENTH-CENTURY
JERUSALEM

1. For definitions of work and women's work see my discussion above, p. 13 and p. 15, note 23.
2. See Welter, 'She hath done her duty'.
3. Eugene Stock, *The History of the Church Missionary Society* (London, 1897) vol. 2, pp. 397–400.
4. Ibid., p. 398.
5. Ibid., vol. 3, p. 369.
6. Ibid., ibid.
7. Ibid., p. 370.
8. 'Statistics of the Palestine Mission in Quinquennial Periods', in *Handbooks of the CMS Missions. The Palestine Mission* (London, 1910).
9. *The Persia and Turkish Arabia Missions* (London, 1909).
10. Eugene Stock, *History of the Church Missionary Society*, vol. 2, p. 528.
11. 'Statistics of the Palestine Mission', *The Palestine Mission*.
12. E. J. Whately, *The Life and Work of Mary Louisa Whately*, p. 79.
13. *JI*, Jan. 1, 1860, p. 14.

14. Ibid., p. 15. There is a euphemistic account of the 'takeover' in the same number. See ibid., p. 9.
15. Julius Richter, *A History of the Protestant Missions.* p. 203.
16. Ibid., pp. 206, 257. For information about the early years of Walker-Arnot's school I am indebted to Ms. Marie Noel Karpik and the principal of the Tabitha School at Jaffa.
17. There is a wealth of literature on missionary activity in Jerusalem. A short-list of publications should include Shaul Sapir, 'The Anglican Missionary Societies in Jerusalem: Activities and Impact', in Ruth Kark (ed.), *The Land that Became Israel Studies in Historical Geography* (New Haven, 1989) pp. 105–20; Sapir, 'The Contribution of the Anglican Missionary Societies Toward the Development of Jerusalem at the End of the Ottoman Empire', MA Thesis (Jerusalem, 1979) (Hebrew). For the London Jews Society in Jerusalem see: Shalom Ginat, 'The Activity of the "London Society for Promoting Christianity Amongst the Jews" Inside the Jewish Yishuv in Jerusalem (1825–1914)', MA Thesis (Haifa, 1986) (Hebrew). For general information about Jerusalem's European population consult Yehoshua Ben-Arieh, *Jerusalem in the 19th century, the Old City* (New York and Jerusalem, 1984) especially pp. 184–201, 250–63.
18. For information on Elisabeth Ann Finn see *Reminiscences* and *Consular Diary of James and Elisabeth Ann Finn* (New York, 1980).
19. For the Sarah Society see *Reminiscences*, p. 117. The records of the society are now not available to the public.
20. F. K. Prochaska, *Women and Philanthropy*, pp. 97–138.
21. For the 'Benevolent Society' see Shalom Ginat, 'The Activity of the London Society', pp. 67–8; *JI*, 1865, pp. 209–10.
22. Dorcas Society, Minutes Book, 1849–54, The Israel Trust Society of the Anglican Church, Archives, Jerusalem.
23. Ibid.
24. Jerusalem Literary Society, Minute Books, PEF, JER 6.
25. James Finn, *Stirring Times, or Records from Jerusalem Consular Chronicles of 1853 to 1856*, 2 vols (London, 1878) p. 191.
26. Ibid., p. 193.
27. 'Digest of the Rules Respecting Members of the Society', PEF, JER 6 (n.d., presumably November 1849), p. 2.
28. Jerusalem Literary Society early November and 30 November 1849, PEF, JER 6.
29. Dorcas Society, Minutes Book (1857) The Israel Trust.
30. There are numerous descriptions of the daily routine at the Institute. See, for example, Mrs Finn, *Reminscences*; Mathilda Cubley, *The Hills and Plains of Palestine*, plate 1; Ellen Clare Miller, *Eastern Sketches, Notes of Scenery, Schools and Tent Life in Syria and Palestine* (Edinburgh, 1871) p. 127.
31. Cubley, plate 6.
32. *JI*, 1 January 1860, p. 15.
33. Emily Ann Beaufort, *Egyptian Sepulchres and Syrian Shrines, Including Some Stay in the Lebanon at Palmyra and in Western Turkey* (London 1861) two vols, vol. I, p. 409.

34. Ibid., p. 410.
35. Elisabeth Ann Finn, *A Third Year in Jerusalem, a Tale Illustrating Customs and Manners in Modern Jerusalem* (London, 1869), p. 151.
36. Ibid., p. 176.
37. Ibid., p. 223.
38. On Creasy, see Finn, *Reminiscences*, p. 172; Blumberg, *A View from Jerusalem*, pp. 295, 311.
39. British-Born Subjects Residing Within the Jurisdiction of the Jerusalem Consulate, June 21, 1859, ISA, Jerusalem 8 (2) 786.
40. Ellen Clare Miller, *Eastern Sketches*, p. 208.

CHAPTER 8: 'DOMESTIC LIFE IN PALESTINE': EVANGELICAL ETHNOGRAPHY, FAITH AND PREJUDICE

1. PEF. Jer 6, 85. The two different locations are given in the minutes. The paper was read by the President of the Society.
2. The full title is 'The Hebrew Women Recorded in the Bible', a lecture, given in the Valley of Hortues (Artas) near Bethlehem, May 1859, pp. 85–100.
3. Ibid., p. 100.
4. Ibid., ibid.
5. Ibid., pp. 86–7.
6. Ibid., ibid.
7. Ibid., p. 85.
8. Ibid., on women in the age of the Patriarchs see pp. 87–8; on the age of Judges see pp. 89–92. On the Monarchy see pp. 92–3.
9. Ibid., p. 100.
10. Ada M. Goodrich-Freer, *Inner Jerusalem*, p. 261. Goodrich-Freer herself devotes a chapter to 'The Moslem in His Relations to Women', pp. 251–65.
11. Ibid., p. 253.
12. Menachem Kedem, 'The Idea of the Restoration of the Jews', *Katedra*, 19 (April 1981). See also Kochav, 'Biblical prophecy'.
13. Elisabeth Ann Finn, Preface, *Home in the Holy Land, a Tale* (London, 1866) p. vi.
14. Ibid., pp. 114–15.
15. PEF, JER, G.I (1849), p. 108.
16. Cubley *The Hills and Planes of Jerusalem*, plates V, VI, XVII.
17. Harriet Catherine Egerton, Countess Ellesmere, *Journal of a Tour in the Holy Land in May and June 1840* (London, 1840) p. 48.
18. Ibid., p. 49.
19. Ibid., p. 50.
20. Mary Mackintosh, *Damascus and Its People*; Mentor-Mott, *Stones of Palestine, Notes on a Rumble Through the Holy Land* (London, 1865), p. 31.
21. Mackintosh, pp. 24–5.
22. Mackintosh, p. 25.

23. Egerton, p. 50; Mackintosh, p. 24.
24. Goodrich-Freer, *Inner Jerusalem*, p. 252.
25. *JI*, August 1856, pp. 254–5.
26. Ibid., p. 253.
27. Ibid., 1865, p. 210.
28. Elizabeth Charles, *Wanderings Over Bible Lands and Seas*, pp. 69–70.
29. Finn, *A Third Year in Jerusalem*, p. 177.
30. *Mackintosh*, pp. 26–7.
31. Beaufort, *Egyptian Sepulchres*, p. 410.
32. The quotation, reproduced in a typed history of the school, was shown to me by M. N. Karpik.
33. Augusta Mento-Mott, *Stones of Palestine*, p. 82.
34. Ibid., p. 84.
35. Mary Eliza Rogers, *Domestic Life in Palestine*, p. 327.
36. Ibid., p. 219; pp. 226–7, for the reversal of the metaphor.
37. Finn, 'I have been careful to avoid bringing forward living persons who might be identified on the spot'; Preface to *Life*, p. vi; *Reminiscences*, p. 225.
38. Finn, *Home*, p. 470.
39. Ibid., p. 284.
40. Ibid, pp. 284–5.
41. For estimates see Ben-Arieh, *Jerusalem in the 19th Century, the Old City*, pp. 260–1, for estimates of the Jewish population of Jerusalem see ibid., pp. 271–4.
42. Martineau, *Eastern Life*, pp. 466–9.

CHAPTER 9:   FEMINISING THE LANDSCAPE

1. See for instance Goodrich-Freer, *Inner Jerusalem* and *In a Syrian Saddle*, the prefaces.
2. On the changes in status of religious paintings and the development of forms of commercial reproduction see Kenneth Paul Bendiner, 'The portrayal of the Middle East in British Painting 1835–60', Ph.D. thesis (Columbia, New York, 1979) and Lynne Thornton, *The Orientalists: Painters and Travellers 1818–1908* (Paris, 1983). For a comparison with France and Germany see Thornton and Phillipe Julian, *The Orientalists: European Painters of Eastern Scenery* (Oxford, 1977). On the influence of evangelical writing on religious painting consult Bendiner, 'The Portrayal' and George P. Landau, *William Holman Hunt and Typological Symbolism* (New Haven, 1979), pp. 1–19; *Victorian Types, Victorian Shadows: Biblical Typology in Victorian Literature, Art and Thought* (Boston, 1980).
3. Percy G. Adams, *Travel Literature and the Evolution of the Novel*, especially pp. 38–103. See also Adams, *Travellers and Travel Liars*.
4. Egerton, *Journal of a Tour*, 'Preface'.
5. Cubley, *Hilles and Plaines*, 'Preface'.
6. Beaufort, *Egyptian Sepulchres*, p. 365.

7. Finn, *Home in Holy Land*, p. 49; pp. 123–5.
8. E. F. Van Der Bilt, 'Proximity and Distance: American Travellers to the Middle East, 1819–1918', Ph.D. Thesis (Cornell, Ithaca, 1985).
9. Benjamin Disraeli, *Tancred, or the New Crusade* (London, 1848, Hergenden, 1881), p. 151.
10. Dea Birkett, *Spinsters Abroad*, especially pp. 103–5, 108–9.
11. Beaufort, *Egyptian Sepulchres*, pp. 212, 230–69.
12. Cubley, *Hills and Plaines*, 'preface'.
13. Ellen Calre Miller, *Eastern Sketches*, p. 3.
14. Landau, *Victorian Types*; Bendiner, 'The Portrayal of the Middle East', pp. 40–2.
15. Quoted in Landau, *William Holman Hunt*, pp. 7–8.
16. Ibid.
17. Frances Power Cobbe, *Cities of the Past*, p. 122.
18. Ibid., p. 123.
19. Ibid., p. 124.
20. Ibid., p. 125.
21. Stafford, *Voyage into Substance*, pp. 49–50.
22. Charles, *Wanderings*, pp. 101–2.
23. Ibid., p. 103.
24. Agnes Smith, *Eastern Pilgrims; Travels of Three Ladies*, pp. 295–6.
25. Erick Aurbach, *Mimesis: The Representation of Reality in Western Literature* (Princeton, 1953) pp. 195–6.
26. Finn, *Home Life*, pp. 59; 89; 63; 127; Mentor-Mott, p. 13.
27. *Mentor-Mott*, pp. 8–9, 15.
28. *Mentor-Mott*, pp. 2–3.
29. *Mentor-Mott*, p. 3.
30. *Mentor-Mott*, p. 24.
31. *Mentor-Mott*, pp. 31–2 (Nablus), p. 25 (Shumem); *Rogers* p. 278, p. 329.
32. Lady Herbert, *Cradle Lands* (New York, n.d., probably 1864) p. 128.
33. Amy Fullerton, *A Lady's Ride Through Palestine and Syria; with Notices of Egypt and the Canal of Suez* (London, 1872) p. 117. See also *Charles* pp. 67; 108–109.
34. Beaufort, *Egyptian Sepulchres*, pp. 394–5.
35. Augusta Cook, *By Way of the East*.
36. Rogers, *Domestic Life*, p. 46.
37. *Rogers*, p. 57; Finn, *Reminicences*. See also Hunt's own litany in *Pre-Raphaelite Brotherhood* (New York, 1905) vol. I, pp. 424–5; vol. II, pp. 22–33.
38. Quoted in Bendiner, 'The Portrayal of the Middle East', p. 80.
39. W. M Rosetti, *The Pre-Raphaelite Journal*, 24 October 1850, quoted in *Bendiner*, p. 79.
40. William Holman Hunt, *Pre-Raphaelitism and the Pre-Raphaelite Brotherhood*, vol. ii, pp.15–16.
41. Finn, *Home*, pp. 513–14.
42. Ibid., p. 514.
43. Ibid., ibid.
44. Ibid., pp. 515–16.

CHAPTER 10: HARRIET MARTINEAU'S ANTI-PILGRIMAGE: AUTOBIOGRAPHY, HISTORY AND LANDSCAPE

1. Harriet Martineau, *Autobiography*, vol. 2, pp. 295–6. Murray maintained that the book was a 'conspiracy against Moses'.
2. Quoted in Valery Kossew Pichanick, *Harriet Martineau, the Woman and her World, 1802–76*, p. 181.
3. Ibid., ibid.
4. Ibid., ibid.
5. Martineau's expression. See *Autobiography*, vol. 2, p. 281.
6. Her critical biographers would endorse this view. See for example Pichanick, *Harriet Martineau*; R. K. Webb, *Harriet Martineau a Radical Victorian* (London, 1960) and Deidre David's 'Harriet Martineau: A Career of Auxiliary Usefulness', in *Intellectual Women and Victorian Patriarchy, Harriet Martineau, Elizabeth Barret Browning, George Eliot* (Ithaca, New York, 1987) pp. 27–97. For a less critical view see Florence Fenwick Miller, *Harriet Martineau* (London, 1884); Vera Wheatly, *The Life and Work of Harriet Martineau* (London, 1957) and Theodore Bosanquet, *Harriet Martineau an Essay in Comprehension* (New York, 1927). See also Mitzi Myers, 'Harriet Martineau's Autobiography: the making of a Female Philosopher', in Estelle C. Jelinck (ed.), *Women's Autobiography: Essays in Criticism* (Bloomington, Indiana, 1980).
7. *Autobiography*, vol. 2, p. 277.
8. For the Victorian notions on history consult: Olive Anderson, 'The Political Uses of History in mid-Nineteenth Century England', *Past and Present* 36 (1967) pp. 87–105; J. W. Burrow, *Evolution and Society, A Study in Victorian Social Theory* (Cambridge, 1966); *A Liberal Descent: Victorian Historians and the English Past* (Cambridge, 1981) and Herbert Butterfield, 'Delays and Paradoxes in the Development of Historigraphy', in K. Bourne and D. C. Watt (eds), *Studies in International History: Essays Presented to W. Norton Medlicott* (London, 1967) pp. 1–15.
9. *Autobiography*, vol. 2, pp. 278–9.
10. Ibid., p. 283.
11. Quoted in *Webb*, p. 288.
12. The expression, Martineau's own, may be found in the obituary, written by herself and published in the *Daily News* on 27 June 1876, two days after her death. Deidre David applies the combination 'auxiliary usefulness' to Martineau's status as a woman intellectual in a male dominated culture. Rather than challenge the values of that culture, Martineau defends and expounds them. David, *Intellectual Women*, pp. 27–40.
13. For a discussion of the Unitarian background and Martineau's education see Francis E. Mineka, *The Dissidence of Dissent: the Monthly Repository 1806–38* (Chapel Hill, N.C., 1944) and R. K. Webb, *Harriet Martineau*, especially Chapters II, III. See also the *Autobiography*, vol. 1, pp. 61–117. For a larger discussion see Josephine Kamm, *Hope Deferred: Girl's Education in English History* (London, 1965).

14. Webb is particularly useful on the Unitarian legacy. See *Webb*, Chapter III.
15. See 'Unitarianism', in F. D. Cross (ed.), *The Oxford Dictionary of the Christian Church*, pp. 1408–9; Owen Chadwick, *The Victorian Church Part I*, pp. 391–8.
16. The *Autobiography* is not very helpful on that point. Most students of Martineau agree that she rewrote her relations with Unitarianism and the history of ther conversion to Necessarianism. See for example Mitzi Meyer's Preface to the Virago edition of the *Autobiography* (London, 1984). See also *Webb*, pp. 79–86.
17. Webb, pp. 87–92.
18. For the influence in Britain of the higher criticism see *Chadwick*, pp. 527–33. See also E. S. Shaffer's excellent, *'Kubla Khan' and the Fall of Jerusalem. The Mythological School in Biblical Criticism and Secular Literature 1770–1880* (Cambridge, 1975). Shaffer is particularly useful on the relations between the Unitarians and the German 'mythologists'. For Martineau's use of the new criticism see Pichanick, *Harriet Martineau*, pp. 178–9.
19. Pichanick, *Harriet Martineau*, pp. 178–9.
20. See Leila Ahmed, *Edward W. Lane*, pp. 40–60.
21. Ibid., p. 52.
22. *Eastern Life*, p. 18.
23. Ibid., p. 89.
24. Ibid., p. 54.
25. See ibid., pp. 90–110 for the ancient historians and chronology.
26. Ibid., Chapter XX, pp. 259–74.
27. Ibid., pp. 150–51.
28. See, for example, ibid., pp. 189, 325–7, 450–51, 155, 566–7.
29. Ibid., p. 189.
30. Ibid., p. 189.
31. Ibid., p. 148.
32. 'Ikhnaton', *Encyclopedia Britannica* (1967 edn), vol. 11, pp. 1074–5; K. Lang, *König Echnaton und die Amarnazeit* (1951).
33. *Eastern Life*, pp. 327–9.
34. On Martineau's belief in human action and progress see Pichanick, *Harriet Martineau*, Chapters 2 and 8.
35. *Eastern Life*, p. 37.
36. Ibid., pp. 38–9.
37. Ibid., pp. 39–40.
38. Ibid., p. 43 on 'pictured language' and for her knowledge of Necessarian literature see notes 18, 19 above.
39. Ibid., p. 122.
40. Ibid., p. 40.
41. Ibid., p. 41.
42. Ibid., p. 326.
43. Ibid., ibid.
44. Ibid., ibid. And for Jesus see ibid., pp. 447–64.
45. Ibid., p. 443.
46. Ibid., ibid.

47. A. S. Shaffer, *'Kubla Khan' and the Fall of Jerusalem*, especially pp. 17–62.
48. *Eastern Life*, p. 442.
49. Ibid., pp. 401, 382, 403.
50. Quoted in the *Autobiography*, vol. II, pp. 288–90.

CHAPTER 11:   QUEEN HATASU'S BEARD: AMELIA EDWARDS, THE SCIENTIFIC JOURNEY AND THE EMERGENCE OF THE FIRST FEMALE 'ORIENTALISTS'

1. There is no full-fledged biography of Edwards. For biographical details see Birkett, *Spinsters Abroad*, pp. 46–50, 163–7, 281; Sutherland, *The Longman Companion to Victorian Fiction*, pp. 206–7, and James, 'Excavating in Egypt'. Martineau recorded her various illnesses in the *Autobiography*, especially vol. 2, the section on 'morbid conditions' and 'causes of illness' pp. 147–82 and in the morbid *Life in the Sickroom*. There are hints in an unknown letter by Edwards of a nervous breakdown about a year before the Mediterranean journey. See letter to Mrs Lane, 30 March 1872. The Edwards Papers, University College, London, Rare Books and Manuscripts Department, Science Division, add. ms. 182 (1–5).
2. Warren R. Dawson, *Who is Who in Egyptology* (London, 1951).
3. See Chapter 1.
4. L. Wm. Winslow, 'Amelia B. Edwards the "Queen of Egyptology"', *The American Antiquarian*, November 1892.
5. Philippa Levine, *The Amateur and the Professional*, pp. 32–3. See also G. E. Daniel, *A Hundred Years of Archaeology* (London, 1950); *The Origins and Growth of Archaeology* (Harmondsworth, 1967) and his *A Short History of Archaeology* (London, 1981).
6. Levine, *The Amateur and the Professional*, pp. 170–2.
7. Levine, pp. 32–4. For Layard see O. Waterfield, *Layard of Ninveh* (London, 1963). For Petrie see his *Seventy Years in Archaeology* (London, 1931).
8. A. Whigham Price, *The Ladies of Casetebrae*, especially pp. 184–211.
9. 'Benson', in Dawson *Who is Who in Egyptology*, p. 25; A. C. Benson, *The Life and Letters of Maggie Benson* (London, 1917).
10. Brodrick in *Dawson*, p. 40.
11. George Clark, *Archaeology and Society. Reconstructing the Prehistoric Past* (London, 1968) p. 17.
12. G. Daniel, *Cambridge and the Back Looking Curiosity* (Cambridge, 1976) p. 5. For the importance of excavation see also Thomas William Davis, 'A History of Biblical Archaeology'.
13. *Levine*, pp. 90–1.
14. J. H. Marsden, *Two Introductory Lectures Upon Archaeology Delivered in the Univesity of Cambridge* (Cambridge, 1852) p. 5.
15. Samuel Birch, 'Inaugural Discourse Delivered in the Section of General Antiquities at the Annual Meeting of the Archaeological

Institute at London, July 1866', *Archaeological Journal*, vol. XLI (1884) pp. 58–78, 59–63.

16. Quoted in J. T. H. James, *Excavating in Egypt*, p. 13.
17. C. Wm. Winslow, 'Amelia B. Edwards', *The American Antiquarian*, November 1892, pp. 7–8.
18. Birkett, *Spinsters Abroad*, pp. 163–4.
19. Amelia Blandford Edwards, *Pharaohs, Fellahs and Explorers* (New York, 1891) Preface.
20. Ibid., 'I The Explorer in Egypt', pp. 3–36.
21. Ibid., pp. 23–4.
22. Ibid., p. 24.
23. Edwards, *A Thousand Miles Up the Nile*, p. 85.
24. Ibid., p. 101.
25. Ibid., p. 183.
26. Ibid., p. 86.
27. Edwards, 'The Social and Political Postion of Women in Ancient Egypt', unpublished paper, *EEF*, p. 1.
28. Ibid., p. 14.
29. Ibid., ibid.
30. Ibid., p. 20.
31. Ibid., p. 22.
32. Ibid., p. 18A (Edwards' pagination).
33. Ibid., ibid.
34. Ibid., p. 42.
35. Ibid., p. 47, second page numbered 50.
36. Ibid., p. 49.
37. Ibid., p. 69.
38. *A Thousand Miles*, 'Preface to the First Edition', p. vii.
39. Ibid., pp. 69–70.
40. Ibid., 'Preface to the First Edition'.
41. Ibid., pp. 232–3.
42. Ibid., p. 319.
43. Nisan Peres, *Focus East*, p. 130.
44. *A Thousand Miles*, pp. 196–7.
45. Ibid., ibid.
46. Barbara Maria Stafford, *Voyage into Substance*, especially pp. 1–33 and Charles L. Batten, *Pleasurable Instruction*.
47. *A Thousand Miles*, p. 236.
48. Ibid., p. 195.
49. Ibid., p. 231.

CHAPTER 12:   AN 'ORIENTALIST' COUPLE: ANNE BLUNT, WILFRID SCAWEN BLUNT AND THE PILGRIMAGE TO NAJD

1. For 'the couple' or 'Writing Couples' see Alice Jardine, 'Death Sentences: Writing Couples and Ideology', in Susan Rubin Suleiman (ed.), *The Female Body in Western Culture* (Cambridge Mass., 1986) pp.

84–99. My usage of the two terms is historical and is not concerned with their ontological meanings.
2. Ibid., p. 85.
3. Gertrude Himmelfarb, 'The Genealogy of Morals from Clapham to Bloomsbury', in *Marriage and Morals among the Victorians*, p. 23; Noel Annan, 'The Intellectual Aristocracy'.
4. Albert Hourani, 'Wilfrid Scawen Blunt and the Revival of the Middle East', in *Europe and the Middle East*, pp. 97–104.
5. Wilfrid S. Blunt, *The Secret History of the English Occupation of Egypt, Being a Personal Narrative of Events* (London, 1907) p. 8.
6. Anne Blunt, BL, add. mss. 53889, 6 Nov. 1878.
7. Anne Blunt, *Bedouin Tribes of the Euphrates*, vol. II, p. 160.
8. Anne Blunt, *Pilgrimage to Nejd*, p. xxxiv.
9. Giovanni Belzoni, *Narrative of the Operations and Recent Discoveries*, quoted in Anthony Satin, *Lifting the Veil, British Society in Egypt, 1768–1956* (London, 1989) p.36.
10. Esmé Scott-Stevenson, *Our Ride Through Syria and Asia Minor*, preface.
11. See for example Hourani, 'Wilfrid Scawen Blunt'; *Said*, pp. 195, 237; Thomas Assad, *Three Victorian Travellers, Burton, Blunt Doughty* (London, 1964) pp. 93–4.
12. In addition to Hourani and Assad see Kathryn Tidrick, *Heart Beguiling Araby* (Cambridge, 1981). The fullest biographical account is Elisabeth Longford, *A Pilgrimage of Passion, the Life of Wilfrid Scawen Blunt* (London, 1976). See also *Edith Finch* and for Blunt's involvement in the nationalist movement Martin Kramer, *Islam Assembled, the Advent of Muslim Congresses (New York, 1986).*
13. See Earl of Lytton, *Wilfrid Scawen Blunt, A Memoir by His Grandson, The Earl of Lytton* (London, 1961); Max Egerton, *The Cousins, the Friendship, Opinions and Activities of Wilfrid Scawen Blunt and George Wyndham* (London, 1977), pp. 53–4. For an exception from the biographer's view, see Longford, *A Pilgrimage of Passion.*
14. BL, add. mss. 54673, 23 April 1873.
15. Quoted in Egermont, *The Cousins*, p. 262.
16. 4 June 1877; 8 June 1877; 19 April 1869. Quoted in Longford, *A Pilgrimage of Passion*, p. 71.
17. The comparison with Lady Byron is Lytton's. See *Wilfrid Scawen Blunt*, p. 291. For sympathetic accounts see Hourani, 'Wilfrid Scawen Blunt'; Longford, *A Pilgrimage*, p. 150; Tidrick, *Heart Beguiling Araby*, p. 120.
18. A letter to Ralph Wentworth, Simla, 19 May 1879, 'Wilfrid proposes to begin at once to write a 'pilgrimage to Nejd' 1 vol [sic] full of pictures . . . He has indeed began looking through my journals with a view of arranging them. I have got the materials for no end of pictures'. BL, add. mss. 54095.
19. *A Pilgrimage to Nejd*, 'preface by the Editor', pp. xv–xviii.
20. Ibid., pp. xvi–xvii.
21. BL, add. mss 53897 10 Jan; 11 January 1879.
22. Letter to Ralph Wentworth, London 15 December, 1879, BL, add.

mss. 54095, vol. CCLXXIX.

23. Thomas Assad, *Three Victorian Travellers*, pp. 114, 118, 134–5.

24. Wilfrid Scawen Blunt, 'A Visit to Jebel Shammar (Nejd). New Routes through Northern and Central Arabia', *Proceedings of the Royal Geographical Society*, no, II, February 1880, p. 82. *Pilgrimage to Nejd*, xxx–xxxi.

25. Gifford Palgrave, *Narrative of a Years' Journey through Central and Eastern Arabia* (1862–3) (London, 1865) vol. I, p. 92.

26. *Pilgrimage to Nejd*, p. 158.

27. Blunt, 'A Visit to Jebel Shammar', pp. 94–5; add. mss. 53897, 23 January; *Pilgrimage to Nejd*, pp. 158–9.

28. Blunt, 'A Visit to Jebel Shammar', pp. 95–6.

29. Ibid., pp. 92–3; *Pilgrimage to Nejd*, pp. 69–70.

30. Palgrave, *Narrative*, vol. I, p. 91.

31. Ibid., p. 92.

32. Ibid., ibid.

33. *Pilgrimage to Nejd*, pp. 155–6.

34. Assad, *Three Victorian Travellers*, pp. 67–9; Mary Joan Reinehr, *The Writings of Wilfrid Scawen Blunt, An Introduction and Study* (Wisconsin, 1940) pp. 158–66; Longford, *A Pilgrimage of Passion*.

35. See *Longford*, ibid.

36. Quoted in *Longford*, p. 59.

37. Ibid., ibid.

38. Ibid., ibid. Lytton, *Wilfrid Scawen Blunt*, pp. 290–91.

39. A letter to Wilfrid, 31 July 1917, quoted in Lytton, ibid., pp. 301–2; Longford, *Pilgrimage*, pp. 148–9.

40. A letter to Ralph Wentworth, Simla, 19 May 1879, BL, add. mss. 54095, vol. CCLXXIX.

41. See above, note 15.

42. *Pilgrimage to Nejd*, p. XX.

43. Ibid., pp. 186, 207–8 (entitled 'The Happy Mountains').

44. Kramer, Martin, 'Pen and Purse: Sabundji and Blunt', unpublished draft.

45. Judith Baroness Wentworth, *The Authentic Arab Horse* (1942), p. 69.

46. *Tidrik*, pp. 5–32.

47. Ibid. pp. 97–8.

48. Assad, *Three Victorian Travellers*; Tidrick 136–57, especially 140–1.

49. Anne Blunt, *Bedouin Tribes of the Euphrates*, vol. II p. 108, for Sheik Medjuel; pp. 314–15, for Faris.

50. Hourani, 'Wilfrid Scawen Blunt', pp. 89–90, 102.

51. 10 December 1878, BL add. mss. 53880.

52. Ibid., ibid.

53. Ibid., ibid.

54. BL, add. mss. 53899 23 January 1879; *Pilgrimage*, p. 216.

55. *Pilgrimage*, pp. 311–12.

56. BL, add. mss. 53903, 16 April 1879.

57. *The Authentic Arabian Horse*, pp. 311–12.

58. Ibid., Chapter VI, 'The Golden Horsemen of Arabia', pp. 109–41, for her knowledge of the written sources.

59. Ibid., p. 312.
60. Ibid., ibid.
61. Ibid., pp. 86–8, 92–4.
62. Ibid., pp. 87–8.

CONCLUSION

1. Isabel Burton, *The Inner Life in Syria*, vol. I, 'preface', p. vii.
2. Gertrude Lowthian Bell, *The Desert and the Sown* (1907, repr. London, 1985).
3. Hornby, *In and Around Constantinople*, vol. I, p. 157; Harvie, *Turkish Harems*, p. 91.
4. Melek Hanîm, *Thirty Years in the Harem, or the Autobiography of Melek Hanîm, Wife of H. H. Kibrizie-Mehmet-Pasha* (London, 1872). For other autobiographical writings consult Mervat Hatem, *Through Each Other's Eyes*.
5. James Clifford, 'On Ethnographic Authority'.
6. Bowman-Dodd, *The Palaces of the Sultan*, p. 456.
7. *Domestic Life in Palestine*, p. 372.
8. Chandra Talpade Mohanty, 'Under Western Eyes: Feminist Scholarship and Colonial Discourses', *Boundary*, 2, 12 (Fall 1984), pp. 333–58.
9. Lucie Duff-Gordon, *Letters from Egypt*, p. 380.
10. Clifford Geertz, quoted in Rosseau and Porter, *Exoticism and the Enlightenment*, p. 1.
11. See Peter Gay, *The Bourgeois Experience*.

Bibliography

A. MANUSCRIPT SOURCES

1. British Library

Anne Blunt, Diaries, Wentworth Bequest, add. mss. 53889–53893, vols 73–7; 53896–53901, vols 80–85.
——, Sketch Books, add. mss. 54048, vol. 232; 54049, vol. 233.
——, Correspondence with Ralph Gordon, Noel Milbanke, Baron Wentworth, add. mss. 54095, vol. 269.
Wilfrid Scawen Blunt, Diaries, Wentworth Bequest, add. mss. 54076.
Duff-Gordon Lucie, letters, Hekekeyan Papers, add. mss. 37463, f. 287; f. 331.
Pardoe Julia, Correspondence, Bentley Papers, add. mss. 46614, f. 308; 46615, ff. 172–3; Biography, add. mss. 28.551.

2. Israel State Archives, Jerusalem

8(2) 786.
6(4) 786.

3. Israel Trust for the Anglican Church, Jerusalem

Minutes for the Dorcas Society (1849–54).

4. Palestine Exploration Fund, London

Jerusalem Literary Society, Minutes, PEF (JER) 6.
Correspondence, PEF (JER) 7.
Water Relief Society, PEF (JER 8–37).

5. Egypt Exploration Fund, London

Amelia Edwards, 'The Social and Political Position of Women in Ancient Egypt', unpublished paper.

6. Royal Geographical Society, London

Gertrude Bell, Notebooks.
Mabel Bent, Correspondence.
Papers related to the admission of women.

Alexandrine Tinné, Notebooks.

7. Somerville College, Oxford

Amelia Edwards' papers and drawings.

8. University College, London, Department of Rare Books and Manuscripts at the Science Division

Amelia Edwards' papers.

9. Private collections

(a) Nathan Schur, Tel-Aviv.
(b) Jacob Wharman, Jerusalem.

B. TRAVEL BOOKS AND ETHNOGRAPHIC LITERATURE

Barclay, Sarah Mathilda, *Hadji in Syria; or Three Years in Jerusalem* (Philadelphia, 1858).

B. M. A., *Diary of Travels through Palestine* (Women's Printing Society, 1898).

Baillie, E. C. L., *A Sail to Smyrna: or, an Englishwoman's Journal: Including Impressions of Constantinople, a Visit to a Turkish Harem, and a Railway Journey to Ephesus* (London, 1873).

Beaufort, Emily, *Egyptian Sepulchres and Syrian Shrines Including Some Stay in the Lebanon, at Palmyra and in Western Turkey* (London, 1861).

Beke, Emily Alston, *Jacob's Flight; or, a Pilgrimage to Harran, and thence in the Patriarch's Footsteps into the Promised Land* (London, 1865).

Bell, Gertrude Lowthian, *Amurath to Amurath* (London, 1911).

——, *Notes on a Journey through Cilicia and Lyconnia* (Paris, 1907).

——, *Palace and Mosque at Ukhaidir, A Study in Early Mohammedan Architecture* (Oxford, 1914).

——, *Syria, the Desert and the Sown* (London, 1907).

Belzoni, Sarah, 'An Account of Women in Egypt, Nubia and Syria', in Giovanni Battista Belzoni, *Narrative of the Operations and Recent Discoveries Within the Pyramids, Temples, Tombs and Excavations in Egypt* (London, 1820).

Bensley, Agnes Dorothee, *Our Journey to Sinai; a Visit to the Convent of St. Catarina with a Chapter on the Sinai Palimpsest* (London, RTS, 1896).

Bent, James Theodore and Mabel V. Anna, *Southern Arabia* (London, 1900).

Bibesco, Marthe Lucie, *The Eight Paradises*, (New York, 1909).

Bird, Mary Rebecca Stewart, *Persian Women and their Creed* (London, CMS, 1899).

Bishop, Isabella Lucy Bird, *Journeys in Persia and Kurdistan Including a*

Summer in the Upper Karun Region and a Visit to the Nestorian Rayahs,
2 vols (London, 1891).

Blunt, Anne Noel, *Bedouin Tribes of the Euphrates* (London, 1878).

——, *A Pilgrimage to Nejd, the Cradle of the Arab Race, a visit to the Court of the Emir and 'Our' Persian Campaign* (London, 1879).

Blunt, Fanny Janet, *The People of Turkey; Twenty Years' Residence Among the Bulgarians, Greeks, Albanians, Turks and Armenians, by a Counsul's Daughter and Wife* (London, 1878).

Blackwood, Alicia, *Narrative of a Personal Experience and Impressions during a Residence on the Bosphorus throughout the Crimean War* (London, 1881).

Bowles, Charles and Susan M., *A Nile Voyage* (Tokyo, 1897) (n.d.).

——, *Sketches of National Character, A Charming Book about a Dahabieh Voyage* (n.d.).

Bowman, Anne, *Travels of Orlando; or, a Tour Round the World* (London, 1853).

——, *The Young Nile Voyagers* (London, 1868).

Brassey, Annie, *A Voyage on the 'Sunbeam', our Home on the Ocean for Eleven Months* (London, 1878).

——, *Sunshine and Storm in the East, or Cruises to Cyprus and Constantinople* (London, 1880).

——, *Egypt after the War* (n.p. 1884).

Bremer, Frederika, *Travels to the Holy Land* (London, 1861).

Brodrick, Mary, *A Handbook for Travellers in Lower and Upper Egypt* (London, 1896).

——, *A Handbook for Travellers in Syria and Palestine* (London, 1903).

Buckingham, James Silk, *Travels in Mesopotamia, Including a Journey from Aleppo, Across the Euphrates to Orfah through the Plains of the Turcomanes, to Diarbeker in Asia Minor* (London, 1827).

Buckhardt, Jean Louis, *Travels in Syria and the Holy Land* (London, 1882).

Burton, Isabel, *The Inner Life of Syria, Palestine and the Holy Land from my Private Journal*, 2 vols (London, 1875).

——*AEI, Arabia, Egypt, India, A Narrative of Travel* (London, 1897).

Burton, Richard, Francis, *Personal Narrative of a Pilgraimage to Al-Madinah and Meccah*, 2 vols (1856, Memorial Edition, 1893).

Butler, Lady Elisabeth Southerden Thompson, *Letters from the Holy Land* (London, 1903).

Butcher, Edith Louisa, *Things Seen in Egypt* (london, 1910).

Cary, Amelia, Viscountess Falkland, *Chow Chow, Being Selections from a Journal Kept in India, Egypt and Syria*, 2 vols (London, 1857).

Cecil, Mary Roberts, *Birds Notes from the Nile* (London, 1904).

Charles, Elizabeth Rundle, *Wanderings Over Bible Lands and Seas* (London, 1862).

Chauteaubriand, F. R. Vicomte de, *Itineraire de Paris à Jerusalem* (Paris, 1811).

Chennels, Ellen, *Recollections of an Egyptian Princess by her English Governess. Being a Record of Five Years Residence at the Court of Ismail Pasha Khedive* (London, 1893).

Cobbe, Frances Power, *Cities of the Past* (London, 1864).

Cobbold, Evelyn, Lady Murray, *Wayfarers in the Lybian Desert* (London, 1912).

Cook, Augusta, *By Way of the East: or, Gathered Light from our Travels in Palestine, Egypt, Smyrna, Ephesus etc.* (London, 1903).

Cowper, Countess, *A Month in Palestine* (London, 1889).

Craven, Elisabeth, margravene of Anspach, *A Journey through the Crimea to Constantinople in a Series of Letters Written in the Year MDCCLXXXVI* (London, 1789).

Cubley, Lucy Mathilda, *The Hills and Plains of Palestine* (London, 1860).

Cumming, Constance Frederica Gordon, *Via Cornwall to Egypt* (London, 1885).

——, *The Gorilla and the Dove. Outlines of a Voyage Without Discovery towards the Source of the Nile* (London, 1864).

Damer, Mary Georgina Emma Dawson, *Diary of a Tour in Greece, Turkey, Egypt and the Holy Land*, 2 vols (London, 1841).

Dautrey, William Cox and Mrs Cox, *The Bible in Palestine, or Hints from them by Which to Determine the Localities of the Crusification , the Transfiguration and other Great Events of Our Savior's Life, together with Notes of a Tour through the Holy Land during the Summer of 1843* (London, 1846).

De Bunsen, Victoria, *The Soul of a Turk* (London and New York, 1910).

Dodd, Anna Bowman, *The Palaces of the Sultan* (New York, 1903).

Doughty, Charles M., *Travels in Arabia Deserta*, 2 vols (New York, 2nd edn, n.d.).

Durham, Edith, *High Albania* (London, 1909).

——, *The Struggle for Scutari* (London, 1919).

Durand, Ella R., *An Autumn Tour in Western Persia* (London, 1902).

Eams, Jane A., *Another Budget: or Things Which I Saw in the East* (Boston, 1855).

——, *The Budget Closed* (Boston, 1860).

Edwards, Amelia Ann Blanford, *Pharaohs, Fellahs and Explorers* (New York, 1891).

——, *A Thousand Miles Up the Nile* (London, 1976).

Egerton, Harriet Catherine Granville, countess Ellesmere, *Egypt, a Description of the Land, People and Produce* (London, 1839).

——, *Egypt, the Peninsula of Mount Sinai and Arabia Petra with the Southern Part of Palestine, Shewing the Journeyings of the Israelites from Egypt to the Holy Land* (New York, 1861).

——, *Journal of a Tour in the Holy Land in May and June 1840* (London, 1840).

Eliot, Frances Minto, *Diary of an Idle Woman in Constantinople* (London, 1871).

Ellison, Grace, *An Englishwoman in a Turkish Harem* (London, 1915).

Ely, Jane, marchioness Loftus, *Mafeesh, or Nothing New: The Journal of a Tour in Greece, Turkey, Egypt, the Sinai Desert, Petra, Palestine, Syria and Russia*, 2 vols (London, 1870).

Elwood, Anne Katherine Curtis, *Narrative of a Journey Overland from England, by the Continent of Europe, Egypt and the Red Sea, to India; Including Residence There and Voyage, in the Years 1825, 26, 27 and 28*, 2 vols (London, 1830).

Evans, Katherine and Cheevers, Sarah, *This is a Short Relation of Some of the Cruel Sufferings of K. E. and S. Cheevers in the Inquisition in the Isle of Malta* (London, 1662).

Fay, Eliza, *Original Letters from India; Containing a Narrative of a Journey through Egypt and the Author's Imprisonment at Calicut* (1817, London, 1926).

Finn, Ann Elisabeth, *Home in the Holy Land, a Tale* (London, 1866).

——, *A Third Year in Jerusalem, a Tale Illustrating Customs and Incidents of Modern Jerusalem* (London, 1869).

——, *Sunrise over Jerusalem* (n.d., n.p.).

Fleming, George see Fletcher, Julia Constance.

Floyer, Edith Louisa, *A Strange Journey; or Pictures from Egypt and the Soudan*, 3 vols (London, 1882).

——, *Egypt as We Knew it* (London, 1911).

Fountaine, Margaret, *Love Among the Butterflies, the Diaries of a Wayward Determined and Passionate Victorian Lady*, ed. W. F. Cater (Harmondsworth, repr. 1983).

Fullerton, Amy, *A Lady's Ride Through Palestine and Syria; with Notices of Egypt and the Canal of Suez* (London, 1872).

G.C., *Fortnight's Tour Amongst Arabs on Mount Lebanon; Including a Visit to Damscus, Ba'albeck, the Cedars, Natural Bridge, etc.* (London, 1876).

Garnett, Mary Lucy Jane, *Home Life in Turkey* (New York, 1909).

——, *Mysticism and Magic in Turkey. An Account of the Religious Doctrines, Monastic Organisation and Ecstatic Powers of the Dervish Order* (London, 1912).

——, *Turkish Life in Town and Country* (New York and London, 1909).

——, *The Turkish People; their Social Life, Religious Beliefs and Institutions and Domestic Life* (London, 1900).

——, *The Women of Turkey and their Folklore*, 2 vols (London, 1890–91).

Gibson, Margaret Dunlop (Smith), *How the Codex was Found, a Narrative of two Visits to Sinai from Mrs Lewis's Journals 1892–3* (Cambridge, 1893).

Goodnow, Elisabeth, Cooper, *The Women of Egypt* (London, 1914).

——, *The Harem and the Purdah: Studies of Oriental Women* (London, 1915).

Goodrich-Freer, Ada M., *In a Syrian Saddle* (London, 1905).

——, *Inner Jerusalem* (London, 1904).

——, *Things Seen in Palestine* (London, 1913).

Gordon, Lady Lucie Duff, *Letters from Egypt* (London, 1870).

——, *Last Letters from Egypt to which are added Letters from the Cape* (London, 1875).

Griffith, M. C., Hume, *Behind the Veil in Persia and Turkish Arabia, an Account of an Englishwoman's Eight Years' Residence Amongst the Women of the East* (London, 1909).

Griswold, Louise M., *A Woman's Pilgrimage to the Holy Land or Pleasant Days Abroad* (Hartford, 1871).

Harvey, Annie, Jane, *Turkish Harems and Circassian Homes* (London, 1871).

——, *Our Cruise in the Claymore, with a Visit to Damascus and the Lebanon* (London, 1861).

Herbert, Mary Elisabeth, baroness, *Cradle Lands* (London, 1867).

Hornby, Emilia Bithynia, Lady Marconi, *In and Around Stamboul* (Philadelphia, 1858).

Hornby, Emily, *Sinai and Petra, the Journal of Emily Hornby in 1899 and 1901* (1907).

——, *Nile Journal* (n.p., 1908).

Hunt, Mrs W. H., *Children at Jerusalem a Sketch of Modern Life in Syria*, (n.p., 1881).

Hutton, Catherine, *The Tour of Africa, Containing a Concise Account of All the Countries in that Quarter of the Globe Hitherto Visited by Europeans; with the Manners and Customs of Inhabitants* (London, 1819).

Janeway, Catherine, *Ten Weeks in Egypt and Palestine* (London, 1908).

Jebb, Louisa, Wilkins, *By Desert Ways to Baghdad* (London, 1908).

King, Annie, Dr. *Liddon's Tour in Egypt and Palestine in 1886* (London, 1891).

Kinglake, Alexander William, *Eothen, or Traces of Travel Brought Home from the East* (1844, repr. Century Books, 1982).

Lane, Edward William, *Manners and Customs of the Modern Egyptian*, 3 vols (London, 1836).

Leland, Lilian, *Travelling Alone, A Woman's Journey Around the World* (New York, 1870).

Lloyd, Susette, Harriet, Smith, *The Daughters of Syria. A Narrative of the Efforts of the Late Mrs Brown Thompson, for the Evangelisation of the Syrian Females*, ed. H. B. Tristram (London, 1872).

Lott, Emmeline, *The English Governess in Egypt, Harem Life in Egypt and Constaninople*, 2 vols (London, 1866).

——, *The Grand Pascha's Cruise on the Nile in the Viceroy of Egypt's Yacht*, 2 vols (Newby, 1869).

——, *The Mohaddehyn in the Palace of Ghezire, or Nights in the Harems*, 2 vols (London, 1867).

Lushington, Sarah Gascoyne, *Narrative of a Journey from Calcutta to Europe, by Way of Egypt in the Year 1827–8* (London, 1829).

Mackintosh, Mary, *Damascus and Its People* (London, 1883).

Martineau, Harriet, *Eastern Life Present and Past* (London, 1848).

Max-Müller, Georgina, *Letters from Constantinople* (London and New York, 1897).

Melek Hanim, *Thirty Years in the Harem* (Berlin, 1872), 2 vols.

Menzies, Sutherland, see Stone, Elisabeth.

Miller, Ellen Clare Pearson, *Eastern Sketches: Notes of Scenery, Schools and Tent Life in Syria and Palestine* (Edinburgh, 1871).

Miller, Ellen E., *Alone Through Syria* (London, 1891).

Montefiore, Judith, *Notes from a Private Journal of a Visit to Egypt and Palestine, by Way of Italy and the Meditteranean* (published privately, 1855).

Montagu, Lady Mary Wortley, *The Complete Letters*, 3 vols, ed. Robert Halsband (Oxford, repr. 1967).

Mott, M. Augusta, *Stones of Palestine. Notes of a Ramble Through the Holy Land* (London, 1865).

Nightingale, Florence, *Letters from Egypt* (London, 1854).

Oliphant, Margaret, *Jerusalem, its History and Hopes from the Days of David to the Time of Christ* (London, 1891).

Osgwood, Irene Andrews, *When Pharaoh Dreams, Being the Impression of a Woman-of-Mode in Egypt* (London, n.d.).

Paine, Caroline, *Palestine Past and Present Pictorial and Description* (n.p., n.d. circa 1900).

——, *Asia Minor, Egypt* (n.p., 1850).

——, *Tent and Harem; Notes of an Oriental Trip* (New York, 1859).

Palgrave, Gifford, *Narrative of a Year's Journey through Central and Eastern Arabia (1862–3)*, 2 vols (London, 1865).

Pardoe, Julia, *The Beauties of the Bosphorus Illustrated in a Series of Views on Constantinople and its Environs from Original Drawings by W. H. Bartlett* (London, 1839).

——, *The City of the Sultan and the Domestic Manners of the Turks in 1836*, 2 vols (London, 1837).

Platt, Miss, *Journal of a Tour Through Egypt, the Peninsula of Sinai and the Holy Land in 1838/9*, 2 vols (private publication, 1841/2).

Poole, Sophia Lane, *The Englishwoman in Egypt: Letters from Cairo Written during a Residence there in 1842, 3 and 4 with E. W. Lane by his Sister* (London, 1844).

Postans, Marriane Young, *Our Camp in Turkey, and the Way to It* (London, 1854).

——, *Facts and Fictions, Illustrative of Oriental Character*, 3 vols (London, 1844).

Ramsay, Mrs W. M., *Everyday Life in Turkey* (London, 1897).

Rattray, Harriet, *Country Life in Syria, Passages of Letters Written from Anti-Lebanon* (London, 1876).

Reute, Emilie, *Memoirs of an Arabian Princess* (n.d., n.p., 1907).

Roberts, Emma, *Notes on an Overland Journey through France and Egypt to Bombay* (London, 1841).

Rogers, Mary Eliza, *Domestic Life in Palestine* (London, 1863).

——, 'Damascus' in C. W. Wilson, *Picturesque Palestine, Sinai and Egypt* (London, 1880).

Romer, Isabella Frances, *The Bird of Passage, or Flying Glimpses of Many Lands* (1849).

——, *A Pilgrimage to the Temples and Tombs of Egypt, Nubia and Palestine in 1845–6*, 2 vols (London, 1846).

Slade, Adolphus, *Records of Travels in Turkey, Greece and of a Cruise in the Black Sea with the Captain Pasha, in the Years 1829, 1830 and 1831* (London, 1833).

Stanhope, Lady Hester Lucy, *Memoirs as Related by Herself in Conversation with her Physician*, ed. Charles Meyron (London, 1845).

——, *Travels of Lady Hester Stanhope, Forming the Completion of her Memoirs* (London, 1896).

Straiton, Mrs M., *Two Lady Tramps Abroad, A Compilation of Letters Descriptive of Nearly a Year's Travel in Asia Minor, Egypt, the Holy Land and Turkey* (Evening Journal Press, 1881).

Stevenson-Scott Esmé, *Our Home in Cyprus* (London, 1880).

——, *Our Ride Through Asia Minor* (London, 1881).

Sykes, Ella Constance, *Through Syria on a Side Saddle* (London, 1898).

——, *Persia and its People* (London, 1910).

Taylor, Frances M., *Eastern Hospitals and English Nurses, the Narrative of Twelve Months' Experience in the Hospitals of Scutari by a Lady Volunteer*, 2 vols (London, 1856).

Temple, A. Augusta, *Flowers and Trees of Palestine* (London, 1907).

Thackeray, William Makepeace, *Notes of a Journey from Cornhill to Grand Cairo by Way of Lisbon, Athens, Constantinople and Jerusalem* (London, repr. 1846).

Thomas, Margaret, *Two Years in Palestine and Syria* (London, 1900).

Tobin, Lady Catherine, *The Land of Inheritance of Bible Scenes Revisited* (London, 1862).

———, *Shadows of the East, or Slight Sketches of Scenery, Persons and Customs from Observations during a Tour in 1853 and 1854 in Egypt, Palestine, Syria, Turkey and Greece* (London, 1855).

Vaka, Demetra Brown, *Haremlik* (Boston, 1909).

Vane, Frances, Anne, *A Narrative of a Visit to the Courts of Vienna* (London, 1844).

Vivanti, Anna, *A Journey to Crete, Constantinople, Naples and Florence* (private publication, 1865).

Walker, Mary Adelaide, *Eastern Life and Scenery with Excursion in Asia Minor, Mytilene, Crete and Rumania*, 2 vols (London, 1886).

West, Maria A., *West and East; on a Tour through Europe and the Holy Land* (London, 1878).

Whately, Mary Louisa, *Among the Huts in Egypt, Scenes from Real Life* (London, 1871).

———, *Behind the Curtain. Scenes from Life in Cairo* (London, 1883).

———, *Letters from Egypt to Plain Folk at Home* (London, 1879).

———, *Lost in Egypt* (London, R.T.S.).

———, *More About Ragged Life in Egypt* (London, 1864).

———, *Stories of Peasant Life on the Nile* (n.p., 1867).

Wheeler, Susan A., *Missions in Eden: Glimpses of Life in the Valley of the Euphrates* (New York, 1899).

C.   LITERARY WORKS CITED

Beckford, William, *Vathek* (1783, repr. Harmondsworth, 1983).

Bunyan, John, *The Pilgrim's Progress* (Harmondsworth, Penguin edn, 1987).

Burton, Richard Francis, *A Plain and Literal Translation of the Arabian Night's Entertainment*, 17 vols (London, 1884–86).

Byron, Lord George Gordon, *The Complete Poetical Works*, ed. J. J. McGann (Oxford, 1980).

Diderot, Denis, *Les Bijoux indiscrets*, in *Oeuvres Romanesques* (col. Paris, 1962).

Disraeli, Benjamin, Lord Beaconsfield, *Tancred, or the New Crusade*, 2 vols (London, 1847).

Flaubert, Gustave, *Oeuvres* (Paris, 1952).

Galland, Antoine, *Le Mille et une nuits* (Paris, 1704–1717) (12 vols).

Lane, Edward William, *The Thousand and One Nights*, 3 vols (London, 1838–40).

Loti, Pierre, *Aziyad* (Paris, 1879).

Marana, Giovanni Paolo, *Letters Writ by a Turkish Spy, who Liv'd five and forty Years Undiscovered at Paris* (1687–99) (8 vols).

Montesquieu, Charles-Louis de Secondat, *The Persian Letters* (1721, repr. Harmondsworth, 1987).

Moore, Thomas, *Lalla Rookh: an Oriental Romance* 6th edn (London, 1817).

Morier, James, *The Adventures of Hajji Baba of Ispahan* (London, 1824) (3 vols).

——, *Ayesha, the Maid of Kars* (London, 1834).

——, *Zohrab, the Hostage* (London, 1832).

Richardson, Samuel, *Clarissa, or the History of a Young Lady* (1747–9, repr. 1986).

Thackeray, William Makepeace, *Vanity Fair* (Signet Classic edn, New York, 1981).

Voltaire, *Candide, or the Optimist. Rasselas, Prince of Abyssinia by Samuel Johnson* (London, 1884).

——, *Zadig or the Book of Fate. An Oriental History* (London, 1749).

——, *The White Bull, an Oriental History. From an Ancient Syrian Manuscript. Communicated by Mr. Voltaire* (London, MDCCLXXVIII).

D. WORKS ON WOMEN AND SEXUAL MORALS CITED

Astell, Mary A., *Serious Proposals to the Ladies for the Advancement of their Own True and Greatest Interest* (London, 1694).

——, *Some Reflections upon Marriage* (London, 1770).

Blackstone, William, *Commentaries on the Laws of England*, 4 vols, 18th edn (1829).

Hume, David, 'On Polygamy and Divorce', *Essays Literary, Moral and Political* (n.d.).

Kames, Lord, *Sketches of the History of Man*, 4 vols (London 1796).

Lecky, W. E. H., *History of European Morals*, 2 vols (London, 1869).

Locke, John, *The Second Treatise on Government* ed. J. W. Vough, 3rd edn (1966).

Martineau, Harriet, *Society in America*, 3 vols (London, 1839).

——, *How to Observe Manners and Morals* (New York, 1838).

Montagu, Lady Mary Wortley, 'the Nonsense of Commonsense', in Lord Wharncliffe (ed.), *The Letters and Works of Lady Mary Wortley Montagu*, 3rd edn (London, 1862), vol. 2.

——, *Women Not Inferior to Men, or a Short and Modest Vindication of the Natural Right of the Fair Sex to a Perfect Equality* by Sophia (n.p., 1743).

Montesquieu Charles-Louis de Secondat, *De l'esprit des lois, The Spirit of the Laws: a Compendium of the first English edition*, ed. David Wallace (Berkeley, 1977).

Westermark, Edward, *The History of Human Marriage* 3rd edn (London and New York, 1907).

E. SCHOLARLY WORKS INCLUDING WRITINGS ON BIBLICAL
GEOGRAPHY, ARCHAEOLOGY AND OTHER CRITICAL WORKS
ON THE SCRIPTURES

Balden, s. ph. j., Penger, 'Women of the East', *PEF Quarterly Statement* (1899)
p. 160 and (1900) pp. 171–90.

Bartlett, William M. *Walks about the City and Environs of Jerusalem* (London,
1842).

Lewis, Agnes Smith, *Select Narratives of Holy Women from the Syro Antiochene
or Sinai Palimpest as Written above the Old Syriac Gospels* (London, 1900).

——, *The Four Gosples Translated from the Sinai Palimpest* (London, 1894).

Maccalister, R. A. S., 'Gleanings from the Minute Books of the Jerusalem
Literary Society.' *Palestine Exploration Quarterly*, Jan. 1908, Jan. 1909, Jan.
1910 pp. 52–60; 42–9, 27–31 and 116–26.

Martineau, Harriet, *Traditions of Palestine* (London, 1830).

Munk, Solomon, *La Palestine: Description géographique historique et
archéologique* (Paris, 1845).

Palestine Exploration Fund, *Our Work in Palestine: Being an Account of the
Different Expeditions Sent Out to the Holy Land by the Committee of the
Palestine Exploration Fund* (London, 1877).

——, *PEQ, Palestine Exploration Quarterly, Embodying the Quarterly Statement
of the Palestine Exploration Fund and the Bulletin of the British School of
Archaeology in Jerusalem*, 1869–1914.

——, *Twenty One Years' Work in the Holy Land* (London, 1886).

——, *Thirty Years' Work in the Holy Land, A Record and Summary, 1865–95*
(London, 1895).

——, *Fifty Years' Work in the Holy Land: A Record and Summary, 1865–1915*
(London, 1915).

Robinson, Edward, *Biblical Researches in Palestine* (London, 1856).

——, *Later Biblical Researches in Palestine* (London, 1856).

Royal Geographical Society, *Proceedings and Monthly Record of Geography*
(1892).

——, *Geographical Journal* (1888–93; 1913).

Strauss, Frederick David, *The Life of Jesus. trans. from the 4th German edn by
George Eliot* (London, 1846).

Thomson, William McLure, *The Land and the Book* (London, 1859).

Tristram, Henry Baker, *A Natural History of the Bible* (London, 1867).

——, *Fauna and Flora of Palestine With the Western Survey of Palestine* (London,
PEF, 1884).

Warren, Charles, *Underground Jerusalem* (London, 1875).

Wilkinson, Sir Gardner, *Manners and Customs of the Ancient Egyptians,
Including their Private Life, Government, Laws, Art, Manufactures, Regligion
and Early History* (London, 1837).

——, *The Egyptians in the Time of the Pharaohs [with] Egyptian Hieroglyphs*
(London, 1856).

F. TRAVEL GUIDES, MANUALS FOR TRAVELLERS AND POPULAR WRITINGS ON TRAVEL

Adams, W. H. Davenport, *Celebrated Women Travellers of the Nineteenth Century* (London, 1883).

Cook, Thomas and Son, *Autumnal Programmes of Personally Conducted, Partially Assisted and Independent Tours to all Parts of the Continent, Algeria, Egypt and Palestine* (1875).

——, *Programmes of Personally Conducted and Independent Palestine Tours with Extensions to Egypt and the Nile, Sinai, Petra, Moab, the Houran, Turkey, Greece and Italy* (1875–6).

Davison, Lilias C., *Hints to Lady Travellers: at Home and Abroad* (London, 1889).

'Lady Travellers', *Blackwood's Magazine*, vol. 160 (July, 1896) pp. 49–67.

'Lady Travellers', *Quarterly Review*, vol. 76 (1845).

Moore, Mary MacLeod, 'Distinguished Women Travellers', *The Lady*, 17 April 1913.

Mundrell, Frank, *Heroines of Travel* (London, 1897).

——, *Stories of Travel Adventure* (London, 1899).

Murray, John, *A Handbook for Travellers in the Ionian Islands, Greece, Turkey, Asia Minor and Constantinople* (1840).

——, *A Handbook for Travellers in Constantinople, the Bosphorus, Dardanells, Brussa and Plain of Troy with General Hints for Travellers in Turkey* (1871).

——, *A Handbook for Travellers in Turkey, Describing Constantinople, European Turkey, Asia Minor, Armenia and Mesapotamia* (1854).

Robins, Elisabeth, 'The New Art of Travel', *The Fortnightly Review*, vol. 84, New Series, p. 470.

'The Romance of Modern Travel', *Quarterly Review*, vol. 149 (1880).

Royal Geographical Society, *Hints to Travellers, Edited by a Committee of Council of the Royal Geographical Society* (1878).

——, *Hints to Travellers, Scientific and General, Edited for the Council of the Royal Geographical Society*, 7th edn (1893).

Wilkinson, Sir Gardner, *Hand-Book for Travellers in Egypt* (London, 1847).

SECONDARY BIBLIOGRAPHY

Abel, Elisabeth; Hirsh, Marianne and Langland, Elisabeth (eds), *The Voyage in: Fictions of Female Development* (Hanover, New Hampshire, 1983).

Adams, Percy G., *Travel Literature and the Evolution of the Novel Before 1800* (Kentucky, 1983).

——, *Travellers and Travel Liars 1660–1800* (New York, repr. 1980).

Ahmed, Leila, *Edward William Lane, A Study of his Life and Works and of British Ideas of the Middle East in the 19th Century* (London, 1978).

Albright, W. F., *Archaeology of Palestine and the Bible* (London, 1949).

——, *From the Stone Age to Christianity: Monotheism and the Historical Process* (Baltimore, 1940).

——, *Archaeology and the Religion of Israel* (Baltimore, 1942).

——, *Archaeology, Historical Analogy and Early Biblical Tradition* (Louisiana, 1966).

Alexander, Sally, 'Women, Class and Sexual Differences in the 1830s and the 1840s: Some Reflections on the Writing of Feminist History', *History Workshop*, no. 17 (1984).

Amelinkx, Franz C., Megay Joyce N. (eds), *Travel, Quest and Pilgrimage as Literary Themes, Studies in Honour of Reino Virtaner.*

Anderson, Michael S., *The Eastern Question, 1774–1923* (London, 1966).

Arberry, A. J., *British Orientalists* (London, n.d.).

Ariés, Philippe and André Béjin (eds), *Western Sexuality, Practice and Precept in Past and Present Times* (Oxford, repr. 1985).

Assad, Thomas, *Three Victorian Travellers, Burton, Blunt, Doughty* (London, 1964).

Auerbach, Nina, *Communities of Women: An Idea in Fiction* (Cambridge, Mass., 1978).

Avitzur, Shmuel, *Daily Life in Palestine in the Nineteenth Century* (Tel-Aviv, 1972) (Hebrew).

Bachelard, Gaston, *The Poetics of Space,* trans. Maria Jolas (New York, 1964).

Baer, Gabriel, *Studies in the Social History of Modern Egypt* (Chicago, 1969).

Ballhatchet, K., *Race, Sex and Class Under the Raj* (London, 1980).

Barker, Francis (ed.), *Essex Conference on the Sociology of Literature: Europe and its Others,* 2 vols (Colchester, 1985).

Batten, Charles, *Pleasurable Instruction: Form and Convention in Eighteenth-Century Travel Literature* (Berkeley, 1978).

Baudet, Henri, *Paradise on Earth: Some Thoughts on European Images of Non-European Man* (New Haven, 1965).

Beck, Lois, Keddie Nikki, *Women in the Muslim World* (Cambridge, Mass., 1978).

Ben-Arieh, Yehoshua, *Jerusalem in the 19th Century, the Old City* (Jerusalem and New York, 1986).

——, *Jerusalem in the 19th Century, the New City* (Jerusalem and New York, 1984).

——, *The Rediscovery of the Holy Land in the 19th Century* (Jerusalem, 1979).

——, 'The Literature of Western Travellers to Palestine in the 19th Century as an Historical Source and Cultural Phenomenon', *Kathedra,* vol. 40 (1986), pp. 159–89 (Hebrew).

Bevis, Richard, *Bibliotheca Cisorientalia, an Annotated Checklist of Early English Travel-Books on the Near- and Middle East* (Boston, 1973).

Bidwell, Robin, *Travellers in Arabia* (London, 1976).

Birkett, Dea, *Spinsters Abroad, Victorian Lady Explorers* (Oxford, 1989).

Black, Jeremy, *The British and the Grand Tour* (London, 1985).

Blumberg, Arnold, *A View from Jerusalem 1849–58, the Consular Diary of James and Elisabeth Ann Finn* (New York, 1980).

Boahdiba, A., *Islam et sexualité* (Paris, 1975).

Booth, Wayne, C., *The Rhetoric of Fiction,* 2nd edn (Harmondsworth, 1983).

Boucé, Paul G., 'Some Sexual Beliefs and Myths in Eighteenth-Century Britain', in Boucé (ed.), *Sexuality in Eighteenth-Century Britain* (Manchester, 1984), pp. 28–47.

Bradley, Ian, *The Call to Seriousness: The Evangelical Impact on the Victorians* (New York, 1976).

Brodie, Fawn, *The Devil Drives, A Life of Sir Richard Burton* (New York, 1967).

Brown, L. Wallace, 'English Travel Books and Minor Poetry about the Near East in the 18th Century', *Philological Review*, vol. XVI, 1937.

Brumberg, Joan Jacobs, *Fasting Girls: The Emergence of Anorexia Nervosa as a Modern Disease* (Cambridge, Mass., 1988).

Burke, John G., 'The Wild Man's Paradise: Scientific Method and Racial Anthropology', in Edward Dudley and Maximilian Novak (eds), *The Wild Man Within: An Image in Western Thought from the Renaissance to Romanticism* (Pittsburg, 1972).

Cairncross, John, *After Polygamy Was Made a Sin, the Social History of Christian Polygamy* (London, 1974).

Callaway, Helen, *Gender, Ideology and Empire. European Women in Colonial Nigeria* (Oxford, 1987).

Cambridge History of English Literature, vol. XIV: *the 19th century*, Ch. VII, The Literature of Travel 1700–1900, pp. 240–57; vol. IV: Ch. V, 'Seafaring and Travel, the Growth of Professional Text-Books and Geographical Literature' (Cambridge).

Cameron, Ian, *To the Farthest End of Earth, the History of the Royal Geographical Society* (London, 1980).

Chadwick, Owen, *The Victorian Church Part I: 1829–59* (London, 1966); *Part II: 1860–1901* (1972).

Chew, Samuel C., *The Crescent and the Rose, Islam and England During the Renaissance* (New York, 1965).

Christ, C., 'Victorian Masculinity and the "Angel in the House"' in Martha Vicinus (ed.), *A Widening Sphere: Changing Roles of Victorian Women* (Indiana, 1977).

Clifford, James, 'Edward Said, Orientalism', *History and Theory*, vol. 19 (1980), pp. 204–24.

——, *The Predicament of Culture, Twentieth-Century Ethnography, Literature and Art* (Cambridge, Mass., 1988).

Codell, Julie F., 'Expression over Beauty: Facial Expression, Body Language, Circumstantiality in the Paintings of the Pre-Raphaelite Brotherhood', *Victorian Studies*, vol. 29, no. 2 (Winter 1986).

Cominos, Peter T., 'Late Victorian Social Respectability and the Social System' *International Review of Social History*, vol. VIII, no. 8 (1963) pp. 8–48, 216–50.

Conant, Maria Pike, 'The Oriental Tale in England in the 18th Century', *Studies in Comparative Literature* (Cambridge, 1908).

Cox, E.G., *A Reference Guide to the Literature of Travel* vol. I, *The Old World* (Washington, 1935); vol. II, *The New World* (1938).

Daniel, Norman, *Islam and the West: the Making of an Image* (Edinburgh, 1960).

——, *Islam, Europe and Empire* (Edinburgh, 1969).

David Deirdre, *Intellectual Women and Victorian Patriarchy, Harriet Martineau, Elizabeth Barrett Browning, George Eliot* (Ithaca, New York, 1987).

Davidoff, Leonore, *The Best Circles: Society and Etiquette and the Season* (London, 1973).

———, 'Class and Gender in Victorian England: the Diaries of Arthur J. Munby and Hannah Cullwick, *Feminist Studies*, no. 5 (1979).

Davidoff, Leonore and Chaterine Hall, *Family Fortunes, Men and Women of the English Middle-Class 1780–1850* (London, 1987).

Davis, Fanny, *The Ottoman Lady, A Social History from 1718 to 1918* (Westport Conn., 1986).

Dawson, Warren R., *Who Was Who in Egyptology* (London, EES, 1951).

Delamont, Sara, 'The Contradictions in Ladies' Education', in Sara Delamont and Lorna Duffin (eds), *The Nineteenth-Century Woman: Her Cultural and Physical World* (London, 1978).

Djavidan, Hanîm, *Harem Life* (New York, 1931).

Dodd, Philip (ed.), *The Art of Travel: Essay on Travel Writing* (London, 1982).

Douglas, Mary, *Purity and Danger, an Analysis of the Concepts of Pollution and Taboo* (New York, repr. 1988).

Egerton, Max, *The Cousins, the Friendship, Opinions and Activities of Wilfrid Scawen Blunt and George Wyndham* (London, 1977).

Elias, Norbert, *The Civilizing Process: the History of Manners* (Oxford, 1978).

Eliav, Mordechai, *Palestine and its Settlement in the Nineteenth Century* (Hebrew)(Jerusalem, 1978).

Ellman, Mary, *Thinking about Women* (New York, 1968).

Elshtain, Jean Bethke, *The Family in Modern Political Thought* (Amherst, 1982).

———, *Meditations on Modern Political Thought: Masculine/Feminine Themes from Luther to Arendt* (New York, 1986).

Esposito, J. L., *Women in Muslim Family Law* (Syracuse New York, 1982).

Etienne, Nona and Eleanor Leacock (eds), *Women and Colonisation: Anthropological Perspectives* (New York, 1980).

Fahnestock, Jeanne, 'The Heroine of Irregular Features: Physiognomy and Conventions of Heroine Description', *Victorian Studies* (Spring 1981).

Fedden, Robin, *English Travellers in the Middle East* (London, 1938).

Field, James A., *America and the Mediterranean World* (Princeton, 1969).

Finch, Edith, *Wilfrid Scawen Blunt* (London, 1938).

Finnie, David, *Pioneers East: the Early American Experience in the Middle East* (Cambridge, Mass., 1967).

Foucault, Michel, *A History of Sexuality*, vol. I: *An Introduction*, trans. Robert Huley (Paris, 1976, repr. 1978); vol. II, *The Use of Pleasure* (Paris 1984, repr. 1987).

Fox, Margaret Schmidt, *Passion's Child; the Extraordinary Life of Jane Digby* (London, 1978).

Frantz, R. W., 'The English Traveller and the Movement of Ideas, 1660–1732', *University Studies*, vols 22–30 (1932–3).

Freeth, Zahra, *Explorers of Arabia from the Renaissance to the End of the Victorian Era* (London, 1978).

Freud, Zigmund, 'A Disturbance of Memory on the Acropolis', *Character and Culture*, ed. Philip Rieff (New York, 1963) pp. 311–20.

Frye, Northrop, *The Secular Scripture, a Story of the Structure of Romance* (Cambridge, Mass., 1976).

Fussell, Paul, *Abroad: British Literary Travelling between the Wars* (Oxford, 1980).

Gail, Marzieh, *Persia and the Victorians* (London, 1951).

Gay, Peter, *The Bourgeois Experience, vol. I: Victoria to Freud* (Oxford, 1984); vol. II: *The Tender Passion* (1986).

Gerhardt, Mia J., *The Art of Story-Telling, A Literary Study of the Thousand and One Nights* (Lieden, 1963).

Gilbert, Sandra M. and Susan Gubar, *The Madwoman in the Attic: The Woman Writer and the Nineteenth-Century Literary Imagination* (New Haven, Conn., 1979).

Goodman, Susan, *Gertrude Bell* (Leamington Spa, 1985).

Goody, Jack, *The Development of Family and Marriage in Europe* (Cambridge, 1983).

Graham-Brown, Sarah, *Images of Women: The Portrayal of Women in Photography of the Middle-East 1860-1915* (New York, 1988).

Groot, Joana de, '"Sex" and "Race": The Construction of Language in Image in the Nineteenth Century', in Susan Mendus and Jane Rendall (eds), *Sexuality and Subordination, Interdisciplinary Studies of Gender in the Nineteenth Century* (London, 1989).

Grosrichard, Allan, *Structures du Sérail, la fiction du despotisme asiatique dans l'Occident classique* (Paris, 1979).

Habermas, J., 'The Public Sphere: an Encyclopedia Article', *New German Critique*, vol. 1, no. 3 (1974).

Hachicho, Mohamad A., 'English Travel Books about the Arab Near-East in the 18th Century, *Die Welt des Islams*, vol. 9, nos. 1–4 (1964), pp. 1–207.

Hall, Catherine, 'The Early Formation of Victorian Domestic Ideology', in Sally Burman (ed.), *Fit Work for Women* (London, 1979).

Halsband, Robert, 'Ladies of Letters in the 18th Century', *Papers Read at the Clark Library Seminar* (Los Angeles, 1969).

——, 'Lady Mary Wortley Montagu, Her Place in the 18th Century, *History Today*, vol. 16 (1966), pp. 94–102.

——, 'Lady Mary Montagu and the 18th Century Fiction', *Philological Quarterly*, vol. 45 (1966), pp. 145–56.

——, *The Life of Lady Mary Wortley Montagu* (Oxford, 1960).

——, 'A New Lady Mary Letter', *Philological Quarterly*, vol. 44 (1966), pp. 180–4.

——, 'A Plain Account of the Innoculating of the Small Pox by a Turkish Merchant', *Journal of the History of Medicine*, vol. 8 (1953) pp. 390–405.

Hamalian, Leo, *Ladies on the Loose, Women Travellers of the 18th and 19th Centuries* (London, 1981).

Hamilton, Malcolm, *Travel Index: A Guide to Books and Articles* (Phoenix, 1988).

Hannam, Michael, 'Some 19th Century Britons in Jerusalem', *Palestine Exploration Quarterly* (June 1982) pp. 53–65.

Harrison, J. F. C., *The Second Coming: Popular Millenarianism 1780–1850* (London, 1979).

Harper, M., 'Recovering the Other: Women and the Orient in Writings of Early 19th Century France', *Critical Matrix*, no. 1 (1985).

Hatem, Mervat, 'Class and Patriarchy as Competing Paradigms for the Study of Middle Eastern Women', *CSSN*, vol. 29, no. 4 (October 1987).

———, 'Through Each Other's Eyes, Egyptian, Levantine-Egyptian and European Women's Images of Themselves and of Each Other (1862–1900)', *Women's Studies International Forum*, vol. 12, no. 2, pp. 183–198 (1989).

Hay, Denys, *Europe: The Emergence of an Idea* (Edinburgh, 1968).

Hyamson, A. M., *The British Consulate in Jerusalem in Relation to the Jews in Palestine* (London, 1934–41).

Heasman, K., *Evangelicals in Action, An Appraisal of their Social Work in the Victorian Era* (London, 1962).

Himmefarb, Gertrude, *Marriage and Morals among the Victorians and Other Essays* (New York, Sept. 1986).

———, *The New History and the Old* (New York, 1986).

Hobsbawm, Eric, *The Age of Empire 1875–1914* (New York, 1989).

Hoggarth, David R., *The Penetration of Arabia, a Record of the Development of Western Knowledge Concerning the Arabian Peninsula* (Khayats, 1966).

Holcombe, Lee, *Victorian Ladies at Work, Middle-Class Working Women in England and Wales 1850–1914* (Hamden, Conn., 1973).

———, *Wives and Property, Reform of the Married Women's Property Law in 19th Century England* (Toronto, 1983).

Houghton, Walter, *The Victorian Frame of Mind 1830–70* (New Haven, Conn., 1957).

Hourani, Albert Habib, *Europe and the Middle East* (London, 1980).

———, *Western Attitudes Towards Islam* (Southampton, 1974).

Howard, Donald R., *Writers and Pilgrims, Medieval Pilgrimage Narratives and their Posterity* (Los Angeles, 1980).

Howard, Shirley Weber, *Voyages and Travels in the Near East and Adjacent Regions Made previous to the Year 1801* (Princeton, 1953).

Hunt, David, *Holy Land Pilgrimage in the Late Roman Empire 312–460* (Oxford, 1982).

Hunter, Robert F., *Egypt Under the Khedives 1805–1879: from Household Government to Modern Bureaucracy* (Pittsburg, 1984).

Hussain, Asaf, *Orientalism, Islam and Islamists* (Vermont, 1984).

Hyde, J. K., *Real and Imaginary Journeys in the Middle-Ages* (1982).

Jammeelah, Maryam, *Islam and Orientalism* (Lahore, Pakistan, 1981).

James, T. G. H., *Excavating in Egypt. The Egypt Exploration Society 1882–1982* (London, 1983).

Jassim, Ali Mushim, *Scherazade in England* (Washington, 1981).

Jauss, Hans Robert, *Toward an Aesthetic of Reception*, trans. Timothy Bathi, *Theory and History of Literature*, vol. 2 (Minneapolis, 1983).

Jullian, Phillippe, *Orientalists: European Painters of Eastern Scenes* (Oxford, 1977).

Kabbani, Rana, *Europe's Myths of Orient, Devise and Rule* (London, 1986).

Kamm, Josephine, *Hope Deferred: Girls' Education in English History* (London, 1965).

Kark, Ruth, *Jaffa, A City in Evolution, 1799–1917* (Jerusalem, 1986).

——, (ed.), *The Land that Became Israel, Studies in Historical Geography* (New Haven and Jerusalem, 1989).

Kausar, Niyazi, *Islam and the West* (Lahore, 1976).

Kedouri, Elie, *England and the Middle East* (London, 1956).

——, and Haim, Sylvia G. (eds), *Palestine and Israel in the 19th and 20th Centuries* (London, 1982).

Kenyon, Kathleen, *Archaeology in the Holy Land* (London, 1965).

Kiernan, V. G., *The Lords of Human Kind, European Attitudes Towards the Outside World in the Imperial Age* (London, 1969).

Knoepflmacher, U. C., 'Genre and the Integration of Gender: from Wordsworth to Virginia Woolf', in James R. Kincaid and Albert J. Kuhn (eds), *Victorian Literature and Society: Essays Presented to Richard D. Altick* (Columbus Ohio, 1984).

Labarge, M. W., *Medieval Travellers* (London, 1982).

Lacan, Jean, *Les Sarrazins dans le haut Moyen-Age Français* (Paris, 1965).

Lander, G. R., 'Homo Viator: Medieval Ideas on Alienation and Order', *Speculum*, vol. 42, (1867).

Landou, George P., *Victorian Types, Victorian Shadows: Biblical Typology in Victorian Literature, Art and Thought* (Boston, 1980).

——, *William Holman Hunt and Typological Symbolism* (New Haven, 1979).

Levine, Philippa, *The Amateur and the Professional. Antiquarian Historian and Archaeologist in Victorian England, 1838–86* (Cambridge, 1986).

Lévi-Strauss, Claude, *Mythologiques, vol. I: Le Crue et le cuit* (Paris, 1964); *vol.II: Du Miel aux cendres* (Paris, 1966); vol. III: L'Origine du maniéres du table (Paris, 1968).

——, *La Pensée sauvage* (Paris, 1962).

——, *Tristes Tropiques* (1955, repr. Harmondsworth, 1989).

Lewis, Bernard, *The Emergence of Modern Turkey* (London and New York, 1961).

——, *Istanbul and the Civilisation of the Ottoman Empire* (Oklahoma, 1963).

——, *The Middle East and the West* (New York, 1964).

——, *The Muslim Discovery of Europe* (New York, 1982).

——, *Race and Colour in Islam* (New York, 1971).

Lipman, Sonia and V. D., *A Century of Moses Montefiore* (Oxford, 1985).

Lloyd, Clare, *The Travelling Naturalists* (London, 1985).

Longford, Elisabeth, *A Pilgrimage of Passion, the Life of Wilfrid Scawen Blunt* (London, 1979).

Lüschburg, Winfried, *A History of Travel*, English Version with Michalis Jena and Patrick Murray J. (Leipzig, 1971).

Lowenthal, D., and Prince H. C., 'English Landscape Tastes', *Geographical Review*, 55 (1965) pp. 186–222.

Lund, Hans Peter, *Elements du voyage romantique* (Copenhagen, 1979).

Lytton, Noel A. S., *Wilfrid Scawen Blunt, a Memoir* (London, 1967).

Macfarlane, Alan, *Marriage and Love in England 1300–1840* (Oxford, 1986).

*Marcus, Stephen, *The Other Victorians: A Study of Sexuality and Pornography in Mid-Nineteenth-Century England* (London, 1966).

Ma'oz, Moshe, *Ottoman Reform in Palestine and Syria* (Oxford, 1968).

——, ed., *Studies in Palestine During the Ottoman Period* (Jerusalem, 1975).

Markham, Clement, *The Fifty Years Work by the Royal Geographical Society*

(London, 1882).

al-Sayyid Marsot, Afaf Lutfi, *Egypt in the Reign of Muhammad Ali* (Cambridge, 1984).

Meester, Marie de, 'Oriental Influences in the English Literature of the 19th Centruy', *Anglistische Forschunger*, Heft 46 (1915).

Melman, Billie, 'Desexualising the Orient: the Harem in English Women's Travel-Writing, 1763–1914, *Mediterranean Historical Review*, vol. 4, 2 (December 1989), pp. 301–39.

——, 'The Widening Spheres, The Journey as Fact and Metaphor in Women's Writing on the Middle East' *Zmanim*, vol. 16 (1986) (Hebrew).

Meltitzki, Dorothee, *The Matter of Araby in Medieval England* (New Haven, Conn., 1977).

Michie, Helena, *The Flesh Made Word, Female Figures and Women's Bodies* (Oxford, 1987).

Middleton, Dorothy, 'Some Victorian Lady Travellers', *Geographical Journal*, vol. 13 (1973) pp. 65–75.

——, *Victorian Lady Travellers* (London, 1965).

——, 'Women in Discovery and Exploration' in Depler Helen (ed.), *The Discoverers: An Encyclopedia of Explorers* (London, 1980).

Milbury-Steen, S. L., *European and African Stereotypes* (London, 1980).

Mill, H. R., *The Record of the Royal Geographical Society* (London, 1930).

Miller, Barnette, *Beyond the Sublime Porte the Grand Seraglio of Stambul* (New Haven, Conn., 1931).

Miller, Nancy K., 'Emphasis Added: Plots and Plausibilities in Women's Fiction' *PMLA*, vol. 96 (1981) pp. 36–47.

Mineka, Francis Edward, *The Dissidence of Dissent: the Monthly Repository 1806–38* (Chapel Hill, N. C. 1944).

Mohanty, Chandra Talpode, 'Under Western Eyes: Feminist Scholarship and Colonial Discourses' *Boundary* 2, no. 12 (Fall, 1984), pp. 333–58.

Mosse, George, *Nationalism and Sexuality, Respectability and Abnormal Sexuality in Modern Europe* (New York, 1985).

Moulin, Anne Marie and Chuvin, Pierre, 'Des Occidentaux à la cour du Sultan', *L'Histoire* tom. 45 (Mai 1981).

Mulvery, Ch., *Anglo-American Landscapes: a Study of 19th Century Anglo-American Travel Literature* (Cambridge 1983).

Mülenbrock, H. J., 'The Political Implications of the Grand Tour: Aspects of a Specifically English Contribution to the European Travel Literature of the Age of Enlightenment', *Terma*, vol. 9 (1984).

Myers, Mitzi, 'Harriet Martineau's Autobiography: The Making of a Female Philosopher' in Estelle C. Jelinek (ed), *Women's Autobiography: Essays in Criticism* (Bloomington, Indiana, 1980).

Nir, Yeshayahu, *The Bible as Image; The History of Topography in the Holy Land, 1839–99* (Philadelphia, 1985).

Nasir, Sari, *The Arab and English* (London, 1979).

Okin, Susan Moller, *Women in Western Political Thought* (London, repr. 1980).

Onne, Eyal, *Photographic Heritage of the Holy Land, 1839–1914* (Manchester, 1980).

*Pastner, Carol, 'Englishmen in Arabia: Encounter with Middle Eastern

Women', *Signs,* vol. 4 (20), pp. 309–27.

Pemble, John, *The Mediterranean Passion, Victorians and Edwardians in the South* (Oxford 1987).

Penzer, Norman H., *The Harem* (Philadelphia, 1936).

Peres, Nissan N., *Focus East, Early Photography in the Near East 1839–85* (New York, 1988).

Pichanick, Valerie Kessew, *Harriet Martineau, the Woman and her Work* (Ann Arbor, 1980).

Porter, Roy, 'Mixed Feelings: The Enlightenment and Sexuality in Eighteenth-Century Britain' in Boucé (ed.), *Sexuality in Eighteenth-Century Britain* (Birmingham, 1986).

——, 'The Exotic as Erotic: Captain Cook at Tahiti' in Rousseau and Porter, *Exoticism and the Enlightenment.*

Pratt, Mary Louise, 'Field Work in Common Places' in Clifford, James and Marcus, George (ed.), *Writing the Poetics and Politics of Ethnography* (Santa Fe, 1986).

Prochaska, David, 'Anthropology, Photography and Colonialism: Thérèse Riviere's Photographs of Colonial Algeria', *Proceedings of the French Colonial Historical Society* (unpublished).

——, 'L'Algerie imaginaire, Jalons pour une histoire de l'iconographie coloniale' *Revue d'histoire et d'archives de l'anthropologie* (Hiver 1989/1990) pp. 29–38.

Prochaska, F. K., *Women and Philanthropy in Nineteenth-Century England* (Oxford, 1980).

——, 'Women in English Philanthropy, 1790–1830', *International Review of Social History,* vol. 19 (1974) pp. 426–45.

Pucci, Suzanne Rodin, 'The Discrete Charms of the Exotic: Fictions of the Harem in Eighteenth-century France' in Rousseau and Porter (eds), *Exoticism in the Enlightenment.*

Pudney, John, *The Story of Thomas Cook* (London, 1936).

Quinlan, Maurice J. , *Victorian Prelude: A History of English Manners 1700–1830* (New York, 1941).

Rashdy, Rashad, *The Lure of Egypt for English Writers and Travellers During the 19th Century* (Cairo, 1953).

——, *The English Travel Books (1780–1850), A Popular Literary Form* (Cairo, 1953).

Rice, Warner G., 'English Travellers to Greece and the Levant', *Essays and Studies in English and Comparative Studies,* vol. 10 (1933).

Richter, Julius, *A History of the Protestant Missions in the Near East* (New York 1910, rep 1970).

Rivlin, J. B., *Harriet Martineau, A Bibliography* (1946).

Roppen, Georg, *Strangers and Pilgrims: an Essay on the Metaphor of Journey* (New York, 1964).

Rossi, Alice S., 'The First Woman Sociologist: Harriet Martineau' (1801–76), in Alice S. Rossi (ed.), *The Feminist Papers: From Adams to de Bouvoire* (New York, 1973).

Said, Edward W., *Orientalism* (London, 1978).

——, 'Reflections on Orientalism' *South Asia Series* no. 8, no. 33.

——, *The World, the Text, and the Critic* (Cambridge, Mass., 1983).

Schiffer, Ronald, 'Turkey Romanticised: Images of the Turks in Early Nineteenth-Century English Travel Literature.' *Materialia Turcia*, vol. 8 (1982).

——, 'Orientalism', a review, *Materialia Turcia*, vol. 5 (1979) pp. 130–4.

Schwab, Raymond, *La Renaissance Orientale* (Paris, 1950).

Searight, Sarah, *The British in the Middle East* (London, 1969).

Shaffer, E. S., *'Kubla Khan' and the Fall of Jerusalem: the Mythological School in Biblical Criticism and Secular Literature, 1770–1880* (Cambridge, 1975).

Shanley, Mary Lyndol, Stillman, Peter G., 'Political and Marital Despotism: Montesquieu's Persian Letters' in Jean Bethke Elshtain (ed.) *The Family in Political Thought*.

Shaw, Stanford and Ezel Kural, *History of the Ottoman Empire and Modern Turkey* (Cambridge, 1976–7), 2 vols.

Shepherd, Naomi, *The Zealous Intruders, the Western Rediscovery of Palestine* (London, 1987).

Showalter, Elaine, *A Literature of their Own: British Women Novelists from Brontë to Lessing* (London, 1978).

——, 'Towards a Feminist Poetics' in Mary Jacobus (ed.), *Women Writing and Writing about Women* (New York, 1979).

Southern, R. W., *Western Views of Islam in the Middle-Ages* (Cambridge, Mass., 1980).

Spack, Patricia Meyer, 'Borderline, Letters and Gossip', *Georgia Review*, vol. 37, no. II (1983), pp. 791–813.

Spivak, Gayatri Chakravorty, *In Other Worlds: Essays in Cultural Politics* (New York, 1987).

Stafford, Barbara Maria, *Voyage into Substance: Art, Science, Nature and the Illustrated Travel Account, 1760–1890* (Cambridge, Mass., 1984).

Stevens, Mary Anne (ed.), *The Orientalists, Delacroix to Matisse, European Painters in North Africa and the Near East* (London, 1984).

Stevenson, Cathrine Barnes, *Victorian Women Travel Writers in Africa* (Boston, 1982).

——, 'Female Anger and African Politics: The Case of Two Victorian "Lady Travellers"', *Turn of the Century Woman*, vol. 2 (1985) pp. 7–17.

Stowasser, Barbara Freyer, 'The Status of Women in Early Islam' in Freda Hussain (ed.) *Muslim Women* (London, 1984) pp. 11–44.

Suleiman, Susan Rubin (ed.) *The Female Body in Western Culture, Contemporary Perspectives* (Cambridge, Mass., 1986).

*Sumption, Jonathan, *Pilgrimage, an Image of Medieval Religion* (London, 1975).

Sutherland, John, *The Longman Companion to Victorian Fiction* (Harlow, Essex, 1988).

Swinglehurst, Edmund, *Cook's Tours, the Story of Popular Travel* (London, 1982).

——, *The Romantic Journey* (London, 1984).

Taylor, Anne, *Lawrence Oliphant, 1829–88* (Oxford, 1982).

Thornton, A. P., *Doctrines of Imperialism* (London, 1965).

Thronton, Lynne, *The Orientalists: Painters and Travellers 1818–1908* (Paris, 1983).

——, *Women as Portrayed in Orientalist Painting* (Paris, 1985).

Tibawi, A. L., *American Interests in Syria 1800–1901, A Study of Education, Literary and Religious Work* (Oxford, 1966).

——, *British Interests in Palestine 1800–1901, A Study of Religious and Educational Enterprise* (Oxford, 1961).

Tidrick, Kathryn, *Heart Beguiling Araby* (Cambridge, 1981).

Toledano, Ehud R., 'The Imperial Eunuchs of Istanbul: from Africa to the Heart of Islam' *Middle Eastern Studies*, vol. 20, no. 3 (1984) pp. 379–90.

——, *The Ottoman Slave Trade and its Suppression, 1840–90* (Princeton, N. J., 1982).

——, 'Slave Dealers, Women, Pregnancy and Abortion: The Story of a Circassian Slave-Girl in Mid-Nineteenth-Century Cairo', *Slavery and Abolition*, vol. 1, no. 1, pp. 53–68.

——, *State and Society in Mid-Nineteenth–Century Egypt* (Cambridge, 1990).

Trollope, Joanna, *Britannia's Daughters, Women of the British Empire* (London, 1983).

Tuchman, Barbara, *The Bible and the Sword, England and Palestine from the Bronze Age to Balfour* (New York, 1957).

Tuchman, Gaye and Nina Fortin, *Edging Women Out, Victorian Novelists and Social Change* (New Haven, Conn., 1989).

Ulucay, Cagatay, *Harem*, (Ankara, 1971) (Turkish).

Vaczek, Louis and Gail Buckland, *Travellers in Ancient Lands: A Portrait of the Middle East, 1839–1919* (New York, 1981).

Vereté, M., 'Why Was a British Consulate Established in Jerusalem', *English Historical Review*, vol. 85 (1970) pp. 316–45.

——, 'The Idea of the Restoration of the Jews in English Protestant Thought', *Middle Eastern Studies*, vol. 8, no. 1 (1972) pp. 3–50.

*Vizeer, Engin, *Photography in the Ottoman Empire* (Paris, 1988).

Webb, R. K., *Harriet Martineau, a Radical Victorian* (New York, 1960).

Welter, Barbara, '"She Hath Done What She Could": Protestant Women's Missionary Careers in the 19th Century America', *American Quarterly*, vol. 30 (1978) no. 5, pp. 624–39.

Wheatly, Vera, *The Life and Work of Harriet Martineau* (London, 1957).

Williams, Arthur S., 'Panegyric Decorum, in the Reign of William and Anne', *Journal of British Studies*, vol. 21, no. 1 (1981) pp. 56–67.

Williams, Raymond, *Communications* (Harmondsworth, 1976).

——, *The Long Revolution* (Harmondsworth, 1980).

——, *Marxism and Literature* (Oxford, 1977).

Winstone, H. V. F., *Gertrude Bell* (New York, 1978).

Women of Istanbul in Ottoman Times, Osmali domeninole Istanbul kadinlah (1984) (Turkish).

Yudkiss, Heda, *Bibliography of Botanical Research of the Middle Eastern Region* (Geneva, 1987).

Zacher, Christian K., *Curiosity and Pilgrimage, the Literature of Discovery in 14th Century England* (1976).

Unpublished Theses and Papers

Abdullah Adel, 'The Arabian Nights in English Literature to 1900', Ph.D.

Dissertation (Cambridge, 1963).

Bendiner, Kenneth Paul, 'The Portrayal of the Middle East in British Painting 1835–60', Ph.D. Dissertation (New York, 1979).

Bonsnes, Margorie P., 'The Pilgrimage to Jerusalem: a Typological Metaphor for Women in Early Medieval Religious Orders', Ph.D. Dissertation (New York, 1982).

Chapman, Rupert III, 'British Archaeology and the Holy Land', Britain and the Holy Land, Conference at the Institute of Jewish Studies, University College London (February 1989).

Davis, Thomas William, 'A History of Biblical Archaeology', Ph.D. Dissertation (Arizona, 1982).

Fallon, Gretchen Kidol, 'British Travel-Books from the Middle East 1890–1914: Conventions of the Genre and Three Unconventional Examples', Ph.D. Dissertation (Maryland).

Gross, Irena Grundzinska, 'Journey through Bookland: The Travel Memoir in the 19th Century', Ph.D. Dissertation (New York).

Ideology and Landscape in Historical Perspective, Seventh International Conference of Historical Geographers (Jerusalem, July, 1989).

Kochav, Sarah, 'Biblical Prophecy, the Evangelical Movement and the Restoration of the Jews to Palestine 1790–1860', Britain and the Holy Land, a Conference at University College London, Institute of Jewish Studies (February 1989).

Knipp, Charles Christopher, Types of Orientalism in 18th Century England, Ph.D. Dissertation (Berkeley).

Swartz, Kathryn C., The Rhetorical Resources of Lady Mary Wortly Montagu, Ph.D. Dissertation (Ohio).

Van der Bilt, E. F., 'Proximity and Distance, American Travellers to the Middle East 1819–1918', Ph.D. Dissertation (Cornell, 1985).

Index